Vol. 1

On the Shoulders of Giants of International Business Scholarship

Standing on the Shoulders of International Business Giants

In Memory of

Yair Aharoni

On the Shoulders of Giants of International Business Scholarship

Series Editors: Arie Y Lewin (*Duke University, USA*)
Elizabeth L Rose (*University of Leeds, UK & Indian Institute of Management Udaipur, India*)

Published:

Vol. 1 *Standing on the Shoulders of International Business Giants: In Memory of Yair Aharoni*
edited by Arie Y Lewin, Ravi Ramamurti & Elizabeth L Rose

Vol. 1

On the Shoulders of Giants of
International Business Scholarship

Standing on the Shoulders of International Business Giants

In Memory of
Yair Aharoni

editors

Arie Y Lewin
Duke University, USA

Ravi Ramamurti
Northeastern University, USA

Elizabeth L Rose
Indian Institute of Management Udaipur, India

World Scientific

NEW JERSEY • LONDON • SINGAPORE • BEIJING • SHANGHAI • HONG KONG • TAIPEI • CHENNAI • TOKYO

Published by

World Scientific Publishing Co. Pte. Ltd.
5 Toh Tuck Link, Singapore 596224
USA office: 27 Warren Street, Suite 401-402, Hackensack, NJ 07601
UK office: 57 Shelton Street, Covent Garden, London WC2H 9HE

Library of Congress Cataloging-in-Publication Data
Names: Aharoni, Yair, honoree. | Lewin, Arie Y., 1935- editor. | Ramamurti, Ravi, editor. | Rose, Elizabeth Louise, editor.
Title: Standing on the shoulders of international business giants : in memory of Yair Aharoni / edited by Arie Y. Lewin, Duke University, USA, Ravi Ramamurti, Northeastern University, USA, Elizabeth L. Rose, Indian Institute of Management, Udaipur, India.
Description: New Jersey : World scientific, [2024] | Series: On the shoulders of giants of international business scholarship ; vol. 1 | Includes bibliographical references.
Identifiers: LCCN 2023054100 | ISBN 9789811287503 (hardcover) | ISBN 9789811287510 (ebook) | ISBN 9789811287527 (ebook other)
Subjects: LCSH: International business enterprises. | International trade. | Globalization--Economic aspects.
Classification: LCC HD2756 .S83 2024 | DDC 338.8/8--dc23/eng/20231130
LC record available at https://lccn.loc.gov/2023054100

British Library Cataloguing-in-Publication Data
A catalogue record for this book is available from the British Library.

For any available supplementary material, please visit
https://www.worldscientific.com/worldscibooks/10.1142/13708#t=suppl

Desk Editors: Soundararajan Raghuraman/Nicole Ong

Typeset by Stallion Press
Email: enquiries@stallionpress.com

https://doi.org/10.1142/9789811287510_fmatter

Preface

This book serves as an introductory volume to Yair Aharoni's remarkable impact on international business (IB) research. Most IB researchers will be familiar with at least one aspect of his work, but relatively few will be familiar with his broader body of work, as it spans so many of the issues addressed today in IB and strategy. This book aims to introduce readers to the depth and breadth of his impact.

Unquestionably a founder of the IB field, over the course of his long career, Aharoni influenced its earliest development and, driven by a deep connection to policy and managerial practice, continually challenged conventional thinking on IB and strategy. He generated seminal insights into many aspects of why and how firms internationalize, including managerial decision-making processes, the strategies employed by state-owned enterprises, the interaction between firms and governments, and the foreign expansion of firms — including small- and medium-sized enterprises (SMEs) and those operating in the service sector — based in small and open economies. His research contributed to several salient research directions, including the behavioral theory of the firm, emerging-market multinationals, international entrepreneurship, the service economy, and non-market strategies.

Aharoni was also an influential educator, having served as the founding dean of two top business schools in Israel. He was deeply engaged with the Israeli business environment — particularly senior executives of start-up companies — and a highly valued advisor to the Israeli government. Few scholars have had such meaningful impact on research, practice, and policy. In honor of these contributions, Aharoni was the first management scholar in Israel to be awarded the prestigious Israel Prize in 2010.

https://doi.org/10.1142/9789811287510_fmatter

About the Editors

Arie Y. Lewin (PhD, Carnegie Mellon University) is a Professor Emeritus of Strategy and International Business, Duke University, with recent appointments as a Visiting Professor at Fudan University School of Management, Shanghai Jiaotong University Antai College, and the School of Economics and Management at Tsinghua University. Professor Lewin is the founding Editor-in-Chief of *Organization Science*, the past Editor-in-Chief of the *Journal of International Business Studies*, and the current Editor-in-Chief of *Management and Organization Review*, which focuses on management research in the context of China and other rising economies. His research and consulting work focus on organization adaptation and change, directed co-evolution of innovation, corporate governance, sustaining open innovation organizations, hidden champions in China and rising economies, and global sourcing of innovation. From 2002 to 2014, he was the Lead Principal Investigator (PI) of the multi-year global Offshoring Research Network (Duke ORN) project that tracked the evolution of unbundling and dispersal of work (especially innovation activities) enabled by advances in information and communication technologies. Recent research and consulting involve case studies of open innovation at Haier, niche and sector SME champions in China, and outsourcing of ITO and BPO at 20 of the largest global banks. His book, *China's Innovation Challenge: Overcoming the Middle-Income Trap*, was published by Cambridge University Press in 2016. The Chinese translation was published by Peking University Press. Professor Lewin has further taken a keen interest in the impact of geopolitical developments on business and management in China and other emerging markets.

In this context, he has initiated and contributed to two Discussion Forums related to the topic of *Management and Organization Review* and a Perspective paper in the *Journal World of Business*.

Ravi Ramamurti (DBA, Harvard University) is the University Distinguished Professor of International Business and Strategy and Director of the Center for Emerging Markets at Northeastern University. He studies strategy and innovation in emerging markets. He earned his MBA from IIM-Ahmedabad and his Doctorate in Business Administration from Harvard University. While studying at Harvard Business School, Ravi worked as a research assistant to Professor Yair Aharoni. Ravi has been a Visiting Professor at Harvard Business School, the Wharton School, MIT-Sloan School, and CEIBS-Shanghai. His eight books include three published by Cambridge University Press on the internationalization of emerging-market firms. In 2011, Niron Hashai and Ravi co-edited a festschrift in honor of Yair Aharoni. Ravi's latest book, *Reverse Innovation in Health Care,* published by HBR Press (2018), was a finalist for the Tata Book award. For the past decade, Ravi has been working on the idea of "reverse innovation". His article (co-authored with V. Govindarajan) "Reverse innovation, emerging markets, and global strategy" won the inaugural prize for Best Article published in *Global Strategy Journal.* In 2008, Ravi was elected a Fellow of the Academy of International Business. Earlier, he was elected to serve as Chair of the Academy of Management's International Management Division. Prior to academia, Ravi worked as a Consultant to the Indian Planning Commission, as an Executive Assistant to the CEO of India's largest engineering company, and as a UN Adviser to Bangladesh and South Korea. Ravi has studied or consulted with firms in more than 20 emerging economies and been a consultant to global organizations, including the *Economist Group,* Fulbright, USAID, UNCTAD, the World Bank's board, and the United Nations.

Elizabeth L. Rose (PhD, University of Michigan) is a Research Chair Professor of Business Policy and Strategy at the Indian Institute of Management Udaipur. A statistician by training, her research addresses various aspects of how firms internationalize and compete across borders. Working at the intersection of international business, international entrepreneurship, and strategy, she is especially interested in the internationalization activities of firms from emerging markets, particularly smaller firms and those operating in the service sector. She is an elected Fellow of the Academy of International Business (AIB) and was named the 2019 Woman of the Year by the Women of the AIB (WAIB). Currently, she is the co-editor of *Academy of Management Collections*. Professor Rose has held leadership roles in several academic professional organizations. She served as Vice President for Administration for the AIB, working closely with AIB chapters around the globe, and was the founding chair of the AIB's Australia and New Zealand Chapter (now AIB-Oceania). She has also been the President of both the Australia and New Zealand International Business Academy (ANZIBA) and the Association of Japanese Business Studies (AJBS) and the Chair of the Strategic Management Society (SMS) Global Strategy Interest Group and the Academy of Management (AOM) International Management Division. She is Vice President of the Board of the European Institute for Advanced Studies in Management (EIASM).

https://doi.org/10.1142/9789811287510_fmatter

List of Contributors

Raj Aggarwal	Kent State University Foundation, USA
Tamar Almor	College of Management, Israel
Christian Bellak	University of Business and Economics, Vienna, Austria
Ingmar Björkman	Hanken School of Economics, Finland
Mary Yoko Brannen	Copenhagen Business School, Denmark
David M. Brock	Ben Gurion University, Israel
Peter J. Buckley	University of Manchester, UK
Jeremy Clegg	University of Leeds, UK
Farok Contractor	Rutgers University, USA
John Daniels (deceased)	University of Miami, USA
José de la Torre (deceased)	University of Bologna, Italy
Avishai Gal	Jerusalem Institute of Management, Israel
Pervez N. Ghauri	University of Birmingham, UK
Robert Grosse	Thunderbird International Business School, USA
Niron Hashai	Interdisciplinary Center, Israel, and University of Manchester, UK
Seev Hirsch	Tel Aviv University, Israel
Steven Kobrin (deceased)	University of Pennsylvania, USA
Ran Lachman	Reichman University, Israel
Arie Y. Lewin	Duke University, USA
Cheng Li	University of Manitoba, Canada
Zvi Oded Maimon	Tel-Aviv University, Israel

Yair E. Orgler	Tel Aviv University, Israel
Rebecca Piekkari	Aalto University, Finland
Ravi Ramamurti	Northeastern University, USA
Elizabeth L. Rose	Indian Institute of Management Udaipur, India
Eli Segev	Tel Aviv University, Israel
Laszlo Tihanyi	Rice University, USA
Louis Wells	Harvard University, USA
Mira Wilkins	Florida International University, USA
Jehiel Zif	Tel Aviv University, Israel

https://doi.org/10.1142/9789811287510_fmatter

Acknowledgments

So many people have participated in making this book a reality. The genesis of the volume was the collection of thoughtful and heartfelt responses from the Fellows of the Academy of International Business (AIB) upon hearing of Yair's death. We are truly grateful to all of the colleagues who have contributed by writing about their perspectives on Yair's many contributions to international business research and practice and their memories of a life well lived.

The financial support of the Coller School of Management of Tel Aviv University and the College of Management, toward the cost of publisher permission fees, is especially appreciated.

Several people have been instrumental in helping us with details regarding different aspects of Yair's life and his deep contributions to business and education in Israel. We are especially thankful to Dean Tamar Almor, Dean Moshe Zviran, Avishai Gal, Niron Hashai, Yair E. Orgler, Yair's daughter Orna Zmiry, and his soul-mate Ofira Wegrzyn. We are also grateful to Kathy Kiessling and Cheng Li for their assistance with accessing the recording of the 2020 AIB conference panel. Thanks are also due to Debra Soled, for her eagle-eyed editing, and to Zvi Ruder, for enthusiastically embracing the idea of this volume as the first in a series.

Ultimately, we are grateful to Yair Aharoni for inspiring all of us.

https://doi.org/10.1142/9789811287510_fmatter

Contents

Part 1

Introduction

https://doi.org/10.1142/9789811287510_0001

Chapter 1

Yair Aharoni Eulogy: Academy of International Business Fellows Business Meeting, June 1, 2021*

Arie Y. Lewin

Strategy and International Business
Duke University Fuqua School of Business

Yair was an outlier. He was an academic entrepreneur. He was trained in accounting, rose to the rank of captain in the Israeli Defense Force, and married his direct report Mira, the love of his life. We know him for his seminal PhD dissertation at Harvard Business School on the decision to internationalize. Yair's seminal qualitative study was about the firm internal logic of appropriateness to internationalize and about reconciling the decision as the consequences reveal themselves. It is a rich example that preceded the formal development of the theory of the Logic of Appropriateness and of the Logic of Consequences by March and Olsen and others, which was still to come. Yair also made important contributions in other areas of IB, including the internationalization of state-owned enterprises and small and medium enterprise ecosystems, and was early to recognize the up-and-coming service-sector economy, generally with a strong contextual focus on his beloved underdeveloped home country economy. His 2013 *Academy of International Business Insights* article

* It is a special honor for me to present this brief eulogy in memory of Yair Aharoni, who passed away on August 6, 2020 in Tel Aviv, Israel.

exemplifies his profound and all-inclusive perspective of international business scholarship.

Yair's academic entrepreneurship encompassed being the founding dean of the Coller Graduate School of Business at Tel Aviv University, becoming the first rector of the College of Management in Rishon LeZion, inaugurating an innovative and farsighted academic institution that opened up new higher education opportunities for young Israelis for whom the small number of elite Israeli universities were not accessible. He also recognized the importance of executive education for the emerging senior managers of the nascent startup companies arising in Israel and became the CEO (1981–1987) of Jerusalem Institute of Management (JIM) at Tel Aviv University. Israel recognized Yair's many contributions by awarding him the 2010 Israel Prize. Yair served on several important government of Israel task forces, including the creation of the office of Israel Chief Scientist, which became renowned for fostering Israel as the high-tech "Startup Nation".

He was recruited to the Fuqua School by Dean Keller in 1985 and single-handedly internationalized the MBA curriculum and established the CIBER at Duke. The book in Yair's memory that Ravi Ramamurti, Elizabeth Rose, and I have co-edited should be published very soon. We are so very pleased to be able to make Yair's contributions readily available to old and new generations of IB researchers.

https://doi.org/10.1142/9789811287510_0002

Chapter 2

Introduction to This Volume

This volume is dedicated to the memory of Professor Yair Aharoni, who died in Tel Aviv, Israel, on August 6, 2020. He was a creative scholar, whose work had both academic and practical impact. He was a dedicated educator, whose vision made him an influential administrator. He was also driven to improve managerial and strategic practice, along with enhancing national policy to support international engagement by Israeli firms. In 2010, he received the Israel Prize, which is the nation's highest cultural honor, in recognition of his extensive contributions to management sciences.

The seminal career of Professor Aharoni, the Daniel and Grace Ross Professor of International Business and the Issachar Haimovic Professor of Business Policy at Tel Aviv University, was noteworthy for foundational contributions to the then-fledgling field of international business, particularly with respect to foreign direct investment (FDI) decisions by globalizing companies. His impact on the field began early in his career; his influential and widely cited book, *The Foreign Investment Decision Process*, published in 1966, grew out of his PhD dissertation. This book offered the first rigorous qualitative study of how top corporate managers arrive at decisions related to FDI, with a focus on behavioral processes. His subsequent work addressed a wide variety of issues, such as the globalization of state-owned enterprises and service-sector firms.

As an international business scholar with a strong interest in practice and a deep attachment to his homeland, Professor Aharoni was preoccupied with the challenges that faced Israel and other small and developing economies that sought to evolve into advanced economies, even though their domestic markets could never hope to create the economies of scale required for effective global competition. He was among the earliest advocates of institutional initiatives (e.g., the role of a national head of science and technology), which would serve to transform Israel's economy from one dependent on exports of low-value-added agricultural products (e.g., the renowned Jaffa oranges or dairy products) into a high-tech, innovation-based economy, epitomized by Israel's emergence as a "Startup Nation".

Professor Aharoni was also a pioneering academic entrepreneur. He was the visionary founding dean of the Recanati Business School (now called the Coller School) at Tel Aviv University and led the establishment and development of management education, research scholarship, and management executive education in Israel. Later, he was the first rector of the College of Management in Rishon LeZion, inaugurating an innovative and farsighted academic institution that opened up new higher education opportunities for young Israelis who lacked access to the small number of elite Israeli universities. He also drove the establishment of executive education for managers in Israel.

A Short Biography

Professor Aharoni was born in Zichron Yaakov, Israel, on September 5, 1931. His father, Israel Arie Halevi, was born in Kleck, Poland (now in Belarus), and was a true Zionist, among the early pioneers who sought a new life in the then-Palestine, which was under the British mandate that went into effect after World War I. Yair's father, who was an accomplished high school mathematics teacher and principal, arrived in Palestine in 1920, having jumped off a cargo ship *en route* to Egypt and swimming to shore in Palestine. He was fluent in many languages but spoke only Hebrew in front of his children.

During the early years of the British mandate, teachers often moved from city to city because the Jewish communities in Palestine were small and dispersed. As a result, Yair was born in Zihron Yaakov, but his sister, Rivka, and brother, Amikam, were born in other cities.

In 1950, after graduating from Gymnasia Herzliya Hebrew High School, Yair served in the Israel Defense Forces (IDF). He retired from the IDF as the rank of captain and as the head of the Statistical Branch of the Israeli Air Force (1954–1956). Yair met his first wife Mira

Zauberman — the love of his life — in the army. In March 1952, the IDF sent Mira to the United States for a course on radar operation. On her return to Israel, she reported to Yair, who, at the time, was the officer in charge of overseas advanced training. They married in December, 1953. Yair and Mira had a daughter, Orna, who was born in 1965. Mira and her twin sister, Nina, were Holocaust survivors, who had been subjected to medical experiments involving radiation; they died within a month of each other in 1974. The following year, Yair married Nili Eisner, who died in 1994. At the time of Yair's death, his partner was Ofira Wegrzyn.

Family was extremely important to Yair. Orna recalls him as a devoted parent. "He always helped me in everything he could, even if he was very tired. When I was in school and did not understand something, he would explain it to me even if it was late." Whenever he was in Israel, Yair made it a priority not to miss the Friday night family gathering, to partake in the *kiddush* (Sabbath prayer) and the *Shabbat* (Sabbath) meal and — most importantly — to catch up with family events. Orna described Yair as a great storyteller, who enjoyed regaling family members and others with tales about his life and his military service. According to Orna, Yair was a devoted grandfather to his four now-adult grandchildren: Mirit, Iddo, Danielle, and Ohad.

After his family, Yair loved teaching and sharing his knowledge. He was an avid reader, with a thirst for learning about any subject, including history, politics, and science. He was also a global traveler, enjoying the opportunity to attend conferences and give talks in locations that were new to him. Over time, he became renowned for his professional and social network, which spanned the world.

Organization of This Volume

This book celebrates the life and multifaceted contributions of Professor Yair Aharoni, with a combination of his own work and tributes and remembrances by a variety of colleagues and friends.

Part 2 showcases Yair's voice, with reprints of some of his key articles. It also includes a transcript of his final academic presentation, along with comments by the organizer of the panel in which he participated.

Part 3 consists of a collection of tributes and recollections from some of his worldwide academic friends and colleagues. Yair was an active member of the Academy of International Business (AIB) and was elected as an AIB Fellow in 1990. The news of his death elicited an outpouring of responses from other AIB Fellows, many of which are represented in this section as essays and remembrances.

Part 4 focuses on Yair's contributions to education, business, and policy in Israel. The essays in this section offer some insight into the depth and breadth of his impact on his home country.

https://doi.org/10.1142/9789811287510_0003

Chapter 3

2010 Israel Prize

Prof. Aharoni was awarded the prestigious Israel Prize for his outstanding academic contribution to the field of management, during an academic career that spanned over half a century. It was the first time, since its establishment in 1953, that the Israel Prize was awarded to a scholar in the field of business management.

Israel Prize Winners List 2010.

2010	Mordechai Shani	Lifetime achievement & special contribution to society and the State
2010	Avishai Margalit	Philosophy
2010	Hanoch Bartov	Literature
2010	Aryeh Sivan	Poetry
2010	Abraham Tal	Hebrew linguistics
2010	Arye Levin	General linguistics
2010	Moshe Adad	Criminology
2010	Yair Aharoni	Administrative science
2010	Abraham Nitzan	Chemistry
2010	Yehoshua Kolodny	Earth sciences
2010	Jonathan Gressel	Agriculture
2010	Peter Mirom	Photography
2010	Suzanne Dellal Center for Dance and Theater	Dance

(*Continued*)

(*Continued*)

2010	Aharon Yadlin	Lifetime achievement & special contribution to society and the State
2010	Yardena Cohen	Lifetime achievement & special contribution to society and the State
2010	Kamal Mansour	Lifetime achievement & special contribution to society and the State

Part 2

Yair Aharoni's Academic Legacy

General

https://doi.org/10.1142/9789811287510_0004

Chapter 4

Introduction to Yair Aharoni's Intellectual Contributions

Arie Y. Lewin[*], Ravi Ramamurti[†], and Elizabeth L. Rose[‡]

[*]*Duke University, Durham, NC, USA*

[†]*Northeastern University, Boston, MA, USA*

[‡]*Indian Institute of Management Udaipur, Udaipur, India*

In this volume, we collect some of Yair Aharoni's most original and impactful journal articles and book chapters.[1] Considering that he wrote more than 72 articles and book chapters and published at least 30 books and monographs, it was challenging to select the articles to highlight in this section; we pooled our collective assessments to choose among them. Of course, this means that the final selection is subjective, and others might have selected a different subset of Yair's work. Our goal was to represent all the major topics on which he wrote. The broad focus of Aharoni's work was management and strategy, but he explored these topics at all levels, from macro (e.g., global and national) to micro (e.g., the role of managers in shaping organizational strategies). Looking back on his lifetime of scholarship, we were struck by how often he was ahead of other scholars in writing about important new trends in management and international business. He was among the first to explore the role of

[1]Parts of this introduction draw heavily on a chapter (Hashai & Ramamurti, 2011) in a *festschrift* for Yair. We are grateful to Niron Hashai for permission to do so.

multinational enterprises (MNEs) from small countries, among the pioneers to study state-owned enterprises and their internationalization, among the earliest to explore the globalization of services, and at the forefront of exploring the complex relationship between MNEs and home/host governments.

Aharoni always preferred to look at real-world implications. He was not interested in abstract theories but only in theories that helped explain real-world phenomena. He believed in integrating theory and practice, which is why his extensive academic contributions are matched by significant real-world contributions, whether establishing a new management school, serving on Israeli government commissions, or transforming how business schools teach international business. This was, perhaps, Aharoni's greatest strength as a researcher: the ability to bounce back and forth, freely, and frequently, between general theories and their application to real-world situations. Every type of exploration fed and nurtured another. Theories helped him to make sense of the real world, and, when the existing theories did not serve this purpose, he did not shy away from proposing new ideas or theories that might be better at explaining the real world. Aharoni's outlook on the importance of having business practice informs research is captured in two articles included in this volume: Aharoni (2011a, 2013). His capacity to straddle theory and practice so effectively is extremely rare among business scholars.

The sections of his academic work selected for this volume can be divided into four areas:

(1) how managers make decisions pertaining to strategy and internationalization, including coping with uncertainty and complexity,
(2) explaining the behavior of state-owned enterprises and the state,
(3) the changing national origin of MNEs, including the rise of new MNEs and internationally active small and medium-sized enterprises (SMEs) from small and large economies,
(4) the shifting focus of multinationals from natural resources and manufacturing to all kinds of services.

As noted earlier, he also wrote books on some of these same topics, and we devote a separate section of this volume to reviews of some of them, printed in leading journals.

Strategic Decision-Making and Internationalization

One of the earliest topics on which Aharoni worked was the process of foreign investment decision-making. This was the subject of his 1961 PhD dissertation, published by Harvard Business School Press in 1966 (Aharoni, 1966 — discussed in this volume by Peter Buckley and others). Aharoni highlighted the decision to engage in foreign direct investment (FDI) as a special case of a strategic decision. He emphasized the complexity of making such a decision, given the multiple attitudes and opinions involved, both internal and external to the organization. Aharoni identified the complex interrelationships among changing attitudes, opinions, and social relationships, and argued that past experiences and views of the future critically affect the decision to engage in foreign investment. He noted that making the decision to do so requires a "champion" who is emotionally invested in the decision and who persuades others that the risk of this investment outweighs the risk of inaction. This champion helps convince leaders that the foreign investment is within the organization's "feasibility zone".

The five articles we selected on this topic show that Aharoni continued to consider this question — how organizations make strategic decisions, such as whether or not to pursue foreign investment — for many years after his first book was published and became a seminal work in the field. In the first of these papers (Aharoni, 2011b), which was included in the *festschrift* for him organized in 2010 at Tel Aviv University by Niron Hashai and Ravi Ramamurti, Aharoni revisited the question that formed the basis of his dissertation: How do managers and managerial discretion influence what organizations do? In this paper, Aharoni urged international business scholars to stop ignoring managers and viewing them as something of a black box. He noted that "managers behave according to different rules than those assumed in much of the IB literature. ... they are not part of a herd but unique" (Aharoni, 2011b: p. 23). He lamented that, as a result, "theory fails to predict actual behavior and does not allow best guidance for policy options" (Aharoni, 2011b: p. 23).

In two other articles, published in *Management Science*, Aharoni and his coauthors explored how managers scan the environment and focus their efforts on managing external dependence. Based on the notion that information is not costless, search takes effort, and managers' time and attention are limited, one of them argues that "managers do not try to identify all environmental forces, [but] identifying the dominant components of the environment focuses the scanning efforts and saves energy and costs" (Aharoni *et al.*, 1978: p. 949). A key finding of the other article is that, unlike other elements in the environment, "different components of the government … were perceived as having conflicting interests, both within the segment and with other segments of the environment" (Aharoni *et al.*, 1981: p. 197). The managerial implication of this reality was that "when a segment of the environment is heterogeneous, it is possible that managers use a tradeoff strategy in which pressures generated by one component of the environment can be used as a means to reduce pressure of the other components" (Aharoni *et al.*, 1981: p. 197).

In the fourth article on this topic, published in the *Journal of Management Studies* in 1993, Aharoni stressed that differentiation is at the heart of any successful strategy and that differentiation requires firms to become unique in some way. Any party who is attempting to evaluate a strategy *ex ante* (e.g., a venture capitalist) must be able to assess whether the firm in question actually possesses any unique capabilities or assets. Aharoni (1993a: p. 31) noted that "success is defined as the ability to gain abnormal profits, not simply to stay alive in a competitive industry, [and] the ability to protect the uniqueness against imitators ensures continued success". He then discussed how difficult it can be, in practice, to make a firm unique or to know, in advance, how likely being unique in a particular manner is to pay off in terms of abnormal returns.

In the fifth article, Aharoni traced the evolution of MNEs over the past century, the forces driving that evolution, and the distinctive features of new MNEs coming out of emerging economies. The first wave of MNEs developed in Europe before World War I. The next big wave was from the United States after World War II, and the third wave was from Japan in the 1980s. The most recent has been from emerging economies in the 2000s. Sagaciously, this article (Aharoni & Ramamurti, 2011: p. 113) warns of the "risk of a backlash against globalization and multinationals in Western societies, even as these trends gain in popularity in developing countries".

Aharoni's early work on strategic decision-making and internationalization was contemporaneous with the highly influential work of other management scholars; for example, his research pertaining to how leaders manage the environment was undertaken at about the same time as the work by Pfeffer and Salancik (1978) on how organizations manage external dependence to enhance their autonomy. Aharoni's thinking also laid the foundation for a stream of work in the 1970s and 1980s on the internationalization process (e.g., Czinkota, 1982; Johanson & Vahlne, 1977; Reid, 1981) and FDI (e.g., Dunning, 1979, 1988, 1993). That said, it is important to note that Aharoni's PhD dissertation was one of the first examples of the development of a behavioral theory of the firm, which was popularized only two years later by Cyert and March (1963).

State-Owned Enterprises

A second area in which Aharoni made pioneering contributions was the study of state-owned enterprises (SOEs). Through the 1970s, only public administrators were interested in studying these organizations, as an extension to their study of government departments. Aharoni recognized that SOEs were an important class of business organizations, because they often operated in regular markets, in competition with private firms; in addition, several SOEs had substantial international operations. In sectors such as mining, utilities, infrastructure, energy, and transportation, SOEs were dominant players in many countries (with the obvious exception of the US). Because he was in Israel, Aharoni saw, firsthand, the role of SOEs in the economy, along with other less-common forms of ownership, such as companies owned by the Histradrut, the national trade union center. Aharoni served on the boards of these companies, as well as on government commissions charged with studying how to reform SOEs; these roles gave him a deep understanding of how SOEs operated. With Raymond Vernon, of Harvard Business School, Aharoni organized one of the first SOE-focused conferences at a US business school, which led to an edited volume (Aharoni & Vernon, 1981). Aharoni then wrote a comprehensive book on SOEs (Aharoni, 1986), synthesizing international experience in managing and reforming SOEs.

The four articles on SOEs included in this volume capture Aharoni's most original contributions to our understanding of these organizations. His 1981 *Management Science* paper highlighted that too much of the SOE literature was normative, discussing how they *should* behave, without sufficient understanding of how they actually behave. As he noted, "Almost no research has been done on why SOEs function as they do" (Aharoni, 1981a: p. 1340). Echoing his recurring theme about the need for rich, descriptive research, especially on the role of managers, he argued that "the paucity of knowledge about the operation of SOEs stems both from insufficient research effort, and from the concern of researchers with formal structures and products of these organizations and not with management behavior or with decision processes" (Aharoni, 1981a: p. 1340).

Aharoni offered three valuable insights in the other selected articles, based on his descriptive research approach and his first-hand experience with SOEs. In Aharoni and Vernon (1981), he noted something in one chapter that few in business or public administration schools seemed to recognize at the time: that leaders of SOEs often worked systematically to increase their autonomy from or discretion with respect to their bosses in government, even if that meant straying from official goals or government directives. In this fascinating article, Aharoni (1981b) laid out a series of tactics that SOE leaders use to increase their managerial discretion.

A second conference on SOEs, this time at Boston University, produced a conference volume that included a contribution by Aharoni, in which he argued that the principal–agent model breaks down when applied to SOEs because "the SOE is an agent without a principal" (Aharoni, 1982: p. 67). This profound point altered how we think about SOEs. We recognize now that a central problem in managing SOEs is the absence of a universally accepted definition of the "public interest" and that every part of the government (e.g., ministry or department) might view the purpose of an SOE or the criteria for evaluating its performance differently. The problem is muddied further by the recognition that, when it comes to SOEs, government officials are themselves agents of the true principal, i.e., the public.

The fourth SOE-related article included here has a title that says it all: "Can the Manager's Mind Be Nationalized?" (Aharoni & Lachman, 1982). The argument here is that, although the SOE executive's adherence to public sector goals is taken for granted, empirical research on Israeli managers shows almost no difference in the goal perceptions of managers at SOEs and private firms. Aharoni and Lachman concluded that "the lack of differences indicates that mere affiliation with nationalized enterprises does not secure 'nationalization' of the executives' goal commitments and goal pursuit and that the achievement of the nationalization objectives may be hindered" (Aharoni & Lachman, 1982: p. 33).

Small Firms and Countries in the Global Economy

Aharoni also contributed substantially to an ongoing shift of focus among international business scholars, from large, industrial MNEs based in developed countries to more moderately sized MNEs and internationally active SMEs, often based in small and/or emerging countries (e.g., Zander *et al.*, 2015). He was troubled by the fact that mainstream theoretical frameworks used in strategy and international business research were influenced too heavily by the US experience and did not always apply to what was observed in other countries. In particular, his embeddedness in his local environment exposed Aharoni to Israeli firms that were internationally competitive, despite their small size and the fact that they were based in a small home economy. At the time, mainstream theoretical perspectives, popularized primarily in the US, seemed to conclude that successful internationalization was heavily dependent on whether a firm had already established a strong position in a large home market.

This discrepancy led Aharoni to initiate a stream of research in which he explained how small MNEs from small countries, such as Israel, could overcome their inherent scale disadvantages, relative to large MNEs based in large home markets (e.g., Aharoni, 1992, 1994, 2000b, 2009; Aharoni & Hirsch, 1996). We include four of these pieces in this volume.

For instance, in a book chapter, Aharoni argued that, for a small firm to globalize successfully, it must "identify a product and a market in a non-global industry, one in which more than a small number of giant firms can operate, and one that does not require economies of scale. Then, dominate a niche" (Aharoni, 1994: p. 9). This simple, but powerful, conclusion may be at the foundation of what became of Israel's remarkable success as the "start-up nation" (Senor & Singer, 2009). Aharoni (1994) recommended that small firms seeking international success customize their products and services in innovative ways, in order to serve niche segments while commanding premium prices. Other strategies that he suggested include the reduction of marketing costs by engaging in large transactions (which often implies a focus on business-to-business [B2B] sales rather than business-to-customer [B2C]), reacting quickly to customer needs by being technologically flexible and providing superior service before and after sales. This was built on the thinking that was reflected in an earlier work, also included in this volume, in which he discussed the necessary conditions for small firms based in developed but smaller countries to enjoy global success. Aharoni (1992) summarized these conditions as the CS^2F^3 strategy: customization, a small number of transactions, superior service, focus, fast response, and flexibility. Importantly, he also distinguished how SMEs enter foreign markets, as original equipment manufacturer (OEM) suppliers to large MNEs or on their own accord.

Aharoni also put thought into the complex interaction among attributes of the firm, its industry, and its home country, viewing an economy as "a portfolio of firms and markets" (Aharoni, 2006: p. 113, in this volume). He had a particular and understandable interest in the international engagement of firms from small economies, whose international business engagement is based on large numbers of smaller firms operating across borders rather than heavy reliance on the scale associated with large MNEs. He argued that contrary to many predictions, globalization offers real benefits to smaller countries: "rather than making the small nation-state obsolete — globalization created opportunities for growth and prosperity for citizens of small states" (Aharoni, 2006: p. 93). In a later article, he took this argument further, noting that "Israel clearly demonstrates that a large home market is not a prerequisite for creating MNEs. On the contrary, the tiny size of the home market is a major incentive for Israeli firms to become multinationals by catering to much larger foreign markets" (Aharoni 2009: p. 353). Today, it is widely accepted that both large and small countries can produce internationally competitive firms and that firm size is not the primary determinant of cross-border success.

Aharoni's work on small MNEs and internationalizing firms from small countries contributed substantially to our understating of the phenomenon of "born global" firms or international new ventures (Oviatt & McDougall, 1994; Knight & Cavusgil, 2004); these are SMEs that internationalize soon after their founding, without having developed a strong domestic business before expanding across national borders. Many of his ideas also have direct relevance for explaining the strategies of new and newly internationalizing multinationals from emerging and developing countries, which often suffer from being small and beginning with a limited set of competitive advantages that are directly applicable to international markets and thus benefit from avoiding head-on conflicts with Western MNEs (Ramamurti, 2009).

Service Firms in the Global Economy

Most of the original theory pertaining to international business and strategy was developed based on large manufacturing firms in developed markets. This context still accounts for most of the theorizing, along with the bulk of the empirical evidence, despite the importance of the service sector in the global economy.

Aharoni was one of the first scholars to discuss the growth of MNEs as service providers as distinct from industrial MNEs that develop, produce, and sell tangible goods. In a substantial stream of research that included articles and edited collections, he studied the specific challenges associated with supplying services abroad; the challenges arise, in part, from the intensive interaction required between the service provider and its customers, particularly in knowledge-intensive services. In the earliest of Aharoni's service-related articles included in this volume (Aharoni, 1993b), he laid out some initial ideas regarding how service firms, in general, internationalize. He also conducted research focused on internationalization processes in specific service-sector industries, including accounting (Aharoni, 1999) and airlines (Aharoni, 2004). Among the insights from this line of work was the importance of reputation in enabling firms to provide services in foreign countries (Aharoni, 2000a). In another paper (Aharoni, 1993b), he emphasized that successful internationalization in the service sector often necessitates the development of alliances with local (domestic) firms, for establishing relationships and credibility (legitimacy) with customers, suppliers, regulators, and other local institutional actors.

Aharoni also addressed strategic and structural considerations associated with the successful internationalization of services. For example, in Aharoni (1996), he emphasized that the integration and centralization of global operations enhance the foreign service provider's ability to compete abroad, facilitating the efficient transfer of firm-specific knowledge between the headquarters and foreign subsidiaries. Because this often means that complex and embedded knowledge needs to be standardized and made explicit, internationalizing service providers face difficult decisions about which aspects of their knowledge base to transfer outside of the home country, in terms of sharing with both subsidiaries and strategic partners. These choices are likely to be influenced strongly by both the firm's strategy and the organizational structure in place to support these transfers, in order to help spread knowledge without the risk of sharing too much and, in doing so, jeopardizing the firm's core competencies or its competitive advantages.

The final services-focused paper included in this volume differs from the others in this section because it is about a special type of service: technology. Aharoni and Hirsch (1996) looked at this issue from the perspective of a developing, rather than a developed, country. They noted that the interaction of technology, trade, and investment and their impact on economic development are poorly understood. Further, they highlighted some challenges that developing countries face when importing foreign technology. For instance, specific imported technology may be appropriate for developed countries but suboptimal for developing countries. In this chapter, these two friends and colleagues noted that it may sometimes be preferable for a developing country to import technology as part of a packaged bundle (i.e., in the form of FDI), and, at other times, it may be better to unbundle the package and select the specific technology that is needed by the developing country.

Conclusion

Throughout his long career, Yair Aharoni made substantial, and truly fundamental, contributions to our understanding of key aspects of international business and strategy. Few scholars have engaged deeply with so many aspects of internationalization, considering nation-states, industries, and firms. A deep understanding of context drove much of Aharoni's work, and this strong involvement in practice and policy enabled him to identify emerging issues long before most other researchers. He was among the first to write about phenomena that remain pertinent in current research, including various aspects of the internationalization of SOEs and smaller firms, along with the challenges (and benefits) of foreign expansion from the home base of an emerging market.

Aharoni's contributions are also distinguished by his strong commitment to studying the processes that led to internationalization and understanding managers' perspectives. This emphasis on process and managerial decision-making meant that he was a very early proponent of detailed qualitative research. Although qualitative work is now mainstream in international business and strategy, much of Aharoni's career was spent resisting the prevailing approach to research in these fields, with respect to both methodological orientation and a focus on a behavioral perspective, rather than a strictly economic one.

In this volume, we have chosen to reprint writings that reflect four aspects of Aharoni's work pertaining to internationalization. The first is foreign direct investment, in which he focused on the questions of "why" and "how", offering nuanced insights that would not have been possible using the then-dominant quantitative research approach. The second aspect pertains to the internationalization of SOEs, which are important organizational forms in many countries, especially emerging markets; Aharoni looked at these organizations early, surfacing insights that remain relevant. The third area represents his work on small and medium-sized enterprises. Although the internationalization of SMEs is now an important focus of international business research, Aharoni was, again, ahead of this development, driven by his deep understanding of the Israeli context, in which smaller firms play such an important role. The fourth aspect of Aharoni's work that we include pertains to the international expansion of services. Today, service industries are seen as the cutting edge of globalization. While we still have much to learn about the internationalization of the service sector, Aharoni's pioneering research laid the foundation for a deeper understanding of this phenomenon.

References

Aharoni, Y. 1966. *The Foreign Investment Decision Process*. Cambridge: Harvard University Press.

Aharoni, Y. 1981a. Performance evaluation in state-owned enterprises: A process perspective. *Management Science*, 29(11): 1340–1347.

Aharoni, Y. 1981b. Managerial discretion in state-owned enterprise. In Vernon, R. & Aharoni, Y. (Eds.) *State-Owned Enterprise in Western Economies*. London: Croom Helm, pp. 184–193.

Aharoni, Y. 1982. State-owned enterprise: An agent without a principal. In Jones, L. (Ed.) *Public Enterprise in Less-Developed Countries*. New York: Cambridge University Press, pp. 67–76.

Aharoni, Y. 1986. *The Evolution and Management of State-Owned Enterprises*. Cambridge, MA: Ballinger.

Aharoni, Y. 1992. The role of small firms in an interdependent world. In Burton, R. M., Forsyth, J. & Obel, B. (Eds.) *Strategies for Players in a Larger World: The Effect of Regulatory and Information Changes*. Amsterdam: Elsevier, pp. 11–32.

Aharoni, Y. 1993a. In search for the unique: Can firm-specific advantages be evaluated? *Journal of Management Studies*, 30(1): 31–44.

Aharoni, Y. 1993b. The internationalization process in professional business service firms: Some tentative conclusions. In Aharoni, Y. (Ed.) *Coalitions and Competition: The Globalization of Professional Business Services*. Abington, UK: Routledge, pp. 280–285.

Aharoni, Y. 1994. How can small firms achieve competitive advantage in an interdependent world? In Agmon, T. & Drobnick, R. (Eds.) *Small Firms in Global Competition*. New York: Oxford University Press, pp. 9–18.

Aharoni, Y. 1996. The organization of global service MNES. *International Studies of Management and Organization*, 26(2): 6–23.

Aharoni, Y. 1999. Internationalization of professional services: Implications for accounting firms. In Brock, D., Powell, M. & Hinings, C. R. (Eds.) *Restructuring the Professional Organization*. London: Routledge, pp. 20–40.

Aharoni, Y. 2000a. The role of reputation in global professional business services. In Aharoni, Y. & Nachum, L. (Eds.) *Globalization of Services: Some Implications for Theory and Practice*. London: Routledge, pp. 125–141.

Aharoni, Y. 2000b. Globalization and the small, open economy. In Almor, T. & Hashai, N. (Eds.) *FDI, International Trade and the Economics of Peacemaking: Papers in Honor of Seev Hirsch*. Rishon LeZion: College of Management Academic Division, pp. 90–116.

Aharoni, Y. 2004. The race for FDI in services: The case of the airline industry. In Ghauri, P. & Oxelheim, L. (Eds.) *European Union and the Race for Foreign Direct Investment in Europe*. Kidlington, UK: Elsevier, pp. 381–406.

Aharoni Y. 2009. Israeli multinationals: Competing from a small open economy. In Ramamurti, R. & Singh, J. V. (Eds.) *Emerging Multinationals in Emerging Markets*. Cambridge: Cambridge University Press, pp. 352–396.

Aharoni, Y. 2011a. Insights into the future of international business. *Academy of International Business Insights*, 11(2): 3–6.

Aharoni, Y. 2011b. Behavioral elements in foreign direct investments. In Ramamurti, R. & Hashai, N. (Eds.) *The Future of Foreign Direct Investment and the Multinational Enterprise*. Bingley, UK: Emerald, pp. 23–60.

Aharoni, Y. 2013. A few lessons from my long experience in IB research. *Academy of International Business Insights*, 13(4): 17–19.

Aharoni, Y. & Hirsch, S. 1996. The competitive potential of technology-intensive industries in developing countries. In Svetlicic, M. & Singer, H. W. (Eds.) *The World Economy: Challenges of Globalization and Regionalization*. London: Palgrave Macmillan, pp. 99–118.

Aharoni, Y. & Lachman, R. 1982. Can the manager's mind be nationalized? *Organization Studies*, 3(1): 33–46.

Aharoni, Y., Maimon, Z. & Segev, E. 1978. Performance and autonomy in organizations: Determining dominant environmental components. *Management Science*, 24(9): 949–959.

Aharoni, Y., Maimon, Z. & Segev, E. 1981. Interrelationships between environmental dependencies: A basis for tradeoffs to increase autonomy. *Management Science*, 28(2): 197–208.

Aharoni, Y. & Ramamurti, R. 2011. The evolution of multinationals. In Ramamurti, R. and Hashai, N. (Eds.) *The Future of Foreign Direct Investment and the Multinational Enterprise*. Bingley, UK: Emerald, pp. 113–135.

Czinkota, M. R. 1982. *Export Development Strategies: U.S. Promotion Policies*. New York: Praeger.

Cyert, R. M. & March, J. G. 1963. *A Behavioral Theory of the Firm*. Englewood Cliffs, NJ: Prentice Hall.

Dunning J. H. 1979. Toward an eclectic theory of international production: Some empirical tests. *Journal of International Business Studies*, 11(1): 9–31.

Dunning J. H. 1988. The eclectic paradigm of international production: A restatement and some possible extensions. *Journal of International Business Studies*, 19(1): 1–31.

Dunning J. H. 1993. *Multinational Enterprises and the Global Economy*. Reading, UK: Addison-Wesley.

Hashai, N. & Ramamurti, R. 2011. Research on FDI and MNEs in a changing world. In Ramamurti, R. & Hashai, N. (Eds.) *The Future of Foreign Direct Investment and the Multinational Enterprise*. Bingley, UK: Emerald, pp. 1–19.

Johanson, J. & Vahlne, J.-E. 1977. The internationalization process of the firm — a model of knowledge development and increasing foreign market commitment. *Journal of International Business Studies*, 8(1): 23–32.

Knight, G. & Cavusgil, T. 2004. Innovation, organizational capabilities, and the born-global firm. *Journal of International Business Studies*, 35: 124–141.

Oviatt, B. M. & McDougall, P. P. 1994. Toward a theory of international new ventures. *Journal of International Business Studies*, 25(1): 45–64.

Pfeffer, J. & Salancik, G. R. 1978. *The External Control of Organizations: A Resource Dependence Perspective*. New York: Harper and Row.

Ramamurti, R. 2009. What have we learned about emerging-market MNEs? In Ramamurti, R. and Singh, J. V. (Eds.) *Emerging Multinationals in Emerging Markets*. Cambridge: Cambridge University Press, pp. 399–426.

Reid, S. D. 1981. The decision-maker and export entry and expansion. *Journal of International Business Studies*, 10: 101–112.

Senor, D. & Singer, S. 2009. *Start-up Nation: The Story of Israel's Economic Miracle*. New York: Twelve.

Vernon, R. & Aharoni, Y. 1981. *State-Owned Enterprises in the Western Economies*. London: Croom Helm.

Zander, I., McDougall-Covin, P. & Rose, E. L. 2015. Born globals and international business: Evolution of a field of research. *Journal of International Business Studies*, 46(1): 27–35.

https://doi.org/10.1142/9789811287510_0005

Chapter 5

Insights Into the Future of International Business*

Yair Aharoni

Tel Aviv University, Tel Aviv, Israel

IN 2002, BUCKLEY ARGUED THAT past IB research has succeeded because it focused on three big research questions: (1) How to explain the flows of foreign direct investment (FDI), (2) How to explain the existence, strategy, and organization of multinational enterprises (MNEs), and (3) How to understand and predict the internationalization of firms and the new developments of globalization (Buckley, 2002: p. 365). He concluded that "the IB research agenda is stalled because no such big question has currently been identified" (Buckley, 2002: p. 370). Buckley & Ghauri (2004) elaborated on the question of globalization as a possible next big question for IB research. Peng (2004) argued that the next big question should be "What determines the international success and failure of firms around the globe?" Perhaps another big question is the ways and means nation-states can cooperate to create a global regime.

The unique contribution of IB researchers is the study of the international/multinational/transnational/global business enterprise/firm/company/corporation. These firms operate in an international environment that has changed profoundly. Technology, macroeconomics, institutions (or as

*This chapter is reproduced from *AIB Insights*, Vol. 11, No. 2.

North, 1990, calls them, the rules of the game) and ideological beliefs — all have changed. Existing multinational enterprises (MNEs) reacted by adapting their strategy and organization. More and different MNEs emerged. The nature of MNEs, their origins, the sectors in which they operate, their size, the drivers for their operations and many other variables have all evolved. IB research was unable to predict these changes and those reactions but did study them after they occurred. The "big questions" turned out to be a moving target. Solutions to some of them became obsolete. The future of IB research is in adapting theory to answer the same big questions given the environmental changes and the emergence of the new players.

The Changing Environment

IB scholars are familiar with the many changes in the last fifty years. *New technologies* impacted quite a few firms. Industries, institutions and the knowledge and skills that provide comparative advantage are under the unremitting assault of change. Major new products created totally different markets and new industries — and many established products became obsolete. Recently, many innovations have originated from emerging markets. Improvements in information and communication technologies and the rapid coverage of the world with internet facilities changed fundamentally the ways people communicate across borders and the time it takes to respond to a message. They have vastly reduced the cost of managing and integrating a globally dispersed value chain and allowed the zooming of outsourcing and offshoring not only of manufacturing but also of business services and R&D.

MNEs have also grown because of fundamental changes in the *international political environment*. The multilateral trading arrangement (GATT and later WTO) has been a necessary precondition to enable zooming of world exports from $60 billion in 1950 to $16,070 billion in 2008. The General Agreement on Services opened up many avenues for FDIs in services. Deregulation of infrastructure services has created opportunities for new FDIs.

These changes stemmed to a large extent from *changing beliefs*. More and more intellectuals — and then government officials — became ardent believers in the efficiency of free markets and disillusioned with the ability of governments to plan and direct the economy. Changing beliefs led to an almost universal urge to contain government intervention, to deregulate but also to coordinate national economic policies, recognizing the fragility of the international financial system. Many economies moved from import substitution policies and domestic firm protection to export-led growth policies. In 1960, US MNEs invested to jump tariff walls and other national restrictions on trade. Since the 1990s, policy changes forced firms to benchmark themselves against best-in-class global competitors and venture abroad, in search of markets, lower costs and resources. In the 21st century world, more and more countries, including developing countries, are fostering internationalization of formerly sheltered industries. To be sure, national authorities still limit movements of labor across borders. Further, confidence in free market economics, until recently virtually impregnable, has been undermined by the financial crisis of 2007–2008.

The *macro economic environment* has also changed dramatically. The direct convertibility of the US dollar to gold and the fixed exchange regime were abandoned. Currencies moved to a full float. The 1985 Plaza Accord realigned the value of the major currencies. The Euro was born and soon rivaled the US dollar as the currency of choice. Further, capital markets became global and more efficient, allowing broadened access to capital for small- and medium-sized firms, including those in developing countries. These changes led also to a shift the global distribution of economic and political power.

The *prevailing views on MNEs* were also altered. In the 1960s, MNEs were perceived as new forms of colonialism and as an arm of American Hegemony (e.g., Levitt, 1970; Saari, 1999: p. 2). Many scholars portrayed national governments as impotent pawns in the hands of powerful MNEs (Barnet & Műller, 1974). Anxiety about the possible dominance of MNEs over countries led to nationalizations and to calls for UN intervention — and the creation of UNCTAD. Since the 1980s MNEs have been increasingly recognized as a prime engine of economic development. Their potential to inject capital without debt servicing obligations, create jobs, transfer technology (including management skills), enhance exports and raise productivity became widely acclaimed in a knowledge-based global economy. The possible conflict of power between the MNEs and the nation-states seems to have been forgotten (but see Eden & Lenway, 2001). The "storm over the multinationals" (Vernon, 1977) has subsided. Instead, MNEs are courted. Nations compete intensively to get MNEs to locate value-added activities within their borders. Governments also encourage home-based MNEs. Government policies in emerging markets have become more welcoming of FDI, not just in manufacturing but also in services. International agreements covering both goods and services

FDI are proliferating at the bilateral, regional and multilateral levels. In addition, cross-border social networks among locals and overseas nationals have accelerated the cross-border flow of information and tacit knowledge and helped new MNEs from emerging economies to penetrate developed markets.

The Changing MNEs

As the industrial world transformed to a knowledge- and information-driven world, established MNEs adapted to different environments and new MNEs were able to emerge. MNEs have proliferated in numbers, areas of operations, national origin and size distribution, and they have changed considerably. First, their numbers grew 11-fold. The UN counted 7,276 MNEs in 1969 (United Nations, 1973) and 82,053 in 2008 (UNCTAD, 2009: 222–223). Second, MNEs were originally dominated by resource seeking and manufacturing MNEs. More recently, MNEs from the service sector have been steadily increasing their share. Third, the home country is now spread. In 1914, 93 percent of MNEs were from Europe (and 50 percent from England). By 1969, 55 percent were US MNEs (Aharoni & Ramamurti, 2008). Today MNEs come from 137 countries (UNCTAD, 2009: 222–223). In 2008 only 2,418 parents out of 82,000 were from the US, while 3,428 were from China (out of 21,425 parents from developing countries). Fourth, in the 1970s, multinationals were regarded as giants, with sales that dwarfed the GNPs of most countries. This is still true of the largest MNEs. However, the vast majority of MNEs counted by UNCTAD are small in size. MNEs are increasingly recognized as market seekers, efficiency seekers and strategic asset and innovation seekers — looking for new ideas. Finally, new MNEs are being spawned at earlier stages of a firm's evolution than before — many are "born global" firms.

Established MNEs have also learned how to collaborate in strategic alliances rather than seeking to be stand-alone superstars. Western MNEs seek knowledge and ideas as keenly as they once sought natural resources or access to closed markets. Managers of MNEs orchestrate assets, coordinate development of new products, eradicate inefficiencies and allocate resources within the firm. They decompose their supply chain, moving the labor intensive production to low labor cost countries and distributing other activities to the best location across the world. Today, half of all trade takes place within the hierarchy of the same MNEs or among different MNEs. In addition, the sales of MNEs' overseas affiliates (international production) are almost double that of world exports. All these changes eradicated certain products and industries that became redundant as a result of new innovations.

Theories Becoming Obsolete

One result of the environmental (and the institution) changes coupled with MNEs' learning is that many theories rooted in an earlier context became obsolete because context and circumstances changed. Thus, the idea that governments can nationalize MNEs because the power of these firms is reduced with time after the large initial investment has been made — the so-called obsolescing bargain model — may be relevant, if at all, for oil and minerals but not for today's innovative MNE. MNEs' advantages today are less based on factors vulnerable to rapid obsolescence and more on the capability to innovate, generate new technologies and manage knowledge across a global network.

> *"...many theories rooted in an earlier context became obsolete because context and circumstances changed."*

As another example, the product life cycle theory (Vernon, 1966) assumed demand led innovations from the home developed country. Vernon himself acknowledged the impact of some changes in Vernon (1979). Cantwell (1995) has shown that clusters of innovations occur in many centers and the greater capability of many MNEs is the broader degree of cross-border specialization that they are able to manage. Today, MNEs search actively for technologies, ideas and products from outside the firm (Huston & Sakkab, 2006; Jones, 2005). Many innovations by MNEs stem from subsidiaries rather than from headquarters. Teece (1986) analyzed how an inventor can profit internationally from his new invention. He suggested the need for what he termed "appropriability regime" — or available patent protection — but also the possession of complementary assets and capabilities. Recently, Hennart (2009) acknowledged that theories are too MNE centric — assuming the choice of entry is unilaterally determined by the MNE. He called for recognition of the need to bundle FSA of MNEs with complementary local assets. Hennart still assumes that the source of innovation is the MNE, and knowledge is transferred from its headquarters. For some MNEs today, FSA lies in distribution. The innovator is a local firm — in many cases one in a developing country (Govindarajan & Ramamurti, 2011).

Other obsolete theories include descriptions of organization of the MNE as portrayed by Stopford & Wells (1972) (see Egelhoff, 1988) or the evolutionary theory of internationalizing (Johanson & Vahlne, 1977).

Further, many theories turned out to be true for manufacturing but not for services. Thus, IB theory posited that MNEs possess a firm-specific exploitable factor that creates an oligopolistic advantage. Based on this line of reasoning one may assume that firms would invest abroad when they possess a clear ownership advantage to compensate for what Zaheer (1995) termed "liability of foreignness". However, world famous universities did not create subsidiaries abroad, despite their clear advantage. Parenthetically, liability of foreignness may be less than it used to be. Further, IB theory assumed that firms seek to control their subsidiaries, demanding full ownership to protect their intellectual property. Only because government, having the advantage of bargaining obsolescence, demands joint ventures, does the firm use this route. Yet hotel chain management seems to prefer joint ventures and use this form even when the government allows full ownership.

As to industries, according to Porter, when competition in each nation is essentially independent the industry is multi-domestic. In contrast, in global industries firms are compelled to compete internationally to achieve or sustain competitive advantage. "But choosing a domestic focus in a global industry is perilous, no matter what the firm's home nation" (Porter, 1990: p. 54). Yet in most professional services many domestic firms operate alongside of a few multinationals. Is the theory wrong or the definition of industry erroneous? Further, according to Porter (1990) and many others, experience in a (large) home country is essential to gain ownership advantages and then invest abroad. However, ISS offers worldwide cleaning services — although its home market (Denmark) is small. Theories may be industry- or home-country specific. Therefore it is essential to clearly define the population discussed.

Definition of Terms

Despite much research on "the MNE", different researchers define the term differently. Vernon looked at giant US-based firms listed in

Fortune 500. He required an investment in at least six countries. His data bank of 187 so-called US MNEs was the source of much important research work. He refused to include, e.g., International Flavors and Fragrances even though it operated in dozens of countries, because it was not in the Fortune 500.

The figures often used — and those quoted above — are based on UNCTAD and its definition of an MNE. UNCTAD requires investment in only one country. Its definitions are based on the balance of payments statistics. Non-equity forms of FDI, e.g., sub-contracting, management contracts, turnkey arrangements, franchising, licensing or product sharing, as well as different forms of strategic alliances are reflected only as receipts of royalty and management fees. In many services non-equity forms are much more important than equity investments.

Rugman (2005: 85) presented the Fortune Global 500 as if it "is an annual ranking (by sales) of the world's 500 largest MNEs", claiming these firms "are the 'unit of analyses' for research in international business" (p. 3).

The proper definition of MNEs "depends to a large extent on the problems discussed" (Aharoni, 1971: p. 36). Given the diversity of MNEs it is crucial that future researchers specify the population they discuss, e.g., Chinese outward FDI (Wei, 2010). Very few characteristics are true for all MNEs. The pioneers of scientific management attempted to discover general rules of behavior, such as number of hierarchical levels, assumed to be pertinent to all organizations. Only decades later were contingent variables introduced. The future of IB is in the introduction of relevant contingent variables and a clear specification of the context in which a certain study has been carried out.

The Future of IB Research

IB is about how firms behave and how managers of firms decide. The firm learns, and it is operating within an environment, including a political and institutional regime. All of these dimensions, except the way managers decide, have seen fundamental changes. MNEs are very different than they used to be and are quite heterogeneous. MNEs are transforming themselves. They learn and adapt to the changing environment. Clearly, theory should adapt too.

IB theory does not have the ability to predict the future. It is context dependent. It does not necessarily apply to different environments and diverse contexts nor is it independent of these factors. It follows that IB research should specify the context to which it applies. A major task of future IB research is to understand the drivers of these differences and their impact on strategy.

IB research should also delineate the differences if any, e.g., in firm specific advantages of firms from different home countries and cultural origins, different size, different sectors and different experience in international operations. IB research should shed light on such questions such as how salient are experience, knowledge and path? Does the home environment shape the pattern of international operations? Are firms based in different countries behaving differently? If so, how? R&D is now globally organized. We need to understand the impact of such outsourcing on intellectual properties and FSAs. In the past, the theoretical constructs and the data led to a concern for the explanation of a Marshallian "representative firm". The temptation of additional rigor called for analysis of a large number of observations. Unfortunately, to achieve rigor researchers find themselves very distant from reality — which is socially constructed rather than objectively determined. The task of IB researchers should not be to gather facts and measure how often certain patterns occur, but to appreciate the different constructions and meanings that people place upon their experience.

Final Reflections

Past IB research ignored managerial behavior and processes. Also, IB often neglects to acknowledge that the MNE is also a political actor, exerting more political power than some governments. Far too much attention — from Vernon to Rugman — has been devoted to the Fortune 500 firms. Researchers may find it rewarding to look at the outlier rather than search for central tendencies in a population of MNEs. The outlier changes the rules of the game and may achieve immutable and sustainable high profits. Careful case studies may unearth rules for identification of successful breakthroughs, means of achieving firm-specific advantages, a better understanding of the behavior of top management teams as well as the interaction of IB and governments.

The success of MNEs is at least as much a function of management ability as it is of industry characteristics or environmental factors. Managers behave according to different rules than those assumed in much of the IB literature. They are not part of a herd, but unique. The result of such a lacuna is that theory failed to predict actual behavior and did not allow the best guidance for policy options (Aharoni, 2010). Environments were treated most of the time as objective facts, independent of the firms. The ability to generate oligopoly rents by political action or through collusion is almost always ignored. The ability to change the environment by innovation of new products that alter the structure of the market was recognized only recently. Hopefully, future IB research will avoid these pitfalls.

References

Aharoni, Y. 1971. On the definition of a multinational corporation. *The Quarterly Review of Economics and Business*, 11(3): 27–37.

Aharoni, Y. 2010. Behavioral elements in foreign direct investment decisions. In Devinney, T., Pederson, T. & Tihanyi, L. (Eds.) *The Past, Present and Future of International Business and Management*. Advances in International Management, Vol. 23. Bingley: Emerald Group, pp. 72–112.

Aharoni, Y. & Ramamurti, R. 2008. The internationalization of multinationals. In Boddewyn, J. J. (Ed.) *International Business Scholarship: AIB Fellows on the First 50 Years and Beyond*. Research in Global Strategic Management, Vol. 14. Bingley: Emerald, pp. 177–201.

Augier, M. & Teece, D. 2007. Dynamic capabilities and multinational enterprise: Penrosean insights and omission. *Management International Review*, 47(2): 175–192.

Barnet, R. J. & Műller, R. E. 1974. *Global Reach: The Power of the Multinational Corporations*. New York: Simon and Schuster.

Buckley, P. 2002. Is the international business research agenda running out of steam? *Journal of International Business Studies*, 33(2): 365–373.

Buckley, P. & Ghauri, P. 2004. Globalization, economic geography, and the strategy of multinational enterprises. *Journal of International Business Studies*, 35(2): 81–98.

Cantwell, J. 1995. The globalisation of technology: What remains of the product cycle model? *Cambridge Journal of Economics*, 19(1): 155–174.

Eden, L. & Lenway, S. 2001. Multinationals: The Janus face of globalization. *Journal of International Business Studies*, 32(3): 383–400.

Egelhoff, W. G. 1988. Strategy and structure in multinational corporations: A revision of the Stopford and Wells model. *Strategic Management Journal*, 9(1): 1–14.

Govindarajan, V. & Ramamurti, R. 2011. Reverse innovation, emerging markets, and global strategy. *Global Strategy Journal*, 1(3-4): 191–205.

Hennart, J.-F. 2009. Down with MNE-centric theories! Market entry and expansion as the bundling of MNE and local assets. *Journal of International Business Studies*, 40(9): 1432–1454.

Huston, L. & Sakkab, N. 2006. Inside Procter & Gamble's new model for innovation. *Harvard Business Review*, 84(3): 58–66.

Johanson, J. & Vahlne, J.-E. 1977. The internationalization process of the firm. *Journal of International Business Studies*, 8(1): 23–32.

Jones, G. 2005. *Renewing Unilever: Transformation and tradition*. Oxford: Oxford University Press.

Levitt, K. 1970. *Silent Surrender: The Multinational Corporation in Canada*. New York: St. Martin's Press.

North, D. 1990. *Institutions, Institutional Change, and Economic Performance*. Cambridge, MA: Harvard University Press.

Peng, M. W. 2004. Identifying the big question in international business research. *Journal of International Business Studies*, 35(2): 99–108.

Porter, M. 1990. *The Competitive Advantage of Nations*. New York: Free Press.

Rugman, A. M. 2005. *The Regional Multinationals: MNEs and "global" Strategic Management*. Cambridge: Cambridge University Press.

Saari, D. J. 1999. *Global Corporations and Sovereign Nations: Collision or Cooperation?* Westport, CT: Quorum Books.

Stopford, J., & Wells, Jr., L. 1972. *Managing the Multinational Enterprise*. New York: Basic Books.

Teece, D. 1986. Profiting from technological innovation: Implications for integration, collaboration and public policy. *Research Policy*, 15(6): 285–305.

UNCTAD. 2009. *World Investment Report: Transnational Corporations, Agricultural Production, and Development*. New York and Geneva: United Nations.

United Nations. 1973. *Multinational Corporations in World Development*. New York: United Nations Department of Economic and Social Affairs.

Vernon, R. 1966. International investment and international trade in the product cycle. *Quarterly Journal of Economics*, 80(2): 190–207.

Vernon, R. 1971. *Sovereignty at Bay*. Boston, MA: Harvard University Press.

Vernon, R. 1977. *Storm over the Multinationals: The Real Issues*. Boston, MA: Harvard University Press.

Vernon, R. 1979. The product cycle hypothesis in a new international environment. *Oxford Bulletin of Economics and Statistics*, 41(4): 255–267.

Wei, Z. 2010. The literature on Chinese outward FDI. *The Multinational Business Review*, 18(3): 73–112.

Zaheer, S. 1995. Overcoming the liability of foreignness. *Academy of Management Journal*, 38(2): 341–363.

Yair Aharoni (yairah@post.tau.ac.il) is Professor Emeritus at Tel Aviv University, Israel. In addition to more than thirty books and monograph he has authored or edited, he has published more than a hundred papers in various journals and chapters in books and has written more than 150 cases. He is a Fellow of the Academy of International Business and of the International Academy of Management.

https://doi.org/10.1142/9789811287510_0006

Chapter 6

A Few Lessons from My Long Experience in IB Research*

Yair Aharoni

Tel Aviv University, Tel Aviv, Israel

MY LONG EXPERIENCE IN IB RESEARCH has taught me several lessons which may resemble or differ from the experiences of other researchers. I offer some of them in order to elicit your comments and generate a discussion among us. This paper is not a summary of my research work. Rather, I wanted to reflect on what I consider a few of the major challenges and implications for IB researchers.

Let me start by arguing the importance of talking to practitioners in order to get a real grasp of a problem or practice — often resulting in case studies rather than analyses of secondary data or questionnaire surveys. In 1959–1961, when I was doing my doctoral research at Harvard Business School, I was distressed by the apparent failure of Israel to attract foreign direct investments, despite the fervent attempts by the government to encourage it by enacting the Law for the Encouragement of Capital Investments. From my training in economics, I assumed that the conferral of tax benefits would induce foreign investors to initiate projects which they would not otherwise have undertaken. The problem seemed to be straightforward — how large did the tax incentives need to be?

*This chapter is reproduced from *AIB Insights*, Vol. 13, No. 4.

I could have designed a questionnaire asking a carefully chosen sample of managers to rank the size of the tax holiday they would require in order to make a foreign investment, and added some other questions on related topics. I am sure that I would have received answers that could have been tabulated and regressed against other variables, and I am equally certain that the answers would have indicated that tax holidays are desirable — after all, what managers would answer that they would not want these tax holidays?

However, Harvard Business School required case writing as an integral part of doctoral research. I made a list of firms that had considered an investment in Israel and wrote about 40 case studies on the history of the decisions, based on interviewing managers and reading correspondence and other documents related to the decision. I soon found out that tax incentives did not play the decisive role I had expected them to play. Moreover, the picture emerging from my field research seemed to be one of utterly irrational behavior. The "decision process" followed by US businesspeople had very little in common with the classical economic theory of capital investment. To understand their behavior, it was necessary to recognize that decisions are made under uncertainty within an organizational and social system. Once I changed my research lens, what seemed irrational made sense. I could offer a behavioral theory that explained how and why decisions are made and how and why commitments accumulate. In 1966, I published a book based on my findings which are well known so I will not repeat them (Aharoni, 1966).

Had I chosen to study foreign investments through a mail questionnaire, however carefully designed, I would never have been exposed to the rich saga of the real foreign investment decision process and to the way real managers in real firms make decisions. Rather I could have suggested wrong policies. Since then, I have written more than 150 cases on all kinds of problems and researched a variety of issues. In this work, I have consistently benefited from the insights of businessmen. To be sure, I did not always rely on case studies and interviews since, in some of my studies, I used carefully designed questionnaires. Yet I have always tried to understand the actual behavior of persons within a firm — not how they *should* behave.

A second key point is that I expect IB scholars to study management rather than economics. IB scholars try to be as scientific as those in the natural sciences. Many of these researchers (including myself) were trained as economists, and economists prefer to apply econometric methods to what is perceived as descriptive research. The quest for additional rigor calls for a solid analysis of a large number of observations. Unfortunately, to achieve rigor, the researchers find themselves very distant from reality, which is socially and politically constructed rather than objectively determined. The pioneers of scientific management attempted to discover general rules of behavior such as the number of hierarchical levels or the span of control which were assumed to be pertinent to all organizations. Only decades later were contingent variables introduced. IB researchers also preferred to look for general rules and ignored contingent variables. Yet human behavior is very complex, and executives are also family members, belong to different clubs and interest groups and are citizens of a nation — and all of these affiliations impact on their behavior. Moreover, as Simon (1955) pointed out in the 1950s, they do not maximize. Since then, generations of behavioral economists — but unfortunately not IB scholars — have followed in his footsteps.

Classical economics-based theory alone is insufficient to understand the complexity of real life. We must incorporate politics, culture and institutions. Only if all of these approaches are woven into our theories may they be helpful for businessmen and for policy makers. One example is what I term "political strategy" — that is, concentrating on getting benefits from the government rather than on achieving competitive advantages in the marketplace. In a democratic society, power is diffused throughout the society, the spectrum of interest groups is wide and business itself is one of the most powerful organized interest groups. Some firms are state-owned and all large firms spend resources on lobbying. They have great political power — particularly, in small countries — but they are also deeply affected by the government and other environmental forces. Thus, when the government abandons its import-substitution policies and exposes firms to foreign competition, many firms go bankrupt.

In 1970, I taught at IMEDE, where I embarked on an intensive case-research effort on business–government interactions (Aharoni & Baden, 1977). I was able to identify the relevant actors in each situation and assess their strengths both in their home as well as in their host countries. I also found that human material needs are being satisfied to a larger extent through political mechanisms rather than through the market. I also studied boards of directors and the differences among state, trade-union and privately owned enterprises in Israel. I found that professional managers have the same objectives, aspirations and belief systems, irrespective of their firms' owners — be they the state, trade unions or private-sector owners. They pursue what they see as the firm's best interests, disregarding instructions. The simplistic views on the efficacy of planning or that of the market mechanism are both wrong. In my view, the key issue is to design objective and transparent systems for electing the best managers and directors and to avoid political appointments. These managers act within an uncertain environment of norms and institutions and, again, economic-based theory is not sufficient to understand the complexity of real life. The examples above illustrate that we must consider political, cultural and social factors, and acknowledge uncertainty.

Third, IB research is very much context-specific. It does not necessarily apply to different environments and diverse contexts nor is it independent of these factors. Researchers may study a large population and reach wrong conclusions because the choice of the population studied was not a representative sample. Thus, many observations on the behavior of manufacturing firms do not hold for services. As one example, many IB scholars have assumed that firms seek to control their subsidiaries to protect their intellectual property and therefore insist on full ownership. Yet hotel chain management seems to prefer joint ventures and uses this form even when the government allows full ownership (more examples may be found in Aharoni, 1997). By the same token, many of the conclusions reached by Porter (1990) are the result of studying mainly US-based large corporations. However, many Israeli, Canadian and Danish firms did not grow first in their home market. In fact, the Israeli high-technology industry exports more than 90 percent of its output, and in several cases, the firm does not sell in Israel at all! Clearly, a tiny country with a very limited market size faces different issues than a large country. Theories based on the experience of US firms may not be applicable to small countries.

My case research showed that successful firms did not attempt to compete head on against foreign giants. Instead, they identified a particular market niche in which they basically had a monopoly — being the only firm that supplied a certain unique product or service. This observation was even more relevant in international operations. Israeli firms cannot even hope to compete head on in the global market against the giant multinational firms. They can, however, be very successful when they define a niche that is either ignored (often because of its size) or unknown to the giant firms in the industry.

Strategy, I suggest as my fourth point, is not about *gaining competitive advantage in an industry* but about *creating a monopoly in a well-defined niche.* In other words, strategy is about being an outlier and being unique — not about being part of the herd. A large flow of statistically based research efforts attempt to connect industry structure with strategy, performance or other variables. Yet a successful competitor *creates* an industry, achieving success by being unique in a certain specific and well-identified niche within which this firm does not compete but which it dominates.

Having studied managerial behavior and its interaction with government in a small and relatively less-developed country, I was curious to find out whether things were different in the United States and other developed countries. The result was a book I called *The No-Risk Society* (1981), which showed that demands for social justice and equity have turned into calls for more publicly provided insurance and fewer private risks. Governments are expected to reduce or shift the risks once borne by individuals, immunize the latter against almost any change and insure them against any conceivable hazard. Ironically, government programs to reduce risks have the effect of encouraging people to be more reckless in a new version of moral hazard — a "culture of dependency", the erosion of individual responsibility, the decline of the entrepreneurial spirit and a "no-risk society" in the end. Both successful entrepreneurs and long-established businesses do take risks, but they do so against a background of extensive protections and hedges, many of them — such as the $500 billion savings and loans bailout in the US — being supplied at the taxpayers' expense. The expense of these programs is not confined to the public budget. Individuals demand less government yet clamor for public benefits so that the public also pays invisible taxes in the form of regulations that protect business from competition. If a firm begins to falter, the government may rescue it through loans, subsidies or protective trade agreements. The new version of moral hazard became apparent when, in the financial crisis of 2008, it was taken for granted that firms may be "too big to fail", thereby reinforcing the importance of political factors.

Finally, the MNEs of several dozens of years ago extracted rents from existing resources and knowledge developed at home. In an ever-shifting turbulent environment, they are learning to adapt themselves to the changing environment and to develop new capabilities through a globally coordinated network. In this network, knowledge can be developed in any subsidiary and then transferred to the whole network. I have offered my ideas on a few of the issues I observed in my IB research and I am interested to read about your experiences in this area.

References

Aharoni, Y. 1966. *The Foreign Investment Decision Process.* Boston, MA: Harvard Business School Press.

Aharoni, Y. 1981. *The No-Risk Society.* Chatham, NJ: Chatham House.

Aharoni, Y. 1993. The internationalization process in professional business service firms: Some tentative conclusions. In Aharoni, Y. (Ed.) *Coalitions and Competition: The Globalization of Professional Business Services.* Florence, KY: Routledge, pp. 280–285.

Aharoni, Y. (Ed.). 1997. *Changing Roles of State Intervention in Services in an Era of Open International Markets.* Albany, NY: SUNY Press.

Aharoni, Y. & Baden, C. 1977. *Business in the International Environment.* London: Macmillan.

Aharoni, Y. & Lachman, R. 1982. Can the manager's mind be nationalized? *Organization Studies*, 3(1): 33–46.

Porter, M. E. 1990. *The Competitive Advantage of Nations.* New York: Free Press.

Simon, H. 1955. A behavioral model of rational choice. *Quarterly Journal of Economics*, 69: 99–188.

Yair Aharoni is Professor Emeritus at the faculty of management, Tel-Aviv University, a Fellow of the International Academy of Management and the Academy of International Business. During his long and distinguished academic career, Aharoni was the Daniel and Grace Ross professor of International Business and later the Issachar Haimovic Professor of Business Policy — both at Tel Aviv University. He was the Thomas Henry Caroll Ford Foundation Visiting Professor of Business Administration, Harvard Graduate School of Business Administration. (1978–1979). He was also the J. Paul Stitch Visiting Professor of International Business at Duke University (1987–1995) and the director of CIBER (Center of International Business Education and Research) (1992–1995). He published several dozen books and monographs in Hebrew and in English, more than hundred papers and chapters in books and more than 150 cases. For his academic achievements he was awarded both Landau Prize (2007) and Israel Prize in management science (2010).

Strategic Decision-Making and Internationalization

https://doi.org/10.1142/9789811287510_0007

Chapter 7

Performance and Autonomy in Organizations: Determining Dominant Environmental Components*,†

Yair Aharoni, Zvi Maimon, and Eli Segev

The Leon Recanati Graduate School of Business Administration, Tel-Aviv University, Tel-Aviv, Israel

The formulation of a strategy for an organization begins with identifying the opportunities and risks in the environment. A full and permanent search — or scanning — of all environmental forces is both too costly and intractable in terms of management time. Our findings indicate that managers do not try to identify all environmental forces. Identifying the dominant components of the environment focuses scanning efforts and saves energy and, costs.

Furthermore, our findings clearly point out that achievement of autonomy may be advanced by organizational performance. An optimal strategy for a manager seeking to increase autonomy would be to concentrate efforts on dominant environmental components. A spillover effect will generalize this autonomy.

---

* This chapter is reproduced from *Management Science*, Vol. 24, No. 9 (1978).

† Accepted by Melvin F. Shakun, former Departmental Editor and Henry Mintzberg, Special Editor; received June 26, 1976. This paper has been with the authors 3 months, for 2 revisions.

Introduction

The environment in which the organization operates is widely recognized as a major determinant of its functioning. The environment is defined as the total of outside factors which influence, or may influence, any aspect of the organization (e.g., goals, structure, size, plans, procedures, operations, input, output, human relations (Ansoff, 1965: p. 10; Denning, 1971: p. 8; Dill, 1958; Emery & Trist, 1965; Steiner, 1969: p. 204; Terreberry, 1967/68)). For some, the environment is constantly changing and organizations have to navigate in turbulent fields (Emery & Trist, 1965). For others, the environment is quite stable; the organization has influence upon its environment which is composed of other organizations with interests similar to its own, or organizations controlled by them (Perrow, 1972). However, as Thompson and McEwen point out, there is a continuum of organizational influence in environmental relations, ranging from the domination of the organization over its environmental relations to the domination by the environment (Thompson & McEven, 1958).

The degree of autonomy, i.e., freedom from influence of the environment (Dill, 1958), depends on strategic choices related to such factors as location, markets to be served or products to be made. Given these basic choices, the study to be reported in this paper indicates that perceived managerial autonomy from the environment varies in a systematic way according to performance.[1]

The role of the environment in the process of strategy formulation varies in different organizations according to their relative influence. However, for any organization, the environment always (1) poses opportunities and risks that have to be identified, (2) constrains managerial activities, and (3) thrusts to modify goals. Of course the environment does not mechanistically change the organization: it is one consideration in managerial strategic choice.

Performance and Perceived Autonomy

In recent years organizational and management theorists have been paying increasing attention to organization-environment relationships. Two major considerations have justified this new interest:

---

[1] For different discussion about the relationships between organizational properties and autonomy, see Azumi & Hage (1972: pp. 91–100).

(a) organizations should be regarded as open-system entities, therefore, the organization-environment relationships are as crucial for functioning as internal relations;
(b) the environments of the organization are often turbulent, unstable, and uncontrollable; this leaves the managers of the organization uncertain as to what they should do and how to do it.

We regard the organizational environment as imposing constraints both on the goals of the organization as well as on the organizational decision-making process. These constraints are most clearly exemplified by the limitations which they impose on the autonomy of the organization management. Such autonomy is probably required in any type of organization in order to enable its management to take advantage of opportunities and to protect the organization against unanticipated or unpredicted damaging events.

We suggest that managerial autonomy is related to the degree to which management satisfies the various interests of the different components in the organizational environment. These various, and often conflicting interests are satisfied by certain organizational outputs, or transactions with the environment. The level of performance is hypothesized to be associated with the degree of perceived managerial autonomy. The present paper investigates this hypothesis on a sample of managers of Israeli business firms.

Hypotheses

1. Perceived managerial autonomy from an environmental component is a monotonic (increasing or decreasing) function of the level of organizational performance. The better one performs the better is one's bargaining position vis-a-vis the environment. This monotonic relationship is conditional, however, upon the degree to which the organization is dependent on the particular environmental factor. In the absence of a strong dependence, the monotonic relationship will be positive; if such a dependence exists, the relationship will be negative. The rationale behind the second part of this hypothesis is based on the assumption that if the organization strongly depends on an environmental factor to produce one of its outputs, the more the organization produces that particular output, the stronger the dependence is. Or, at least, the degree of dependence does not decrease.

The environment is composed of several segments and the autonomy from each one may be gained in different ways. One may ignore, avoid, oppose, the interests of a certain environmental segment, or one may collude with, or satisfy them. In this paper we argue that the way managers perceive their autonomy from each one of the specific environmental segments, i.e., from their interests, is related to performance variables.

A critical problem in the analysis of the organizational-environment relationship is the relative degree of importance attached to different environmental segments. Put differently, is it necessary to gain the same degree of autonomy from all the segments of the environment, or is it enough to concentrate on particular segments? If the latter is the case, how does one go about identifying these particular ones? Thus:

2. Managers tend to perceive certain components of the environment as being the dominant ones. Once autonomy from the dominant components has been achieved, it is likely to spill over to the nondominant components as well, even though achieving autonomy from each component individually may require different actions.

The data

The studied population is that of general managers of industrial plants in Israel, which, based on 1969 census of the Central Bureau of Statistics, employed 100 employees or more. Out of this population of 302 plants, 12 of the managers were, at the time of the study, out of the country, 38 refused to be interviewed before the fieldwork was completed. Several other managers are not included in the data because of one or more of the following reasons: their addresses were incorrect, a few of the firms merged after the list had been prepared, and a few others reduced the number of their employees below 100. The data, therefore, consists of interviews with 141 general managers of the largest industrial plants in Israel.

Although our sample is not a probability sample of the population, we have no evidence to suspect that a probability sample would result in substantially different conclusions.

Indicators

We chose six segments of the environment which, in our opinion, are perceived by Israeli business firms as having an influence on the functioning of the firm. We speculate, furthermore, that these segments ought to be considered in other industrial economies as well. The six are: the government, the workers, the market, suppliers, owners, and public opinion.

The government. The government in Israel, as a segment of the relevant environment of business firms, has at least two salient features: its impact on business is overwhelming, and it is far from being a monolithic body in terms of its interests. Consequently, we had to choose a few governmental agencies to capture a wide range of impacts and interests.

The choice of agencies was based on five criteria:

(1) The degree to which the agency allocates financial inducements;
(2) The degree to which the agency influences price controls;
(3) The degree to which the agency is responsible for the initiative in developing export industries;
(4) The degree to which the agency provides assistance in organization and promotion of foreign sales; and
(5) The degree to which the agency is involved in enforcing tax laws or granting tax concessions.

Based on these criteria, we chose the Treasury, The Ministry of Commerce & Industry, and a semi-autonomous agency established to encourage investments — The Investment Center.

The workers. Four different components of this segment of the environment were selected. This was necessary since for many years, the multitude of problems in labor relations in the country has been unsettled. Thus, the line of demarcation between the various bodies representing the workers is unclear. For this reason, we included both the General Federation of Labor and the Local Branch of the Federation of Labor as well as the Plant Union and the Employees.

The market. Here we used two indicators: the Customers and Competitors.

Suppliers. Two components were included here: Banks and other Suppliers.

Owners. We included three different types of environmental factors which we considered to be worth examining: Owners, The Board of Directors, and Interests of the Board of Directors' Members. This last one was included on the assumption that personal interests of the board of directors' members need not always coincide with the interests of the board of directors as an entity.

The public. We used Public Opinion as a surrogate for the public interest perceived by the managers of the firms.

The perceived degree of managerial autonomy from each one of the environmental components was estimated by the responses to the following question: "You are requested to rank the following entities according to the amount of influence they exercise on your freedom of decision". By reversing the scores we obtained a measure of the degree of perceived relative autonomy, given those specific environmental components.

The choice of indicators of organizational performance was highly influenced by the need to test our hypotheses that different aspects of performance are related to perceived managerial autonomy from different components of the environment. Using that guideline, four aspects of performance were chosen[2]:

(1) Volume of sales,
(2) The organizational past growth,
(3) The organizational projected growth, and
(4) The size of the organization.

Volume of sales is a rather common indicator of business organizations' performance. This aspect of performance is measured by two indicators: Volume of sales in 1969, and volume of export, both in Israeli Pounds (IL). Since, during its whole existence, one of the major economic problems of Israel has been an acute shortage of foreign currency, exports are highly valued in Israel as important contributions to the economy.

[2]Another possible measure of performance is net income, However, in the specific case of Israel, this measure is considered less relevant — both because of conceptual measurement problems and because of managerial values and was therefore not used. Reported net income at that period was not adjusted for changes in the price level, and given the significant rate of inflation in the country, the figures were not comparable. Moreover, many of the state-owned enterprises received subsidized loans of a substantial size and various other subsidies of inputs. The size of these loans affected profits more than performance; *certain firms were also required to freeze price*. In addition, profit considerations were dominant only in the private sector. Both state-owned and Histaduth-owned managers were motivated more by the desire to create employment, develop certain regions of the country or other social goals than by the profit motives. The performance aspects chosen seem to reflect better the perception of managers about their success.

Major exporters receive considerable financial incentives and also many intangible rewards.

Another major indicator of organizational performance is its rate of growth over the years. Past growth is important as a measure of the achievements at the time of the interview, and future growth — as an indicator of the manager's views of his future performance. These views may be based on hopes, aspirations, actual sales orders or some combination of all these variables. Past growth was estimated by the response of the managers to following questions: (a) "During the last five years, what has been the annual average growth rate of sales?" and (b) "During the last five years, what has been the annual average growth rate of export?" Future growth was estimated by the responses to the following questions: (a) "What is the average rate of growth of sales that you project for the next three years?" and (b) "What is the average annual rate of growth of exports that you project for the next three years?"

Finally, since Israel stresses full employment as a major national goal, the size of the organization, in terms of the number of employees, is examined. This aspect was estimated by the responses to the question: "What is the number of employees in the firm today?"

Design

In our conceptual framework we argue that:

(1) Autonomy from the environment, whether real or perceived is some monotonic function of the level of organizational performance. The interests of the environmental segments to be taken into consideration may be similar, unrelated, or even conflicting ones. But whatever the interrelationship among the various interests may be, the more they are taken into consideration, the more likely they are to satisfy a necessary condition for perceived managerial autonomy.

(2) The degree of autonomy from a certain environmental factor is a monotonic and positive function of taking into consideration its interests if, and only if, this is not associated with high dependence on that component of the environment. If such a dependence exists, the relationship is likely to be still monotone, but negative.

This implies weak monotonic relationships between each one of the organizational performance indicators and the environmental components.[3]

Notice that by assuming weak monotonic relationships we explicitly argue that by satisfying wants one does not necessarily increase perceived autonomy. Rather, the better the firm performs, using our criteria of performance, the higher the probability that the present level of perceived autonomy is not impaired. Or, put differently, satisfying various wants of the relevant environment is a necessary condition for the manager's perceived autonomy, but not a sufficient one. This, of course, is conditional upon the absence of strong dependence of the firm on that particular component of the environment. If such a condition does not hold, the better the firm performs, the higher the probability that the present level of dependence does not decrease.[4]

Findings of the empirical study

Table 1 presents a matrix of weak monotonicity correlation coefficients between the organizational performance indicators and the degree of perceived autonomy from the environmental components.

---

[3] By weak monotonic relationship we mean a type of relationship which may be expressed by the following statement: "If *X* increases, *Y* does not decrease", and "if *X* increases, *Y* does not increase". For discussion of this type of relationship, see Guttman (1968), and Wilson (1974).

[4] An appropriate weak monotonicity coefficient has been suggested by Levy & Guttman (1975). This particular coefficient (μ_2) is especially suited to our case, where one set of variables is measured on an interval scale (the performance indicators), while the other set of ranks creates an ordinal scale. Another coefficient of weak monotone relationship would be Goodman and Kruskal's Gama (Goodman & Kruskal, 1954). It seems to us that μ_2 is a more useful coefficient in this case, since it takes into account not only the rank order, but also the magnitude of the distances between any pair of ranks. μ_2 has a range between +1 and −1. Given *n* pairs of observations on numerical variables (X, Y): (X_i, Y_i) $(1, 2, \ldots, n)$ then

$$\mu_2(X,Y)\frac{\sum_{i=1}^{N}\sum_{j=1}^{N}(X_i - X_j)(Y_i - Y_j)}{\sum_{i=1}^{N}\sum_{j=1}^{N}|X_i - X_j||Y_i - Y_j|}$$

Table 1. Weak monotonicity correlation coefficients between organizational performance and the degree of relative autonomy from environmental components.

		Government			Workers				Market		Suppliers		Owners			The Public
Organizational Performance	Relative Autonomy From	The Treasury	Ministry of Commerce and Industry	The Investment Center	Employees	Plant Union	The General Federation of Labor	Local Branch of the Federation of Labor	Customers	Competitors	Banks	Suppliers	Stock Owners	Board of Directors	Interests of the Board of Directors' Members	Public Opinion
Sales	Sales (IL)	0.317	0.136	−0.095	0.218	0.177	0.162	0.055	0.069	0.064	0.186	0.116	0.128	0.089	0.054	0.183
	Export (IL)	−0.358	−0.256	−0.101	−0.271	−0.424	0.193	0.213	−0.535	−0.225	−0.153	−0.261	−0.024	−0.058	−0.011	0.495
Past	Sales (%)	0.024	0.359	−0.645	−0.051	−0.372	−0.038	−0.268	0.057	0.112	0.140	0.217	−0.243	−0.142	−0.439	−0.215
Growth	Export (%)	−0.384	−0.264	−0.725	−0.378	−0.304	−0.399	−0.210	0.034	−0.279	0.040	−0.124	0.002	−0.012	−0.022	0.114
Projected	Sales (%)	0.273	−0.343	0.451	−0.201	−0.145	0.069	−0.156	0.053	0.242	−0.280	−0.144	0.295	−0.265	0.032	−0.090
Growth	Export (%)	0.083	−0.579	0.250	0.150	0.320	0.393	0.193	0.457	0.285	−0.242	0.070	0.143	0.464	−0.142	0.242
Size	Number of Employees	0.138	0.111	−0.475	0.359	0.210	−0.407	−0.622	0.271	0.372	0.440	−0.129	−0.521	−0.685	−0.238	0.308

Looking at the first two rows in Table 1, one can discern some support for our first hypothesis. The greater dependence of exporting firms on the Government for financial incentives and assistance in organizing and promoting foreign sales, results in negative correlations between the performance indicators and autonomy from government. Tougher competition abroad may mean higher vulnerability to workers' demands, especially where time schedules are concerned. And, naturally dependence on banks for interim finance may be higher than in the case of local sales. This explains most of the negative correlations in the second row. When such a dependence is sharply reduced, as in the case of domestic sales, the correlations between the performance variables and perceived autonomy turn out to be positive for almost all cases.

It is interesting to note that the negative correlations are, on the average, stronger than the positive ones. While the median correlation in the first row is 0.12, the same value for the second row is −0.19 Altogether, though, the small to moderate size of the correlations suggests that the relationships between performance and perceived autonomy do exist. However, it also suggests that performance need not be the only factor, or even the dominant factor in determining autonomy.

In the design of the study and the choice of indicators it was assumed that the various governmental agencies do not form a homogeneous body. The same was assumed to be true for the workers' representatives. This was the rationale behind the inclusion, in the analysis, of more than a single component is each one of these two environmental segments. The figure in Table 1 clearly show that the different governmental agencies, as well as the different workers' representatives, are not perceived by the managers as monolithic entities. For example, while autonomy from the Treasury seems to increase with high volume of sales, this is not the case for the Investment Center. The same applies to the workers' representatives: while increase in export increases dependence on the employees and the plant union, the opposite is true for the other two bodies of workers' representatives (this is probably so because the latter are much more sensitive to macro-level considerations than the former, and export is a highly valuable national goal in Israel). Still, except for the three positive correlations in the second row (and the explanation for the third positive correlation is the same as for the first two) the basic prediction holds: sales increase autonomy while export is likely to reduce it.

Another example for the argument that the representatives of the workers are not perceived as a single body can be seen in the bottom row: the differential effects of the number of employees on autonomy are clearly demonstrated by the fact that two correlations are positive while the other two are negative. This is interpreted by us as representing a conflict of interest between the employees and the plant union on the one hand, and the General Federation of Labor and its Local Branch on the other hand. The General Federation of Labor concentrates its attention on the relationships between management and workers of large firms. This is because of the large number of Federation's members involved and because of precedent setting by the results of negotiations in large firms. Both for these reasons and for the greater sensitivity of the Federation to Macro-Economic considerations, the large firm has a greater autonomy from its local employees than from the outside representatives of these employees.

The first stage in identifying dominant components in the organizational environment is the presentation, in Table 2, of the relationships among the indicators of perceived autonomy.[5]

As can easily be seen, only 3 of the 105 correlations have a negative sign and another 6 are smaller than 0.10. The rest of the correlations are

---

[5]In this case we preferred to assume strong monotonic relationships in the following manner: "if *X* increases, *Y* increases, and if *X* does not vary, neither does *Y*" and "if *X* increases, *Y* decreases, and if *X* does not vary, neither does *Y*" (Wilson, 1974). A proper measure of similarity, or association, between any pair of measures of autonomy, should have at least two properties: (1) it should have the constraint of strong monotonicity, (2) it should also take into account the magnitude of the distances in the rank ordering of the two variables, Daniels (1944) showed that Pearson's product-moment correlation satisfied all these requirements. He used the following formula for the product-moment correlation:

$$r_{XY} = \frac{\sum_i^N \sum_j^N (X_i - X_j)(Y_i - Y_j)}{\sqrt{\sum_i \sum_j (X_i - X_j)^2} \sqrt{\sum_i \sum_j (Y_i - Y_j)^2}}$$

A matrix of Pearson's correlations was, therefore, computed for all fifteen measures of perceived managerial autonomy. The data appear in Table 2.

Table 2. Pearson's correlations among indicators of perceived managerial autonomy.

Government	(1)	The Treasury	0.43*								
	(2)	Ministry of Commerce and Industry	0.001								
	(3)	The Investment	0.44*	0.40*							
		Center	0.001	0.001							
	(4)	Employees	0.04	0.49*	0.34*						
			0.346	0.001	0.001						
Workers	(5)	Plant Union	0.17*	0.24*	0.09	0.49*					
			0.036	0.004	0.180	0.001					
	(6)	The General	0.21*	0.29*	0.14	0.31*	0.53*				
		Federation of Labor	0.014	0.001	0.069	0.001	0.001				
	(7)	Local Branch	0.26*	0.14	0.26*	0.35*	0.49*	0.75*			
		of Federation of Labor	0.003	0.067	0.004	0.001	0.001	0.001			
Market	(8)	Customers	0.03	0.31*	−0.14	0.55*	0.51*	.0.25*	0.10		
			0.393	0.001	0.079	0.001	0.001	0.004	0.142		
	(9)	Competitors	0.10	0.51*	0.37*	0.77*	0.28*	0.19*	0.12	0.45*	
			0.135	0.001	0.001	0.001	0.001	0.020	0.092	0.001	
Suppliers	(10)	Banks	0.42*	0.68*	0.50*	0.60*	0.24*	0.22*	0.18*	0.16*	0.68*
			0.001	0.001	0.001	0.001	0.004	0.010	0.032	0.041	0.001

		(1)	(2)	(3)	(4)	(5)	(6)	(7)	(8)	(9)	(10)	(11)	(12)	(13)	(14)
	(11) Suppliers	0.07	0.54*	0.35*	0.61*	0.35*	0.34*	0.23*	0.25*	0.61*	0.62*				
		0.227	0.001	0.001	0.001	0.001	0.001	0.008	0.003	0.001	0.001				
Owners	(12) Stock Owners	0.12	0.19*	0.04	0.17*	0.11	0.20*	0.18*	0.19*	0.20*	0.14	– 0.09			
		0.110	0.021	0.356	0.035	0.115	0.020	0.032	0.025	0.019	0.072	0.187			
	(13) Board of	0.13	0.31*	0.23*	0.53*	0.10	0.12	0.12	0.23*	0.43*	0.33*	0.22*	0.41*		
	Directors	0.078	0.001	0.008	0.001	0.146	0.105	0.099	0.005	0.001	0.001	0.009	0.001		
	(14) Interests of	0.13	0.36*	0.46*	0.65*	0.14	0.26*	0.41*-	0.10	0.61*	0.56*	0.48*	0.19*	0.46*	
	Directors	0.085	0.001	0.001	0.001	0.070	0.004	0.001	0.140	0.001	0.001	0.001	0.029	0.001	
The Public	(15) Public Opinion	0.30*	0.25*	0.32*	0.26*	0.33*	0.38*	0.43*	0.18*	0.40*	0.36*	0.16*	0.26*	0.07	0.34*
		0.001	0.003	0.001	0.002	0.001	0.001	0.001	0.026	0.001	0.001	0.044	0.004	0.225	0.001
		(1)	(2)	(3)	(4)	(5)	(6)	(7)	(8)	(9)	(10)	(11)	(12)	(13)	(14)

Note: $^*p < 0.05$.

positive, with a range from 0.10 to 0.77.[6] Thus, environmental components are perceived to impose complementary, rather than conflicting, demands on managerial autonomy.

One way to identify dominant components in the organizational environments would be to rank the variables in Table 2 according to the mean correlations for each variable. That is, since we are dealing with a symmetric matrix, the mean of each column or row might give us a clue as to the degree of association of the other variables with that particular one. Table 3 presents the mean correlations for each of the variables in Table 2.

Table 3 can be interpreted in at least two competing manners. Both interpretations show that our approach is a useful one, since it provides us with information on the degree of success in acquiring autonomy for the

Table 3. Mean correlations for the indicators of perceived managerial autonomy (mean of variables in Table 2).

Variable	Mean Correlation
Employees (4)	0.44
Competitors (9)	0.41
Banks (10)	0.41
Ministry of Commerce and Industry (2)	0.37
Suppliers (11)	0.34
Interests of Directors (14)	0.33
The General Federation of Labor (6)	0.30
Plant Union (5)	0.29
Local Branch of the Federation of Labor (7)	0.29
Public Opinion (15)	0.29
The Investment Center (3)	0.27
Board of Directors (13)	0.26
Customers (8)	0.22
The Treasury (1)	0.20
Stock Owners (12)	0.16

[6] Part of the reason for the positive correlations probably stems from the fact that the managers ranked autonomy from several environmental components similarly. In such a case, if the rank order of the few united cases is similar, the correlations will be nonnegative. Nevertheless, it is our belief that there is a nonstatistical explanation as well, which is presented in the text.

managers. One interpretation could be that the higher the value of the mean correlation, the higher the importance of that variable and the higher the autonomy from that dominant component of the environment, the easier it is to achieve autonomy from other parts of the environment. This may tell us how managers should allocate their efforts in order to obtain autonomy. One could, however, argue that a high mean correlation is by no means sufficient evidence for a particular variable being a dominant aspect of the environment; at most, this is an acceptable predictor of the degree of taking various interests in the organizational environment into consideration, which happens to be associated with that particular variable. This still provides the manager with some indication of success or failure in acquiring autonomy.

According to Table 3, the more one acquires autonomy from employees, competitors, banks, and the Ministry of Commerce & Industry, the higher the probability that one acquires autonomy from the rest of the environment as well. Notice also that each of the four variables just mentioned represents a different segment of the environment, and the differences in the magnitude of the mean correlations are negligible. Thus, in order to gain autonomy from the environment, one has first to identify the major segments of the relevant environment. Given that the relevant important environmental segments have been identified, one cannot assume *a priori* that the interests of the different components of that environmental segment are to be taken into consideration in a similar manner. The results of Table 1, and especially the discussion of the first conclusion from that table support this hypothesis.

In each segment of the environment, there is likely to be one or more dominant aspects to be taken into account. Although different things may be required to satisfy various components in the environment, once autonomy from the dominant components has been achieved, there is likely to be a spill-over to the nondominant components as well. Table 2 provides some support for this hypothesis.

This spill-over, or generalizing effect, however, is far from perfect. Autonomy from the dominant components is likely to be followed by autonomy from the other components, but the degree of autonomy may vary, which stresses the point that the interests in the environment may still be different. This is evident from Table 2, when one notices the usually moderate and medium size correlations between the dominant variables mentioned in Table 3 and the rest of the variables in Table 2.

Implications

Our point of departure has been that managers of industrial enterprises aspire to gain autonomy or even to control the relevant environments of their firms. It was suggested that both the achievement of autonomy and the gaining of control, may be advanced by the organizational performance. It was further suggested that since the relevant environment is likely to be composed of a number of heterogeneous interests and may be controlled by a variety of means, management in organizations face the problems of both setting priorities in dealing with the environment and allocating the necessary resources according to these priorities. Since the determination of a suitable strategy for an organization begins in identifying the opportunities and risks in the environment, an essential part of the process of strategy formulation is the identification of the pattern of external conditions that will affect the life of the business. It is also necessary to predict all possible changes in the environment as well as their probable impact on any given organization. In order to adapt action to a changing environment, it is necessary to institute systems of surveillance of all relevant factors and trends in the environment and their impact on the organization and to watch for signs of changes which require shifting priorities or a major revamping of strategy. In practice, however, it is generally agreed that a full and permanent search — or scanning — of all environmental forces is both too costly and inretractable in terms of management time. Even when the search is limited and at least partly structured, it may still be too costly in terms of energies and attention it consumes, let alone other resources. It is often recommended that management, instead of trying to monitor every part of its environment that might change, will take steps to identify major and crucial aspects of the environment. This assertion still leaves unanswered the important question: how does one go about identifying the crucial variables, and how can one be sure that all these variables have been identified?

The crucial need of taking the environment into account in devising strategy is widely acknowledged, but no systematic approach for organizing knowledge about a company's changing environment has yet been developed. In fact, there is reason to believe that such a system is impossible — because of man's limited capacity and his tendency to reach "satisficing" rather than optimizing decisions.

Our findings strongly suggest that, at least as far as managers of industrial plants in Israel are concerned, managers do not try to identify all environmental factors. To the extent that our findings are not culture-bound but can be interpreted as representing universal behavior, it may well turn out that managers classify what they perceive to be relevant environment into certain segments, each consisting of various components. Once these segments have been classified, the managers concentrate their search on the identification of a dominant component in each segment. By a dominant component we mean an environmental component which, when satisfied or controlled, results in a larger management autonomy from, or control of, that segment of the environment than existed before this component had been satisfied.

The identification of the dominant components not only saves energy and attention for the permanent search of the environment, but it also saves resources that might have been allocated to satisfy or control non-dominant components. Furthermore, one can probably assume that dominant components are not very sensitive to non-major changes in the environment. This means that the amount of resources directed at scanning the environment may be reduced by resorting to only periodic checks as to whether or not there have been changes in the dominant components.

If this is indeed the case, an optimal strategy for a business firm manager seeking to increase autonomy would be to concentrate his efforts on one or more components in the relevant environmental segments and secure the degree of desired autonomy from them. The spill-over effect will probably generalize this autonomy, though to various degrees, to other environmental components as well. Therefore, future research should concentrate on the ways used to identify relevant environmental factors and the amount of possible spill-over. The identification of relevant environmental factors should start from a quite refined list of possible factors. Thus, in our study, "government" was found to be a nonmonolithic body that should' be broken down to various components, while the various components of the union were strongly correlated among themselves.

Another important conclusion is that perceived autonomy is not always positively related to performance. In some cases, increased performance will reduce autonomy, as clearly demonstrated by our findings about export performance in Israel: the more one exports, the less autonomy one perceives to have. Therefore, desired autonomy is not always achieved by increasing performance. In fact, certain strategic decisions may reduce autonomy. One may even hypothesize that those managers who value autonomy do not always agree to respond to government's pressures because such a response might be associated with reduced autonomy.

References

Ansoff, H. I. (1965). *Corporate Strategy.* New York: McGraw-Hill.

Azumi, K. & Hage, J. (Eds.) (1972). *Organizational Systems.* Lexington, MA: Heath.

Daniels, H. E. (1944). The relation between measures of correlation in the universe of sample permutations. *Biometrika,* 33: 129–135.

Denning, B. W. (Ed.) (1971). *Corporate Planning, Selected Concepts.* London: McGraw-Hill.

Dill W. R. (1958). Environments as an influence on managerial autonomy. *Administrative Science Quarterly,* 2(4), 409–443.

Emery, F. E. & Trist, E. L. (1965). The causal texture of organizational environments. *Human Relations,* 18: 21–32.

Goodman, L. & Kruskal, W. (1954). Measures of association for cross classifications I. *Journal of the American Statistical Association,* 49 (December 1954): 732–764.

Guttman L. (1968). A general nonmetric technique for finding the smallest coordinate space for configuration of points. *Psychometrika,* 33: 469–506.

Levy, S. & Guttman, L. (1975). On the multivariate structure of well being. *Social Indicators Research,* 361–368.

Perrow, C. (1972). *Complex Organizations: A Critical Essay.* Glenview, IL: Scott, Foresman.

Steiner, G. A. (1969). *Top Management Planning.* New York: Macmillan.

Terreberry, S. (1967/68). The evolution of organizational environments. *Administrative Science Quarterly,* 12: 590–613.

Thompson, J. D. & McEven, W. J. (1958). Organizational goals and environment: Goal-setting as an interaction process. *American Sociological Review,* 23: 23–31.

Wilson, T. P. (1974). Measures of association for bivariate ordinal hypotheses. In Blalock, H. M. (Ed.) *Measurement in the Social Sciences.* Chicago: Aldine, pp. 327–342.

https://doi.org/10.1142/9789811287510_0008

Chapter 8

Interrelationships Between Environmental Dependencies: A Basis for Tradeoffs to Increase Autonomy*

Yair Aharoni, Zvi Maimon, and Eli Segev

Graduate School of Business Administration, Tel Aviv University, Ramaf Aviv, Tel Aviv, Israel

Summary

General managers of large industrial plants in Israel were asked to evaluate the effects of environmental dependencies on their freedom of action. It was found that most segments of the environment were perceived as homogeneous — affecting the firms' autonomy in similar ways. Different components of government, however, were perceived as having conflicting interests both within the segment and with other segments of the environment. When a segment of the environment is heterogeneous, it is possible that managers use a tradeoff strategy, in which pressures generated by one component of the environment can be used as a means to reduce pressure of the other components.

*This chapter is reproduced from *Strategic Management Journal*, Vol. 2, pp. 197–208 (1981).

Introduction

The environment in which the organization operates is widely recognized as one of the major determinants of its functioning. The environment is defined as the total of outside factors which influence, or may influence, any organizational aspect (e.g., goals, structure, size, plans, procedures, operations, input, output, human relations (Ansoff, 1965: p. 10; Denning, 1971: p. 8; Dill, 1958; Duncan, 1972; Emery & Trist, 1965; Hage & Aiken, 1970; Lawrence & Lorsch, 1967; Pugh *et al.*, 1969; Steiner, 1969: p. 204; Terreberry, 1967/68; Thompson & McEven, 1958). Recently it was suggested that "... organizations are other-directed, involved in a constant struggle for autonomy and discretion, confronted with constraint and external control" (Pfeffer & Salancik, 1978: p. 257).

At least three approaches to the environment–organization interrelationships are used in theory and research (Aldrich & Pfeffer, 1976; Aldrich & Mindlin, 1978). The ecological perspective adopts the natural selection mechanism to study the rise, success, and fall of organizations (Glover, 1966). The information, or uncertainty, perspective studies the effects of perceived uncertainty of environmental information on organizations (Aldrich & Mindlin, 1978). The resource perspective views the environment as a source of scarce resources (inputs) which are sought after by a population of organizations that competes for, as well as shares, them (Pfeffer & Salancik, 1978). Yuchtman & Seashore (1967) defined organizational effectiveness as the ability of the organization to obtain scarce resources, hold its bargaining position, and maintain its autonomy. Benson identified four types of resources on the availability of which the organization is dependent: personnel, information, products and services, and operating funds, including accumulation of capital (Benson, 1975). The resource-dependence school of thought defined conditions for dependence, identified environmental dimensions relevant to dependence, and studied the effects of dependence on organizational behavior, structure, and strategy formulation (Aldrich, 1972; Aldrich & Mindlin, 1978; Blau, 1964; Burns & Stalker, 1961; Emerson, 1962).

Works of the resource-dependence school of thought stress the dependence of the organization on the environment for resources, that is, the input dependence. However, the possible number of variables in the environment on which an organization may be dependent is much larger. An organization may be dependent on the environment not only for the availability of inputs and for the consumption of its output, but also for constraints on its operations. A few examples: an organization may be dependent on its environment for new technology; its freedom of action may be constrained by a whole gamut of governmental regulations on safety standards, taxation, employment of women or of minority groups; and it also may be dependent on the sociopolitical system for the legitimacy of its activities. Each one of the myriad of forces in the environment may decrease the organization's freedom of action, and with it its managerial discretion.

It is a generally accepted hypothesis today that managers, as a rule, strive to increase or maintain their relative autonomy within the organization as well as in the outside environments.

The desire to maintain autonomy may stem from several sources: personal needs (e.g., need for power, self-esteem, status, consideration), functional needs of the job (e.g., the need to demonstrate power, success, and independence to subordinates, peers, and superiors, as well as to outsiders), and advancement of the bargaining position of the organization (e.g., maintaining some capability to handle unanticipated and undesirable events, or maintaining some slack to take advantage of sudden or unforeseen opportunities).

In a previous paper we provided some evidence to support the proposition that there exists some interdependence between the degree of perceived autonomy from the various components of the same segment in the environment or from various segments in the relevant environment (Aharoni *et al.*, 1978). By segment of the environment we mean those parts of the environment which can be regarded as distinguishable from others, each consisting of some components. We suggested that managerial autonomy is monotonely related to the degree to which managers satisfy the various interests of the different components in the relevant organizational environment. These various interests are satisfied by certain organizational outputs, or transactions, with the environment. Furthermore, we suggested that in each one of the segments in the relevant environment, there is likely to be one or more dominant components. An optimal strategy for a business firm manager seeking to increase his autonomy could be to concentrate his efforts on one or more components in each segment and secure the degree of desired autonomy from them. A spill-over effect will probably generalize this autonomy, though to various degrees, to other environmental components as well.

In this paper, we report further results of environmental dependence. It is shown that when a segment of the environment is heterogeneous,[1] the strategy of satisfying the interests of a dominant component may not work as effectively as in homogeneous segments. In some cases the requirements of different segments of the environment may be so diverse that no dominant factor can be found. One such case is the government: in an earlier study it was shown that in Israel the various governmental agencies are clearly perceived by general managers of industrial firms to have different interests and goals (Aharoni *et al.*, 1978). We believe this is the case in other countries as well. Thus, in the United States government, its different branches may have different claims; the demands of the EPA, for example, may be contradictory to those of the OSHA.

In other words, government is not a monolithic body, and the manager therefore will not be able to achieve autonomy by satisfying an important (or a dominant) environmental component. In such cases it is plausible that an alternative strategy could be possible: the use of constraints imposed by one component of the environment to achieve more autonomy from another. For example, a manager who is constrained by governmental policies from raising prices, may use this constraint (or dependence) in order to relieve himself from the constraint of achieving a certain target rate of return on investment, or a certain dividend payout. By the same token, in a situation in which the firm is not free to raise prices without governmental approval, a manager who is forced by a strong union to raise wages can use the increase in wages as a bargaining weapon to get approval to raise prices, thus effectively reducing his dependence on the government.[2] Finally, one would expect managers to resort to the excuses of governmental dependencies while dealing with clients. A simple example could be the case of restricted credit terms to clients because of governmental monetary policy. In other words, dependency does not necessarily imply weakness, but can be used as a source of strength:

[1]The more similar the interests of the various components of a certain environmental segment are, the more homogeneous that segment; and the more divergent the interests are, the more heterogeneous that segment.

[2]Another example is the dependence of major customers, mainly government and large industrial users, which tends to reduce competitive market pressures when the dependence is mutual (Grinyer *et al.*, 1980).

pressure from a certain environmental component to do a certain thing, can be reduced and even eliminated, by demonstrating how a particular course of action followed by the firm had been imposed on it by other components in the environment.

One could even imagine situations where the firm might invite pressures from certain components in order to reduce pressure from others or to improve its bargaining position in other contexts (Pfeffer & Salancik, 1978: 96). For example, union pressures have been invited to secure governmental contracts, to receive subsidies in development regions or to prevent reduction in tariffs or to induce import restrictions. Thus, a resourceful manager may be able to turn environmental threats into opportunities using as his weapon a tradeoff process among a variety of dependencies. In this process, a manager may use his dependence on a certain environmental force as leverage in order to reduce his dependence on another environmental factor. These offsetting, rather than complimentary dependencies, which make possible a tradeoff process, are likely to be perceived among government components and between government and other environmental segments, mainly firm's owners and market elements. More generally, the following hypothesis is suggested.

Hypothesis: The more homogeneous a particular segment is, the more it is perceived to affect the firm's autonomy in a similar way; and the more heterogeneous a segment is, the more differentially it is perceived to affect the firm's freedom of action.

The rationale behind the hypothesis is that components which affect the degree of autonomy, or dependence, through the same means (e.g., revenues, costs, etc.) are likely to have similar impacts on the organization more than components affecting the firm through different means. A homogeneous environmental segment, the components of which affect the organizational autonomy through the same means, is therefore more likely to affect the firm in a uniform way than a more heterogeneous segment.

To the extent that this hypothesis is empirically supported, it will provide us with a guideline as to which strategy can be effectively adopted in order to increase one's autonomy. If the impact of the particular segment is uniform, then concentration on satisfying the interests of a dominant component or components is, probably, the efficient strategy to follow, but if a particular important environmental segment affects the organizational or managerial autonomy in different ways, then playing the components of that particular segment against each other may be a more promising approach.

Method and Design

The data

The population which was studied was that of general managers of industrial plants in Israel which employed 100 employees or more according to the 1969 census of the Central Bureau of Statistics. Out of this population of 302 plants, 12 of the managers were abroad at the time of the study, and 38 refused to be interviewed before the fieldwork was completed. Several other managers were not included in the data because of one or more of the following reasons: their addresses were incorrect; a few of the firms merged after the list had been prepared; and a few others reduced the number of their employees to below 100. The data, therefore, consist of interviews with 141 general managers of the largest industrial plants in Israel.

Although our sample is not a probability sample of the population, we have no evidence to suspect that a probability sample would lead to substantially different conclusions.

The conceptual framework

The research design is expressed by a mapping sentence which assigns, or observes for each respondent (**X**) a value of the range (**R**) for each item classified by the content facets of the domain (facet **A** and **B** in this case). For a discussion of the concept and some examples of its application in the social sciences, see Borg (1977), Elizur & Guttman (1976), Guttman (1970), Levy (1976), and Levy & Guttman (1975).

General Manager (X) evaluates the dependencies of his organization on

$$\begin{array}{ccc} \textit{A. Segments in the environment} & & \textit{B. Types of dependencies} \\ \left\{\begin{array}{l} a_1 \text{ government} \\ a_2 \text{ workers} \\ a_3 \text{ market} \\ a_4 \text{ suppliers} \\ a_5 \text{ owners} \\ a_6 \text{ public} \end{array}\right\} & \text{through their impact on the} & \left\{\begin{array}{l} b_1 \text{ revenues} \\ b_2 \text{ costs} \\ b_3 \text{ liquidity} \\ b_4 \text{ long range plans} \\ b_5 \text{ general functioning} \end{array}\right\} \end{array}$$

$$\text{of his organization} \rightarrow \left\{\begin{matrix} \textit{Range} \\ \text{very strong} \\ \text{to} \\ \text{very weak} \end{matrix}\right\} \text{dependencies.'}$$

The elements in facet A distinguish between the various segments in the environment. Each one of these segments consists of one or more components, representing different parts of that segment. Facet **B,** on the other hand, distinguishes among some of the more important types of dependencies of an organization on the various environmental components which reduce the freedom of action of its managers.

The mapping sentence calls for at least 30 = (6 × 5) operational definitions if each one of the profiles (combinations) is to be measured by at least one indicator. However, when the variables were operationalized it soon became clear that certain profiles were not relevant or meaningful (e.g., only a_6b_5 is really relevant, but a_6b_4 or a_6b_3 or a_6b_1 are not very meaningful). At the same time, quite a few profiles were operationalized by two or more indicators to better represent various environmental segments. The operational definitions of the variables are presented below.

Operational definitions of the profiles in the mapping sentence

Facet **A** consists of six segments of the environment which, we suggest, are perceived by Israeli business managers as having an influence on the functioning of the firm. Furthermore, we speculate that these segments ought to be considered in other industrial economies as well. The following is a description of the criteria used to operationalize the indicators for these six segments.

The government

The government in Israel, as a segment of the relevant environment of business firms, has at least two salient features: it has an overwhelming impact on business, and it is far from being a monolithic body in terms of its interests. Consequently, we had to choose a few governmental agencies to capture a wide range of impacts and interests.

The choice of agencies was based on five criteria:

(1) the degree to which the agency allocates financial inducements;
(2) the degree to which the agency influences price controls;

(3) the degree to which the agency is responsible for the initiative in developing export industries;
(4) the degree to which the agency provides assistance in organization and promotion of foreign sales; and
(5) the degree to which the agency is enforcing tax laws or granting tax concessions.

Based on these criteria we chose the Treasury, the Ministry of Commerce and Industry, and a semi-autonomous agency established to encourage investments — the Investment Centre.

The workers

Four different components of this segment of the environment were selected. This was necessary since the line of demarcation between the various bodies representing the workers is unclear. For this reason, we included both the General Federation of Labor and the local branch of the Federation of Labor, as well as the plant union and the employees.

The market

Here we used two indicators: the customers and competitors.

Suppliers

Two components were included here: banks and other suppliers.

Owners

We included three different types of environmental factors which we considered to be worth examining: owners, the board of directors, and interests of members of the board of directors. This last component was included on the assumption that personal interests of members of the board of directors need not always coincide with the interests of the board of directors as an entity.

The public

We used public opinion as a surrogate for the public interest perceived by the managers of the firms.

Facet **B** consists of a minimal list of the major kinds of dependencies through which the environment may affect the business firm and, thus, the freedom of decision of its managers. Two sets of questions were presented to the general managers concerning the effects of environmental dependencies on their freedom of decision making:

1. "You are requested to rank the following factors according to the amount of influence they exercise on your freedom of decision:
   - a_1b_2 direct taxes
   - a_1b_2 wage policy
   - a_1b_1 development area incentives
   - a_1b_4 tariff reduction
   - a_1b_1 export incentives
   - a_1b_3 monetary policy
   - a_1b_2 indirect taxes
   - a_3b_4 the European Common Market."
2. "You are requested to rank the following entities according to the amount of influence they exercise on your freedom of decision:
   - a_1b_2 the Treasury
   - a_1b_3 Ministry of Commerce and Industry
   - a_1b_1 the Investment Centre
   - a_2b_2 employees
   - a_2b_2 plant union
   - a_2b_2 General Federation of Labor
   - a_2b_2 local branch of the General Federation of Workers
   - a_3b_1 clients
   - a_3b_1 competitors
   - a_4b_3 banks
   - a_4b_2 suppliers
   - a_5b_4 stock owners
   - a_5b_4 board of directors
   - a_5b_4 interests of the board of directors members
   - a_6b_5 public opinion."

The hypothesis predicts that the interrelationships between components in homogeneous segments are likely to be positive and strong, while the interrelationships between components of heterogeneous segments are likely to be more often negative.

Notice that the hypothesis does not imply that a change in the degree of a certain dependency is a sufficient condition for a change in another dependency. Rather, as perception of autonomy from one component of the environment increases, the perception of autonomy from another component does not decrease. That is, it remains unchanged or increases.

This is the case of positive association. For the negative case, the hypothesis suggests that as the perception of autonomy from a certain component increases, the perception of autonomy from another component does not increase. That is, it remains unchanged or decreases.

This rules out the possibility of resorting to a strong monotonicity measure of association, such as the Pearson's correlation coefficient (Maimon, 1978). Instead, such a design requires a weak monotonic analysis. An appropriate measure to test such a hypothesis is Guttman's correlation coefficient of weak monotonicity[3] (Guttman, 1977; Lingoes, 1973).

Results

The hypothesis is tested by analyzing a matrix of weak monotonicity correlation coefficients for all 23 variables.

Table 1 supports our hypothesis. Out of the 253 off-diagonal coefficients, 30 are negative. Of the positive ones, 44 indicate no monotone relationship or a very weak one ($\mu_2 \leq 0.20$). 140 coefficients indicate moderate weak monotonicity ($\mu_2 \leq 0.59$), and 39 provide evidence of highly complementary monotone relationships ($\mu_2 \geq 0.60$).

Note that these are the results that should be expected if our hypothesis is to be supported. The reasons are as follows:

(a) Two segments, workers and owners, are completely uniform in their impacts. The various components of the workers segment affect autonomy through their impacts on costs, while the owners influence autonomy through long range plans. Therefore, the interrelationships between any pair of components in each one of those segments should be positive. And indeed, inspection of Table 1 (the intersection of

---

[3]This is a symmetrical coefficient which varies from −1 to +1. Its formula is:

$$\mu_2 = \frac{\sum_{p\in P}\sum_{q\in P}\left(x_p - x_q\right)\left(y_p - y_q\right)}{\sum_{p\in P}\sum_{q\in P}\left|x_p - x_q\right|\left|y_p - y_q\right|}$$

where x and y are numerical variables and p and q are different members of the set P. Since the sampling distribution of μ_2 has not yet been sufficiently investigated to formulate accurate probabilistic statements, and the sample is not a simple random sample, no significance levels are provided.

Table 1. Weak monotonicity correlation coefficients for all variables (decimal points omitted).

Environmental Segment	Environmental Component or Constraint		1	2	3	4	5	6	7	8	9	10	11	12	13	14	15	16	17	18	19	20	21	22	23
Government	Direct Taxes	(1)	—	19	22	32	57	−06	68	21	18	34	22	09	−13	09	25	−05	30	43	−14	05	−14	−04	41
	Wage Policy	(2)	19	—	46	−26	01	71	12	43	47	62	32	30	29	40	51	−01	19	51	52	−44	−37	41	14
	Development Area Incentives	(3)	22	46	—	38	53	21	15	31	29	43	29	10	09	17	45	06	23	11	18	01	12	−09	11
	Tariff Reduction	(4)	32	−26	38	—	45	−46	−05	03	24	−33	53	53	38	27	00	63	41	14	16	43	37	−22	17
	Export Incentives	(5)	57	01	53	45	—	−14	63	56	47	16	22	21	−10	−01	19	28	46	55	11	27	25	−15	40
	Monetary Policy	(6)	−06	71	21	−46	−14	—	40	38	28	66	−03	01	33	49	44	−31	−17	22	38	−16	−17	29	10
	Indirect Taxes	(7)	68	12	15	−05	63	40	—	41	23	38	22	21	17	49	39	−05	41	48	15	21	06	33	70
	The Treasury	(8)	21	43	31	03	56	38	41	—	60	61	08	25	30	38	58	04	20	62	12	19	25	26	43
	Ministry for Commerce and Industry	(9)	18	47	29	24	47	28	23	60	—	54	67	37	45	21	23	50	68	83	70	30	67	50	21
	Investment Centre	(10)	34	62	43	−33	16	66	38	61	54	—	51	14	22	38	57	−23	53	67	48	06	34	65	49
Workers	Employees	(11)	22	32	29	53	22	−03	22	08	67	51	—	82	60	50	08	77	88	75	76	27	68	79	39
	Plant Union	(12)	09	30	10	53	21	01	21	25	37	14	82	—	70	67	30	74	52	40	55	18	18	28	48
	General Federation of Workers	(13)	−13	29	09	38	−10	33	17	30	45	22	60	70	—	50	25	77	88	36	75	27	22	59	54
	Local Branch of the General Federation of Workers	(14)	09	40	17	27	−01	49	49	38	21	38	50	67	50	—	56	17	18	26	33	30	18	59	59

(Continued)

Table 1. *(Continued)*

Environmental Segment	Environmental Component or Constraint		1	2	3	4	5	6	7	8	9	10	11	12	13	14	15	16	17	18	19	20	21	22	23
Market	The Common Market	(15)	25	51	45	00	19	44	39	58	23	57	08	30	25	56	—	−08	42	33	04	18	−04	43	59
	Clients	(16)	−05	−01	06	63	28	−31	−05	04	50	−23	77	74	77	17	−08	—	68	27	41	32	40	−18	30
	Competitors	(17)	30	19	23	41	46	−17	41	20	68	53	88	52	88	18	42	68	—	82	76	30	55	74	56
Suppliers	Banks	(18)	43	51	11	14	55	22	48	62	83	67	75	40	36	26	33	27	82	—	76	22	44	70	70
	Suppliers	(19)	−14	52	18	16	11	38	15	12	70	48	76	55	75	33	04	41	76	76	—	−13	29	62	24
Owners	Stock Owners	(20)	05	−44	01	43	27	−16	21	19	30	06	27	18	27	30	18	32	30	22	−13	—	59	30	39
	The Board of Directors	(21)	−14	−37	12	37	25	−17	06	25	67	34	68	18	22	18	−04	40	55	44	29	59	—	59	12
	Interests of the Board of Directors Members	(22)	−04	41	−09	−22	−15	29	33	26	50	65	79	28	59	59	43	−18	74	70	62	30	59	'—	51
The Public	Public Opinion	(23)	41	14	11	17	40	10	70	43	21	49	39	48	54	59	59	30	56	70	24	39	12	51	—

rows and columns 11–14 and 20–22) shows that not only are all correlations positive, but they also have quite high values.

(b) On the other hand, in the market segment, clients have a negative correlation with the European common market. Although the two components belong to the same environmental segment, they affect autonomy through different means (i.e., revenues and long range plans).

(c) The government is clearly the most heterogeneous and probably the most important segment in the environment. We would expect, therefore, most of the negative correlations to be related to government. Indeed they are, as can be seen from Table 2: only three out of 30 negative correlations do not involve at least one component of the government segment.

Table 2. Analysis of the negative correlations.

	Variables			
	First Variable		Second Variable	
μ_2	Name	Profile	Name	Profile
−0.46	Monetary policy	a_1b_3	Tariff reduction	a_1b_4
−0.44	Stock owners	a_sb_4	Wage policy	a_1b_2
−0.37	The Board of Directors	a_sb_4	Wage policy	a_1b_2
−0.33	The Investment Centre	a_1b_1	Tariff reduction	a_1b_4
−0.31	Clients	a_3b_1	Monetary policy	a_1b_3
−0.26	Tariff reduction	a_1b_4	Wage policy	a_1b_2
−0.23	Clients	a_3b_1	The Investment Centre	a_1b_1
−0.22	Interests of the Board of	a_5b_4	Tariff reduction	a_1b_4
	Directors members		Direct taxes	a_1b_2
−0.18	Interests of the Board of	a_5b_4	Monetary policy	a_1b_3
	Directors members		Competitors	a_3b_1
−0.17	Board of Directors	a_5b_4	Stock owners	a_5b_4
−0.17	Monetary policy	a_1b_3	Interests of the Board of	
−0.16	Monetary policy	a_1b_3	Directors members	a_5b_4
−0.15	Export incentives	a_1b_1	Direct taxes	a_1b_2
−0.14	Board of Directors	a_5b_4	Direct taxes	a_1b_2
−0.14	Suppliers	a_4b_2	Export incentives	a_1b_1
−0.14	Monetary policy	a_1b_3	Suppliers	a_4b_2
−0.13	Stock owners	a_5b_4	General Federation of Workers	a_2b_2
−0.13	Direct taxes	a_1b_2	General Federation of Workers	a_2b_2

(*Continued*)

Table 2. (*Continued*)

	Variables			
	First Variable		Second Variable	
μ_2	Name	Profile	Name	Profile
−0.10	Export incentives	a_1b_1	Interests of the Board of	
−0.09	Development area incentives	a_1b_1	Directors members	a_5b_4
−0.08	Clients	a_3b_1	The Common Market	a_3b_4
−0.06	Direct taxes	a_1b_2	Monetary policy	a_1b_3
−0.05	Direct taxes	a_1b_2	Clients	a_3b_1
−0.05	Indirect taxes	a_1b_2	Clients	a_3b_1
−0.05	Indirect taxes	a_1b_2	Tariff reduction	a_1b_4
−0.04	Direct taxes	a_1b_2	Interests of Board of	
−0.04	The Common Market	a_3b_4	Directors members	a_5b_4
−0.03	Monetary policy	a_1b_3	Board of Directors	a_5b_4
−0.01	Wage policy	a_1b_2	Employees	a_2b_2
−0.01	Export incentives	a_1b_1	Clients	a_3b_1
			Local branch of the Federation	a_2b_2

Finally, since the impact of the various governmental agencies and policies is far from homogeneous, some agencies or policies are likely to be regarded as performing certain functions of other environmental segments. The Ministry of Commerce and Industry, for example, may be regarded as a resource supplier, like banks or other suppliers (inspection of the ninth row in Table 1 shows that the highest correlations in that row are with suppliers).

Discussion

The environment has been viewed as a source of scarce resources sought after by a population of organizations, which compete as well as share them (Yuchtman & Seashore, 1967). There is a whole variety of possible responses of an organization to environmental demands. In a previous study, we suggested one possible response: satisfaction of the demands of the dominant component in each one of the segments of the environment. This strategy was shown to allow an organization to generate a spillover that should satisfy, or at least neutralize, other components of the environment.

Table 1 shows that general managers of business firms in Israel perceive most environmental dependencies as complementary. Table 1 also shows, however, that within the government segment, various components have conflicting interests. Moreover, components of the government may have conflicting interests with other segments of the environment. In this case, the strategy of satisfying the dominant component is counterproductive: satisfying demands of one segment of the environment may well not reduce demands of others. In such cases an alternative strategy is appropriate. A useful strategy could be to identify conflicts of interests between different agencies and policies of the government, and between government agencies and policies and other segments and components in the environment. Once these conflicts have been identified, they may well be the best means by which autonomy — restricting pressures and constraints in the environment — could be attained. Indeed, it is an interesting hypothesis for students of organization–environment relationships to test whether the right manipulation of conflicting interests and demands in the environment are an important determinant of "success" of business firms. This strategy may be termed a tradeoff strategy, in which pressures generated by one component of the environment are used as a means to reduce pressures by other components. Since the output of the focal organization serves as input to other organizations, a clever manipulation of this output should not only provide the focal organization with the means of survival, but could also increase its bargaining position in the environment beyond that of similar organizations with similar outputs.

The specific findings of this study, of course, do not indicate that managers are actually using such a strategy, nor is it claimed that tradeoff is the only possible strategy. Managers may use other methods to increase organizational autonomy from the government (e.g., political action, lobbying, co-optation of regulatory agencies). Pfeffer and Salancik hypothesized that in order to cope with government dependence, firms or industries are more likely to increase the relationships with other organizations by diversification, merger, long term contracts, interlocking directorates, and so on (Pfeffer & Salancik, 1978). Further research is needed to establish which strategy is best in each particular case. Thus, relationships with other organizations may be effective in reducing dependency on the government as a buyer, supplier or even owner and may be ineffective in reducing other dependencies on the government: for example, organizations cannot merge with the government or diversify into its business.

We propose that a tradeoff strategy is likely to be more efficient in gaining autonomy, the more heterogeneous the environment is and the more intense and encompassing its impacts are on the firm. Although this proposition is not directly tested in this paper, we believe that the idea and the partial test are a useful contribution to the organizational environment theory of management.

References

Aharoni, Y., Maimon, Z. & Segev, E. 1978. Performance and autonomy in organizations: Determining dominant environmental components. *Management Science*, 24 (May 1978): 949–959.

Aldrich, H. 1972. Technology and organizational structure: A re-examination of the findings of the Aston group. *Administrative Science Quarterly*, 17 (March 1972): 26–43.

Aldrich, H. & Pfeffer, J. 1976. Environments of organizations. In Inkeles, A., Coleman, J. & Smelser, N. (Eds.) *Annual Review of Sociology*, Vol. 2. Annual Reviews Inc., Palo Alto, California, pp. 79–105.

Aldrich, H. & Mindlin, S. 1978. Uncertainty and dependence: Two perspectives on environment. In Karpik, L. (Ed.) *Organization and Environment-Theory, Issues, and Reality.* London: Sage.

Ansoff, H. I. 1965. *Corporate Strategy*. New York: McGraw-Hill.

Benson, J. K. 1975. The interorganizational network as a political economy. *Administrative Science Quarterly*, 20 (June 1975): 229–249.

Blau, P. (1964). *Exchange and Power in Social Life.* New York: Wiley.

Borg, I. 1977. Some basic concepts of facet theory. In Lingoes, J. C. (Ed.) *Geometric Representation of Relational Data.* Ann Arbor, Michigan: Mathesis Press, pp. 65–102.

Burns, T. & Stalker, G. M. 1961. *The Management of Innovation.* London: Tavistock.

Denning, B. W. (Ed.). 1971. *Corporate Planning, Selected Concepts*. London: McGraw-Hill.

Dill, W. R. 1958. Environments as an influence on managerial autonomy. *Administrative Science Quarterly*, 2 (March 1958): 409–443.

Duncan, R. 1972. Characteristics of organizational environments and perceived environmental uncertainty. *Administrative Science Quarterly*, 17 (September 1972): 313–327.

Elizur, D. & Guttman, L. 1976. The structure of attitudes toward work and technological change. *Administrative Science Quarterly*, 21 (December 1976): 611–622.

Emerson, R. 1962. Power-dependence relations. *American Sociological Review*, 27 (February 1962): 31–41.

Emery, F. E. & Trist, E. L. 1965. The causal texture of organizational environments'. *Human Relations*, 18 (February 1965): 21–32.

Glover, J. D. 1966. *Strategic Guidance of Corporations — A System of Concepts and Analysis.* Draft, Harvard Business School.

Grinyer, P., Al-Bazzaz, S. & Yasai-Ardekani, M. 1980. Strategy, structure, the environment, and financial performance in 48 United Kingdom companies. *Academy of Management Journal*, 23 (June 1980): 193–220.

Guttman, L. 1970. Integration of test design and analysis. *Proceedings of the 1969 Invitational Conference on Testing Problems.* Princeton: Educational Testing Service.

Guttman, L. 1977. What is now what in statistics. *The Statistician*, 26: 81–107.

Hage, J. & Aiken, M. 1970. *Social Change in Complex Organizations.* New York: Random House.

Lawrence, P. R. & Lorsch, J. W. 1967. *Organization and Environments.* Boston: Harvard Graduate School of Business Administration.

Levy, S. 1976. The use of mapping sentences for coordinating theory and research. *Quality and Quantity*, 10: 117–125.

Levy, S. & Guttman, L. 1975. On the multivariate structure of well being. *Social Indicators Research*, 361–368.

Lingoes, J. C. 1973. *The Guttman-Lingoes Non-Metric Program Series.* Ann Arbor, Michigan: Mathesis Press.

Maimon, Z. 1978. The choice of ordinal measures of association. *Quality and Quantity*, 12: 255–264.

Pfeffer, J. & Salancik, G. R. 1978. *The External Control of Organizations: A Resource Dependence Perspective.* New York: Harper and Row.

Pugh, D., Hickson, D. J., Hinings, C. R. & Turner, C. 1969. The context of organization structures. *Administrative Science Quarterly*, 14 (March 1969): 91–114.

Steiner, G. A. 1969. *Top Management Planning.* New York: The Macmillan Co.

Terreberry, S. 1967/68. The evolution of organizational environments. *Administrative Science Quarterly*, 12: 590–613.

Thompson, J. D. & McEven, W. J. 1958. Organizational goals and environment: Goal-setting as an interaction process. *American Sociological Review*, 23–31.

Yuchtman, E. & Seashore, S. 1967. A systems resources approach to organizational effectiveness. *American Sociological Review*, 32 (December 1967): 891–903.

https://doi.org/10.1142/9789811287510_0009

Chapter 9

In Search for the Unique: Can Firm-Specific Advantages Be Evaluated?*

Yair Aharoni

Tel Aviv University, Tel Aviv, Israel

Duke University, Durham, NC, USA

Abstract

Strategy, whatever its different definitions, entails an attempt by a firm to achieve and sustain competitive advantage against other firms. Competitive advantage can be achieved if the firm is able to be *different.* Success is based on using a unique strategy. Success is defined as the ability to gain abnormal profits, not simply to stay alive in a competitive industry. The ability to protect the uniqueness against imitators ensures continued success.

Strategy theory research is diverse, and can be divided into distinct schools of thought. Certain researchers describe the process of strategy formation. Others are prescriptive, concerned with analytical tools for strategy formulation. Among strategy content researchers, much recent research concentrates on industry analysis techniques. Since strategy is defined as the ability to gain an advantage, a cross-sectional study of industry conditions can show the constraints on such a strategy, but is far less useful in defining how to achieve and sustain a competitive advantage. A

*This chapter is reproduced from *Journal of Management Studies*, Vol. 30 (1993).

critical aspect in understanding competitive advantage is that of the identification of firm-specific advantages, particularly in an outlying rather than the average "representative" firm. The process by which managers of such firms gain insights on strategic vision often affects the results.

This article calls for understanding the unique or — as a minimum — learning to recognize uniqueness (e.g., as someone running a venture fund reviewing proposals for investment). It is concerned with how a strategy can be evaluated *ex ante* by outsiders to predict its probability of success.

The strategy research field is not mature enough to settle on only some conceptual boxes. The article also calls for several accepted modes of investigation, including history and political behavior, to understand better the process by which firms attempt to achieve unique advantages and the evolution of resource deployment.

Introduction

Strategy may be defined as a pattern or stream of decisions taken to achieve the most favorable match between external environment and organizational capabilities (Chakravarthy, 1982; Hofer, 1975; Lawrence & Dyer, 1980; Mintzberg, 1978). Organizational environment includes such dimensions as uncertainty, directness, change, dynamism, homogeneity, complexity, and munificence (Aldrich, 1979; Duncan, 1972; Ford & Slocum, 1977; Jurkovich, 1974; Tung, 1979).

The empirical and theoretical literature on strategic management has been growing exponentially over the past three decades since the seminal Chandler (1962) research, and the work of early pioneers among faculty members at Harvard Business School (Learned *et al.*, 1965). These early efforts emphasized not only the alignment of the firm with its environment, but also the uniqueness of each strategy. Early configurations also differentiated between business and corporate strategy (Ansoff, 1965).

Selznick (1957: p. 42ff) coined the term *distinctive competence* — a skill or an activity in which a firm excels compared to rival firms. Two decades later, Quinn (1980) defined strategy as a means for allocating resources into a *unique* and viable posture. Henderson (1989) cites Gause's Principle of Competitive Exclusion: two competing species cannot coexist if they make their living in an identical way. A good strategist is advised to concentrate efforts within a defined strong area of operations while avoiding calamities by anticipating potentially hostile forces. He must ensure "fit" with both internal strengths and external opportunities and threats. For that fit, a strategist is expected to show vision, to choose the environment in which to operate by setting missions and goals. Strategy is designed to generate higher profits by being unique and maintain these high profits by preventing imitation.

The importance of unique attributes of a firm's strategy, characteristics and actions and the need to explain why competing firms earn different efficiency rents, are generally recognized. Caves (1980), in a survey of strategy contributions, pointed out that strategy implies "that competing firms earn different efficiency rents and that they can serve the same market by quite different input combinations" (p. 65). He argued, however, that strategy researchers "lacked the tools to follow [their] blueprints" and proposed that "errors and omissions" (p. 88) can be avoided by using economic models. Despite "professional modesty" he concluded that "well-trained professional economists could have carried out many of the research projects cited in this paper more proficiently than did the authors, who were less effectively equipped by their own discipline" (Caves, 1984: pp. 163–164). Porter (1981) also recommended the application of economic reasoning to business strategy issues. Other researchers bemoaned the lack of a dominant research paradigm for strategy and were concerned that strategy research was not subjected to rigorous analysis (e.g., Montgomery, 1988: p. 3). Others were worried that if concepts were loosely defined, much confusion could develop. These legitimate concerns may have led too early to freezing other possible avenues of strategic research. In the search for precision, it became easier to look for the common ingredients in a population (e.g., Fiegenbaum *et al.*, 1987; Schamlensee, 1985) rather than to understand differences, explain them and predict their impact on a firm's success in the market place.

By incorporating ideas and concepts developed by industrial organization (IO) economists to strategy, Porter (1979, 1980, 1985) blazed a new trail in both corporate and business level strategy. Porter made examination of industry structure a cornerstone of identifying the driving forces causing its evolution and, from that, a key concern for the strategic analysis of firms. The understanding of industry's structure was shown to be a major prerequisite for identification of the key factors required for success (see also Ohmae, 1983: pp. 84–85). Strategy has been assumed to be generic, largely determined by environmental forces.

Many of Porter's followers paid more attention to industry characteristics than to unique means of achieving competitive advantage. A large flow of statistically based research efforts attempt to connect industry's structure (meaning sometimes organization's structure, sometimes industry's structure) with strategy, with performance or with other variables. More and more researchers propose normative prescriptions (how firms *should* decide on their strategy).

While this research output allowed important insights, it also ignored or left unanswered many problems. First, in most cases for this type of research, the firm is taken as a black box. We are not told how organizations decide on a strategic vision, or on a change of strategy. The question of the earlier choice of a strategy domain is left unanswered. Yet, by deciding missions and visions, the firm chooses the environment in which to operate. Second, the environment is assumed to be fixed, ignoring possibilities of *changing* the environment through political action, by collusion or by innovation. To be sure, in the international business strategy area, much attention has been devoted to the impact of government on strategy, to questions of political risks, to issues of conflict and bargaining between multinational enterprises (MNEs) and governments. There were also some studies pointing out the "unnatural market imperfections" that the state can generate in the competition among firms (for a catalog of these efforts, see Boddewyn, 1990). Third, most of the empirical work in strategy deals with larger, multidivisional companies. Research often implicitly assumes strategy process and content are identical in different cultures and tests of theories are carried out almost exclusively on large industrial firms in a domestic environment: databases include only a few service firms, or small firms, or global firms. Fourth, very little work has been done on the rate of success and failure and mainly the reasons for failure and success in small entrepreneurial firms. One problem is that many of the key mechanisms are invisible to the researcher, since they are buried in the minds of the actors. As a result, we know very little about how entrepreneurs in our own or other environments make "bold stroke" decisions, or how a new and completely different strategy is designed. Fifth, most variables were tested and explained by cross-sectional rather than longitudinal analysis. These tests do not tell us much about strategic changes resulting, for example, from industry's evolution or how innovations changed the structure of competition.

To be sure, given the vast, mushrooming and diverse work on strategy, one can identify some research that did look inside the firm, or that analyzed attempts to change the environment. The limitations of using only large firms as a research field have also been recognized. A few researchers also carried out some very innovative and interesting longitudinal research (e.g., Cool & Schendel, 1987; Fiegenbaum & Thomas, 1990; Mintzberg & Waters 1982, 1984). There were also many studies on innovation, although they are rarely linked to study of strategy. Lieberman & Montgomery (1988) in a path-breaking paper, address the advantages and disadvantages of first-mover firms. Yet, all these studies made a major omission. The theoretical constructs and the data led to a concern with an explanation of a Marshallian "representative firm", sometimes operating in an environment of deterministic paradigms in which firms are selected out with very little choice allowed. Very little research has been carried out studying the outlier (the best or the worst performers) as opposed to the average, representative firm. Some well-known exceptions are, of course, Peters & Waterman (1982) and Heskett *et al.* (1990). As a result, we do not even have adequate tools to predict the success of a unique strategy once it is proposed by an entrepreneur. How many strategy researchers would have been able to increase the success rate of a venture capitalist who has to decide on the probable success of new and unique ideas? The unfortunate result is a very primitive state-of-theory development on the essential part of a business strategy: that of its uniqueness. Even the resource-base school (Barney, 1986; Dierickx & Cool, 1989; Lippman & Rumelt, 1982; Rumelt, 1984, 1987; Wernerfelt, 1984) emphasizes population of firms with heterogeneous resources. In attempting to achieve scientific rigor, strategy research abandoned its major *raison d'être*: the search for the unique.

This article argues that one reason for this state of affairs is that strategy theory does not benefit enough from multiple perspectives. The challenge is to expand the legitimate paradigms used, or to use Daft & Lewin's (1990) terminology on organization theory, "to break out of the normal science straitjacket". The objective should be not simply to predict the behavior of a large number of firms, learning about regular profits, the average firm, or a gambler, but to predict the success of the actions and characteristics of unique firms. This objective may be achieved by a careful scrutiny of the outlying firm. Hopefully, the lessons learned could also enable us to help a venture capitalist to make choices. The article analyses differences between a "population" point of view and the uniqueness of the strategy and between a cross-sectional analysis of an industry and the formulation of strategy. We also look at the research on strategic groups. It then considers the implications of studies in international business theory of firm-specific advantages (FSAs) in understanding unique strategies.

The article then examines some issues related to the shaping of the environment and concludes with a plea to widen the conceptual paradigms used in strategy research, to include history and political science ideas and mainly to study the best and the worst in populations (the outlier) in addition to the average firm.

Population v. Specifity

Social scientists are trained to avoid studying actions seen as purely random or idiosyncratic and to study the behavior of groups of firms, not that of any particular one. They attempt to discover universal (or contingent) rules of behavior characterizing a population of individuals or of organizations. Key research issues are defined by shared paradigms. The pioneers of scientific management attempted to discover general rules of behavior, such as span of control or number of hierarchical levels, assumed to be pertinent to *all* organizations. In economics, Alfred Marshall attempted to characterize the behavior of a "representative firm". In sociology, the population ecology school emphasized evolution of populations of organizations, seeing survival as based on natural selection and luck in achieving a fit with a changing environment (e.g., Hannan & Freeman, 1977). Later, researchers looked for contingency variables.

To many, scientific interpretation is expected to be based on solid analysis of a large enough number of observations to allow statistical testing of the significance of results. In the 1970s and 1980s, a growing stream of research in strategy has indeed analyzed large aggregates of firms, often within an artificial boundary of "an industry", conducted in the hope of capturing the essential constraints on and opportunities for effective strategic choice. This approach was bolstered by the availability of large databases such as PIMS or Compustat. An increasing number of studies has been made using industrial organization (IO) methodologies. Other researchers, perhaps influenced by their training in organization behavior, relied on large-scale questionnaires, not always assessing the validity and reliability of their results. Dozens of these types of studies have been adding to our stock of knowledge of the theory of strategic content.

Industry effects may explain far more variance than firm effects (Wernerfelt & Montgomery, 1988). It might also explain some of the constraints faced by the strategist. It does not explain strategy in the sense that it does not explain the creative processes that combine resources in a new configuration to create new values. By definition, strategy is tailored to achieve distinctive competence. The distinctive competence, or the unique definition of the environment or of customers' needs are all relegated to an unexplained variance. Nor does it allow the researcher to assess the strategic lessons one can learn from the outlier firm — which is strongest in achieving unique competitive advantages, or which firm's weak performance can illustrate major foibles, frailties and mistakes to be avoided.

The seminal work of Chandler (1962) was carried out in only four firms, but proposed important conclusions for generations of scholars to research. A painstaking longitudinal historical research of archival data can generate important insights not only on how strategies are formulated (Mintzberg, 1981) but also on the types of possible unique advantages designed, nurtured and protected by managers in outlier firms. A strategist should explain how the outlying firm achieves and maintains "abnormal" profits so that our theory could help others to achieve such results.

It is intriguing to attempt to speculate why so many, but by no means all, strategy researchers moved to study industries rather than firms, ignoring issues of distinctive competence. One possibility, already mentioned, is the seductive appeal of the availability of large databases. Another is the long time it takes a researcher to conduct a historical study. A third is the temptation of the additional rigor allowed when one uses IO economics tools. Whatever the reason, one result is that strategy content theory may be devoid of predictive capability, when certain questions are analyzed.

Industry Analysis v. Strategy Identification

In the 1960s, a persistently high relative profitability among firms in a given line of business would be interpreted by business school scholars as emanating from a competitive advantage, based on skilled use of some unique resources. Rivals would not be able to imitate easily the unique advantage without very substantial costs and uncertainty, and the development of a corporate strategy involving managerial decisions. For the IO scholar at Harvard, the explanation was the existence of monopoly behavior, or collusion and discouraging entry or predation. The "abnormal" profits were proof of a basic conflict between public policy, seeking competition, and corporate managers, seeking monopoly (Thomas, 1986: p. 16).

In the conventional neoclassical economics formulation, an industry is a collection of homogeneous firms in all economically important aspects except size. Optimal size, in turn, is determined by the cost conditions. In the long run and in the absence of barriers to entry, the profit of any firm in any industry is zero. Attempting to explain why some firms are able to command higher market share than others, IO economic theories recently recognized that firms within industries are not identical. Since Coase (1937), it is accepted that markets and firms (employing hierarchies) are alternative means of providing a product or a service. Williamson's transaction cost theory (1975, 1985) purports to show when each mode of organizing economic activities should be preferred. Firms are viewed as a collection of rent-yielding heterogeneous assets and factors, co-ordinated by their management through semi-permanent or long-term contractual relationships. The configuration of firms' asset bundles may differ considerably across firms, depending on their initial and subsequent strategic choices (Caves, 1984; Porter, 1985).

For an IO economist, the concept of strategy is applicable only when firms operate in oligopolistic structures. Strategic actions are designed to create an asymmetry in the ability of firms to compete, and some firms may be able to gain higher than average profits or a high market share (Gale, 1972; Shepherd, 1986).

IO researchers believe that industry conditions determine the strategies appropriate for a business to pursue in order to maximize performance. Industry, claims Porter, "is the arena in which competitive advantage is won or lost" (Porter, 1986: p. 11). Yet sources of asymmetry may be disparate across industries. Therefore, the search for variables that make for the asymmetry must be firm-specific. Again, strategy research should be able not only to catalog these asymmetries, but to predict their success and to identify differences across nations or cultures. A strategy is unique, specific to the resources of the firm and tailored to achieve the highest profits in a specific, often changing, sometimes turbulent, environment.

Researchers may study the structure of the "garment industry". The manager of a firm in this industry attempts to achieve a unique position by differentiating the product through design, brand name, technology or service. Benetton or Yves St. Laurent are, for at least some segment of the consuming population, not just another clothing manufacturer. Each enjoys higher profits as a result of some unique attributes. These should be explained and predicted by strategy research. "Cross" and "Bic" both produce pens, and Omega, Seiko and Timex all produce watches. These firms belong to the same industry and are in the same population. Yet their strategy is designed to make them unique, using differentiated FSAs to achieve better performance, not an average firm in a population. These attempts to achieve unique distinctive competition are a never-ending process involving management trade-offs on questions of R&D, technology transfer, production, marketing, information systems, organizational design, even time spent on lobbying. In this sense, process and content are interconnected.

As another example, all universities are in the same industry: all are teaching and doing research. Yet each university attempts to be unique and to develop certain specific attributes. These allow it to attract faculty, to lure students, and to charge tuition fees different from other universities (and therefore to afford a different cost structure).

Empirical tests fail to show a very strong match between environmental characteristics and generic strategies. Miller & Friesen (1986a, 1986b), studying Porter's generic strategies and performance, concluded that successful performance was a result of having strategic advantages, not strictly adhering to Porter's generic strategies. These statistical results are not surprising. The more firms are assumed to attempt to achieve asymmetry and heterogeneity, the less it should be expected that the perceived environment will be homogeneous. Many successful firms not only identified existing strengths and weaknesses, or attempted to compete by being as efficient as others; instead, they transformed current capabilities, changed technology, affected market parameters and shaped the environment. Those firms that were extremely successful in their efforts created the boundaries of the industry studied later by strategy researchers. A successful outlier firm changes the dynamics of its industry and the key factors of success within it. L.M. Ericson did so with modular technology (Hout *et al.*, 1982). In some cases, the firm redefines the boundaries of the industry, as Canon did with the innovation of the personal copier. The world watch industry changed leaders several times in the last few decades, and each time the new leader (Timex, Seiko) changed the rules of the game and the key factors of success. In several industries today, outlier firms introduced delivery time as a new measure of performance, or achieved dominance by reducing inventories through the Kanban system. Honda created new markets in the United States. In all these cases, the basic economics of an industry is changing — while many IO scholars implicitly assume no change or a very slow rate of change. They suggest that established industries show patterns of stability (Porter, 1980). This is in contrast to a Schumpeterian firm. For Schumpeter (1934) the rules of the game are never stable. Technology, the nature of demand, government rules, are all in a state of flux. In a Schumpeterian dynamic view of the world, a firm must adapt continuously to a complex set of shifts (see Mintzberg & Waters, 1982). Unique strategic innovations become crucial to gain advantage (Hampden-Turner, 1990; Nelson & Winter 1982).

Even in a relatively stable world, once intra-industry heterogeneity of firms is accepted and explained by the firm's strategic decisions in an imperfect market, one must search for unique differences. The unique could be a result of a major breakthrough, or an outcome of a collection of many small improvements in work methods and managerial practices that in combination yield significant productivity gains. To understand how firms can achieve competitive advantage, one may be advised to start with an identification of the firm-specific advantages (FSAs), defined as the core skills or unique know-how. FSAs can be people-embodied or machine-embodied. Thus, Spence (1977, 1981) showed the theoretical significance of learning economies and capacity investment; and Lieberman (1987) explored the implications of the learning curve for competitive strategy under a range of assumptions regarding the nature of the learning process and competition. Many have discussed the intertemporal gap in technology, and others drew attention to differentiation through brand loyalty or service quality (e.g., Gronroos, 1990). Several authors also pointed out that above-normal returns may be based on resources specific to the firm (Barney, 1986; Wernerfelt, 1984) or on specific assets (Aaker, 1989). Superior resources are able to earn rent only if there are inferior resources employed in production. Of course, sustainability of a firm's resources position depends on how easily the resources can be imitated or replaced (Dierickx & Cool, 1989; Lippman & Rumelt, 1982).

If FSAs are easily copied by another firm, and the first firm does not erect entry barriers, it has no sustainable advantage. In agriculture, for example, a new product innovation or a new method of cultivation is copied by other firms almost instantaneously, and the innovator does not enjoy any first-mover advantages. On the other hand, if the innovative firm is able to create very high switching costs, it does enjoy an advantage over any competitors. In other words, FSAs must be translated speedily into actual sustainable competitive advantages in the market place.

In summary, an industry is a compilation of firms, each one of which must constantly learn, adapt and innovate, attempting to carve itself a different niche, arrange its business in a different way, market its products differently to a defined customer group or use a different technology. In short, each firm attempts to gain competitive advantage by following a unique strategy. To test empirically for asymmetry among firms, the sources for firms' specific advantages and the degree they are sustainable must be ascertained. This can be done by longitudinal historical analysis of outlier firms, much more than by looking at the structure of an industry.

Strategic Groups

The outlier firm may be able to achieve unique non-imitable advantages. Many other firms may not be so successful, and the strategy they follow may be very similar to that of other firms, but not to all firms in the industry. In the 1970s, emphasis shifted from structural barriers to stressing strategic barriers, based on corporate acts. Hunt (1972) coined the term "strategic groups" in an industry for a group following the same or similar strategy along the strategic dimensions (Porter, 1980: p. 129). The group is separable from others by mobility barriers (Caves & Porter, 1977), that deter entry to the group.

The concept of strategic groups has attracted a plethora of empirical and theoretical studies — often defining groups *ad hoc* (McGee, 1985). For a survey, see Cool, 1985; Fiegenbaum *et al.*, 1987; McGee & Thomas, 1986. The empirical research did demonstrate the existence of performance differences among strategic groups (Fiegenbaum & Thomas, 1990; Harrigan, 1985; Hatten & Hatten, 1987; Mascarenhas & Aaker, 1989). A cross-sectional analysis of firms does not show, of course, the movements across time, and the study does not often take into account Dierickx & Cool's (1989) distinction between asset stock accumulation and flows. A longitudinal study may demonstrate that the number and composition of strategic groups has changed over time (e.g., Fiegenbaum & Thomas, 1990). Such studies demonstrate again the need to look for dynamic Schumpeterian characteristics. Although firms in a group use the same strategy, again, one can gain much richer insights by looking at the outlier.

The success of a firm in a market economy is crucially dependent on its ability to achieve unique attributes in the eyes of all of its stakeholders. Consumers may be willing to pay more to get a brand *A* washing machine rather than brand *B*. Engineers may prefer to work for firm *A* than for firm *B*. Raw material suppliers may rather sell to firm *A* than to firm *B* when the supply is limited. Workers may prefer working for the firm *A* rather than firm *B* even though the salary in firm *A* is lower than in firm *B*. A highly respected scientist, whose services are essential for a firm's success, may prefer to work for the firm rather than move to a competitor or work on his own because of a plethora of factors, including long-term competence of the firm in certain scientific endeavors, or the "culture" of the firm, its distinctive competence in creating a different environment in order to attract workers, taking care of human beings, allowing dignity, self-respect or innovation to flourish. Strategy research should be able to catalog these variables and predict their impact on performances.

Some firms were able to become a major force in the global economy. These are the multinationals, perceived by some as a boon to mankind and considered by others as imperialistic predators. To understand the existence of these powerful firms, researchers had to explain how they were able to compete against their domestic uninational rivals, despite the costs of doing business abroad. Some explanations assume multinational enterprises (MNEs) possess FSAs: scale, expertise or internalizing. This line of thinking is very relevant as a guideline for strategy research.

Firm-Specific Advantages and Entry Barriers in the International Arena

For international production to exist it should be less costly to serve foreign markets by establishing a subsidiary than by exporting or licensing (Caves, 1971; Dunning, 1977, 1981, 1988). Free trade is based on assumptions of a frictionless world and a high level of homogeneous products. When government-imposed transaction costs create barriers to trade or, more generally, when transaction costs are important, the need to internalize a firm-specific advantage would lead to foreign direct investments (FDIs) by MNEs. MNEs are operating in oligopolistic industries, and must have firm-specific advantages in intangible assets that they can internalize (for a summary see Buckley & Casson, 1976; Caves, 1982; Rugman, 1986). "Internalizing" provides a key source of competitive advantage over other domestic firms. For any potential to be realized, managers must make conscious decisions to achieve the benefits, and develop an effective organization capable of carrying out the tasks. Thus, benefits must be managed; they do not accrue automatically.

Typically, MNEs have some resource advantage, either capital, technology, or managerial expertise. Depending on the requirements of the host or parent countries, the MNE capital may or may not be invested in foreign countries; its technology may or may not be fully diffused. Successful MNEs also learn very quickly; they can transfer any good ideas emanating in one country in the process of manufacturing or sales of a given good to other countries in the system, having to manufacture, sell and service the same standard good.

MNEs may be differentiated by managerial cognition toward international business: they may be ethnocentric or home-country dominated; polycentric, treating each subsidiary on a country-by-country basis; or geocentric—having integrative, global and cosmopolitan style (Perlmutter, 1969). An FSA can be management attitudes and ability of the firm to digest different cultures and employ managers of many nationalities and other attributes of the organization. These management styles effect behavior and therefore decisions.

Perlmutter's emphasis on firms implies that a firm's strategy is decoupled from the industry's structure. Several other models attempt to identify organizational forces that drove MNEs to develop global capabilities and are not summarized here (e.g., Bartlett & Ghoshal, 1987, 1989; Ghoshal & Bartlett, 1990; Hedlund, 1986; Prahalad & Doz, 1987). Identification of FSAs is essential in explaining any strategy, not only that of MNEs competing against other firms. Transaction-cost analysis and agency theory allow researchers at least some access (and legitimation) to the organizational issues in real-life firms. Hansen & Wernerfelt (1989), for example, have shown that what they termed the organizational factors explained about twice as much in profit rates as economic factors. Economists did learn to incorporate "firm-specific advantages" and "first-mover's advantages" into their theories. Incorporating variables of this sort into the theory of the firm is a first step in creating a theory of searching for the unique strategy.

Shaping the Variety of Environments

Environments are treated most of the time as objective facts, independent of firms. Much of the empirical testing of strategy is based on environmental determinism. Some strategy theories see business performance as a function of controllable or strategic variables and non-controllable or environmental variables (Hatten *et al.*, 1978). In some cases environments are treated as perceptually determined and enacted. Bourgeois (1980) proposed that the issue was not whether measures should be objective or perceptual. To him, both the objective and the perceived environments are real and relevant to an organization's strategy. Objective environment is relevant to primary strategy-making (domain selection), while perceived environment is a prime input to secondary strategy-making (domain navigation). Firms can shape the environment by tacit collusion, advancing values, influencing governmental policies, advancing the technology or altering the terms of competitive rivalry.

A firm that does not enjoy a competitive advantage can still be able to command higher-than-average profits by generating oligopoly rents through political action, and also by collusion. Maintaining such a collusion for a long time is possible but not easy. The international oil firms were able to develop mechanisms to maintain market share agreements for a relatively long time, even during periods of oil glut, despite the diverse interests of the rivals (for an analysis see Jacoby, 1974; Moran, 1987; Penrose, 1968). Other raw material producers were less successful. Paul Eckbo (1976) shows that only 19 out of 51 attempts at raw materials cartelization were successful, and the life spans of even the successful ones were only four to five years.

A firm may also be able to survive despite competitive disadvantage if it is able to enlist political support that would prevent more efficient firms' imports. Marginal oil firms in Texas, sugar producers in the US, car firms lobbying for local contents regulations in Europe, import substitutors in Latin America or many state-owned airlines are some examples of such a political rather than a competitive strategy. Firms — in particular, large firms — can and do influence the political agenda (Doz, 1986; Poynter, 1985; Prahalad & Doz, 1987), changing seemingly exogenously determined environmental parameters. Of course, a government can protect a firm only within its country, much less so in the international arena. Still, the "political strategy" should be part of strategy research (on this idea, see Boddewyn, 1988; Yoffie & Milner, 1989).[1]

Firms are also able to change the environment by innovations: Canon's personal copier expanded the definition of industry and changed the structure of the copier market (Yamanouchi, 1989).[2]

Proactive development of new capabilities or effective organization of the manufacturing function may enable a firm to have different strategies (Hayes & Wheelwright, 1984). A firm may avoid competition by dominating a well-defined segment. The competitive advantages required may differ across segments, reflecting the unique preferences of consumers (Tremblay, 1985). Intra-industry competitive asymmetry may be a result of other factors, among them technological innovation, that may have created a transient monopoly between the first-mover and the followers. (For a survey, see Lieberman & Montgomery, 1988; see also Nelson & Winter, 1982; Schamlensee, 1982.) Technology is often not a single, coherent body of knowledge. Rather, it may be extremely heterogeneous, due to diversity of needs. One firm may have an advantage in a certain area of technology application but not in another. In all these cases, managers attempt to shape a new environment and create a unique strategy.

The New, the Untested, the Outlier Firm

If a manager had fallen asleep for three decades, and awakened in 1990, he would be amazed at the rate of transformation: he might not recognize many flexible manufacturing systems, would not have ever seen major products that created totally different markets and new industries: fax, copier, laser printer, microprocessors, VCRs, electronics, personal computers and so on. Our manager may be amazed to learn that so many strategy researchers attempt to establish possible causalities of strategy, structure and performance (Hrebiniak *et al.*, 1989), or to understand the limitations imposed by industry structure on possible strategy, ignoring much of its historical evolution. He would understand of course that some issues were studied less than others because of technical problems such as variable definition or data availability, but may conclude that the field of strategy has prematurely settled on a rather narrow scope of problems to be studied, ignoring process, politics, technological changes and dynamics.

The manager may also conclude that Schumpeterian dynamic theory may be a better starting point to understand strategy in an ever-shifting, turbulent world than some of the IO basic assumptions. Research in strategy should look at the ways new and untried strategies are designed. To capture the richness of real-life situations, one has to look at such questions as (1) how does an entrepreneur decide on the strategy of a new venture; (2) how does a CEO decide on a changing direction of the firm (and what are the forces triggering a major strategic change); (3) how does a new entrant decide on where to attack the existing firms in an existing industry structure. In all these situations, strategic theory should give guidance *ex ante*, not only explain behavior *ex post.* Explaining asymmetry *ex post* may be of interest, but the challenge is to identify a successful strategic posture *ex ante*; for example, when the posture is designed or proposed, say, to a venture capitalist.

Technological innovations, major shifts in relative cost, new consumer needs, are some examples of economic, social and technological changes, the result of which is to elevate a new product or service to the level of a potentially viable business opportunity. Ideally, strategy theory should help a venture capitalist in assessing several business plans presented to him for financing and, once the ideas have been presented, choose those among them that have a higher probability of success.

Research should provide essential insights into the basic dimensions that make a strategy for a new product a successful one. The complexity of such situations and the dilemmas encountered by the strategist cannot be captured by statistical tests of significances. In most cases of important innovations, sceptics doubted the success of the new product and certainly did not predict that the new innovation would revolutionize the industry. Miles & Snow's (1978) proposed typology of strategies attracted many researchers. (For a recent review see Segev, 1989; Shortell & Zajac, 1990). The prospectors in their typology — those consistently first in developing new ideas — are those of greatest interest.

Conclusions

Any observation of the profits of various firms in the same industry would show significant variance in returns of real-life firms in a given industry. Persistently high profits, unless they are explained away as an accounting error, must be accounted for as a result of some competitive advantage — or a consequence of a strategy. For quite a long time, IO researchers believed that the so-called abnormal profits could be explained by tacit collusion or other monopoly behavior, allowing economies of scale or brand loyalty through advertising. If, however, profits depend on scale, why do some firms continue to be small? Moreover, in several industries, e.g., real estate, some firms enjoy what an IO economist would see as persistent windfall profits, which cannot be explained by predation, monopoly, collusion or deterrence. Instead, these firms have some specific assets that allow them to get high rent. Of course, for the profits to be persistent, these assets must be induplicable.

Researchers may find it rewarding to look for the unique and the different rather than search for central tendencies in a population of firms. The outlier firm changes the rules of the game and creates new breakthroughs. To the extent that it can also maintain barriers to entry, it achieves immutable and persistently high returns. A cross-sectional analysis of firms, as repeatedly argued, may be very misleading. A longitudinal study of the outlier firm would identify not only the vision and the unique strategy but also the means by which it was made sustainable, and the dynamics of the shifts and changes.

Managers attempt to create unique FSAs, and to make their organization, as perceived by its major stakeholders, *unique*. Each manager strives to create a unique product, distinctive market presence, special relations with customers and suppliers, different price structure, better services, or some distinct competence for the firm to excel. The uniqueness may also be an image, or the customer's perception of the differences.

Business strategy researchers using IO methodology attempt to propose plausible generalizations based on carefully designed empirical research or to prove hypotheses based on a large population of firms. In doing so, researchers gain mathematical elegance, statistical rigor, parsimony and persuasive power. Unfortunately, the price of this elegance is ignoring the task of identifying the lessons one can learn from the particularly successful or unsuccessful outliers. An exceptionally successful firm may have learned better how to assess business opportunities or how to improve certain weaknesses or how to assess and improve the organization or how to ensure alignment of an organization to a changing environment. All these important lessons may be lost when researchers rely on industry averages to identify generic strategy domains, implicitly assuming a slowly changing static environment. Empirical studies may demonstrate the existence of perceived environmental heterogeneity is a single industry (e.g., Kim & Lim, 1988: p. 821). Careful case studies or longitudinal work can identify rules for identifying successful new ideas, successful breakthroughs, or new ways to create new environments. Such studies may provide a basis for new theoretical ideas to be tested on a larger population.

A strategy, after all, must be a unique action plan and must be predicated on building, maintaining and defending a competitive advantage. In strategy, as in biology, identical ways of making a living do not allow competitive species to exist, unless collusion is possible. Incorporating "firm-specific advantages" into the theory of the firm is a first step in searching for the unique strategy and evaluating it. Our ability to interpret and evaluate the imaginative and integrated visions of the entrepreneur may be aided more by research based on the tools of the historian than those of the economist.[3]

Notes

[1] The importance of these factors may also be country specific. In Austria, "social partnerships" appear to have been operating for several decades without any serious frictions (Katzenstein, 1984). In such a case, all firms may pursue the same strategy, in effect colluding to allocate market share. The degree to which one can trust one's competitors not to cheat or freeride is extremely important in maintaining a cartel arrangement. Perhaps such arrangements are easier in certain cultures.

[2] The relationship between innovation and competition has recently been explored by Nelson & Winter (1982), Rosenberg (1982), and Rosenbloom & Burgelman (1989). Much of this work has been categorized and summarized by Adler (1989). Abernathy & Clark (1985) mapped the various roles innovations play in competition, proposing what they termed the transilience map; positing that innovations may change the technology alone or the markets/customers alone, or both, creating what they termed "architectural" innovation — one that departs from established forms of production and also opens new linkages to markets and users. Such innovations may create new industries or reformulate an existing one. Friar & Horwitch (1986) stress the importance of technology strategy as a competitive weapon.

[3] Since this article was written, the *Strategic Management Journal* has published a special issue on "Strategy and economics". Some of the articles there are very relevant to our topic here, including the editors' summary. See also, Jacobson, R. 1992. The Austrian school of strategy. *Academy of Management Review,* 17(4) (October): 182–207.

References

Aaker, D. 1989. Managing assets and skills: The key to a sustainable competitive advantage. *California Management Review* (Winter): 91–106.

Abernathy, W. J. & Clark, K. B. 1985. Innovation: Mapping the winds of creative destruction. *Research Policy*, 14: 3–22.

Adler, P. S. 1989. Technology strategy: A guide to the literature. In Rosenbloom, R. S. (Ed.) *Research on Technological Innovation, Management and Policy*, Vol. 4. Greenwich, CT: JAI Press.

Aldrich, H. E. 1979. *Organizations and Environments.* Englewood Cliffs, NJ: Prentice-Hall.

Andrews, K. R. 1980. *The Concept of Corporate Strategy* (Revised edn.). Homewood, IL: Irwin.

Ansoff, H. I. 1965. *Corporate Strategy: An Analytic Approach to Business Policy for Growth and Expansion.* New York: McGraw-Hill.

Barney, J. B. 1986. Strategic factor markets: Expectation, luck and business strategy. *Management Science*, 32(10): 1231–1241.

Barlett, C. A. & Ghoshal, S. 1987. Managing across borders: New organizational responses. *Sloan Management Review* (Fall): 45–53.

Bartlett, C. A. & Ghoshal, S. 1989. *Managing across Borders: The Transnational Solution.* Boston, MA: Harvard Business School Press.

Boddewyn, J. J. 1988. Political aspects of MNE theory. *Journal of International Business Studies*, 19(3): 341–363.

Boddewyn, J. J. 1990. New directions in international-business political-behavior research. Paper Presented at Academy of International Business Conference in Toronto.

Bourgeois, L. J. 1980. Strategy and environment: A conceptual integration. *Academy of Management Review*, 5: 25–39.

Buckley, P. J. & Casson, M. 1976. *The Future of the Multinational Enterprise.* London: Macmillan.

Casson, M. 1987. *The Firm and the Market: Studies on the Multinational Enterprise and the Scope of the Firm.* Cambridge, MA: MIT Press.

Caves, R. E. 1971. International corporation: The industrial economics of foreign investment. *Economica*, 38: 1–27.

Caves, R. E. 1980. Industrial organization, corporate strategy and structure. *Journal of Economic Literature*, 18 (March): 64–92.

Caves, R. E. 1982. *Multinational Enterprise and Economic Analysis.* New York: Cambridge University Press.

Caves, R. E. 1984. Economic analysis and the quest for competitive advantage. *American Economic Review*, 74 (May): 127–136.

Caves, R. E. & Porter, M. E. 1977. From entry barriers to mobility barriers. *Quarterly Journal of Economics*, 61: 241–261.

Chakravarthy, B. S. 1982. Adaption: A promising metaphor for strategic management. *Academy of Management Review*, 7: 35–44.

Chandler, A. 1962. *Strategy and Structure: Chapters in the History of the Industrial Enterprise.* Cambridge, MA: MIT Press.

Coase, R. H. 1937. The nature of the firm. *Economica*, 4: 385–405.

Cool, K. O. 1985. Strategic Group Formation and Strategic Group Shifts: A Longitudinal Analysis of the U.S. Pharmaceutical Industry, 1963–1982. Unpublished PhD dissertation, Purdue University, May.

Cool, K. O. & Schendel, D. E. 1987. Strategic group formation and performance: The case of the U.S. pharmaceutical industry, 1963–1982. *Management Science*, 33(9): 1102–1124.

Daft, R. L. & Lewin, A. Y. 1990. Can organization studies begin to break out of the normal science straitjacket? An editorial essay. *Organization Science*, 1(1): 1–10.

Dierickx, I. & Cool, K. O. 1989. Asset stock accumulation and sustainability of competitive advantage. *Management Science*, 35(12): 1504–1514.

Doz, Y. 1986. *Strategic Management in Multinational Companies.* Oxford: Pergamon. Duncan, R. B. 1972. Characteristics of organizational environments and environmental uncertainty. *Administrative Science Quarterly*, 17: 313–327.

Dunning, J. H. 1977. Trade, location and economic activity and the MNE: A search for an eclectic approach. In Ohlin, B., *et al.* (Eds.) *The International Allocation of Economic Activity, Proceedings of Nobel Symposium Held in Stockholm.* London: Macmillan.

Dunning, J. H. 1981. *International Production and the Multinational Enterprise.* London: Allen & Unwin.

Dunning, J. H. 1988. The eclectic paradigm of international production: A restatement and some possible extensions. *Journal of International Business Studies*, 19(1): 1–31.

Eckbo, P. L. 1976. *The Future of World Oil.* Cambridge, MA: Ballinger.

Fiegenbaum, A. & Thomas, H. 1990. Strategic groups and performance: The U.S. insurance industry, 1970–1984. *Strategic Management Journal*, 11(3): 197–216.

Fiegenbaum, A., McGee, J. & Thomas, H. 1987. Exploring the linkage between strategic groups and comparative strategy. *International Studies of Management and Organization*, 18(1): 6–25.

Ford, J. D. & Slocum Jr., J. W. 1977. Size, technology, environment and the structure of organizations. *Academy of Management Review*, 2: 561–575.

Friar, J. & Horwich, M. 1986. The emergence of technology strategy: A new dimension of strategic management. In Horwich, M. (Ed.) *Technology in Society*, 7(2/3): 50–85.

Gale, B. 1972. Market share and rate of return. *Review of Economics and Statistics*, 54 (November): 412–423.

Ghoshal, S. & Bartlett, C. A. 1990. The multinational corporation as an interorganizational network. *Academy of Management Review*, 15(4): 603–625.

Gronroos, C. 1990. *Service Management and Marketing: Managing the Moments of Truth in Service Competition.* Lexington, MA: Lexington Books.

Hampden-Turner, C. 1990. *Charting the Corporate Mind: Graphic Solutions to Business Conflicts.* New York: Free Press.

Hannan, M. T. & Freeman, J. H. 1977. The population ecology of organizations. *American Journal of Sociology*, 82(5): 929–964.

Hansen, G. S. & Wernerfelt, B. 1989. Determinants of firm performance: The relative importance of economic and organizational factors. *Strategic Management Journal*, 10: 399–411.

Harrigan, K. 1985. An application of clustering for strategic group analysis. *Strategic Management Journal*, 6: 55–73.

Hatten, K. J. & Hatten, M. L. 1987. Strategic groups, asymmetrical mobility barriers and contestibility. *Strategic Management Journal*, 8: 329–342.

Hatten, K. J., Schendel, D. E. & Cooper, A. C. 1978. A strategic model of the U.S. brewing industry: 1952–1971. *Academy of Management Journal*, 21: 592–610.

Hayes, R. H. and Wheelwright, S. C. 1984. *Restoring Our Competitive Edge: Competing through Manufacturing.* New York: Wiley.

Hedlund, G. 1986. The hypermodern MNGL a heterarchy? *Human Resource Management*, (Spring): 9–35.

Henderson, B. D. 1989. The origin of strategy. *Harvard Business Review*, 67: 139–145.

Heskett, J. L., Sasser Jr., W. E. & Hart, C. W. L. 1990. *Service Breakthroughs: Changing the Rules of the Game.* New York: Free Press.

Hofer, C. W. 1975. Toward a contingency theory of business strategy. *Academy of Management Journal*, 18: 784–810.

Hout, T., Porter, M. E. & Rudden, E. 1982. How global companies win out. *Harvard Business Review*, 60 (September–October): 98–108.

Hrebiniak, L. G., Joyce, W. F. & Snow, C. C. 1989. Strategy, structure and performance: Past and future research. In Snow, C. C. (Ed.) *Strategy, Organization Design, and Human Resource Management.* Greenwich, CT: JAI Press.

Hunt, M. S. 1972. Competition in the Major Home Appliance Industry, 1960–1970. Unpublished PhD dissertation, Harvard University.

Jacoby, N. H. 1974. *Multinational Oil: A Study of Industrial Dynamics.* New York: Macmillan.

Jurkovich, R. 1974. A core typology of organizational environments. *Administrative Science Quarterly*, 19: 380–394.

Katzenstein, P. J. 1984. *Corporatism and Change: Austria, Switzerland and the Politics of Industry.* Ithaca, NY: Cornell University Press.

Kim, L. & Lim, Y. 1988. Environment, generic strategies, and performance in a rapidly developing country: A taxonomic approach. *Academy of Management Journal*, 31(4): 802–827.

Lawrence, P. & Dyer, D. 1980. Toward a theory of organizational and industrial adaptation. Working Papers HBS 80–57, Graduate School of Business Administration, Harvard University.

Learned, E. P., Christensen, C. R., Andrews, K. R. & Guth, W. D. 1965. *Business Policy: Text and Cases.* Homewood, IL: Irwin.

Lieberman, M. B. 1987. The learning curve, diffusion and competitive strategy. *Strategic Management Journal*, 8: 441–452.

Lieberman, M. B. & Montgomery, D. B. 1988. First-mover advantages. *Strategic Management Journal*, 9 (Summer): 41–58.

Lippman, S. A. & Rumelt, R. P. 1982. Uncertain imitability: An analysis of interfirm differences in efficiency under competition. *Bell Journal of Economics*, 13(2): 418–438.

McGee, J. 1985. Strategic groups: Reviews and prospects. In Thomas, H. & Gardner, D. M. (Eds.) *Strategic Marketing and Management.* Chichester: Wiley.

McGee, J. & Thomas, H. 1986. Strategic groups: Theory, research and taxonomy. *Strategic Management Journal*, 7: 141–160.

Mascarenhas, B. & Aaker, D. A. 1989. Mobility barriers and strategic groups. *Strategic Management Journal*, 10(5): 475–485.

Miles, R. E. & Snow, C. C. 1978. *Organizational Strategy, Structure and Process.* New York: McGraw-Hill.

Miller, D. & Friesen, P. H. 1986a. Porter's 1980 generic strategies and performance: An empirical examination with American data, (part I). *Organizational Studies*, 7: 37–55.

Miller, D. & Friesen, P. H. 1986b. Porter's 1980 generic strategies and performance: An empirical examination with American data, (part II). *Organizational Studies*, 7: 255–261.

Mintzberg, H. 1978. Patterns in strategy formulation. *Management Science*, 24: 934–948.

Mintzberg, H. 1981. What is planning anyway? *Strategic Management Journal*, 2: 319–324.

Mintzberg, H. & Waters, J. A. 1982. Tracking strategy in an entrepreneurial firm. *Academy of Management Journal*, 25: 465–499.

Mintzberg, H. & Waters, J. A. 1984. Researching the formation of strategies: The history of Canadian Lady, 1939–1976. In Lamb, R. B. (Ed.) *Competitive Strategic Management.* Englewood Cliffs, NJ: Prentice-Hall, pp. 62–93.

Montgomery, C. 1988. Guest editors's introduction to the special issue on researching in the content of strategy. *Strategic Management Journal*, 9: 3–8.

Moran, T. H. 1987. Managing an oligopoly of would-be sovereigns: The dynamics of joint control and self-control in the international oil industry past, present and future. *International Organization*, 41(4): 575–608.

Nelson, R. & Winter, S. 1982. *An Evolutionary Theory of Economic Change.* Cambridge, MA: Harvard University Press.

Ohmae, K. 1983. *The Mind of the Strategist.* New York: Penguin.

Penrose, E. T. 1968. *The Large International Firm in Developing Country: The International Petroleum Industry.* Westport, CT: Greenwood Press.

Perlmutter, H. V. 1969. The tortuous evolutions of the multinational corporation. *Columbia Journal of World Business*, (January–February): 9–18.

Peters, T. J. & Waterman, R. H. 1982. *In Search of Excellence: Lessons from America's Best-Run Companies.* New York: Harper & Row.

Porter, M. E. 1979. The structure within industries and companies' performance. *Review of Economics and Statistics*, 61 (May): 215–227.

Porter, M. E. 1980. *Competitive Strategy: Techniques for Analyzing Industries and Competitors.* New York: Free Press.

Porter, M. E. 1981. The contributions of industrial organization to strategic management. *Academy of Management Review*, 6(4): 609–620.

Porter, M. E. 1985. *Competitive Advantage.* New York: Free Press.

Porter, M. E. 1986. Changing patterns of international competition. *California Management Review* (Winter): 9–40.

Poynter, T. A. 1985. *International Enterprises and Government Intervention.* London: Croom Helm.

Prahalad, C. K. & Doz, Y. L. 1987. *The Multinational Mission: Balancing and Global Vision.* New York: Free Press.

Quinn J. B. 1980. *Strategies for Change: Logical Incrementalism.* Homewood, IL: Irwin.

Rosenberg, N. 1982. *Inside the Black Box: Technology and Economics.* Cambridge, MA: Cambridge University Press.

Rosenbloom, R. S. & Burgelman, R. A. 1989. Technology strategy: An evolutionary process perspective. In Rosenbloom, R. S. (Ed.) *Research on Technological Innovation, Management and Policy*, Vol. 4. Greenwich, CT: JAI Press.

Rugman, A. M. 1986. New theories of the multinational enterprise: An assessment of internalization theory. *Bulletin of Economic Research*, 38(2): 101–118.

Rumelt, R. P. 1984. Toward a strategic theory of the firm. In Lamb, R. (Ed.) *Competitive Strategic Management.* Englewood Cliffs, NJ: Prentice-Hall.

Rumelt, R. P. 1987. Theory, strategy and entrepreneurship. In Teece, D. (Ed.) *The Competitive Challenge.* Cambridge, MA: Ballinger.

Schamlensee, R. 1982. Product differentiation advantages of pioneering brands. *American Economic Review*, 72(3): 349–365.

Schamlensee, R. 1985. Do markets differ much? *American Economic Review*, 75 (June): 341–351.

Schumpeter, J. A. 1934. *The Theory of Economic Development.* Cambridge, MA: Harvard University Press.

Segev, E. 1989. A systematic comparative analysis and synthesis of two business-level strategic typologies. *Strategic Management Journal*, 10(5): 487–505.
Selznick, P. 1957. *Leadership in Administration.* Evanston, IL: Row, Peterson.
Shepherd, W. 1986. On the core concepts of industrial economics. In de Jong, H. W. & Shepherd, W. (Eds.) *Mainstream of Industrial Organization, Book I. Theory and International Aspects.* Dordrecht: Martinus.
Shortell, S. M. & Zajac, E. J. 1990. Perceptual and archival measures of Miles and Snow's strategic types: A comprehensive assessment of reliability and validity. *Academy of Management Journal*, 33(4): 817–832.
Spence, A. M. 1977. Entry, capacity investment and oligopolistic pricing. *Bell Journal of Economics*, 8 (Autumn): 534–544.
Spence, A. M. 1981. The learning curve and competition. *Bell Journal of Economics*, 12 (Spring): 49–70.
Thomas, L. G. Ill (Ed.) 1986. *The Economics of Strategic Planning: Essays in Honor of Joel Dean.* Lexington, MA: Lexington Books.
Tremblay, V. 1985. Strategic groups and the demand for beer. *Journal of Industrial Economics*, 32(2): 183–198.
Tung, R. L. 1979. Dimensions of organizational environment: An exploratory study of their impact on organization structure. *Academy of Management Journal*, 22: 672–693.
Wernerfelt, B. 1984. A resource-based view of the firm. *Strategic Management Journal*, 5: 171–180.
Wernerfelt, B. & Montgomery, C. 1988. Tobins *q* and the importance of focus in firm performance. *American Economic Review*, 78 (March): 246–250.
Williamson, O. E. 1975. *Markets and Hierarchies: Analysis and Antitrust Implications.* New York: Macmillan, Free Press.
Williamson, O. E. 1985. *The Economic Institutions of Capitalism.* New York: Macmillan, Free Press.
Yamanouchi, T. 1989. Breakthrough: The development of the Canon personal copier. *Long Range Planning*, 22(117): 11–21.
Yoffie, D. B. & Milner, H. V. 1989. An alternative to free trade or protectionism: Why corporations seek strategic trade policy. *California Management Review*, 3(4): 113–131.

https://doi.org/10.1142/9789811287510_0010

Chapter 10

Behavioral Elements in Foreign Direct Investment Decisions*,†

Yair Aharoni

Tel Aviv University, Tel Aviv, Israel

Abstract

The success of multinational enterprises (MNEs) is at least as much a function of management ability and behavior as it is of industry characteristics or environmental factors. These managers display human limitations that affect judgment. Yet international business (IB) researchers tend to ignore management in their research, treating the firm as a black box. To the extent top management team (TMT) is considered, rational behavior in classical economic sense is assumed. Behavioral elements were studied by others in different fields. Clearly, managers behave according to different rules than those assumed in much of the IB literature. Further, managers are not part of a herd but unique. The result of such a lacuna is that theory fails to predict actual behavior and does not allow best guidance for policy options. The chapter summarizes research on behavioral decision making and calls for its application in future research in international business.

---

*This chapter is reproduced from *The Future of Foreign Direct Investment and the Multinational Enterprise*, pp. 23–60 (2011), Emerald Group Publishing.

†An earlier version of this chapter was originally published in "The Past, Present and Future of International Business and Management", *Advances in International Management* (Vol. 23, pp. 73–112).

Keywords: Managerial decision-making bounded rationality; behavior; multinational enterprise; foreign direct investment; environmental uncertainty; judgment; heterogeneity; top management teams.

> Nothing is more fundamental in setting our research agenda and informing our research methods than our view on the nature of the human beings whose behavior we are studying. It makes a difference. A very large difference. (Simon, 1985: p. 303)

> There is no general principle that prevents the creation of an economic theory based on other hypotheses than rationality. (Arrow, 1987)

Introduction

In 1960 I was a young doctoral student. I was distressed by the apparent failure of less developed countries (LDCs) to attract US manufacturing investments. Specifically, I noted that the fervent attempts to encourage foreign direct investments (FDI) by enacting the Law for Encouragement of Capital Investments did not in fact materialize. Therefore, I resolved to study the way foreign investment decisions are made by US manufacturing firms. I hoped that by finding out the considerations business persons took into account in making FDI decisions I could unearth ways and means to increase FDIs in LDCs. I assumed that tax incentives permit a higher rate of return and therefore can make otherwise unpromising investments attractive. The conferral of tax benefits will induce foreign investors to initiate projects which they would not otherwise have undertaken. The problem seemed to be straightforward: how large should the incentives be?

I soon found out that the tax incentives did not play the decisive role I expected them to play. Moreover, the picture emerging from my field research seemed to be one of utterly irrational behavior and a complete lack of economic logic. The decision process had very little in common with the classical economic theory of capital investments. It was necessary to look at the system as a whole, recognizing that decisions are made under uncertainty within an organization and a social system. Once I changed the lens what seemed irrational made sense.

I submitted my doctoral thesis in 1961. Sometimes thereafter, a spate of publications appeared that bore many similarities to the major themes of my thesis. One important contribution that laid out a conceptual basis for looking at the decision-making process was *a behavioral theory of the firm* by Cyert & March (1963). I incorporated these contributions and others when I wrote the Foreign Investment Decision Process (1966a).

Many things have changed since then. These changes made some theories obsolete and modified the nature of the multinational enterprise (MNE). New technologies impacted quite a few firms. Major new products created totally different markets and new industries. Search engines, dial up modems, and internet browsers — all mitigate transaction costs; connect people and the dispersed components of MNEs worldwide. The rapid coverage of the world with internet facilities changed fundamentally the ways people communicate across borders and the time it takes to respond to a message (Kogut, 2003). One result has been an increased offshore outsourcing of business services — leading Thomas Friedman (2005) to declare that the world is flat. Another result is the surge of electronic trade. In addition, in a growing number of industries, that is, aerospace, telecommunications, or pharmaceuticals, even the largest national market is too small to amortize the enormous research and development expenses associated with new products. The firm must expand into many national markets (Mytelka & Delapierre, 1999).

International operations have grown also because of fundamental changes in the *international political environment*. World exports have increased from $60 billion in 1950 to $16,070 billion in 2008. The multilateral trading arrangement under the auspices of GATT and later World Trade Organization (WTO) has been a necessary precondition to enable this growth. The General Agreement on Services opened up many avenues for FDIs in services — an area not long ago regarded as nontradable. World trade in commercial services grew from $365 billion in 1980 to $3,778 billion in 2008. In the 1960s, managers of international oil firms were able to maintain market share agreements even during periods of oil glut — generating oligopoly rents through political behavior and collusion (Jacoby, 1974; Moran, 1987; Penrose, 1968). Other firms were able to survive by enlisting political support to prevent imports of more efficient firms. A "political strategy" was an important ingredient to gain competitive advantage (Yoffie & Milner, 1989). Stopford & Strange (1991: p. 1) argued that "Firms have become more involved with governments and governments have come to recognize their increased dependence on the scarce resources controlled by firms". As a result, states have become increasingly dependent on MNEs to achieve technological competitiveness. In some countries, "social partnerships" appear to have been operating without serious frictions, allowing firms to collude to allocate market share (Katzenstein, 1984). However, a collusion strategy may be less successful in some cultures than in others (Eckbo, 1976). Deregulation of many infrastructure services has also created opportunities for more international investment. These changes stemmed to a large extent from *changing beliefs*. More and more intellectuals — and then government officials — became ardent believers in the efficiency of free markets or at least disillusioned with the ability of governments to plan and direct the economy. These beliefs led to an almost universal urge to contain the extent of government intervention in the management of resource allocation and to coordinate economic policies, recognizing the fragility of the international financial system. As a result of globalization, the options open to national governments are severely constrained.

In 1960, US MNEs invested to jump tariff walls and many other national restrictions on trade. Since the 1990s, it is generally accepted that open and competitive markets are necessary to ensure economic growth. The Berlin Wall crumbled in November 1989. Since then, the former Soviet Empire disaggregated, its different components moved toward liberal economic policies. Most economies moved from import substitution policies and protection of domestic firm to policies aimed to achieve export-led growth through reduction of government's intervention. These policy changes forced domestic firms to upgrade their products and services, trim costs, and benchmark themselves against best-in-class global competitors. Several of these firms also ventured abroad, in search of markets, lower costs, and resources. To be sure, many economic activities, for example, agriculture or airlines are still highly protected. Capital is being globalized, but national authorities try hard to limit movements of labor across borders. Further, confidence in free market economics, until recently virtually impregnable, has been undermined by the financial crisis of 2007–2008.

The macro economic environment has also changed dramatically. The direct convertibility of the US dollar to gold and the Bretton Woods fixed exchange regime were abandoned. Currencies in the developed world moved to a full float, followed by two oil crises in 1973 and 1979, a decade of high interest rates in the United States, and a debt crisis in many developing countries. The Plaza Accord in 1985 realigned the value of the major currencies and Japanese FDIs zoomed. The Euro Zone was created in 1998; in 1999 the Euro was born (as electronic currency, becoming a cash currency in 2002), and soon rivaled the US dollar as the currency of choice for international business. A financial crisis gripped Thailand, spreading to many Asian countries (Kaufman *et al.*, 1999). All these changes also led to a shift in the distribution of economic and political power in the world. As one example, in 2008 China became the world's largest manufacturing exporter.

The prevailing views on MNEs were also altered fundamentally. In the world of neoclassical economics, FDI had little place (Kindlebeger, 1969). During the 1990s, intrafirm trade (trade within the same MNE) accounted for one-third of all world trade. These transactions are not determined by the market and are valued by the MNE using transfer prices — based on tax and tariff considerations. Another third of world trade is accounted for by the exports of MNE parent firms and foreign affiliates to unaffiliated firms. Thus, nearly two-thirds of international trade in the 1990s was shaped by MNEs (UNCTAD, 1995: p. 193, 1996: p. 121). By 2007, the share of trade within the MNEs, according to WTO, reached 27.5%. In addition, the sales of MNEs' overseas affiliates (international production) are almost double that of world exports. In the 1960s, MNEs were perceived as new forms of colonialism or imperialism and as an arm of American Hegemony (e.g., Levitt, 1970; Saari, 1999: p. 2). Many scholars portrayed national governments as pawns in the hands of powerful MNEs, impotent and incapable of achieving national goals (Barnet & Műller, 1974). Some observers even claimed that the "nation-state is just about through as an economic unit" (Kindlebeger, 1969: p. 207) and would be finished off by powerful MNEs (see Gilpin, 1975: p. 220) that would make the state impotent. (For a description and rebuttal of these arguments, see Wolf, 2004: Chap. 11.) In the 1970s, such fears led to nationalizations and expropriations of MNE assets, and to efforts to amend the world economic order. The growing anxiety about the possible dominance of MNEs over countries led also to a request by the United Nations to study the role of MNES and their impact on the process of development. The result was the first systematic efforts at data gathering by the United Nations, identifying 7,276 parent MNEs in the world in 1969 with book value of global FDI stock at US$108.2 billion. Eight of the 10 largest multinational corporations were based in the United States (UN, 1973: p. 77).

Since the 1980s, MNEs have been increasingly recognized as a prime engine to foster long-term economic development. FDIs potential to inject capital without debt servicing obligations, create jobs, transfer technology (including management skills), enhance exports, and raise productivity is now widely acclaimed. The possible disadvantages of FDIs or the possible conflict of power between the MNEs and the nation-states seem to have been forgotten or assumed to be manageable. It is now widely agreed that the advantages of MNEs are less based on factors vulnerable to rapid obsolescence and more on the capability to innovate, generate new technologies, and manage knowledge across a global network of subsidiaries. The MNE is therefore courted as a major engine of development in a knowledge-based global economy. Different nations compete intensively with each other to get MNEs to locate value-added activities within their borders (Oxelheim & Ghauri, 2004: Chap. 1).

MNEs themselves are constantly changing. First, their numbers are growing — to a large extent as a response to changing environment. From 7,276 firms in 1969, the number of MNEs worldwide mushroomed by 2008 to 82,053 parent corporations with 807,353 foreign affiliates (UNCTAD, 2009: pp. 222–223). Second, the home country is now spread. Today MNEs come from almost all countries. In 2008, only 2,418 parents were from the United States, while 21,425 parents were from developing countries (Aharoni & Ramamurti, 2008). Third, MNEs were dominated by resource seeking and manufacturing MNEs. Later, MNEs from the service sector have been steadily increasing their share. In 2008, there were 26 service MNEs among the top 100, compared to 14 in 1993. Fourth, in the 1970s, multinationals were regarded as giants, with sales that dwarfed the GNPs of most countries. This is still true of the largest MNEs. The 100 largest MNEs accounted since 2000 for about 4% of world GDP and to about 9% of foreign assets and 16% of foreign sales of all MNEs. However, the vast majority of firms counted by UNCTAD as MNEs are small in size. Fifth, MNEs are increasingly recognized as market seekers or efficiency seekers and more and more they are strategic asset seekers — looking for new ideas attempting "to innovate by learning from the world" (Doz *et al.*, 2001: p. 1). Sixth, MNEs shifted from hierarchical organizations to horizontally networked alliances, most of which are not based on equity links. While in the past FDI has been distinguished from portfolio investment by the element of control — assumed to be a function of ownership — today, in Dunning's (1994) terms, hierarchical enterprises are being replaced by alliance capitalism — that do not appear in official statistics. One reason is that MNEs decompose their supply chain, outsourcing operations that can be digitized and decomposed into a cheap labor location and distributing other activities to the best location across the world. They also interconnect all markets and knowledge centers. FDI inflows according to UNCTAD (2009) reached a historic high of \$1,979 billion. As a result of the world recession, it went down to \$1,697 billion in 2008 and further declined in 2009.[1] Again, these figures do not include alliances and other nonequity forms of cooperation. MNEs have become centers of knowledge and innovation. Managers of MNEs orchestrate assets, coordinate development of new products, eradicate inefficiencies, and allocate resources within the firm. New theories of MNEs indeed emphasized learning, capabilities, and innovation (Kogut & Zander, 1993; Augier & Teece, 2007; Pitelis, 2007). More recently MNEs were recognized as networks rather than as markets or hierarchies. Knowledge within MNEs flows now in all directions within the network and MNEs are knowledge-seekers, not just transferring knowledge from home to their foreign affiliates in host countries (Gupta & Govindarajan, 2000).

The growing sophistication and shrinking costs of transportation and of information and communication technology (ICT) facilitates global integration of operations. To be sure, the world of business is still mainly a domestic one and most production is domestically oriented. Large firms operating in a huge domestic market remain in that market as long as they find enough growth opportunities within it. The larger this market, the more can a domestic firm grow and prosper without ever extending its operations to other markets. Firms from small countries (and those operating in large scale, expensive R&D industries) do not enjoy such a luxury. They must enter lucrative foreign markets in order to grow — and the new technologies allow such a strategy. New technologies also foster a major enhancement of cooperation among firms in diverse locations in different parts of the globe. Rangan & Sengal (2009) convincingly argue that MNEs employing more ICT exhibit a reduced propensity for transnational integration. Instead, they cede ownership to foster decentralized value creation. The most recent transformation is the flurry of FDI in the acquisition of farmland (Von Braun & Meinzen-Dick, 2009; Cotula, 2009).

The changes summarized above were of course noted by international business (IB) scholars. Unfortunately, I cannot identify any seminal papers that predicted any of these changes. IB scholars did propose adaptations for theories that became obsolete because of the rapid changes. As one example, Vernon's product life theory (1966) assumed demand led innovations from the home developed country. This and other parts of his model were discredited with time. Vernon himself acknowledged the impact of some changes in Vernon (1979). Cantwell (1995) has shown that the hypothesis that innovation is concentrated in the home country is not true anymore. In fact, clusters of distinctive innovations occur in many centers and the greater capability of many MNEs manifests itself not just in the wider geographical dispersion of their investments, but in the broader degree of cross-border specialization that they are able to manage. Today, many of the innovations by MNEs originate from subsidiaries rather than from headquarters. Teece (1986) analyzed how an inventor can profit internationally from his new invention. He not only suggested the need for what he termed "appropriability regime" — or available patent protection — but also the possession of complementary assets and capabilities. Recently, Hennart (2009) pointed out that theories are too MNEs centric — assuming the choice of entry is unilaterally determined by the MNE. He called for recognition of the need to bundle firm-specific advantages (FSA) of MNEs with complementary local assets. His model also predicts how entry modes evolve with time. Despite quoting Teece (1986), Hennart assumes that the source of innovation is the MNE, knowledge is transferred from its headquarters and local firms enjoy domestic market position. In fact today MNEs FSA can be in distribution and the innovator is a local firm. MNES search actively for technologies, ideas, and products from outside the firm. Procter and Gamble expects half of its future products to be based on technologies and concepts it will acquire from third parties (Huston & Sakkab, 2006; Jones, 2005).

In the field of strategy, since the seminal Chandler (1962), the theoretical literature has been growing exponentially. By incorporating ideas and concepts developed by industrial economics (IO) to strategy. Porter (1979, 1980, 1985) blazed a new trail in strategy. He made examination of industry structure a cornerstone of identifying the key factors required for success. He was followed by many who attempted to connect industry's structure and performance of firms — including their international operations. Another strand — the resource-based view (RBV) offered an explanation for interfirm variations in performance. Its central tenets are path dependence and firm heterogeneity. Firms are able to sustain competitive advantage because of the ownership of firm-specific resources that must be valuable, rare, and inimitable and nonsubstitutable (VRIN) (Barney, 1991). As the external environment changes, firms need to renew their stock of VRIN resources. Dynamic capabilities are needed to cope with changing environment (Teece & Pisano, 1994). These capabilities and the strategic decisions are made by top management teams (TMTs) — the study of which builds on upper-echelon theory (Hambrick & Mason, 1984). These studies influenced also the IB field. Many recent IB studies stressed the salience of experience, knowledge, as well as path dependence — an evolution of the firm that depends on its past history. Indeed, Jones & Khenna (2006) convincingly argued that "history matters".

One thing did not change: lack of information about alternatives and the impossibility of foreseeing the future makes managers of MNEs "satisficers". Their rational behavior is bounded by the cost of obtaining information, by their cognitive ability and because they are working under uncertainty within a social system. A whole new field of economics was developed — stressing behavioral elements, cognitive bias leading to a search in a relatively familiar domain and other seemingly irrational behavior, including the malleability and context dependence of preferences and behavior. Yet, despite the rich findings of behavioral economics, behavioral marketing, and behavioral finance, it is quite amazing that "the role that managers play in achieving certain internationalization positions is, to a great extent, underdeveloped in the IB literature ... One important commonality is that they do not leave much scope for discretionary management decision-making" (Hutzschenreuter *et al.*, 2007: pp. 1056–1057). Most IB researchers assumed perfect rationality in their models and managers do not have any role (Kogut *et al.*, 2002). To the extent individual managers are incorporated into conceptual frameworks, it is assumed they act based on their own self-interest or, if appropriate governance mechanisms is in place, in accordance with interests that are aligned with that of the MNE's owners (see Carpenter *et al.*, 2004; Werner, 2002 for reviews). It is tempting to speculate why IB did not incorporate bounded rationality, decision-making biases, and judgments by managers in their models. It may be more constructive to enumerate these findings, hoping that future researchers would consider their meaning. In the following sections I shall summarize my findings on the foreign investment decision process and the important advances in behavioral theories. I shall then demonstrate the relevance of behavioral findings in prescribing policies and enumerate future research implications.

The Foreign Investment Decision — A Complex Process

The foreign investment decision process is not a single, identifiable act. Rather, it is a complex succession of acts. It is "a dynamic social process of mutual influences among various members of an organization, constrained by the organization's strategy, its resources and the limited capacity, goals and needs of its members, throughout which choices emerge" (Aharoni, 1966a: p. 15). The foreign investment decision process is made by a group of individuals in an organization all of which are busy. It is a long process, involves different organizational levels. The process is made under uncertainty both because of lack of information and because of the limited capacity of the human mind. The decision process starts because of an outside force that causes a *decision to look abroad*. The strength of this force determines the *investigation process* — throughout which decision makers accumulate psychological commitments toward other organizations and individuals. The more committed they become, the higher the probability of a *decision to invest*. In this sense, the *decision to invest* is not necessarily the last part of the decision process. Thus, if the force that caused the look abroad is strong enough, the decision to invest abroad is already made and the investigation process may concentrate on minimizing the size of the investment and the risks involved. The process is changing with the accumulation of experience and the result of organizational modifications such as the creation of an international division.

Any decision process includes several elements. First, any choice made by an organization depends on the *social system*. The social elements focus on the decision maker's relations with other individuals both within and outside the MNE, such as customers, suppliers including financial suppliers, government agencies in host and home countries and competitors. Second, the process takes a long *time*. Third, decisions are made under *uncertainty*. Therefore, the decision maker's perception of uncertainty is a major element. This perception changes as a result of experience and knowledge. Decision makers also vary regarding how comfortable they are with uncertainty surrounding the decision. Fourth, organizations have *goals*. Finally, there are many constraints on the freedom of action of the decision makers.

The decision-making process is spread over a long period of time. Implicit and explicit negotiations, both inside the organization and with outsiders, may drag on for years. During that period there are many changes, it is often found that certain factors were not taken into account or proved to be unpredictable. These changes invariably require more modifications, more approvals, and sometimes new round of negotiations has to be started.

When a series of investment decisions are examined another important factor emerges: "the accumulation of experience by executives in various echelons regarding foreign investments creates profound changes in the organization itself … Gradually, organizations may evolve into multinational corporations, vigorously looking for opportunities abroad"

(Aharoni, 1966a: p. 174). Organizations learn and with learning the perception of uncertainty in foreign operations changes. Investments previously perceived as risky become acceptable. When the process is put in a historical perspective it may be found that the firm received an export order long time in the past. The foreign market was developed by a foreign agent with top management paying little or no attention to foreign development. With the growth of export business, sometimes even without any deliberate action from headquarters, an export department may have been created. This in turn forms a group of people in the company who feel obligated, driven by their vested interest, to expand the international operations. The very existence of an international division gives a momentum to international operations and these operations are expanded. The assignment of a group of executives to an international division creates several institutional as well as individual commitments. The cost of investigation in an international division is generally lower: knowledge has been accumulated from previous investigations. Further, both because of their role and because of their experience the international executives perceive the risk of foreign operations to be lower. They have more knowledge about remote control operations. With time, foreign investments become a substantial part of total operations. The level of the international division in the firm's hierarchy is much higher and the involvement of top management increases. When the expansion of existing foreign operations is considered, the investigation is much more expeditious.

The location pattern also evolves: very often Canada was the first country selected for foreign operations. The Canadian subsidiary exported to the British Commonwealth. "Most United States investments in Asia and Africa have been made by companies which have had considerable experience in foreign operations in more developed countries. This phenomenon may perhaps be attributed to the idea of 'experience first': companies may have preferred to get their feet wet in safer water" (*ibid.*: p. 180). Because of path dependence, the history of the firm is an important variable.

The population I studied was US firms. A similar incremental process of learning and experience as well as the choice of familiar countries first was found by Johanson & Vahlne (1977) in their observations of Swedish firms. Firms are inhibited by lack of knowledge about markets. Therefore, firms proceed in small steps adjusting as they gain knowledge through experience. The internationalization is evolutionary, continuous process from export, to joint venture representation, to sales subsidiary, to resource development subsidiary. Further, based on experience and knowledge acquisition firms enter new markets with successively greater psychic distance. These explanations are considered at the firm — not the individual — level. "In our model, we consider knowledge to be vested in the decision-making system. We do not deal explicitly with the individual decision maker" (Johanson & Vahlne, 1977: p. 26).

In subsequent work, Johanson & Vahlne (1990, 2009) expanded the notion of knowledge development to include knowledge gained through relationships with other bodies on the foreign market. They posit markets as networks of relationships among firms. Insidership in relevant networks is necessary for successful internationalization. Relationships offer potential for building trust and commitments, which in turn shapes a firm's market knowledge.

IB theory developed significantly since the early attempts to understand the foreign investment decision process, the modes of operations and the sequence of entry to different locations. An extensive academic literature used cross-sectional design to study the choice of modes of operation. Brouthers & Hennart (2007) have documented about 100 empirical studies in the last 15 years. Most of these theoretical developments relied heavily on the pioneering efforts of Coase (1937) to explain the existence of firms. Coase stressed the relative costs of internalizing transactions versus operating in external markets. Williamson (1975) developed the transaction costs approach to a general theory of the firm. Buckley & Casson (1976) combined internalization with location effects — portraying the MNE as an internal market operating across borders. Other researchers followed Williamson's transaction cost theory (Hennart, 1982; Anderson & Gatignon, 1986). Dunning (1980) offered a theory attempting to combine the role of ownership and location advantages in explaining why an MNE would engage in FDI — thus demonstrating (I) advantage — rather than exports. This theory was later presented as paradigm — that was updated many times (For the latest version see Dunning & Lundan, 2008). Later, influenced by resource-based theory and premised on the idea that organizations learn from experience (Levitt & March, 1988), the MNE was recognized as knowledge-based (Kogut & Zander, 1993). Organizational learning theory is primarily concerned with experience accumulation. It also addresses knowledge articulation and knowledge codification (Zollo & Winter, 2002).

These theories were all based on some — often implicit — assumptions about human behavior. Williamson, for example, relied heavily on bounded rationality and also assumed opportunism, defined as self-interest seeking with guile (Williamson, 1985). Indeed this assumption was the major reason for rejecting the application of TCE to practice (Ghoshal & Moran, 1996). Other theories ignored managerial behavior totally. As pointed out by one of the founders of internalizing, Mark Casson, "Transaction cost analysis … explains the boundaries of the firm very welly … What lies inside the boundaries of the firm is not explained so well because this is not the focus of the theory" (Casson, 2000: p. 118). It seems that many of the IB scholars were willing to assume managers are omnipotent, possessing all the information needed to make rational decisions. As a minimum, it is assumed "that the decision-maker can identify a set of options, and has an objective by which these options can be ranked, and an ability to identify the top-ranked option and select it" (Buckley & Casson, 2009: p. 1568). Thus, the vast literature on entry mode choice tends to assume that firms will move their transferable FSA to locations enjoying country-specific advantages (CSAs). Based on the relative strengths of the CSA the MNE would choose both the initial and the subsequent modes of entry. It is taken for granted that all the relevant information is known. To be sure, relevant does not imply complete. "A rational decision-maker will collect only sufficient information to make the risks surrounding the decision acceptable" (Buckley & Casson, 2009: p. 1568). What is sufficient, how is the information collected and evaluated, how the decision maker knows which information to collect, and what is an acceptable risk are left unanswered. The OLI paradigm also assumes rationality in the classical economic sense. The behavioral elements in decision making were unfortunately ignored. Theoretical developments, clearly demonstrating departures from rationality both in judgment and in choices were extensive — as will be shown in the next section.

Theoretical Developments on Behavior

In 1955, Herbert Simon received the Nobel Memorial Prize for his ideas on behavior of bounded rational actors. Simon criticized the classical economists' rational choice model and the reliance of economists, following physics, on equilibrium as unrealistic. Simon pointed out that because of their cognitive limitations; bounded-rational actors do not attempt to maximize profits or utility. The rationality of individuals is limited by the information they have, the cognitive limitations of their minds, and the finite amount of time they have to make decisions. Decision makers lack the ability and resources to arrive at the optimal solution; they instead apply their rationality only after having greatly simplified the choices available (Simon, 1947, 1955; March & Simon, 1958).

Since Simon, behavioral theories have undergone steady developments in different fronts. One has been information processing psychology, using computer simulation. Extensive empirical evidence demonstrates that problem solving involves selective search, based on rules of thumb or "heuristics". Over time these rules of thumb change as outcomes are evaluated. The same process was shown in decisions on investments in securities or medical diagnosis and in many other case studies of organizational decision making (Newell & Simon, 1972).

Another major field has been the empirical refutations of the theory that human beings maximize subjective expected utility (SEU) — reported mainly by Kahneman and Tversky but also by Kunreuther and his colleagues (1978) in studies of individual decisions to purchase or not to purchase flood insurance. Kahneman & Tversky (1979 — Tversky & Kahneman, 1974), based on a series of experiments in different countries, developed a theory they termed prospect theory. It distinguishes two phases in the decision-making process: an *editing* phase, which is a preliminary analysis of the offered prospects, and an *evaluation* phase, which is when the prospect with the highest value is chosen from among the edited prospects. They also demonstrated a *certainty effect* — meaning people overweight outcomes that are certain, relative to outcomes that are merely probable even when the expected value of each is the same. People tend to avoid a loss, even if it means taking even greater risks. *Loss aversion* might depend on *framing* the safer option as the *status quo* and the complexity of the suggested alternatives.

In order to simplify the choice between alternatives, people frequently disregard components that the alternatives share. They focus on those that distinguish them. Since different choice problems can be decomposed in different ways, this can lead to inconsistent preferences. Kahneman & Tversky (1979) call this phenomenon the *isolation effect*. Prospect theory replaces the notion of utility with value. Whereas utility is usually defined only in terms of final assets or net wealth value is defined in terms of gains and losses relative to a reference point (*framing effect* — Tversky &

Kahneman, 1981). Decision makers may be more risk averse when they frame a strategic decision as potential for loss and less risk averse than when a decision is framed as potential for gain (March & Shapira, 1987; Miller & Chen, 2004). Attitude of persons toward risk are very different when gain is concerned than when loss is anticipated. For losses the value function is convex and relatively steep, for gains it is concave and not quite so steep. Second, the value of each outcome is a function of "decision weights". These weights do not always correspond to probabilities. Specifically, prospect theory postulates that decision weights tend to overweigh small probabilities and underweigh moderate and high probabilities. Reference points are selected based upon internal capabilities and external conditions considered over time (Shoham & Fiegenbaum, 2002). Decisions have two elements — judgment and choice. Judgment research deals with the processes people use to estimate probabilities. Choice deals with the processes people use to select among actions, taking account of any relevant judgments they may have made. Judgment was shown to be based on extrapolation, overconfidence, and optimism.

In their 1992 paper, Tversky and Kahneman developed an updated form of prospect theory, which they termed *Cumulative Prospect Theory*. The theory incorporates rank-dependent functional that transforms cumulative, rather than individual, probabilities and satisfies stochastic dominance, which the original form of prospect theory does not.

Prospect Theory helps to illuminate experimental results that show individuals often make divergent choices in situations that are substantially identical but framed in a different way. Therefore, managerial choice is not determined uniquely by the objective characteristics of the problem situation. Rather, it depends on the particular heuristic process that is used to reach the decision. Prospect theory has had an enormous influence across a range of disciplines, including economics, marketing, finance, and consumer choice.

Several theories of business firms incorporated bounded rationality. Cyert & March (1963) and Cyert & DeGroot (1974) incorporated adaptive learning and Nelson & Winter (1973) stressed evolution. In these theories profit maximization is replaced by goals defined in terms of targets. A mechanism of some sort, for example, "organizational slack", prevents maximization. Organizational learning could help reaching maximization equilibrium but only if the environment remains unchanged for a very long time. Even if the environmental conditions are identical, different decision mechanisms can produce different results.

More than 40 years after the publication of *A behavioral theory of the firm*, *Organization Science* published a special issue (Organization Science, 2007). It reports the most recent research in this area. None of the papers in that issue — not even any of the hundreds of papers cited — is in international business! The most direct descendents of Cyert and March's work are presented as the organizational learning (Argote, 1999) and evolutionary economics (Nelson & Winter, 1982). In both fields, process-oriented models are important, "In these fields, much theorizing concerns how certain events and experiences set in motion processes of decision making, routine, development, or routine selection that change organizational behavior" (Argote & Greve, 2007: p. 338). Lessons learned are captured by routines such that the lessons are accessible to organizational members. Both used the behavioral theory as a tool for providing basic concepts on which they could build a theory of change. Organizational learning theory has helped to explain the formation, performance, and likelihood of survival of international joint ventures (Barkema *et al.*, 1997; Parkhe, 1991).

Behavioral economists, too, challenged conventional economic analysis, modifying unbounded rationality, unbounded willpower, and unbounded selfishness, adding significant behavioral findings to today's mainstream economics (for reviews, see Camerer, 2000; Camerer *et al.*, 2003; Fudenberg, 2006; Rabin 1998, 2002; Sunstein & Thaler, 2008; DellaVigna, 2009). In 1997 a special issue of the *Quarterly Journal of Economics* was devoted to behavioral economics. Areas of research by behavioral economists include *anchoring* (a cognitive bias one relies too heavily on one trait or piece of information), availability *heuristic* (when people predict the frequency of an event based on how easily an example can be brought to mind. One result is people tend to overstate risks and a result purchase unnecessary insurance, or governments pursuing social goals at the expense of other more fruitful ones), *representativeness heuristic* — where people judge the probability or frequency of a hypothesis by considering how much the hypothesis resembles available data, Status quo bias when people are very likely to continue a course of action since it has been traditionally the one pursued and *herd mentality* — where people are heavily influenced by actions of others. It also includes *loss aversion* (Tversky & Kahneman, 1991), *quasi hyperbolic of intertemporal choice* (Laibson, 1997), *cognitive dissonance* (Akerlof & Dickens, 1982), *endowment effect* (the tendency to place a greater value on an item when it might be given up from one's possession than when it is not in one's possession — Knetsch, 1989; Knetsch & Sinden, 1984; Kahneman *et al.*, 1990), social preferences (Gneezy & Rustichini, 2000a, 2000b), fairness (Kahneman *et al.*, 1986), and mental accounting (Thaler, 1999). Rabin demonstrated that people cooperate in ultimatum games — in which a proposer suggests to a respondent how much of a given sum each should get. If the respondent rejects the offer both get nothing. If the respondent accepts both get what was offered. Economic theory would predict the proposer would offer a token amount. Experiments show respondents reject offer of less than 20% — because of "fairness" (Rabin, 1993). As another example Camerer *et al.* (1997) studied New York cab drivers. The profit maximizers should work hard in good days and quit early on bad days. Instead the cabbies had a target earning treating shortfalls from target as a loss. They thus quitted early in good days and work longer on bad days.

Arieli *et al.* (2003) followed reference ideas of Kahneman and Tversky and similarly provided some reference values to their subjects and then asked them what compensation they would require to hear an unpleasant sound for certain duration. The subjects quoted arbitrary values linked to the reference values. When the subjects were asked to quote the price they would want for longer duration the subjects quoted values consistent with the initial price. When the initial price is arbitrary and the subsequent price consistent with the initial price, the behavior is termed coherent arbitrariness. We do not value goods (or shares) based on "fundamentals". The experiments show that this combination of coherent arbitrariness (1) cannot be interpreted as a rational response to information, (2) does not decrease as a result of experience with a good, (3) is not necessarily reduced by market forces, and (4) is not unique to cash prices. The results imply that demand curves estimated from market data need not reveal true consumer preferences, in any normatively significant sense of the term.

A famous study conducted by Solomon Asch clearly shows peer social pressure can make a person say something that is obviously false. These errors and mistakes that human beings are subject to are well summarized by Sunstein & Thaler (2008). They also coined the term choice architecture — or the way in which decisions are influenced by how the choices are presented. The book asserts that "the notion that each of us thinks and chooses unfailingly well, and thus fits within the textbook picture of human beings offered by economists" is false (Sunstein & Thaler, 2008: p. 6) Unlike members of *homo economicus*, human beings make predictable mistakes that are the result of widely occurring biases, heuristics, and fallacies, and because of the way they are influenced by their social interactions. Behavioral research raises "serious questions about the rationality of many judgments and decisions that people make" (Sunstein & Thaler, 2008: p. 7).

In the last decade or two, a new branch of economics termed neuroeconomics attempts to combine economics, behavior, and scanning of the brain or use eye tracking and pupil dilation in order to compare the roles of the different brain areas that contribute to economic decision making. (For reviews see Camerer *et al.*, 2004, 2005.) In one study, Rubinstein (2008) found different patterns of choice among fast and slow respondents among subjects who were asked to express their preferences in the context of the Allais Paradox. He suggests that we try to identify types of economic agents by the time they take to make their choices. For him, one potentially important task for the neuroeconomics approach is to identify "types" of economic agents, namely to determine characteristics of agents that predict their behavior in different choice problems. It is difficult to do this simply by observing behavior.

Behavioral economists attempt to merge psychology and economics. Most of their studies concentrate on the behavior of individuals. Behavioral finance experts study behavior of individual investors. Many behavioral studies were carried out by marketing experts — trying to understand how consumers make choices. Organization science experts attempted to integrate prospect theory into organizational literature and behavioral decision theory (Slovic *et al.*, 1977). Significant attention is paid to issues of managerial decision making (Miller & Chen, 2004; Schwenk, 1995) and commitment (Schwenk, 1986) and for a search of new and increasingly complex biases and heuristics (e.g., Gilovich *et al.*, 2002; Kahneman, 2003).

One important issue is the consequences of the rapid pace of technological change. Industries, institutions, and the knowledge and skills that constitute core capabilities are under a relentless onslaught and unremitting assault of change. Firms have difficulties in adapting and core capabilities may become core rigidities. These difficulties are clearly a result of behavior of managers — not of rational economic calculations. Thus, Christensen (1997) demonstrates in a study of the disk drive industry the difficulties managers face in changing strategy when what he termed — disruptive as opposed to sustaining — technologies are discovered. Trispas & Gavetti (2000) analyzed how managers in Polaroid coped with the arrival of digital imaging. They provide an example of where mental filters impede evolution of core capabilities in face of radical technological change. As the digital image technology evolved, Polaroid were successful in developing digital image technology but stayed with their original business model and failed to develop manufacturing and product development capabilities, which prevented them from competing efficiently in this new market (Trispas & Gavetti, 2000). In all of these cases and many others, managers' mental models can reduce the companies' ability to react to changes in their environment (Foster & Kaplan, 2001). Managers develop an implicit mental success model and use it as a mental filter to sort information and make decisions in their daily work (Ansoff & McDonnel, 1990). When the environment in which the company is acting is changing a new mental filter must be developed. As long as signals of change in the environment are handled according to an old mental filter the acceptance of new realities will be delayed, which could affect the information system, decision-making process, executive capabilities, and control system (Foster & Kaplan, 2001; Ansoff & McDonnel, 1990). In the world of the 21st century, characterized by a relentless pursuit of new technologies and dynamic markets, mental processes that facilitate rather than hinder adaptation to new environment are of great importance. When managers face fading product-market domains they are often inertial in their response to such decline Martin & Eisenhardt (2004) call for a corporate entrepreneurship response whereby managers move their businesses into new market opportunities as the value of current-market domains inevitably begins to fade. They emphasize exiting from declining markets while simultaneously capturing and exploiting opportunities in more promising markets.

Managers are often overconfident (Biais *et al.*, 2005; Kőszegi, 2006) and their forecasts suffer from hubris (Hayward & Hambrick, 1997). They therefore fail to consider adequately the possible impact of rare but earth-shattering events (Taleb, 2007). In fact, delusional optimism is one of the forces that drive capitalism.

To summarize, studies of the psychology of decision-making acknowledge human limits on computational power, willpower, and self-interest. They posit functional heuristics for solving problems that are often so complex that they cannot be solved exactly by even modern computer algorithms. They show decision makers are influenced by a wide range of factors, such as personal goals, evaluation criteria, and identity. They sometimes make choices that are not in their long run interests and are often willing to sacrifice their own interests to help others. They may make mistakes because of several factors. First, cognitive biases impair decision makers' abilities to select optimal choices (Barnes, 1984; Schwenk, 1984; Clapham & Schwenk, 1991). Second, they transform intractable decision problems into tractable ones by using routines that short-circuit individuals' autonomous judgments (Nelson & Winter, 1982; Teece *et al.*, 1997). Third, managers are dominated by superior logic that orients behavior and result in blind spots and escalation of commitments (Prahalad & Bettis, 1986; Coff, 1999; Staw & Ross, 1987) and may be dominated by inertia. Further, organizations may develop more blind spots even beyond any individual constraints. Research to date emphasized individual behavior — and less so organizational responses (Das & Teng, 1999).

Two streams of research should be briefly mentioned: TMTs and MNE governance. Both recognize the influence of executives, for example, in determining international strategies. TMT research builds on upper-echelon theory (Hambrick & Mason, 1984) to explore the role of TMT in making international business decisions. The upper-echelon perspective focuses on executive cognition, perceptions, biases, and values and their influence on strategic choice. Managers face information overload, ambiguous cues, and competing demands. Complex decisions require reliance upon simplification heuristics, making cognitive processes increasingly important (Einhorn & Hogarth, 1981). In upper-echelon studies, biases and heuristics are assumed to be relatively consistent across similar demographic characteristics such as age, functional background, and educational experience. Empirical research has linked upper-echelon characteristics and experience with strategic choices such as internationalization (Carpenter *et al.*, 2004). However, there are significant problems with using individual-level demographic variables as indicators of decision making in TMTs (e.g., Lawrence, 1997). Markóczy (1997), for example, suggests that individual demographic characteristics are poor measures of managerial cognition. Kilduff *et al.* (2000) found no evidence of any effect of demographic diversity on cognitive diversity. Similarly, Priem *et al.* (1999) encourage TMT researchers to eschew demographic variables in favor of measures that are more difficult to capture. Others have added that, even if demographic characteristics are representative of cognitive constructs, they cannot be treated independently because executives embody a bundle of attributes that continuously interact with each other (Harrison *et al.*, 1998). A few studies of TMT deal specifically with internationalization. Thus, Herrmann & Datta (2005) examine the relationships between TMT characteristics and international diversification among large, internationally diversified US-based manufacturing firms. Findings indicate that firms with higher levels of international diversification are likely to have TMTs characterized by higher educational level, shorter organizational tenures, younger executives, and greater international experience. In addition, findings indicate that the relationships between TMT characteristics and international diversification are more dominant in better-performing than in lower-performing firms. Glunk *et al.* (2001) found that the national diversity of TMTs in Sweden and the Netherlands have not progressed in proportion to the level of internationalization of the companies.

An alternative perspective to upper-echelon research is offered by agency theory. The managers — the agents — have substantial discretion as to the actions they take because the principals — the shareholders — are dispersed and cannot coordinate to share monitoring and control costs (Jensen & Meckling, 1976). The managers pursue private benefits. The divergence of interests is greater the lower the managers' equity stake and the lower the likelihood of them getting caught and punished for nonvalue maximizing behavior. Another problem identified by agency theory is that of entrenchment: top executives with high-equity stakes enjoy more freedom to misallocate resources (Stulz, 1988). These executives cannot be removed in a proxy fight or cast out by hostile raiders attracted by low share prices. Jensen & Meckling (1976) argue that ownership gives TMT an incentive to assume risk and aligns their goals with those of other firm owners. They have less incentive to misallocate corporate resources. Stulz (1988) argues that higher equity stakes gives insiders more freedom to misallocate resources, on the corporate decision-making process.

In these studies managers are portrayed as motivated by their own gains — at the expense of the owners of the firm. They ignore studies that clearly demonstrated that fairness is an important motivator. It may well be that managers are motivated by ego and want to do better than the competitors. They demand higher remuneration or a larger bonus only because they compare their paycheck to those of others (see Arieli, 2008). Further, most of these studies are based on the United States with its separation of ownership and control. Morck *et al.* (2005) review a very large body of studies. They point out that "outside the United States and the United Kingdom, large corporations usually have controlling owners, who are usually very wealthy families. Pyramidal control structure, cross shareholding, and super voting rights let such families control corporations without making a commensurate capital investment" (p. 655). Their paper reviews many studies of different countries. They offer several conclusions. First, corporate governance problem in most countries is that of a conflict between the controlling shareholder and public shareholders — not a conflict between atomistic shareholders and professional managers. Second, the highly concentrated control leads to a range of market power distortions and may curtail investment in innovations. Finally, public policy is much influenced by the power of the rent-seeking controlling groups. Clearly, if one looks for viable policy prescriptions, it is crucial to base public policies on a coherent understanding of behavioral elements that affect the decision process.

Relevance of Behavioral Findings to Prescriptions of Policies

Ceteris paribus, better predictions are likely to result from theories with more *realistic* assumptions. Policies should be tailored to influence actual, as opposed to an assumed, behavior. To quote Douglas North, "the uncritical acceptance of the rationality assumption is devastating for most of the issues confronting social scientists and is a major stumbling block in the path of future progress. The rationality assumption is not wrong, but such an acceptance forecloses a deeper understanding of the decision-making process in confronting the uncertainties of the complex world we have created" (2005: p. 5). Thaler & Benartzi (2004: p. 167) suggest that "before writing a prescription one must know the symptoms of the disease being treated". Indeed, many mistakes made that led to the recent financial crisis could have been avoided if the decision-making process would be considered when policies were implemented.

One example is policies designed to attract FDIs — or some types of specific FDIs. Economic theory would have a clear and straightforward prescription: grant some type of tax exemption or reduction. The rationale is straightforward: if the rate of return on investment is low and the risks involved are very high tax incentives may change the rate of return. However, my doctoral study showed that the granting of income tax exemptions is not an important factor in the foreign investment decision process. The reasons for this conclusion were detailed in Aharoni (1966a: pp. 234–242) and will not be repeated here.

Based on the behavioral findings, a much better use of taxpayers' funds is to market the country (Aharoni, 1966b), to reduce perceived risk and create the decision to look abroad. The marketing program should acquaint the consumer with the product. In our case — acquaint the investor with the foreign country. It should supply up to date, accurate, and adequate information and neutralize the basic apprehension of uncertainty. It should also suggest concrete projects for considerations and demonstrate the advantage to the firm of investing in these projects. Above all, the program should be well integrated and should aid the investor throughout the decision process. The cost of investigation should be minimized — mainly by supply of relevant information and perhaps by sharing the investigation costs.

My ideas seem to have been ignored by IB scholars. The only study I unearthed on the same marketing theme is Wells and Mint (1990, revised 2000). These authors define promotional techniques to consist of (a) providing information to potential investors; (b) creating an attractive image of the country as a place to invest; and (c) providing services to prospective investors. Both the original paper and the revised one appeared as a Foreign Investment Advisory Service (FIAS) occasional papers — not in an academic journal. In the real world many countries established investment promotion agencies to facilitate FDIs. Today there are 228 such agencies from 156 countries that are members of the World Association of Investment Promotion Agencies (WAIPA) — established in 1995. These agencies directly aim at encouraging FDIs — generally inward FDIs but in many cases also outward FDIs. The effectiveness of these agencies in attracting FDI was studied by Morisset & Andrews-Johnson (2003) — again as an FIAS occasional paper. These authors found that agencies with some kind of participation from the private sector do better than those that are purely governmental. They also provide evidence to suggest that, at least for many countries, a dollar spent on investment promotion yields a better return than a dollar provided as a subsidy or given up through a tax. I did not find even one paper on these agencies in the IB academic journals.

Many more examples of policy prescriptions may be cited from behavioral economics that proposed design of institutions that would help people make better choice. As one example, Shefrin & Thaler (1988) portray the life cycle of savings as much different as classical economic theory. They take account of households' lack of self-control and procrastination (tendency to postpone unpleasant tasks). Procrastination, in turn, produces a status quo bias. Samuelson & Zeckhauser (1988) found that the median number of changes, made by TIAA-CREF participants in the asset allocation over the life time, was zero. Since then, several researchers studied retirement account portfolio behavior — relating it to various demographic variables and other participant characteristics such as age, gender, marital status, time in the 401(k) plan, salary, and time on the job (Agnew *et al.*, 2003). Of course, a policy that will achieve a desired result should take into account the behavioral elements. In the specific case of savings behavior, the elements are bounded rationality, self-control, procrastination, and nominal loss aversion. Based on consideration of these elements, a plan was designed to increase savings rate and recognizing, households may lack the self-control to reduce current consumption in favor of future consumption (Thaler & Shefrin, 1981). The plan allows workers to commit themselves now to increase their savings rate each time they get a pay increase in the future (Thaler & Benartzi, 2004).

Recognizing that decisions are driven by emotions, Sunstein and Thaler endorse what they term libertarian paternalism, claiming it is not an oxymoron. Sunstein and Thaler state that "the libertarian aspect of our strategies lies in the straightforward insistence that, in general, people should be free to do what the like — and to opt out of undesirable arrangements if they want to do so". The paternalistic portion of the term "lies in the claim that it is legitimate for choice architects to try to influence people's behavior in order to make their lives longer, healthier, and better" (Sunstein & Thaler, 2008: p. 5). Sunstein & Thaler (2008) use their notion of nudge within the context of choice architecture to propose policy recommendations that they believe are in the spirit of libertarian paternalism in a variety of policy programs. They examine how people can be nudged into making better decisions for themselves on a range of issues, such as buying more healthy food or opting to save more. IB researchers up to now rarely offer such policies.

Future Research Implications: What Are the Things We Do Not Know and Have to Study

We have shown that psychological aspects of decision making were largely ignored by IB researchers. Further, structured experiments are virtually unknown.[2] Of course, a theory susceptible of mathematical measurement is much more elegant and may win applause for sound and profound thinking. However, as March points out, "Variables that can be measured tend to be treated as more 'real' than those that cannot, even though the ones that cannot be measured may be more important" (2006: pp. 203–204). It is quite unlikely that researchers ignored behavioral elements because they have considered them to be wrong or too deterministic.[3] Therefore, IB theory should acknowledge heuristics and other aspects of bounded rationality, incorporate a theory of search, and include dynamic aspiration levels that would change with experience. It must also take account of the social and legal structures within which market transactions are carried out. Studies of actual cases of FDIs may also substantiate the salience of commitment to different stakeholders, including policymakers, accumulated during the investigation process. In fact, each of the areas discussed in IB literature offers ample opportunities for a fruitful future research by using the insights gained by behavioral decision-making and behavioral economics and apply them to different issues of international business. Several examples may be illustrative. Thus, a study of the trade-offs between competition and cooperation in networks should borrow from explanations of fairness. Note that many MNEs achieve competitive advantage by cooperation with other firms rather than by internalizing operations. Further, nonequity forms of FDI, for example, subcontracting, management contracts, turnkey arrangements, franchising, licensing, or product sharing as well as different forms of strategic alliances all increased in importance, even if they are not recorded as FDI. In many service industries, nonequity forms are much more important than equity investments. In professional services, the ownership advantage of the firm are reflected in intangible assets such as reputation or organizational capabilities, information processing, or managerial skills and knowledge (Aharoni, 2000b). For very different reasons, airlines are globalizers that are not allowed to globalize. Inward FDI in airlines has been constrained by ownership requirements in bilateral Air Service Agreements (ASAs). They therefore are forced to use various forms of strategic alliances to augment international competitiveness (see Aharoni, 2002, 2004).[4] These developments affect any discussion of modes of entry: the choice is not only about the degree of ownership, but also about cooperation with independent firms. Cultural differences may also affect entry mode choices (Schneider & DeMeyer, 1991). For example, Japanese managers tend to prefer entry modes that allow higher control over technology (Bartlett & Ghoshal, 1989). Chinese TMTs are very different than their Western equivalents (Zhang, 2007). "Born global" may be a result of managers' experience and more knowledge about world affairs, cultural differences, and international operations in many countries of the world — not only a consequence of technological changes. Research should establish whether MNE managers exhibit greater variance in perceived uncertainty than their counterparts did 50 years ago.

One area of great importance is the ways to avoid inertia given fast changes in the business environment and in technologies. How can an MNE keep its core capabilities dynamic and adjustable in the face of new technologies, different customers, and new suppliers? Behavioral theory is predominantly based on study of individuals and their behavior. Clearly, organizations are composed of individuals. Yet organizations might condition judgment even beyond any individual inefficiency.

The population of MNEs today is much more heterogeneous in a variety of aspects: home countries, their size and their level of development as well as industries, the industry in which they operate; size of the firm as well as years of experience as MNEs. Whether or not the behavior of such a diverse group of firms is the same or alternatively different MNEs behave differently is an important area for future research. Behavioral economists claim that the behavior they unearthed, that is, loss aversion is a universal trait, true in all countries and in all cultures. IB researchers argue that since decision makers in MNEs come from different cultures, they make choices differently. Cultural differences are said to affect MNE strategies (e.g., Benito, 1997; Brouthers & Brouthers, 2001) and performance (e.g., Li & Guisinger, 1992; Park & Ungson, 1997). Furthermore, the role of environmental uncertainty for managers has been explicit in many studies on cultural distance (Barkema & Vermeulen, 1998). Shifting the focus from underlying country-level cultural indicators to indicators of managerial decision making may address some of the recent criticism of cultural distance research (e.g., Shenkar, 2001; Tihanyi *et al.*, 2005). *Managerial distance* could capture variations in decision-making heuristics and biases across managers from different cultural traditions. Measuring how managers from different cultures perceive similar decisions could enhance upper-echelon and governance research (see Aharoni *et al.*, 2011).

Second, even if the environmental conditions are identical, different decision mechanisms can produce different results. Therefore, one cannot assume that process-independent predictions would hold. In fact, these predictions may turn out to be totally wrong and misleading. Third, some firms attempted to become multinational and failed while other firms in the same industry or home country were very successful in their internationalization efforts. Some MNEs clearly perform better than others. Future research should identify the sources of variability in response to environmental conditions. Fourth, we know very little about the determinants of success in managing an MNE and integrating its activities across the globe or within a region. Ownership advantages eluded as the reason for success are not easy to define. There is no real satisfactory explanation why some firms and industries became global while other firms in the same industry were not. Moreover, early research on the operation of MNEs has seen the primary task of the firm as tangible, repeated, measurable, and defined by the producer. All of these attributes are applicable neither to professional business service firms nor to many networks. Professional firms offer an intangible service, selling expertise that is generally customized, and is based on a close interaction between client and the supplier of the service with little or no economies or scale or of scope, and few possibilities of standardization. Networks are based on trust, not on hierarchy. In this context, research shedding light on what makes an MNE successful by focusing on the inner working of the MNEs is badly needed.

Received IB explanations often ignore not only managerial decision making but also the ability to create a novel strategy and to invent new products. Of course it is hard to avoid noticing that for a large number of MNEs the distinctive competence is based on innovation that *created* new markets — markets that did not exist and thus the costs of conducting market transactions could not be compared to the costs of using internal hierarchies.

Certain managers of firms in small countries decide to make the firm they lead a global firm to avoid the restrictions of growth from a small market base. Small firms sometimes enter international market immediately upon inception producing highly specialized goods for niche markets (Knight & Cavusgil, 1996, 2004). A strategy, after all, must be unique. It "must be predicated on building, maintaining and defending a competitive advantage" (Aharoni, 1993: p. 45). Clearly it is easier to study a large population by mathematical manipulation of a database than to follow trajectories of a unique strategy. Bandwagon behavior explains some foreign investment decisions but certainly not all or even most of them. Outliers adopt more proactive routes toward globalization by the innovation of a new path. Strategies of firms are very heterogeneous and such differences cannot be explained by economic models (or, for that matter, by population ecology explanations; Hannan & Freeman, 1977, 1984). Further, different managers may lead the same firm in similar environmental conditions to different strategies and to different locations around the globe.

Most past research on MNEs from Vernon (1971) to Rugman (2005) concentrated on the giant firms. Yet, there are about 80,000 MNEs most of which are small- and medium-sized. We should learn about these firms at least to find out if they face different problems and obstacles in the path toward globalization of operations. We should also learn about the working of MNEs from small countries — in which the firm is a significant part of the GNP and thus may have much too strong political, not only economic, clout (Aharoni, 2000a). It is true that the largest MNEs account for 90% of the world's FDI stock. Yet IB theory must also be able to explain internationalization of small firms and of firms from small economies, which present different challenges than large economies (Aharoni, 1994). Perhaps one can learn from outliers more than from a study of averages and populations.

Several researchers have demonstrated the existence of a home bias in portfolio selection (French & Poterba, 1991; Tesar & Werner, 1995). Despite the well-documented gains and reduced risk from international diversification, investors overwhelmingly prefer investments in domestic firms and in firms whose headquarters is in their country of residence (Coval & Moskowitz, 1999). Researchers also unearthed home bias in trade — preferring trade with neighbor countries or even states (McCallum, 1995; Wolf, 2000). Several explanations were offered for the home bias, from an emphasis on barriers to international movements to preference of geographic proximity and amplification of information asymmetries between countries. All of the explanations seem quite inadequate given the globalization of capital. Research is badly needed on behavior that causes home bias and to prescribe how a home bias could be eliminated or reduced.

In the specific area of top management, past research has focused on two dimensions of TMT characteristics: TMT demographics and heterogeneity of the team (Tihanyi *et al.*, 2001). TMT heterogeneity refers to the differences among team members in demographics and important cognitive aspects, values, and experiences. Hambrick & Mason (1984) assumed that heterogeneous TMT can obtain information from different sources and different opinions on the problem from team members. This difference in opinions would allow the TMT to make high-quality decisions and obtain a greater capability to solve problems. Diversity provides a TMT with a range of different viewpoints and causes a cohesive team to be more receptive to the need for change (Hambrick & Mason, 1984). On the other hand, diversity reduces team cohesion and increased miscommunications, thereby leading to slower pace of strategic change (Hambrick & Mason, 1984). However, while greater homogeneity lead to faster decision making, it may also lead to insular thinking, and therefore, to strategic persistence in conditions when strategic change is appropriate. There is a lack of agreement among academicians as to whether heterogeneous or homogeneous TMT is better for firm performance (Amason, 1996; Amason & Sapienza, 1997; Boone & Hendriks, 2009). Moreover, the contexts and dynamics of TMT vary across countries (Glunk *et al.*, 2001). Therefore, the impact on the performance of the firm may be different in different cultures. Cultural differences affect the attitudes, values, and faith of managers (Ronen & Shenkar, 1985), thereby influencing their strategy selection. Further, a study of TMT heterogeneity should take account of the impact of social context in which team members are embedded (Rau, 2008; Zhang, 2007).

Conclusions

International business research has become more rigorous over the past 50 years, owing to developments in computing technology and statistical software and to broader availability of international databases. Unfortunately, increased mathematical manipulation has often come at the cost of practical relevance. In their search for elegance and rigor, IB researchers ignored the rich evidence on psychological aspects of decision making, the complexity of decision making under uncertainty, and the accumulation of commitments. In most studies, outcomes are deterministic, the firm is treated as a black box and managers — if they are mentioned at all — are assumed to be rational calculators of costs and benefits. To be sure, certain differences among firms originating from different nations (and therefore cultures) are acknowledged.

The study of decision making in MNEs should take into account the many insights from a long line of research in behavioral decision making. It should also determine what is universally applicable and what is specific — to a culture, country, industry, size of firm, or other variables. This chapter presented a large compilation of demonstrations from experimental data showing framing effects, hyperbolic discounting of intertemporal choice, endowment effect, fairness, and other circumstances under which rationality as defined by classical economists does not hold. It is hoped that these demonstrations will motivate and inspire young researchers to look for applications for IB theories.

Notes

1. The Economist Intelligence Unit shows slightly different figures: US$2.09 trillion in 2007, US$1.73 trillion in 2008, plunging by 44% in 2009 (Kekic, 2009).
2. One exception is the structured experiment carried out by Buckley *et al.* (2007). In this experiment the roles of information, biases, and managerial experience were very different in two phases of an FDI investment decision process. The first ("consider") stage is a choice of potential investment options. The second ("invest") stage is the actual choice of the investment. Managers employed more rational measures, including return ratios, cost measures, and market conditions. In the investment-choice phase, however, managers focused more on FDI experience and host country specific factors, such as the political environment and language.
3. Langlois & Csontos (1993: p. 118) argue that behaviorists portray agents as hard headed rule followers or preprogrammed satisficers. These agents act in a deterministic way.
4. The number of airlines alliances has risen markedly from around 20 in the early 1990s to a total of 1,221 by 2001 (UNCTAD, 2004).

References

Agnew, J., Balduzzi, P. & Sundén, A. 2003. Portfolio choice and trading in a large 401(k) plan. *American Economic Review*, 93: 193–205.

Aharoni, Y. 1993. In search of the unique. *Journal of Management Studies*, 30(1): 31–49.

Aharoni, Y. 1994. How small firms can achieve competitive advantages in an interdependent world. In Agmon, T. E. & Drobbnick, R. (Eds.) *Small Firms in Global Competition*. New York: Oxford University Press, pp. 9–18.

Aharoni, Y. 1966a. *The Foreign Investment Decision Process*. Boston: Harvard Business School.

Aharoni, Y. 1966b. How to market a country. *Columbia Journal of World Business*, 1(2): 41–49.

Aharoni, Y. 2000a. Globalization and the small, open economy. In Almor, T. & Hashai, N. (Eds.) *FDI, International Trade and the Economics of Peacemaking.* Rishon Le'Zion, Israel: Academic Studies Division, The College of Management.

Aharoni, Y. 2000b. The role of reputation in global professional business services. In Aharoni, Y. & Nahum, L. (Eds.) *Globalization of Services: Some Implications for Theory and Practice*. London: Routledge, pp. 125–141.

Aharoni, Y. 2002. European Air Transportation: Integration, Globalization and Structural Changes. Swedish Network for European Studies in Economics and Business (May). Mölle, Sweden.

Aharoni, Y. 2004. The race for FDI in services — The case of the airline industry. In Oxelheim, L. & Ghauri, P. (Eds.) *European Union and the Race for Foreign Direct Investment in Europe*. Amsterdam: Elsevier, pp. 381–406.

Aharoni, Y. & Ramamurti, R. 2008. The internationalization of multinationals. In Boddewyn, J. J. (Ed.) *The Evolution of IB Scholarship: AIB Fellows on the First 50 Years and Beyond*, Vol. 14. Emerald Research in Global Strategic Management, pp. 177–201.

Aharoni, Y., Tihanyi, L. & Connelly, B. L. 2011. Managerial decision making in international business: A forty-five year retrospective. *Journal of World Business*, 46(2): 135–142.

Akerlof, G. A. & Dickens, W. T. 1982. The economic consequences of cognitive dissonance. *American Economic Review*, 72(3): 307–319.

Amason, A. & Sapienza, H. 1997. The effects of top management team size and interaction norms on cognitive and affective conflict. *Journal of Management*, 23(4): 495–516.

Amason, A. C. 1996. Distinguishing the effects of functional and dysfunctional conflict on strategic decision making: Resolving a paradox for top management teams. *Academy of Management Journal*, 39: 123–148.

Anderson, E. & Gatignon, H. 1986. Models of foreign entry: A transaction cost analysis and propositions. *Journal of International Business Studies*, 17: 1–26.

Ansoff, I. & McDonnel, E. 1990. *Implanting Strategic Management.* Hemel Hempstead: Prentice Hall Europe.

Argote, L. 1999. *Organizational Learning: Creating, Retaining and Transferring Knowledge.* Norwell, MA: Kluwer Academic Publishers.

Argote, L. & Greve, H. R. 2007. A behavioral theory of the firm — 40 years and counting: Introduction and impact. *Organization Science*, 18(3): 337–349.

Arieli, D. 2008. *Predictably Irrational.* New York: HarperCollins Publishers.

Arieli, D., Loewenstein, G. & Prelec, D. 2003. "Coherent arbitrariness": Stable demand curves without stable preferences. *Quarterly Journal of Economics*, 118(1): 73–105.

Arrow, K. J. 1987. Rationality of self and others in an economic system. In Hogarth, R. M. & Reder, M. W. (Eds.) *Rational Choice: The Contrast between Economics and Psychology*. Chicago: University of Chicago Press, pp. 201–216.

Augier, M. & Teece, D. 2007. Dynamic capabilities and multinational enterprise: Penrosean insights and omission. *Management International Review*, 47(2): 175–192.

Barkema, H. G., Shenkar, O., Vermeulen, F. & Bell, J. H. J. 1997. Working abroad, working with others: How firms learn to operate international joint ventures. *Academy of Management Journal*, 40: 426–442.

Barkema, H. G. & Vermeulen, F. 1998. International expansion through start-up or acquisition: A learning perspective. *Academy of Management Journal*, 41: 7–26.

Barnes, J. H. 1984. Cognitive biases and their impact on strategic planning. *Strategic Management Journal*, 5(2): 129–137.

Barney, J. B. 1991. Firm resources and sustained competitive advantage. *Journal of Management*, 17: 99–120.

Barnet, R. J. & Műller, R. E. 1974. *Global Reach: The Power of the Multinational Corporations*. New York: Simon and Schuster.

Bartlett, C. & Ghoshal, S. 1989. *Managing across Borders*. Boston: Harvard Business School Press.

Benito, G. R. G. 1997. Divestment of foreign production operations. *Applied Economics*, 29: 1365–1377.

Biais, B., Hilton, D., Mazurier, K. & Puget, S. 2005. Judgmental overconfidence, selfmonitoring and trading performance in an experimental financial market. *Review of Economic Studies*, 72: 287–312.

Boone, C. & Hendriks, W. 2009. Top management team diversity and firm performance: Moderators of functional-background and locus-of-control diversity. *Management Science*, 55(2): 118–165.

Brouthers, K. & Hennart, J. F. 2007. Boundaries of the firm: Insights from international entry mode research. *Journal of Management*, 33(3): 395–425.

Brouthers, K. D. & Brouthers, L. E. 2001. Explaining the national cultural distance paradox. *Journal of International Business Studies*, 32: 177–189.

Buckley, P. & Casson, M. 1976. *The Future of the Multinational Enterprise*. London: Macmillan.

Buckley, P. & Casson, M. C. 2009. The internalization theory of the multinational enterprise: A review of the progress of a research agenda after 30 years. *Journal of International Business Studies*, 40(9): 1563–1580.

Buckley, P. J., Devinney, T. M. & Louviere, J. J. 2007. Do managers behave the way theory suggests? A choice-theoretic examination of foreign direct investment location decision-making. *Journal of International Business Studies*, 38(7): 1069–1094.

Camerer, C. 2000. Prospect theory in the wild. In Kahneman, D. & Tversky, A. (Eds.) *Choices, Values and Frames*. New York: Russell Sage.

Camerer, C. F., Babcock, L., Loewenstein, G. & Thaler, R. 1997. Labor supply of New York City cabdrivers: One day at a time. *Quarterly Journal of Economics*, 112 (May): 407–441.

Camerer, C. F., George Loewenstein, G. & Prelec, D. 2004. Neuroeconomics: Why economics needs brains. *Scandinavian Journal of Economics*, 106(3): 555–579.

Camerer, C. F., Loewenstein, G. & Rabin, M. (Eds.). 2003. *Advances in Behavioral Economics*. New York: Russel Sage Foundation.

Camerer, C., Loewenstein, G. & Prelec, D. 2005. Neuroeconomics: How neuroscience can inform economics. *Journal of Economic Literature*, 43: 9–64.

Cantwell, J. 1995. The globalization of technology: What remains of the product cycle model? *Cambridge Journal of Economics*, 19: 155–174.

Carpenter, M. A., Geletkanycz, M. A. & Sanders, W. G. 2004. Upper echelons research revisited: Antecedents, elements, and consequences of top management team composition. *Journal of Management*, 30: 749–778.

Casson, M. (Ed.). 2000. *The Economics of International Business*. Cheltenham, UK: Edward Elgar.

Chandler, A. 1962. *Strategy and Structure: Chapters in the History of the Industrial Enterprise*. Cambridge, MA: MIT Press.

Christensen, C. M. 1997. *The Innovator's Dilemma When New Technologies Cause Great Firms to Fail*. Boston: Harvard Business School Press.

Clapham, S. E. & Schwenk, C. R. 1991. Self-serving attributions, managerial cognition, and company performance. *Strategic Management Journal*, 12(3): 219–229.

Coase, R. 1937. The nature of the firm. *Economica*, 4(3): 386–405.

Coff, R. W. 1999. How buyers cope with uncertainty when acquiring firms in knowledge-intensive industries: Caveat emptor. *Organization Science*, 10(2): 144–161.

Cotula, L. 2009. Land grab or development opportunity? International farm land deals in Africa. *Columbia FDI Perspectives*, No. 8, June 22.

Coval, J. D. & Moskowitz, T. J. 1999. Home bias at home: Local equity preference in domestic portfolios. *Journal of Finance*, 54(6): 2045–2074.

Cyert, R. M. & DeGroot, M. H. 1974. Rational expectations and Bayesian analysis. *Journal of Political Economy*, 82: 521–536.

Cyert, R. M. & March, J. G. 1963. *A Behavioral Theory of the Firm*. Cambridge, MA: Blackwell Publishers.

Das, T. K. & Teng, B. S. 1999. Cognitive biases and strategic decision processes: An integrative perspective. *Journal of Management Studies*, 36(6): 757–778.

DellaVigna, S. 2009. Psychology and economics: Evidence from the field. *Journal of Economic Literature*, 47(2): 315–372.

Doz, Y., Santos, J. & Williamson, P. 2001. *From Global to Metanational: How Companies Win in the Knowledge Economy*. Boston: Harvard Business School Press.

Dunning, J. H. 1980. Towards an eclectic theory of international production: Some empirical test. *Journal of International Business Studies*, 11(1): 9–31.

Dunning, J. H. 1994. Globalization, economic restructuring and development. Geneva: UNCTAD.

Dunning, J. H. & Lundan, S. 2008. *Multinational Enterprises and the Global Economy* (2nd edn.). Cheltenham, UK: Edward Elgar.

Eckbo, P. 1976. *The Future of World Oil*. Cambridge, MA: Ballimger.

Einhorn, H. J. & Hogarth, R. M. 1981. Behavioral decision theory: Processes of judgment and choice. *Annual Review of Psychology*, 32: 53–88.

Foster, R. & Kaplan, S. 2001. *Creative Destruction — Why Companies That Are Built to Last Underperform the Market and How to Successfully Transform Them*. New York: Doubleday.

French, K. & Poterba, J. 1991. Investor diversification and international equity markets. *American Economic Review*, 81(2): 222–226.

Friedman, T. L. 2005. *The World Is Flat: A Brief History of the Twenty-First Century*. New York: Farrar, Straus & Giroux.

Fudenberg, D. 2006. Advancing beyond advances in behavioral economics. *Journal of Economic Literature*, XLIV (September): 694–711.

Ghoshal, S. & Moran, P. 1996. Bad for practice: A critique of the transaction cost theory. *Academy of Management Review*, 21(1): 13–47.

Gilovich, T., Griffin, D. & Kahneman, D. 2002. *The Psychology of Judgment: Heuristics and Biases*. New York: Cambridge University Press.

Gilpin, R. 1975. *U.S. Power and the Multinational Corporation*. New York: Basic Books.

Glunk, U., Heijltjes, M. G. & Olie, R. 2001. Design characteristics and functioning of top management teams in Europe. *European Management Journal*, 19(3): 291–300.

Gneezy, U. & Rustichini, A. 2000a. A fine is a price. *Journal of Legal Studies*, 29(1, part 1): 1–17.

Gneezy, U. & Rustichini, A. 2000b. Pay enough or don't pay at all. *Quarterly Journal of Economics*, 115(3): 791–810.

Gupta, A. K. & Govindarajan, V. 2000. Knowledge flows within multinational corporations. *Strategic Management Journal*, 21(4): 473–496.

Hambrick, D. C. & Mason, P. A. 1984. Upper echelons: The organization as a reflection of its top managers. *Academy of Management Review*, 9(2): 193–206.

Hannan, M. T. & Freeman, J. 1977. The population ecology of organizations. *American Journal of Sociology*, 82: 929–964.

Hannan, M. T. & Freeman, J. 1984. Structural inertia and organizational change. *American Sociological Review*, 49(2): 149–164.

Harrison, D. A., Price, K. H. & Bell, M. P. 1998. Beyond relational demography: Time and the effects of surface- and deep-level diversity on work group cohesion. *Academy of Management Journal*, 41: 96–107.

Hayward, M. L. & Hambrick, D. C. 1997. Explaining premium paid for large acquisitions: Evidence of CEO hubris. *Administrative Science Quarterly*, 42(1): 103–127.

Hennart, J. F. 1982. *A Theory of Multinational Enterprise*. Ann Arbor, MI: University of Michigan Press.

Hennart, J. F. 2009. Down with MNE-centric theories! Market entry and expansion as the bundling of MNWE and local assets. *Journal of International Business Studies*, 40: 1432–1454.

Herrmann, P. & Datta, D. K. 2005. Relationships between top management team characteristics and international diversification: An empirical investigation. *British Journal of Management*, 16(1): 69–78.

Huston, L. & Sakkab, N. 2006. Inside Procter & Gamble's new model for innovation. *Harvard Business Review*, 84(3): 58–66.

Hutzschenreuter, T., Pederson, T. & Volberda, H. W. 2007. The role of path dependency and, managerial intentionality: A perspective on international business research. *Journal of International Business Studies*, 38(7): 1055–1068.

Jacoby, N. H. 1974. *Multinational Oil: A Study of Industrial Dynamics*. New York: Macmillan.

Jensen, M. C. & Meckling, W. H. 1976. Theory of the firm: Managerial behavior, agency costs and ownership structure. *Journal of Financial Economics*, 3(3): 305–360.

Johanson, J. & Vahlne, J. E. 1977. The internationalization process of the firm — A model of knowledge development and increasing foreign market commitments. *Journal of International Business Studies*, 8: 23–32.

Johanson, J. & Vahlne, J. E. 1990. The mechanisms of internationalization. *International Marketing Review*, 7: 11–24.

Johanson, J. & Vahlne, J. E. 2009. The Uppsala internationalization process model revisited: From liability of foreignness to liability of outsidership. *Journal of International Business Studies*, 40: 1411–1431.

Jones, G. 2005. *Renewing Unilever: Transformation and Tradition*. Oxford: Oxford University Press.

Jones, G. & Khenna, T. 2006. Bring history (back) into international business. *Journal of International Business Studies*, 37: 453–468.

Kahneman, D. 2003. A perspective on judgment and choice: Mapping bounded rationality. *American Psychologist*, 58: 697–720.

Kahneman, D., Knetsch, J. L. & Thaler, R. H. 1990. Experimental tests of the endowment effect and the Coase theorem. *The Journal of Political Economy*, 96(6): 1325–1348.

Kahneman, D., Knetsch, J. & Thaler, R. 1986. Fairness as a constraint on profit seeking: Entitlements in the market. *American Economic Review*, 76(4): 728–741.

Kahneman, D. & Tversky, A. 1979. Prospect theory: An analysis of decision under risk. *Econometrica*, 47 (March): 263–291.

Kahneman, D. & Tversky, A. 1982. On the study of statistical intuitions. In Kahneman, D., Slovic, P. & Tversky, A. (Eds.) *Judgment under Uncertainty: Heuristics and Biases*. Cambridge: Cambridge University Press.

Katzenstein, P. J. 1984. *Corporatism and Change: Austria, Switzerland and the Politics of Industry*. New York: Cornell University Press.

Kaufman, G. G., Krueger, T. H. & Hunter, W. C. 1999. *The Asian Financial Crisis: Origins, Implications and Solutions*. Springer.

Kekic, L. 2009. The global economic crisis and FDI flows to emerging markets. Columbia FDI Perspectives, No. 15, October 8. Available at www.vcc.Columbia.edu.

Kilduff, M., Angelmar, R. & Mehra, A. 2000. Top management-team diversity and firm performance: Examining the role of cognitions. *Organization Science*, 11: 21–34.

Kindlebeger, C. 1969. *American Business Abroad*. New Haven, CT: Yale University Press.

Knetsch, J. L. 1989. The endowment effect and evidence of nonreversible indifference curves. *The American Economic Review*, 79: 1277–1284.

Knetsch, J. L. & Sinden, J. A. 1984. Willingness to pay and compensation demanded: Experimental evidence of an unexpected disparity in measures of value, the endowment effect and evidence of nonreversible indifference curves. *The Quarterly Journal of Economics*, 99: 507–521.

Knight, G. A. & Cavusgil, S. T. 1996. The born global firm: A challenge to traditional internationalization theory. In Lindmark, L., Christensen, P. R., Eskelinen, H., Forsstrom, B., Sorenson, O. J. & Vatn, E. (Eds.) *Advances in International Marketing*, Vol. 8. Bingley, UK: JAI, pp. 11–26.

Knight, G. & Cavusgil, S. T. 2004. Innovation, organizational capabilities, and the born-global firm. *Journal of International Business Studies*, 35(2): 124–141.

Kogut, B. 2003. *The Global Internet Economy*. Cambridge, MA: MIT Press.

Kogut, B., Walker, G. & Anand, J. 2002. Agency and institutions: National divergences in diversification behavior. *Organization Science*, 13: 162–178.

Kogut, B. & Zander, U. 1993. Knowledge of the firm and the evolutionary theory of the multinational corporation. *Journal of International Business Studies*, 24: 625–645.

Kőszegi, B. 2006. Ego utility, overconfidence, and task choice. *Journal of the European Economic Association*, 4(4): 673–707.

Kunreuther, H., Ginsberg, R., Miller, L., Sagi, P., Slovic, P., Borkin, B. & Katz, N. 1978. *Disaster Insurance protection: Public Policy Lessons*. New York: Wiley.

Laibson, D. 1997. Golden eggs and hyperbolic discounting. *Quarterly Journal of Economics*, 112: 443–478.

Langlois, R. N. & Csontos, L. 1993. Optimization, rule following, and the methodology of situational analysis. In Mäki, U., Gustafsson, B. & Knudsen, C. (Eds.) *Rationality, Institutions, and Economic Methodology*. London: Routledge.

Lawrence, B. S. 1997. The black box of organizational demography. *Organization Science*, 8: 1–22.

Levitt, K. 1970. *Silent Surrender: The Multinational Corporation in Canada*. New York: St. Martin's Press.

Levitt, B. & March, J. G. 1988. Organizational learning. *Annual Review of Sociology*, 14: 319–340.

Li, J. & Guisinger, S. 1992. The globalization of service multinationals in the triad regions: Japan, Western Europe and North America. *Journal of International Business Studies*, 23: 675–696.

March, J. G. 2006. Ideas as art (interview by Diane Coutu). *Harvard Business Review*, 84 (10): 82–89.

March, J. G. & Shapira, Z. 1987. Managerial perspectives on risk and risk taking. *Management Science*, 33: 1404–1418.

March, J. G. & Simon, H. A. 1958. *Organizations*. New York: Wiley.

Markóczy, L. 1997. Measuring beliefs: Accept no substitutes. *Academy of Management Journal*, 40: 1228–1242.

Martin, J. A. & Eisenhardt, K. M. 2004. Coping with decline in dynamic markets. Corporate entrepreneurship and the recombinative organizational form. *Advances in Strategic Management*. Bingley, UK: JAI, pp. 357–382.

McCallum, J. T. 1995. National borders matter: Canada-U.S. regional trade patterns. *American Economic Review*, 85: 615–623.

Miller, K. D. & Chen, W. R. 2004. Variable organizational risk preferences: Tests of the March-Shapira model. *Academy of Management Journal*, 47: 105–115.

Moran, T. H. 1987. Managing an oligopoly of would-be sovereign: The dynamics of joint control and self-control in the international oil industry: Past, present and future. *Industrial Organization*, 41(4): 575–608.

Morck, R., Wolfenzon, D. & Yeung, B. 2005. Corporate governance, economic entrenchment and growth. *Journal of Economic Literature*, XLIII (September): 655–720.

Morisset, J. & Andrews-Johnson, K. 2003. The Effectiveness of Promotion Agencies at Attracting Foreign Direct Investment. FIAS Occasional Paper no. 16. Foreign Investment Advisory Service, Washington, DC.

Mytelka, L. K. & Delapierre, M. 1999. Strategic partnerships, knowledge-based networked oligopolies and the state. In Cutler, C., Haufler, V. & Porter, T. (Eds.) *Private Authority and International Affairs*. Binghamton, NY: Suny University Press, pp. 129–148.

Nelson, R. & Winter, S. 1982. *An Evolutionary Theory of Economic Change*. Cambridge, MA: Harvard University Press.

Nelson, R. R. & Winter, S. 1973. Toward an evolutionary theory of economic capabilities. *American Economic Review*, 63: 440–449.

Newell, A. & Simon, H. A. 1972. *Human Problem Solving*. Englewood Cliffs, NJ: Prentice Hall.

North, D. C. 2005. Introduction to understanding the process of economic change. In *Understanding the Process of Economic Change*. Princeton, NJ: Princeton University Press.

Organization Science. 2007. Special issue on Cyert and March's a behavioral theory of the firm. *Organization Science*, 18(3): 337–542.

Oxelheim, L. & Ghauri, P. (Eds.). 2004. *European Union and the Race for Foreign Direct Investment in Europe*. Oxford: Elsevier.

Park, S. H. & Ungson, G. R. 1997. The effect of national culture, organizational complementarity, and economic motivation on joint venture dissolution. *Academy of Management Journal*, 40: 279–307.

Parkhe, A. 1991. Interfirm diversity, organizational learning, and longevity in global strategic alliances. *Journal of International Business Studies*, 22: 579–601.

Penrose, E. T. 1968. *The Large International Firm in Developing Country: The International Petroleum Industry*. Westport, CT: Greenwood Press.

Pitelis, C. 2007. Edith Penrose and a learning-based perspective on the MNE and OLI. *Management International Review*, 47(2): 207–220.

Porter, M. E. 1979. The structure within industries and companies' performance. *Review of Economics and Statistics*, 61 (May): 215–227.

Porter, M. E. 1980. *Competitive Strategy: Techniques for Analyzing Industries and Competition*. New York: Free Press.

Porter, M. E. 1985. *Competitive Advantage*. New York: Free Press.

Prahalad, C. K. & Bettis, R. 1986. The dominant logic: A new linkage between diversity and performance. *Strategic Management Journal*, 7(6): 485–502.

Priem, R. L., Lyon, D. W. & Dess, G. D. 1999. Inherent limitations of demographic proxies in top management team heterogeneity research. *Journal of Management*, 25: 935–953.

Rabin, M. 1993. Incorporating fairness into game theory and economics. *American Economic Review*, 83 (December): 1281–1302.

Rabin, M. 1998. Psychology and economics. *Journal of Economic Literature*, 36 (March): 11–46.

Rabin, M. 2002. A perspective on psychology and economics. *European Economic Review*, 46: 657–685.

Rangan, S. & Sengal, M. 2009. Information technology and transnational integration: Theory and evidence on the evolution of the modern multinational enterprise. *Journal of International Business Studies*, 40(9): 1496–1514.

Rau, D. 2008. Top management team social processes and changes in organizational strategy. *Journal of Business and Management*, 14: 1.

Ronen, S. & Shenkar, O. 1985. Clustering countries on attitudinal dimensions: A review and synthesis. *Academy of Management Review*, 10: 435–454.

Rubinstein, A. 2008. Comments on neuroeconomics. *Economics and Philosophy*, 24: 485–494.

Rugman, A. 2005. *The Regional Multinationals*. Cambridge, UK: Cambridge University Press.

Saari, D. J. 1999. *Global Corporations and Sovereign Nations: Collision or Cooperation?* Westport, CT: Quorum Books.

Samuelson, W. & Zeckhauser, R. J. 1988. Status quo bias in decision making. *Journal of Risk and Uncertainty*, 1 (March): 7–59.

Schneider, S. & DeMeyer, A. 1991. Interpreting and responding to strategic issues: The impact of national culture. *Strategic Management Journal*, 12: 307–320.

Schwenk, C. R. 1984. Cognitive simplification processes in strategic decision-making. *Strategic Management Journal*, 5(2): 111–128.

Schwenk, C. R. 1986. Information, cognitive biases, and commitment to a course of action. *Academy of Management Review*, 11: 298–310.

Schwenk, C. R. 1995. Strategic decision making. *Journal of Management*, 21: 471–493.

Shefrin, H. M. & Thaler, R. H. 1988. The behavioral life-cycle hypothesis. *Economic Inquiry*, 26 (October): 609–643.

Shenkar, O. 2001. Cultural distance revisited: Towards a more rigorous conceptualization and measurement of cultural differences. *Journal of International Business Studies*, 32: 519–535.

Shoham, A. & Fiegenbaum, A. 2002. Competitive determinants of organizational risk-taking attitude: The role of strategic reference points. *Management Decision*, 40: 127–141.

Simon, H. A. 1947. *Administrative Behavior*. New York: Macmillan.

Simon, H. A. 1955. A behavioral model of rational choice. *Quarterly Journal of Economics*, 69(1): 99–118.

Simon, H. A. 1985. Human nature in politics: The dialogue of psychology with political science. *The American Political Science Review*, 79(2): 293–304.

Slovic, P., Fischhoff, B. & Lichtenstein, S. 1977. Behavioral decision theory. *Annual Review of Psychology*, 28: 1–39.

Staw, B. M. & Ross, J. 1987. Behaviors in escalation situations: Antecedents, prototypes, and solutions. In Cummings, L. G. & Staw, B. (Eds.) *Research in Organizational Behavior*. Greenwich: JAI Press, pp. 39–78.

Stopford, J. & Strange, S. (with Henley, J. S.). 1991. *Rival States, Rival Firms: Competition for World Market Shares*. Cambridge: Cambridge University Press.

Stulz, R. 1988. Managerial control of voting rights: Financing policies and the market for corporate control. *Journal of Financial Economics*, 20: 25–54.

Sunstein, C. & Thaler, R. H. 2008. *Nudge: Improving Decisions about Health, Wealth, and Happiness*. New Haven, CT: Yale University Press.

Taleb, N. N. 2007. *The Black Swan: The Impact of the Highly Improbable*. New York: Random House.

Teece, D. 1986. Profiting from technological innovation: Implications for integration, collaboration and public policy. *Research Policy*, 15(6): 285–305.

Teece, D. & Pisano, G. 1994. The dynamic capabilities of firms: An introduction. *Industrial and Corporate Change*, 3(3): 537–556.

Teece, D. J., Pisano, G. & Shuen, A. 1997. Dynamic capabilities and strategic management. *Strategic Management Journal*, 18(7): 509–553.

Tesar, L. & Werner, I. 1995. Home bias and high turnover. *Journal of International Money and Finance*, 14(4): 467–492.

Thaler, R. 1999. Mental accounting matters. *Journal of Behavioral Decision Making*, 12: 183–206.

Thaler, R. & Benartzi, S. 2004. Save more tomorrow: Using behavioral economics to increase employee savings. *Journal of Political Economy*, 112(1): 164–187.

Thaler, R. H. & Shefrin, H. M. 1981. An economic theory of self-control. *Journal of Political Economy*, 89(2): 392–406.

Tihanyi, L., Ellstrand, A. E., Daily, C. M. & Dalton, D. R. 2001. Composition of the top management team and firm international diversification. *Journal of Management*, 26(6): 1157–1177.

Tihanyi, L., Griffith, D. A. & Russell, C. J. 2005. The effect of cultural distance on entry mode choice, international diversification, and MNE performance: A meta-analysis. *Journal of International Business Studies*, 36: 270–283.

Trispas, M. & Gavetti, G. 2000. Capabilities, cognition, and inertia: Evidence from digital imaging. *Strategic Management Journal*, 21: 1147–1161.

Tversky, A. & Kahneman, D. 1974. Judgment under uncertainty: Heuristics and biases. *Science*, 185(4157): 1124–1131.

Tversky, A. & Kahneman, D. 1981. The framing of decisions and the psychology of choice. *Science*, 211: 453–458.

Tversky, A. & Kahneman, D. 1991. Loss aversion in riskless choice: A reference-dependent model. *Quarterly Journal of Economics*, 106: 1039–1061.

Vernon, R. 1966. International investment and international trade in the product cycle. *Quarterly Journal of Economics*, 80: 190–207.

Vernon, R. 1971. *Sovereignty at Bay*. Cambridge, MA: Harvard University Press.

Vernon, R. 1979. The product cycle hypothesis in a new international environment. *Oxford Bulletin of Economics and Statistics*, 41: 255–267.

Von Braun, J. & Meinzen-Dick, R. 2009. Land Grabbing by Foreign Investors in Developing Countries: Risks and Opportunities. Washington, DC: International Food Policy Research Institute. Available at www.ifpri.org/bp/bp013.asp.

United Nations Department of Economic and Social Affairs. 1973. *Multinational Corporations in World Development*. New York: United Nations.

UNCTAD. (1995, 1996, 2004, 2009). *World Investment Report*. Geneva: U.N.

Wells, L. & Mint, A. 1990. *Marketing a Country*. FIAS Occasional Paper no. 1. Foreign Investment Advisory Service, Washington, DC.

Wells, L. & Mint, A. 2000. *Marketing a Country: Promotion as a Tool for Attracting Foreign Investment* (Revised edn.). FIAS Occasional Papers no. 13. Foreign Investment Advisory Service, Washington, DC.

Werner, S. 2002. Recent developments in international management research: A review of 20 top management journals. *Journal of Management*, 28: 277–305.

Williamson, O. E. 1975. *Markets and Hierarchies: Analysis and Antitrust Implications*. New York: The Free Press.

Williamson, O. E. 1985. *The Economic Institutions of Capitalism*. New York: The Free Press.

Wolf, H. C. 2000. Intranational home bias in trade. *Review of Economics and Statistics*, 82(4): 555–563.

Wolf, M. 2004. *Why Globalization Works*. New Haven, CT: Yale University Press.

Yoffie, D. B. & Milner, H. V. 1989. An alternative to free trade or protectionism: Why corporations seek strategic trade policy. *California Management Review*, 3(4): 113–131.

Zhang, P. 2007. Top management team heterogeneity and firm performance: An empirical research on Chinese listed companies. *Frontiers in Business Research in China*, 1(1): 123–134.

Zollo, M. & Winter, S. G. 2002. Deliberate learning and the evolution of dynamic capabilities. *Organization Science*, 13: 339–351.

https://doi.org/10.1142/9789811287510_0011

Chapter 11

The Evolution of Multinationals*,†

Yair Aharoni‡ and Ravi Ramamurti§

‡*Tel Aviv University, Tel Aviv, Israel*

§*Northeastern University, Boston, MA, USA*

Abstract

As an institution, the multinational enterprise has evolved in complexity. From having roots in just a few Western nations, it now has roots in dozens of nations, including many developing countries. Its scope has likewise expanded from natural resource-based industries and manufacturing to a variety of services. And firms are becoming multinational earlier in their lives and at smaller sizes than in the past. This chapter analyzes the evolution of multinationals over the last century, the forces driving that evolution, and distinctive characteristics of the latest wave of multinationals coming out of developing countries. It also explores the risk of a backlash against globalization and multinationals in Western societies, even as these trends gain in popularity in developing countries.

---

*This chapter is reproduced from *The Future of Foreign Direct Investment and the Multinational Enterprise,* Vol. 15, pp. 113–135 (2011), Emerald Group Publishing.

†This is an updated and revised version of Aharoni, Y., & Ramamurti, R. (2008). The Internationalization of Multinationals. In: J. Boddewyn (Ed.), *International Business Scholarship: AIB Fellows on the First 50 Years and Beyond* (pp. 177–201). Bingley, UK: Emerald.

It concludes with questions that international business scholars might want to pursue in their future research.

Keywords: MNE evolution; origin of MNEs; emerging-market MNEs; backlash against MNEs; future research questions.

Introduction

The importance, diversity, and scope of MNEs in the global economy have grown exponentially in the post-World War II period, despite short-term ups and downs. From merely a few billion dollars per year in the 1950s, global FDI outflows grew to $51.5 billion in 1980, $239.1 billion in 1990, and $1.231.6 billion in 2000, before falling off sharply as a result of the dotcom bust (Economist Intelligence Unit, 2007). The outflows recovered after 2004, reaching an all-time high in 2007 of $2,146.5 billion, before the global financial crisis caused flows to collapse again in 2008 and 2009. A slow recovery in 2010 was expected to be followed by more robust growth in 2011.

The sales of foreign affiliates of multinational of all nationalities stood at about one-half of world exports in 1960, but by 1982 the two were about equal (US$2.7 trillion and $2.4 trillion, respectively), and by 2007 the former was almost double the latter ($31 trillion vs. $17 trillion, respectively; see UNCTAD, 2008: p. 10). In 1982, the ratio of outward FDI to worldwide gross fixed capital formation was just 1%, but by 1999 it had risen to about 14% (UNCTAD, 2000: p. 4) and by 2007 to 16.2% (UNCTAD, 2008: p. 10). In 2008, there were 82,000 MNEs with 810,000 foreign affiliates, which was 11.3 times the number in 1969 (UNCTAD, 2009). Outward FDI from developed countries consisted of 81% of the world total in 2008, compared to 90% between 1995 and 2000 — the rest of outward FDI originated from developing countries and from transition economies, which, together, are referred to now as emerging markets. The global financial crisis changed the investment landscape, at least temporarily, raising the share of emerging economies in global FDI flows to 43% in 2008 and almost one-half in 2009 (UNCTAD, 2009).

Thus, the growth in FDI has come about not only because existing MNEs have spread their tentacles globally but because wholly new MNEs have emerged in different countries at different times. Indeed, the first survey of MNEs carried out by the United Nations in 1973 identified 16 countries as having outward FDI in 1969 (United Nations, 1973). By 2007, the number of MNE home countries had grown to 135, including 89 developing countries and 9 members of the Commonwealth of Independent States and South-East Europe (UNCTAD, 2008: p. 211).

All in all, a large percent of international economic transactions are accounted for by MNEs, which weave a network of economic linkages across many economies. Since Hymer's pioneering doctoral thesis in 1960, researchers have attempted to understand how is it possible for foreign firms to compete against domestic competitors when they face the extra costs of learning how to operate in a foreign market. The answer proposed was that these firms enjoy some monopolistic advantages, for example, from superior technology, brand recognition, or management skills. Another question was why the MNE makes products abroad rather than export from home or resort to options such as licensing. Instead, different plants in different countries are brought under common control. The answer was the prevalence of transaction costs and their reduction by internalizing transactions within the firm (Buckley & Casson, 1985; Dunning, 1979). This explanation begs another question: why was the United States dominant in creating MNEs when its vast market could sustain multiplant operations. Internalization arguments alone would lead one to expect that MNEs will be based in small countries where multiplant internalization could be achieved only by moving to other countries. At any rate, one interesting unresolved question is why certain countries became home to many MNEs and others did not. The main point of this chapter is that MNEs today are a very diverse species, originating from a very large number of home countries, spawned in many industries, starting at earlier stages of the firm's evolution than before, and including firms of all sizes. This broadening of the origins of MNEs in the last few decades is the result of major shifts in the global economic and political environment, such as the emergence of new technologies, new attitude toward MNEs, and new government policies.

We begin by identifying four major stages in the evolution of MNEs.

Four Stages of MNE Evolution

In the first phase, MNEs followed the flag of a colonial power. One of the oldest MNEs was the Dutch East India Company, which was granted a monopoly in 1602 for 21 years to carry out colonial activities in Asia. It operated for almost two centuries and was formally dissolved in 1800. The British East India Company — a private enterprise backed by the British crown — operated in the East Indies from 1608 until its dissolution in 1858. French, Portuguese, and Spanish firms also invested in their respective nations' colonies. At this time, the major motivation for internationalization was to extract, transport, and process natural resources, which usually flowed from the colonies to the colonial center, with manufactured goods flowing in the reverse direction. The major force enabling the creation of these firms was the political power of the home government. A few US firms were also starting to globalize: Around 1900, Rockefeller's Standard Oil ventured abroad in search of oil reserves (Wilkins, 1974), followed by still other US oil companies (Yergin, 1991). Between 1870 and 1913 — the golden age of rapid growth — a few US manufacturing firms pioneered foreign operations in search of markets, led by Singer Sewing Machine, and followed later by others, such as Ford Motor Company. Yet, MNEs from Europe dominated the world stage, accounting for 93% of worldwide FDI stock, having built international networks on the backs of their home governments' colonialism (see Table 1). The United States' share at this time was estimated at only 6% (Buckley & Casson, 1985: p. 200).

Technological advantage, built on the industrial revolution, which began in Europe, not only gave European firms ownership advantages

Table 1. Share of worldwide stock of outward FDI (OFDI) (various years).

Region/Country	1914	1969	1980	1990	2006
Europe[a]	93%	43.2%	41.1%	49.5%[a]	57.0%[a]
UK	50%	16.2%	14.1%	12.8%	11.9%
France	43%	n.a.	4.2%	6.1%	8.7%
Germany		n.a.	7.5%	8.5%	8.1%
Netherlands		n.a.	7.4%	6.0%	5.2%
United States	6%	55%	37.7%	24.3%	19.1%
Japan	0%	1.3%	3.4%	11.2%	3.6%
Emerging Markets	0%	0%	12.7%	8.3%	12.8
Worldwide OFDI stock (US$ bill.)	n.a.	n.a.	571	1,791	12,474
No. of countries required to account for 93% of global OFDI stock[b]	4[b]	9[b]			24[b]

Notes: [a]Europe's share fell secularly from 1914 to 1980 but then began to reverse course, possibly because of growth in intra-EU FDI, following the Single European Act (1986) and the creation of the euro. [b]The countries involved were as follows: in 1914, UK, France, Germany, and Netherlands; in 1969, the previous four plus USA, Canada, Switzerland, Sweden, and Italy; and in 2005, the previous nine countries plus Australia, and nine EU nations (Belgium, Spain, Norway, Italy, Denmark, Ireland, Finland, Austria, and Luxembourg) and five emerging economies (Hong Kong, Russia, Singapore, Taiwan, and Brazil).

Source: Data for 1914 from Buckley and Casson (1985: p. 200); for 1969, from UN (1973: p. 139); for remaining years from http://www.unctad.org/Templates/Page.asp?intItemID=3277&lang=1. Table on "Outward FDI stock by Host Region and Economy (1980–2005), World Investment Report 2006, 16/10/06".

over foreign rivals but also enabled their home governments to establish military superiority and build global empires. One outlier was Switzerland (Agmon & Kindleberger, 1977).

The two World Wars and the collapse of empires devastated the European MNEs, as foreign subsidiaries were seized by rival powers or nationalized by newly independent countries. In the postwar period, European leaders were determined to foster policies that would prevent a third World War. They initiated a series of market integrating programs that stimulated intra-European FDI as well as FDI from countries outside the bloc, principally the United States, to take advantage of the new opportunities. American firms, which already operated multidivisional and multiregional organizations in the United States, transferred those capabilities relatively easily to the fledgling common market in western Europe.

For approximately two decades, between 1949 and 1971, the economies of the developed nations grew rapidly: reconstruction raised European GDP growth to 5% per year, while Japan galloped along at 10% per year. The US economy grew at 3.8% per year. In the same period, growth in international trade outstripped growth in world output. FDI grew at twice the rate of GNP. European multinationals, mainly those from the United Kingdom, rebuilt their global presence, but the vast majority of new FDI came out of the United States, based on the technological and managerial superiority of its giant firms. The stock of outward FDI by US MNEs rose sharply from $7.2 billion in 1946 to $74.4 billion in 1970.

One of the first systematic efforts at data gathering by the United Nations found that of the 7,276 parent MNEs in the world in 1969, as many as 33.9% were from the United States, 23.3% were from the United Kingdom, and most of the rest were from other western European countries (UN, 1973: p. 138). The same report also showed the book value of global FDI stock at US$ 108.2 billion, of which 55.0% was from the United States, 16.2% from the United Kingdom, and only 1.3% was from Japan (UN, 1973: p. 139). The report also noted "a further central characteristic of multinational corporations is that they are in general the product of developed countries. Eight of the 10 largest multinational corporations are based in the United States" (UN, 1973: p. 7). Note, however, that 3,357 out of the 7,276 firms — nearly half the total — had affiliates in only one foreign country. (Vernon, 1971 required a firm to have subsidiaries in at least six countries to be considered an MNE.) Research on MNEs was mainly on US multinationals, with some attention paid to UK multinationals.

Meanwhile, Japan was successfully rebuilding its shattered economy. When the US occupation of Japan ended in 1952, the government launched an ambitious program to create comparative advantage. For two decades, Japan was the best modern example of a "miracle economy", and her prowess in manufacturing skill- and capital-intensive products was established in these years. Between 1950 and 1990, Japan's real income per capita in constant 1990 prices grew by 7.7% per annum to reach US$ 23,970 (Economist, 1993). Japan's exports grew at 15% per year, even faster than her GDP, as firms took advantage of access to markets in the United States and Europe that were opening up as a result of successive rounds of GATT negotiations. The favorable trade balance enabled Japan to increase overseas investments. But it wasn't until the 1985 Plaza Accord that dictated a very strong yen that Japanese firms began to shift production from Japan to assembly plants in export markets (rich countries) and component factories in low-cost Asian neighbors (developing countries).

FDI outflows from Japan rose from a mere US$5 billion in 1980 to a peak of US$ 89 billion in 1989. In this decade, FDI grew at rates of 20–30% per annum, more than four times as fast as world GNP, but the United States was no longer the dominant source; quite the contrary, it became the largest recipient of FDI inflows, including several large investments from Japan. By the late 1980s, the third generation of MNEs had emerged and the multinational firm was very much a Triad phenomenon (see Table 1).

The fourth generation of multinational firms took off in the 1990s, as economic liberalization measures in many countries forced firms even in developing countries to experience global competition for the first time in the postwar period (Amsden, 2001). At the same time, new IT technologies facilitated the creation of "born globals". Both these trends convinced many entrepreneurs that to be successful they had to invest abroad and become internationally competitive.

In China, economic liberalization began as early as 1978, albeit on an experimental basis. Initially, China received FDI mainly from overseas Chinese based in places like Hong Kong, Singapore, and Taiwan. By the 1990s, inward FDI flooded in from other countries, and following China's accession to the WTO on December 11, 2001, FDI skyrocketed to US$ 72.4 billion in 2005. In the 1990s, Chinese firms, including several that were partly or wholly state-owned, began to invest overseas, in search of raw materials or markets, and in the 2000s those investments included acquisitions in Europe and the United States.

When the Berlin Wall crumbled in November 1989, the former Soviet Empire disaggregated and its different components moved toward liberal economic policies. At about the same time, several Latin American economies began to cut government spending and subsidies, privatize state-owned firms, and deregulate industry. They pushed their economies into export-oriented free market strategies. So did other long-time bastions of protectionism, such as Ireland, Israel, or India, all of which opened their market in the 1990s to more competition, foreign trade, and inward FDI.

In India, for instance, this forced many old-time firms to upgrade their products and services, trim costs, benchmark themselves against best-in-class global competitors, and buttress their positions in the home market against foreign competitors that were entering India. Several of these firms then also ventured abroad, in search of markets and resources (Ramamurti & Singh, 2009). At the same time, a new breed of postliberalization firms competed globally from the beginning (Pradhan & Sahoo, 2005). Many of the India's leading firms were not in labor-intensive manufactures, as in East Asia, but in skill-intensive products and services, such as IT services, pharmaceuticals, and engineered products and services (Kapur & Ramamurti, 2001; Boston Consulting Group, 2009).

From being a Triad-dominated phenomenon, the fourth generation of MNEs saw the multinational firm become a much broader phenomenon — in terms of the geographical distribution of home countries, the explosion of FDI in service industries, and the size of individual MNEs. Although developing countries remained net importers of FDI, several of them become important outward investors. At its peak, total FDI outflows from firms in emerging markets reached $304.3 billion in 2007 — thirty times that in 1990. This represented about 15% of world outward flows in 2007; in 1990 that share was only 5%. In terms of outward FDI stock, with $1.3 trillion in 2005, emerging markets accounted for 12% of the world total (see Table 1). Three-quarters of the top 100 MNEs from developing countries hailed from Asia.

Another striking trend was the growing number of small- and medium-sized enterprises that were multinationals. In the 1970s, multinationals were regarded as giants, with sales that dwarfed the GNPs of many countries. Although this is still true of the largest MNEs, the vast majority of firms counted by UNCTAD as MNEs in the 2000s were small in size.

Changing Drivers of Multinationalization

Dunning's (1979) OLI framework highlights the need for a firm to have ownership advantages that offset the search and transaction costs and the "liability of foreignness" (Hymer, 1976; Zaheer, 1995), which refers to the costs borne by firms operating outside their home country. The timing of when firms in a country multinationalize may therefore be explained partly by when those firms acquire sufficient international competitive advantages to offset the cost of multinationalization. That, in turn, may depend on when a country's firms are exposed to international competition and opportunities. UNCTAD (1998) identified three sets of determinants of FDIs: the economic situation, the regulatory framework for FDI, and investment promotion. These theories and others do not consider explicitly neither they anticipated the role of general technological change, which has reduced the cost of overcoming distance and time-zone separation and expanded the range of goods and services that could be traded internationally. The railroad, the refrigerator, the steamship, the telegraph, and the laying out of the first transatlantic cable in 1866 expanded the scope for trade and investment at the end of the 19th century. In the 20th century came the radio, transcontinental telephones, giant tankers and airliners, and later satellites, computers, and the Internet. Technological change reduced significantly the cost of international transport and communication, and that of computing, as well as the liability of foreignness, all of which promote the multinationalization of firms. New technologies also allowed firms to outsource more activities to the lowest-cost location.

Aside from economic liberalization and technological change, another factor that has helped certain firms become multinationals is improved access to capital. High savings in Asia, coupled with high raw material prices (which boosted the current account surpluses of resource-rich countries) and low interest rates, combined to fuel the internationalization of local firms. The globalization of capital markets improved access to capital for firms in many parts of the world.

Another important factor was the availability of a large number of overseas nationals who could be approached for help to gain access to foreign markets. There were about 50 million Chinese living outside China, mostly in other parts of Asia. When China opened up, it was these overseas Chinese that helped China ramp up its exports of manufactured goods, by transferring their technical expertise, capital, and marketing know-how to small assembly operations in China's special economic zones. Likewise, overseas Indians, many of whom were knowledge workers based in the United States, helped India ramp up its exports of knowledge- and skill-intensive services (Kapur & Ramamurti, 2001). Today, skilled professionals from both countries circulate between Silicon Valley and their home countries, helping to close the knowledge gap between developed and developing countries (Saxenian, 2002).

Technological change and economic liberalization also promoted the growth of "micro-multinationals" (Copeland, 2006). For instance, the popular website, Craigslist.com, was a US company with estimated sales of $100 million that reached customers online in a few dozen countries but employed only 20 people. In fact, technological development and better knowledge of management methods allowed the rise of "born global" small- and medium-sized firms, whose competitive advantage was based on the ability to divide the value-chain activities and disperse it across different countries (Knight & Cavusgil, 1996). In this sense, we now live in a "Lego world" of value-chain building blocks. Even a relatively small firm headquartered in country A, can manufacture components in countries B and C, assemble them in D and E, perform R&D in F and G — and sell the finished products in still other countries. In the post-dot.com bubble era, venture capitalists expect start-ups to tap into the best locations worldwide for every task from the very beginning. This business model has become feasible because of the rise of specialized intermediary firms to which many steps of the value chain can be outsourced and offshored. A sharp decline in IT and communication costs have put the IT systems necessary to coordinate complex supply chains within the reach of even small firms.

Further, domestic firms in many small countries, Switzerland, but also, for example, Finland, Norway, Denmark and Israel, have become multinationals in growing numbers in the last two decades (Aharoni, 2006). Most MNEs from these countries were small compared to giants like General Electric (GE), and depended much more on international business (IB) for survival. Nokia, to cite one example, derived 97% of its sales from outside Finland. These firms developed competitive strengths unrelated to the location advantage of their home countries. They achieved scale economies by using the world as their oyster. Most important, they gained world competitiveness by acquiring a "portfolio of locational assets" (UNCTAD, 1995), thereby reaping the benefits of an international division of labor, with each part of the value chain produced in the most efficient location. They also raised capital in foreign markets, while retaining corporate headquarters and the top management in the home country. In the future, MNEs from many more economies are likely to join their ranks, as firms realize that focusing operations exclusively in the home country may deprive them of major efficiency gains and hurt competitiveness (Dunning, 1996). The MNE will become an even more important institution in the global economy.

The United States and the European Union still account for major shares of the world's GDP and therefore also global FDI flows. It is well known that the world's largest three or four hundred MNEs account for about 90% of the world stock of FDI. Since the larger MNEs dominate international business, IB scholars sometimes dismiss the value of studying small MNEs. In our view, IB theory should explain not only the obvious dominance of giant firms and countries but also the flourishing of MNEs from many countries, the growth of born-global MNEs, and the emergence of MNEs from emerging markets.

The MNE is best explained as an interconnected network of business and other relationships with crucial ties to a complex international business environment (IBE). Organizations are not unitary hierarchies but looser linked coalitions of shifting interest groups. The MNE today does not internalize production with all other transactions based in the market. Rather it governs a global network of loosely coupled units with different capabilities (for more on this idea, see Buckley's chapter in this volume). It enjoys command of a specific — as opposed to universal — knowledge and minimizes the risk of its proprietary knowledge being dissipated. It specializes in specific knowledge creation and is a vehicle for knowledge sharing across distance and differentiated contexts. To achieve its business goals, it may compete with rivals, but it also cooperates with its suppliers. By its very nature it can influence nations, competing for inward FDI in a world of mobile productive activities, capital, technology and labor, emphasizing its needs of political and economic stability. IBE is an aggregate of several elements that differ along geographical, social, political, and economic dimensions. Changes in IBE transform the way MNEs operate. In the world of the 21st century, any country can become the home base of MNEs.

The Newest Breed: MNEs from Developing Countries

Although MNEs from developing countries have appeared on a significant scale only since the 1990s, there was in fact a spurt in the number of such firms in the 1960s and 1970s. That spurt involved annual FDI outflows from developing countries in the hundreds of millions of dollars, not billions of dollars, although by 1980 it had risen to $3 billion. The next spurt did not occur until the 1990s, and accelerated thereafter, peaking in 2000 at $147 billion, followed by a slump until 2002, and a recovery since 2003. By 2007, as stated earlier, outward FDI from developing and transition economies had risen to $304.3 billion (UNCTAD, 2008: p. 2).

The latest wave of MNEs from developing countries raises several interesting questions. In what ways was the second spurt of outward FDI from developing and transition economies similar to or different from the first spurt? In what ways is their outward FDI similar to or different from that which took place from developed countries (e.g., Mathews, 2002)? Specifically, how do the competitive advantages and strategies of MNEs from developing countries compare with those from developed countries? And how consistent is this phenomenon with predictions of the investment development path (IDP) model (Dunning, 1981)? We offer some facts and a few educated guesses on these questions.

One obvious difference between the first and the second spurts in outward FDI from developing countries is that the second one has involved substantially larger flows, even if one excludes countries that serve as way stations for FDI flows from other countries ("overseas financial centers", such as Bermuda, the British Virgin Islands, the Cayman Islands, and to some extent, Hong Kong). Netting out overseas financial centers, FDI outflows from developing countries reached $292.7 billion in 2008, compared to $3 billion in 1980 and $13 billion in 1990. With a faster increase from China and India (UNCTAD, 2009), outward FDI from emerging markets has grown faster than inward FDI into those countries.

South-South FDI is entirely consistent with the expectation that capital would flow from richer to poorer countries — inasmuch as most of these flows occur from a handful of the more prosperous and advanced developing countries (Hong Kong, Taiwan, Singapore, Malaysia, Brazil, Mexico, and so on) to dozens of less prosperous developing countries. This kind of flow is qualitatively similar to that observed by Wells (1983), and is based on emerging market firms having products, and using processes, that are better suited to developing countries than those possessed by Western MNEs. It is also consistent with the expectation that firms will first invest in their own regions before venturing farther away (Johanson & Vahlne, 1977). Perhaps as Rugman (2005) has argued, many firm-specific advantages are more readily transferred to countries in the same region.

Another similarity in the outward FDI of developing countries in the 1970s and the 2000s was the high degree of concentration: in both periods, the top 10 countries accounted for 80% or more of outward FDI. However, the relative importance of different regions changed; for example, Latin America lost its place as the leading source of outward FDI. Taking their place were several Asian economies.

One surprising development in the 2000s was that about one-fourth of the outward FDI from developing countries went to developed countries; in some years, that share was as high as one-third. This is unprecedented, and such substantial flows from poor to rich countries run counter to the argument that firms in poor countries cannot possess technologies or applications of value compared to developed countries. Most of these investments are in services, including those that support trade. With the increase in outward FDI flows, there has been a rise in the number of multinational firms from developing economies. UNCTAD (2009) counted more than 21,000 such firms — 3,500 of which were from China and 815 from India.

The rapid increase in outward FDI from low-income countries, such as China and India, or even middle-income countries, such as Malaysia and Mexico, does not fit the predictions of the "investment development path" IDP model (UNCTAD, 2006: p. 141). Outward FDI from developing economies has occurred sooner than IDP theory would predict. The relationship between level of development (measured by, say, per capita income) and outward FDI, or that between inward and outward FDI, is more complex than IDP theory suggests. For instance, the recent surge in outward FDI by developing countries has come not from the countries that received the most inward FDI in the past — namely, those in Latin America — but rather from countries in Asia, some of which were quite closed to FDI earlier (e.g., India). Such mismatches are also evident in the experience of industrialized countries: Spain, for instance, though quite advanced relative to developing countries, did not become a major source of outward FDI until it joined the European Union in 1986 (Guillen, 2005: p. 68), and Japan emerged as a major supplier of outward FDI after the mid-1980s without ever being open to inward FDI. (Navaretti & Venables, 2004, note that "Japan's economy is virtually closed to foreign MNEs, which account for less than 1% of manufacturing employment", p. 5.)

The important determinant of outward FDI may not be level of development per se, but home country economic policies toward trade and FDI and natural endowments such as the supply of local entrepreneurs (e.g., see discussion in Thomas & Meuller, 2000: pp. 289–291). If a government exposes the economy to greater competition from domestic and multinational firms, its firms are more likely to become internationally competitive. Once these firms develop ownership-specific advantages, they will exploit them overseas or augment them by acquiring complementary or knowledge-based assets abroad.

Government policies allowing or encouraging outward FDI are also important. In the past, many governments viewed outward FDI as an undesirable transfer of capital and jobs to other countries, but in the 2000s they have viewed it as a way to build globally competitive firms. Sovereign wealth funds are also a new player — albeit a negligible one. More important are state-owned enterprises, mainly from China. Thus, the Chinese government reportedly encouraged state-controlled firms to build global organizations (Buckley *et al.*, 2006), as did the Singaporean government. India (UNCTAD, 2004: pp. 8–10), South Africa (Goldstein & Pritchard, 2006: p. 11), and many other governments simplified procedures and increased the size of overseas investments that their companies could make. Firms in transition economies experienced a radical change in national policies for FDI, compared to the years before 1989, when their economies were closed to FDI from outside the Soviet Bloc. There are a myriad of other examples.

In 2011, EM-MNEs were to be found in many industries. Some were resource seekers, looking for oil, gas, or minerals, often in competition with developed-country counterparts; others operated in knowledge-intensive businesses, financial services, infrastructure services, or products not easily traded, such as cement (Cantwell & Barnard, 2006). Still others operated in industries highly exposed to global competition, such as automotives, fast-moving consumer goods, white goods, or pharmaceuticals (for more on this, see Ramamurti & Singh, 2009).

There is surely more room for growth of such firms. For one thing, significant parts of the world are still outside the domain of free markets. Countries like Cuba, North Korea, and parts of sub-Saharan Africa are not integrated into the global economy, nor are poor peasants in rural China or India as integrated into it as counterparts in prosperous urban areas. As pointed out by Stiglitz (2006), poor countries that don't have the roads or other infrastructure to move products cannot enjoy the fruits of open markets, nor do they have the skills to maximize their interests in complex international negotiations. Moreover, despite deregulation and major reductions in tariffs and government intervention, many economic activities are still highly protected in all countries; for example, farmers are subsidized in most developed countries, and airlines still operate in a regime that does not allow foreign ownership of national carriers (Aharoni, 2002).

Another pocket of underglobalized firms involves state-owned enterprises, many of which were created by governments as instruments of national policy and still enjoy preferential access to public resources and contracts. Many are already involved in international production in industries such as in aerospace, armaments, energy, and consumer durables (see Aharoni, 1980; Anastassopoulos *et al.*, 1987; Vernon & Aharoni, 1981). Others have already been privatized. However, over time, many more will be placed squarely in private hands, as a result of which they are likely to become more aggressive players in international markets (Vernon, 1979). In China, one can see such aggressive behavior even among state-owned enterprises that have been partly privatized or that have entered into joint ventures with foreign firms (Park *et al.*, 2006).

One indicator of the status of MNEs from any country is a comparison of its share of worldwide FDI outflows and worldwide GDP. By this yardstick, emerging markets are still underrepresented in global FDI outflows: in 2009, at official exchange rates, they accounted for 25% of world GDP but only 17% of world FDI outflows. Using purchasing power parity (PPP), the gap was much bigger because developing countries accounted for 44% of the world's GDP in real terms. However, the gap was closing, and in another decade or two the shares at official exchange rates are likely to be closely matched. In other words, globalization still has a long way to go in emerging markets, and as it advances, the national origin of MNEs is likely to diversify even further, the size distribution of MNEs will become more skewed, and the number of industries in which MNEs operate will increase.

Backlash against Developing Country MNEs?

MNEs have not always been seen as a positive force in society. In the 1960s and 1970s, anxiety about the growing power of American MNEs was high around the world, including in Europe, while in the developing world that anxiety applied to foreign MNEs of all stripes. The proliferation of MNEs in the subsequent three decades should not be misunderstood to mean that the old fears about MNEs in host countries have dissipated. Quite the contrary, many of the old fears still persist, but with one key difference: today, those fears are high not only in emerging economies but also in the developed world, including the United States.

In the 1970s, the rallying cause was the fear that MNEs would dominate the weaker and less sophisticated nation-state. Their ability to move resources across borders or to use transfer pricing to minimize tax liabilities was resented. Servan-Schreiber (1967), in his best-selling book, *Le Défi Américain*, warned that US MNEs would take over the French economy. Latin American economists railed against *dependencia* (e.g., Evans, 1979), and others feared the MNE's control of the commanding heights — or the strategic sectors — of the economy.

Since the 1980s, new views of the MNE took hold as governments substituted regulation and intervention with greater scope for free markets and competition. Deregulation, privatization, and competition became the major slogans everywhere. The collapse of communist regimes and the breakup of the Soviet Empire silenced any remaining skeptics of free markets and competition. Transition economies moved as quickly as they could to a market economy and integration with the world economy.

Accordingly, governments all over the world chose to ignore tensions with MNEs and instead to court them to invest within their territories (Ramamurti, 2001). The advantages of additional jobs, technology transfers, exports, and knowledge creation were perceived as outweighing the risks, such as loss of national sovereignty, tax evasion through transfer pricing, "crowding out" of local private enterprise, suboptimal technology choices, or other negative spillovers in the host economy. UNCTAD documented in its annual *World Investment Report* the proliferation of investment promotion agencies, the mushrooming of bilateral investment treaties, and the tendency to create a more hospitable environment for MNEs through regulatory changes. The share of FDI laws that made the investment climate less welcoming to MNEs was 6% during 1992–2002, 12% in 2003–2004, as high as 21% in 2005–2007, and hit a record 30% in 2009 (UNCTAD, 2010: pp. 76–77).

At the dawn of the 21st century, there was considerable anxiety about globalization in the developed economies at least as much as in the developing economies. This reversal of the traditional roles — in which the rich countries championed free markets and international openness, and the poor countries resisted it — occurred over the previous two decades. Going forward, there may well be a serious backlash against globalization in the European Union and the United States. If that were to happen, the expansion of MNEs from emerging markets into developed countries may get slowed down.

FDIs from countries such as China or India are already viewed with some suspicion in the West, and arguments of national security may be advanced to limit the acquisition of developed-economy firms by MNEs from developing countries. This was seen, for instance, in Lenovo (China)'s acquisition of IBM's global PC business in December 2004, where the risk of China acquiring dual use technologies or obtaining a US platform for industrial espionage was among the concerns of the Committee on Foreign Investment in the United States (CFIUS), a multiagency federal panel. Dubai Ports World, a firm owned by the UAE government, got quick CFIUS approval for its indirect acquisition of US ports when it purchased the British firm P&O Steam Navigation Co. but later ran into a storm of protests from Congress and had to abandon its quest. Firms being acquired are declared as a part of a "strategic sector" particularly when the acquirer is a state-owned enterprise or sovereign wealth fund.

Wolf (2004) and others identify several grounds on which acquisitions by emerging-market firms in developed countries might be opposed. The foreign owner might be accused of competing unfairly, spoiling the environment, of shifting jobs from the United States or Europe to low-wage workers back home, or of being unqualified to run the acquired operations. But the most common worry is that the acquisition would threaten national security, and these concerns are amplified if a foreign government owns the MNE. Three-quarters of the Chinese firms in Boston Consulting Group's list of the top 100 MNEs in emerging markets were partly or wholly owned by the state (Boston Consulting Group, 2009).

The potential loss of jobs to emerging economies is yet another source of anxiety for rich countries. In the 19th century, people moved freely across borders in search of jobs and better opportunities. During the 1890s, the inflow of immigrants to the United States equaled 9% of the initial population, in Argentina 26%, and in Australia 17% (Baldwin & Martin, 1999: p. 19). In the century following 1815, around 60 million people left Europe to find better lives in America, South and East Africa, and Oceania (Hirst & Thompson, 1999: p. 23). In the 20th century, on the other hand, products, technology, and capital began to move freely across borders, but the movement of people became more restricted. In such a world, workers couldn't move to where the jobs were, but it became easier for jobs to move to where the workers were. In rich countries, this boosted fears that jobs would move to places where they could be performed at the least cost, thereby hollowing out industries in the rich countries. Digitization and improvements in communications and computing technology made many services, including knowledge-intensive activities and even R&D, susceptible to the same kind of global optimization, striking fear in the hearts of not just blue-collar workers but white-collar workers as well.

Indeed, in one developed country after another, protectionism has raised its head more in the investment area than on the trade front. Both US and European governments have sought to check takeover bids, citing security reasons. Predictions of the demise of the nation-state and the creation of a borderless world have not been realized (Ohmae, 1995). Expectations that national business systems would converge to form a seamless global system have not materialized. According to Doremus *et al.* (1999), multinationals continue to be shaped by the policies and cultures of their home countries even though they globalize their assets and liabilities. It is thus highly likely that developed countries would attempt to restrict what they would perceive as the takeover of their precious assets by foreign firms (Hitt, 2007). In this sense, we may encounter a selective globalization, wherein some areas of economic activity are governed by market forces, while others are restricted on grounds of "fair trade", market failure, or national security considerations.

Conclusion and Research Questions

Multinationals have proliferated since they first appeared, in numbers, areas of operations, and national origin. They have changed considerably in response to four major shifts in the environment:

> Government policy, which has become increasingly more welcoming of FDI, especially in emerging markets, not just in manufacturing but also in services;
>
> Improvements in information and communication technologies, which have vastly reduced the cost of managing and integrating a globally dispersed value chain;
>
> Bigger and more efficient capital markets, which have broadened access to capital for small- and medium-sized firms, including those in developing countries; and

The strengthening of cross-border social networks among locals and overseas nationals (sometimes referred to as Diaspora), which has accelerated the cross-border flow of information and tacit knowledge and helped firms internationalize.

As a result of these trends, MNEs are being spawned in more countries, in more industries, and at earlier stages of a firm's evolution than before. The vast majority of the world's MNEs are small, and in the extreme some are "born global" firms. These changes have also transformed the well-established Triad-based MNE. As the industrial world has given way to a knowledge- and information-driven world, established MNEs have learned how to manage across national borders, and how to adapt to different markets and cultures. They have also learned how to collaborate in strategic alliances rather than seeking to be stand-alone superstars. More important, from a start as raw-material seekers and tariff-jumpers, they have become efficiency-seekers and innovation-seekers. Today, Western MNEs seek knowledge and ideas as keenly as they once sought natural resources or access to closed markets. They have learned to scan the world for new ideas, acquire start-ups, absorb knowledge from foreign subsidiaries, and to integrate knowledge acquired in all parts of the firm. Their competitive advantages are based less and less on hard assets — such as factories, inventories, or production skills — and more on intangibles, such as knowledge, intellectual property, and relationships.

These developments raise several questions that future research must address. A necessary condition for becoming an MNE is that the firm possesses firm-specific advantages relative to competitors. Precisely what ownership advantages do the newer MNEs from emerging markets enjoy and how did they develop those advantages in a relatively short period of time? What enables emerging market firms to invest "up-market", that is, in countries richer and more advanced than their home countries, as opposed to "down-market", as the product cycle theory would predict? And, how do the strategies of these firms resemble or differ from those of European, Japanese, or American MNEs (Johanson & Vahlne, 2000)? What is in fact the impact of an MNE's country of origin on its strategy? We have educated guesses on these issues (e.g., Khanna & Palepu, 2006; Ramamurti & Singh, 2009) but more research is needed to provide definitive answers.

Existing theory is not very clear on why some countries spawn MNEs and others do not, and precisely why the number of countries spawning

MNEs has proliferated in the last two decades. Aliber (1970) suggested that the home country's advantage is related to the strength of its currency. Other explanations are related to the supply of local entrepreneurial talent, the behavior of managers, the ability of the firm to innovate, the impact of governmental policies, as well as the impact of technological changes.

Another intriguing issue is whether the world will be dominated by a handful of megacorporations, as Larry Bossidy, former vice chairman of GE, predicted in 1989: "By the latter part of the 1990s, there may well be fewer than 25 megacorporations in the world, about equally divided among United States, European and Far Eastern companies ... The medium-to-large-size-generalists, serving a limited geographic market and without a specific niche, won't be around anymore" (p. 10). Yet, as discussed, the number of multinationals in the world increased more than 10-fold after 1969. In contrast to Porter's (1986) prediction, giant firms do not dominate many economic fields, even in global industries, which are sometimes populated by a large number of domestic players. One example is the accounting industry, but this is also true of some other service industries (Aharoni, 1999).

Rugman (2005) would recommend that scholars focus only on giant firms since other firms are unimportant in the overall picture of world MNEs. We strongly argue that the emergence of new born globals, the expansion of home countries to many more nation-states, and the emergence of MNEs from developing economies may not be earthshaking in size but must have a place in IB theory. Such a theory should guide managers and policy makers in small firms and states as well as in the large ones.

We thus suggest other questions for future research: How and why do small firms survive and thrive in a global world? When are they doomed to be acquired by industry giants and when can they quickly develop and sustain competitive advantages that allow them to remain independent? How does the behavior of large and small MNEs differ? What are the implications for IB theory as firms become MNEs not necessarily to seek resources but also to gain markets, increase efficiency, absorb new knowledge, or be service-centered MNEs?

More research is also needed on the relationship between MNEs and politics, including their impact on national sovereignty. As early as 1969, Charles Kindleberger claimed "the nation-state is just about through as an economic unit" (Kindleberger, 1969). The expansion of globalization since the end of the Cold War was seen by some scholars as making the nation-state obsolete. Yet, the last century has seen, on the one hand, the amalgamation of states into larger blocs, such as the European Union, and on the other hand, the fragmentation of states into smaller countries. The number of countries has more than doubled in the last three decades of the 20th century, rising from 96 in 1960 to 192 in 1998. The number of countries with less than 1 million people has almost tripled — from 15 to 43. Contrary to expectations, the MNE does not dominate over host countries, and globalization has not made states impotent. Why did earlier predictions prove incorrect? The relationship between globalization and the importance of the nation-state thus deserves more research.

Most economists seem to agree that the benefits of FDI exceed its costs (Oxelheim & Ghauri, 2004: p. 10), and that both inward and outward foreign investments are beneficial, contributing to growth that might otherwise not occur (Moran *et al.*, 2005; Kokko, 2006). Others have argued for putting limits on foreign investments, for example, restricting outward FDI that impinges on national security, although defining the national security interest is often controversial, or restricting inward FDI in the "commanding heights of the economy", although this seems to have lost much of its former appeal. Underlying these policy choices is the assumption that a firm's nationality matters, but this too deserves more study. For instance, what changes when an American firm (such as Ford or General Motors) acquires a Swedish firm (such as Saab or Volvo)? Robert Reich (1990) claimed that what really matters is where economic activities are carried out, rather than who carries them out because at the end of the day the outcome of interest is employment and job creation. For him, a Japanese firm producing in the United States is more beneficial to the US economy than a US firm producing (and thus creating employment) in Asia. Yet, an American-owned Intel may be readier than an Israeli-owned firm to close a factory in Israel. These, however, are hypotheses that need to be thought through carefully and tested in future studies (for a deeper discussion of these ideas, see Seev Hirsch's chapter in this volume).

There are also a host of questions about the welfare implications and political fallout from globalization.[1] How and why is globalization affecting income inequality across countries and within countries? Is globalization sustainable if income inequality within countries increases as globalization intensifies? The sustainability of globalization depends on finding satisfactory answers to policy questions of this sort.

Hopefully, researchers of these and other related topics will be careful in defining the population they study, remembering that MNEs are now quite heterogeneous — in terms of their national origin, size, reasons for overseas investments, industries in which those investments are made, and perhaps also their strategy and structure.

Note

1. We are grateful to Nakiye Boyacigiller for bringing this set of issues to our attention.

References

Agmon, T. & Kindleberger, C. P. (1977). *Multinationals from Small Countries.* Cambridge, MA: MIT Press.

Aharoni, Y. (1980). The state-owned enterprise as a competitor in international markets. *Columbia Journal of World Business*, XV(1): 14–22.

Aharoni, Y. (1999). Internationalization of professional services: Implications for accounting firms. In Brock, D., Powell, M. & (Bob) Hinings, C. R. (Eds.) *Restructuring the Professional Organization.* London: Routledge, pp. 20–40.

Aharoni, Y. (2002). The globalizer that cannot globalize — The airline transportation industry European International Business Association Annual conference, Athens, December. Available at http://64.233.169.104/search?q=cache:DUe51KvA1xcJ:www.aueb.gr/deos/EIBA2002.files/PAPERS/C214.pdf+%22the+globalizer+that+cannot+globalize%22&hl=en&ct=clnk&cd=1&gl=us.

Aharoni, Y. (2006). Debunking management myth. *CIIM Management Review*, 2(2): 10–16.

Aliber, R. Z. (1970). A theory of foreign direct investment. In Kindleberger, C. F. (Ed.) *The International Corporation.* Cambridge, MA: The MIT Press.

Amsden, A. H. (2001). *The Rise of "the Rest": Challenges to the West from Late-Industrializing Economies.* New York: Oxford University Press.

Anastassopoulos, J. P., George, B. & Pierre, D. (1987). *State-Owned Multinationals.* Chichester, UK: Wiley.

Baldwin, R., & Martin, P. (1999). Two Waves of Globalization: Superficial Similarities, Fundamental Differences. National Bureau of Economic Research Working Paper no. 6904 (January). Available at www.nber.org.

Boston Consulting Group. (2009). *The 2009 BCG 100 New Global Challengers: How Companies from Rapidly Developing Economies Are Contending for Global Leadership.* Boston: Boston Consulting Group.

Buckley, P. & Casson, M. (1985). *The Economic Theory of the Multinational Enterprise.* New York: St. Martin's Press.

Buckley, P., Clegg, J., Cross, A., Voss, H., Rhodes, M. & Zheng, P. (2006). Explaining China's outward FDI: An Institutional Perspective. Paper Presented at the International Conference on "The Rise of Transnational Corporations from Emerging Markets: Threat or Opportunity?" Columbia University, New York. October 24–25.

Cantwell, J. & Barnard, H. (2006). Do Firms from Developing Countries Have to Invest Abroad? Outward FDI and the Competitiveness of Firms. Paper Presented at the International Conference on "The rise of transnational corporations from emerging markets: threat or opportunity?" Columbia University, New York. October 24–25.

Copeland, M. V. (2006). The mighty micro-multinational. Business 2.0, July 28. Available at http://money.cnn.com/magazines/business2/business2_archive/2006/07/01/8380230/index.htm.

Doremus, P., Keller, W. W., Pauly, L. W. & Reich, S. (1999). *The Myth of the Global Corporation.* Princeton, NJ: Princeton University Press.

Dunning, J. H. (1979). Explaining changing patterns of international production: In defense of the eclectic theory. *Oxford Bulletin of Economics and Statistics*, 45: 269–295.

Dunning, J. H. (1981). Explaining the international direct investment position of countries: Towards a dynamic or developmental approach. *Weltwirtschaftliches Archiv*, 117: 30–64.

Dunning, J. H. (1996). The geographical sources of the competitiveness of firms: Some results of a new survey. *Transnational Corporations*, 5(3): 1–30.

Economist Intelligence Unit. (2007). *World Investment Prospect to 2011: Foreign Direct Investment and the Challenge of Political Risk.* London: Economist Intelligence Unit.

Economist. (1993). Turning point: A survey of Japanese economy. *Economist*, March 6.

Evans, P. (1979). *Dependent Development.* Princeton, NJ: Princeton University Press.

Goldstein, A. & Pritchard, W. (2006). South African Multinationals: South-South Cooperation at Its Best? Paper Prepared for the SAIIA Doing Business in Africa volume. Mimeo.

Guillen, M. (2005). *The Rise of Spanish Multinationals: European Business in the Global Economy.* Cambridge, UK: Cambridge University Press.

Hitt, G. (2007). A higher bar for foreign buyers: Security terms in Alcatel's deal for Lucent signals new era. *Wall Street Journal*, 5 (January): A6.

Hirst, P. & Thompson, G. (1999). *Globalization in Question: The International Economy and the Possibilities of Governance* (2nd edn.). Cambridge: Polity Press.

Hymer, S. H. (1976). *The International Operations of National Firms: A Study of Direct Foreign Investment.* Ph.D. thesis, 1960, The MIT Press, MA.

Johanson, J., & Vahlne, J. E. (1977). The internationalization process of the firm: A model of knowledge development and increasing foreign market commitments. *Journal of International Business Studies*, 8(1): 23–32.

Johanson, J. & Vahlne, J. E. (2000). New technology, new companies and new internationalization processes? A critical review of the internationalization process model. Paper for the Marcus Wallenberg Symposium on Internationalization, January 10–11, Uppsala, Sweden.

Kapur, D. & Ramamurti, R. (2001). India's emerging competitive advantage in services. *Academy of Management Executive*, 15(2): 20–33.

Khanna, T. & Palepu, K. (2006). Emerging giants. *Harvard Business Review*, October–November.

Kindleberger, C. P. (1969). *American Business Abroad: Six Lectures on Direct Investment.* New Haven, CT: Yale University Press.

Knight, G. A. & Cavusgil, S. T. (1996). The born global firm: A challenge to traditional internationalization theory. In Lindmark, L., Christensen, P. R., Eskelinen, H., Forsstrom, B., Sorenson, O. J. & Vatn, E. (Eds.) *Advances in International Marketing*, Vol. 8. Greenwich, CT: JAI Press, pp. 11–26.

Kokko, A. (2006). *The Home Country Effects of FDI in Developing Economies.* Mimeo. The European Institute of Japanese Studies, Stockholm.

Mathews, J. A. (2002). *Dragon Multinationals: A New Model for Global Growth.* Oxford, UK: Oxford University Press.

Moran, T. H., Graham, E. M. & Blomström, M. (Eds.). (2005). *Does Foreign Direct Investment Promote Development?* Washington, DC: The Institute for International Economics.

Navaretti, G. B. & Venables, A. J. (2004). *Multinational Firms in the World Economy.* Princeton, NJ: Princeton University Press.

Ohmae, K. (1995). *The End of the Nation State.* New York: Simon and Schuster.

Oxelheim, L., & Ghauri, P. (Eds.). (2004). *European Union and the Race for Foreign Direct Investment in Europe.* Oxford: Elsevier.

Park, S. H., Li, S. & Tse, D. K. (2006). Market liberalization and firm performance during China's economic transition. *Journal of International Business Studies*, 37: 127–147.

Pradhan, J. P. & Sahoo, M. K. (2005). *Case Study on Outward Foreign Direct Investment by Indian Small- and Medium-Sized Enterprises.* New York: UNCTAD.

Porter, M. E. (1986). *Competition in Global Industries.* Boston: Harvard Business School Press. Ramamurti, R. (2001). The obsolescing 'bargaining model': MNC-host developing country relations revisited. *Journal of International Business Studies*, 32(1): 23–39.

Ramamurti, R. & Singh, J. V. (Eds.). (2009). *Emerging Multinationals from Emerging Markets.* Cambridge, UK: Cambridge University Press.

Reich, R. B. (1990). Who is us? (The changing American corporation). *Harvard Business Review*, 68: 53–64.

Rugman, A. (2005). *The Regional Multinationals: MNEs and 'Global' Strategic Management.* Cambridge, UK: Cambridge University Press.

Saxenian, A. (2002). *Local and Global Networks of Immigrant Professionals in Silicon Valley.* San Francisco: Public Policy Institute of California.

Servan-Schreiber, J. J. (1967). In Steel, R. (Trans.), *Le Défi Américain Paris: Denoel* (The American Challenge). New York: Atheneum Press.

Stiglitz, J. E. (2006). *Making Globalization Work.* New York: W.W. Norton.

Thomas, A. S. & Meuller, S. L. (2000). A case for comparative entrepreneurship: Assessing the relevance of culture. *Journal of International Business Studies*, 31(2): 287–301.

UNCTAD. (1995). *World Investment Report: Transnational Corporations and Competitiveness.* New York: United Nations.

UNCTAD. (1998). *World Investment Report: Trends and Determinants.* New York: United Nations.

UNCTAD. (2000). *World Investment Report: Cross-Border M&A and Development.* New York: United Nations.

UNCTAD. (2004). India's Outward FDI: A Giant Awakening? Paper no. UNCTAD/DITE/IIAB/2004/1, October 20, 2004. Available at http://www.unctad.org/sections/dite_iiab/docs/ diteiiab20041_en.pdf.

UNCTAD. (2006). *World Investment Report: FDI from Developing and Transition Economies: Implications for Development.* New York: United Nations.

UNCTAD. (2008). *World Investment Report: Transnational Corporations and the Infrastructure Challenge.* New York: United Nations.

UNCTAD. (2009). *World Investment Report: Transnational Corporations, Agricultural Production, and Development.* New York: United Nations.

UNCTAD. (2010). *World Investment Report: Investing in a Low Carbon Economy.* New York: United Nations.

United Nations Department of Economic and Social Affairs. (1973). *Multinational Corporations in World Development.* New York: United Nations.

Vernon, R. (1971). *Sovereignty at Bay: The Multinational Spread of U.S. Enterprise.* New York: Basic Books.

Vernon, R. (1979). International aspects of state-owned enterprises. *Journal of International Business Studies*, 10(3): 7–15.

Vernon, R. & Aharoni, Y. (Eds.). (1981). *State-Owned Enterprises in Western Economies.* London: Croom Helm.

Wells Jr., L. T. (1983). *Third World Multinationals.* Cambridge, MA: MIT Press.

Wilkins, M. (1974). *The Maturing of Multinational Enterprise: American Business Abroad from 1914 to 1970.* Cambridge, MA: Harvard University Press.

Wolf, M. (2004). *Why Globalization Works.* New Haven, CT: Yale University Press.

Yergin, D. (1991). *The Prize: The Epic Quest for Oil, Money, and Power.* New York: Simon and Schuster.

Zaheer, S. (1995). Overcoming the liability of foreignness. *Academy of Management Journal*, 38(2): 341–363.

State-Owned Enterprises

https://doi.org/10.1142/9789811287510_0012

Chapter 12

Managerial Discretion*

Yair Aharoni

Tel Aviv University, Tel Aviv, Israel

It is generally agreed that state ownership presents a different management situation from private ownership, that the behavior of managers in state-owned enterprises differs from that of managers in private enterprises, and that these differences vary according to the national setting. This paper argues that differences in management behavior are best analyzed in terms of managerial discretion. Managerial discretion, according to Williamson, is defined as the ability of managers to choose and pursue objectives and strategies that differ from those of the owners.[1]

We shall assume that the owners of private firms are largely motivated to maximize profits. According to Williamson, managers of private firms have discretion to the extent that they operate for reasons other than the maximization of profits, such as the expansion of staff or the increase of on-the-job leisure.

State-owned enterprises, on the other hand, do not exist solely to maximize profits; they have multiple objectives reflecting conflicting public needs and political pressures. Managerial discretion in state-owned enterprises cannot be stated simply in terms of divergence from profit maximization or from any other single objective. The absence of clearly

*This chapter is reproduced from *State-Owned Enterprise in the Western Economies*, pp. 184–193 (1981), St. Martin's Press.

defined goals for state-owned enterprises forms the basis for differences in managerial discretion between private and state-owned enterprises.

Managerial Discretion as an Agency Cost[a]

An agency relationship exists when one party, the agent, acts on behalf of another, the principal. The principal who uses an agent incurs certain costs. These costs arise from the fact that the interests of the agent and the principal are not identical, and that the agent will sometimes act to maximize his own interests. Therefore, the principal must include provisions in his agreement with the agent that will induce the agent to act as if he were maximizing the principal's interests. The costs incurred when the agent fails to maximize the principal's interests plus the cost of creating, monitoring and enforcing the contract between principal and agent are considered agency costs.

Relationships between owners and managers of business firms are examples of agency relationships. Managers of private firms contract to act on behalf of their shareholders. A perfect contract would structure the manager's incentives to correspond exactly to the shareholders' interests; however, given the uncertainties and complexities of actual situations, such perfect contracts are probably rare. Shareholders often choose to permit a degree of managerial discretion that entails some costs, especially if the only option of the shareholders is to replace the manager.

The existence of distinctive managerial interests, costs of monitoring and costs of replacement affect the relationships between managers and their principals in both state-owned and private enterprises. However, in state-owned enterprises, the principal cannot be identified. The owner of a state-owned enterprise is not a person, nor even a single organization. The state acts through a variety of people — ministers, legislators, civil servants — who are themselves agents of the general public. In many cases these agents lack the knowledge to determine and the power to enforce goals for state-owned enterprises. Moreover, different agents have different perceptions of their jobs. A government official concerned with foreign affairs may seek an increase in a public firm's research and development budget in order to reduce the state's dependence upon imported technology. The Minister of Labor may support an increase in

[a]Editors' note: the principal-agent relationship explored here differs from that discussed in Raiffa where the manager's relationship to his subordinates is studied. Here it is the relationship of the owner to the manager that is being studied.

labor-intensive procedures in order to maximize employment. The Minister of Finance, perceiving himself as a shareholder, may want the public firm to pay higher dividends. An entity that buys from the public firm may seek to reduce output prices. Who among these competing government representatives can be considered the principal of the firm? And which interests are to be paramount in the contract between principal and agent?

In the absence of clearly defined goals, state-owned enterprises often find themselves struggling with generalized, vague and conflicting interests. The statutes laying out the responsibilities of the British Steel Corporation and National Coal Board in the United Kingdom exemplify this struggle.

> ... to promote the efficient and economic supply of iron and steel products in such quantities and at such prices as may seem to them best calculated to meet the reasonable demands of customers and to further the public's interest.[2]
>
> ... making supplies of coal available of such qualities and sizes, and in such quantities and at such prices, as may seem to them best calculated to further the public interest in all respects, including the avoidance of any undue or unreasonable preference or advantage.[3]

A legislative proposal in a Canadian Privy Council report provides another example of the struggle state-owned enterprises face.

> It is hereby declared that every Crown corporation is constituted an instrument for advancing the national interests of Canada and that in order to best advance those national interests it is the duty of the directors of every Crown corporation when managing the Crown corporation to take into consideration the national interests of Canada as well as the interests of the Crown corporation and, within the scope of their powers and the powers of the Crown corporations, to pursue those corporate policies that best advance such national interests.[4]

Defining and Measuring Managerial Discretion

Because governments have a tendency to state their goals in general, vague and conflicting terms, measuring the performance of a state-owned enterprise becomes difficult, if not impossible. In a private enterprise, the principal can measure performance, can use an incentive contract that ties rewards to measured performance, and can apply sanctions if measured performance differs significantly from expected performance. In state-owned enterprises, the existence of many goals and the vagueness in the definition of goals render measurement almost impossible. That situation increases the possibility of managerial discretion.

The managers of private enterprises may be able to respond to some secondary goals as they pursue their primary goal of profit maximization; the managers of state-owned enterprises, however, are usually free to choose much more widely, determining what goals are to be primary and what secondary.

Although managers of state-owned enterprises may be freer to choose their goals, they are, however, more constrained than private managers in their choice of strategies. Private managers are usually free to choose their strategies as long as they pursue profit maximization. Public managers may have to recognize employment policies, pricing policies, location policies and foreign investment policies as constraints on managerial discretion.

Managerial discretion may also vary depending upon the issue and the specific situation. For example, a union in a state-owned enterprise, confident of governmental support, may exert stronger pressure for higher wages or more job security than a labor union in a private firm. Such pressure, if supported by the government, may reduce managerial discretion. Indeed, managers of state-owned enterprises are subject to many different pressures from labor unions: unions demand generous wages, fringe benefits, labor conditions and job security; unions expect state-owned enterprises to commit themselves to policies beneficial to workers; unions use state-owned enterprises to set standards that later can be demanded of private enterprises; and unions use their political clout on government to receive concessions in collective bargaining.[5] When Labor governments are in power, these pressures become particularly strong. Indeed, in some cases, collective bargaining, which formally appears to be taking place between unions and management, is actually conducted between unions and ministers, who subsequently pressure managements to accept the resulting agreements.

The degree to which the managers of state-owned enterprises are obliged to respond to the pressures of outside groups, according to the record, seems quite overwhelming. The managers of state-owned enterprises are expected to choose domestic suppliers over foreign suppliers, even if foreign suppliers are able to fill orders more rapidly and less expensively. Managers of state-owned enterprises are also encouraged to choose other state-owned enterprises as suppliers rather than private enterprises. At the same time, constraints are placed on state-owned enterprises to prevent them from competing with private firms. Their ability to expand into new lines of business is constrained by treaty (as in the case of the Rome Treaty creating the European Economic Community), by the law of different countries and by government direction. For example, El Al, the Israeli state airline, is prevented from acquiring a major interest in a hotel, as a result of a government decree issued after pressure from private hotel owners. In many countries military industries are not allowed to produce goods for the civilian market, even if these industries have idle capacity and the machinery and expertise to produce these goods.

As other papers in this volume point out, state-owned enterprises are also expected to do many other things in support of the national interest: to refrain from raising prices in periods of inflation; to invest more during recessions; to borrow abroad in order to bring in needed foreign currency; not to borrow abroad in order to avoid balance-of-payments problems; and to act as trust busters by competing against strong private monopolies. The government also exerts pressure on state-owned enterprises to purchase ailing industries and to invest in laggard regions and weak sectors of the economy.[b]

To be sure, management does have some autonomy. Nevertheless, it would be premature to conclude that the managers of state-owned enterprises are hedged in any more than those of private enterprise. While the demands on the public managers may be greater and more diverse, their special privileges can restore some of the discretion that such demands have curbed. While governments may be reluctant to provide equity capital to their public enterprises, for instance, they are forthcoming in granting enterprises sizeable amounts of loans at subsidized rates of interest, in guaranteeing loans, in waiving requirements for the repayment of loans and in providing operating subsidies. State-owned enterprises at times are also offered special protection for their domestic markets, special waivers from government regulations, special exemptions from taxation.

What, then, are the net effects of these special duties and special privileges upon the discretion of public managers? Andrew Shonfield, a scholar of modern capitalism, believes that some state-owned enterprises successfully resist intervention:

> a fighting company like ENI [Ente Nazionale Idrocarburi], commanded by a dominant personality like Signor Mattei does not readily accept any form of outside supervision. Indeed it seems nowadays that the bosses

---

[b]Editors' note: see the papers by Anastassopoulos and Grassini in this volume.

> of great public enterprises often operate with greater personal freedom of decision than the typical head of the big corporation in private industry. Few of them, however, have carried the method of personal rule to such lengths as Signor Mattei did in ENI. He worked on the *condottieri* principle: he had been handed fief to look after and he saw it as his task to enlarge its power and extent wherever possible — if at the expense of rivals, so much better.[6]

Nor is Signor Mattei altogether a unique case. Most managers of state-owned enterprises have much more discretion than would be supposed from scanning official documents. A French public committee on the state enterprises (the Nora Committee) reported that controllers who were set up to oversee state-owned enterprises became the advocates of the enterprise in the ministry, and that they neither had the expertise nor the inclination to control the enterprises. To be sure, these controllers did have very broad powers, including investigatory powers. However, most of them were superannuated civil servants unable to utilize the powers they enjoyed. The same high level of managerial discretion has been found in other countries.

Nevertheless, despite such cases, it is clear that some managers of state-owned enterprises are docile and passive receivers of governmental orders and parliamentary requests. In extreme cases, managers may develop what Phatak called the "don't rock-the-boat syndrome".[7] With this approach, managers avoid changes that may alienate any powerful groups: redundant workers are not dismissed, erring staff are not disciplined, obsolete plants remain open and faulty organizational structures remain unchanged. In short, managers simply develop apathy.

In the end, broad generalizations about the discretion of managers of state-owned enterprises prove elusive. In some cases, the formal discretion of the manager can be defined in fairly precise terms. In other cases, the manager's perception of his discretion can be precisely stated. But the actuality is more difficult to capture. Yet, if one day that actuality could be recorded in some meaningful way, it would surely reveal a very wide range of outcomes.

Key Variables Affecting Discretion

What is possible, however, is to reflect on the factors that are likely to determine the degree of the manager's discretion from case to case. If we disregard the personal traits of the manager, and assume he is eager to increase discretion, his ability to do so depends on a number of identifiable factors.

First and foremost, a manager who does not need to go to the government to ask for funds is a manager that has more discretion. This, of course, is why officials in Ministries of Finance grant little equity capital to state-owned enterprises, forcing the management to come back to the ministry with requests for funds.

Another variable that affects the discretion of the manager is the legal organization of the firm. Usually managers of enterprises that operate as integral parts of government departments have minimal discretion: their budgets are subject to annual legislative appropriations, they are not permitted to accumulate reserves and their employees are civil servants whose salaries, fringe benefits and incentives are controlled by the state. State-owned enterprises organized as corporations generally have much more discretion. Their employees are not usually civil servants, they are allowed to accumulate funds and they are subject to fewer day-to-day government directives.

In addition, governments tend to allow managers of joint ventures — that is, state-owned enterprises which have private partners — more discretion than is allotted to enterprises fully owned by the state. When a government goes into a joint venture with private partners, the government implicitly assumes certain constraints on its ability to force the enterprise to undertake social tasks, or even to take risks unacceptable to the private owners. Managers of joint ventures have been known to use the existence of private shareholders as a reason for rejecting a governmental intervention and have recruited the private shareholders to aid them in the conflict. Indeed, the private partners may have legal ways to impose their will and to avoid social or political direction.

Still another factor affecting discretion is the number and complexity of the goals that are associated with the enterprise. For the manager, the responsibility of responding to many masters may prove to be the privilege of responding to no masters at all.

Managers may also acquire more discretion from the fact that controllers perceive the very act of control as necessitating resources: their time, energy and attention. If the enterprise is large or is considered important for the national interest, it is monitored more carefully than otherwise. Thus, the manager of a state-owned electricity utility is subject to much closer scrutiny and may therefore have considerably less discretion than the manager of a small state-owned hotel.

Control functions are largely executed by civil servants. This point has particular importance because the capacity for control is a scarce resource in most countries. The degree of expertise and knowledge of these civil servants is necessarily limited, especially in relation to the enterprises which they confront. One reason is that the enterprises often pay higher salaries than the civil service and can attract more talented personnel. Another is that it is usually more challenging professionally to work for an enterprise than to control it. Pilots or aeronautical engineers usually work for the airline or the aerospace industry, not for the government. Generally, therefore, the more technical the information needed to operate the enterprise, and the more expertise concentrated at the management and firm level, the higher the managerial discretion.

Managers who are scarce and hard to replace also gain discretion by that very fact. A good manager may be hard to find, and not all good managers may be willing to work in the uncertain and ambiguous environment of the state-owned enterprise. The higher the perceived costs of replacing a manager, the higher his discretion. Very successful and effective managers can get away with ignoring many government demands, since the government may perceive the costs of replacing the manager as higher than the benefits.

Managerial discretion also depends on market structure. For example, state-owned, monopolistic firms, particularly public utilities, have less discretion than comparable firms in a competitive market. In one sense, the firm in the competitive market is already constrained, being obliged to match the prices of its competitors. Accordingly, a public enterprise that is expected to compete with other firms has to be compensated for its discretionary social activities, since it cannot recoup them through higher prices. On the other hand, if a monopolist is required to perform social services, it can be authorized by the government to recoup the costs of these services through higher prices, without the need for budgetary expenditures. Monopolies, therefore, are often the preferred social instrumentalities of governments, thus reducing the manager's discretion.

Another variable that affects discretion is the internationalization of the firm's operations. International enterprises enjoy greater discretion than domestic enterprises because of their ability to avoid foreign exchange controls and to avoid revealing the details of their offshore operations.

And, finally, a strategy of diversification on the part of the state-owned enterprise often proves to provide an escape toward increased discretion. With a large number of product lines, a state-owned enterprise enjoys added freedom. Many of its transactions are internalized, beyond the gaze of outsiders. If one product line becomes enmeshed in a web of government-imposed restrictions, the others may still be beyond the reach of government.

Techniques for Increasing Discretion

The various techniques for increasing discretion generally involve exploiting one or another of the factors mentioned above. But the manager can employ these factors in several different ways.[8]

One strategy of managers is to try to prevent apparent controls from becoming actual constraints. For instance, by appearing to pursue the objectives demanded by one government agency, managers can reduce the control of another government agency. Thus, managers may refuse to introduce pollution abatement equipment on the grounds that low-cost electricity was being demanded; they may refuse to pay dividends by pointing to the demand to maintain low prices; they may refuse to add workers to the plant on the grounds that profits were being demanded.

Managers of state-owned enterprises can also prevent the government's controls from becoming actual constraints by limiting the extent to which ministries have access to pertinent information. For example, if the state demands that the use of nuclear energy be safe, managers of state-owned enterprises can provide assurances that appropriate safety measures have been taken. In industries requiring specialized knowledge, particularly high-technology industries, government may be forced to defer to the expertise of the managers in determining whether the desired goals have been achieved.

A second line of strategy for managers, implicit in many of the factors listed earlier, is to reduce the firm's dependence on the government. As noted earlier, profitable firms increase their discretion by developing an internal source of discretionary funds for investment purposes and by reducing the opportunities for the media and legislature to scrutinize their operations. The strategy of diversification also reduces the risk of dependence for the firm by buffering it against possible losses in any one product.

Finally, managers of state-owned enterprises can sometimes affect the context in which control of their operations takes place, and can thereby increase their discretion. If managers are in a position to determine the rules that apply to the use of foreign exchange, for example, they may be able to place themselves in a position of using foreign currency without seeking government approval. If managers represent their governments in international negotiations, as they commonly do in the case of state-owned airlines, they may be able to negotiate international rules, such as the rules governing air fares, that increase their discretion. In complex technological fields, decisions on the extent and direction of research and development may be based upon the recommendations of experts inside the organization; and these recommendations may be aimed at increasing discretion.

Managers of state-owned enterprises, therefore, are not to be thought of as passive agents, required to live with the degree of discretion that the conditions of the environment produce.

This paper has put forth a number of variables and factors that may affect managerial discretion in state-owned enterprises. The actual weight of these factors in the management of public firms is still unknown. It is clear, however, that in the absence of a principal to dictate specific goals and monitor enterprises' activities, managerial discretion becomes a critical factor in the successful performance of state-owned enterprises. A better understanding of the mechanism of managerial discretion, its uses and the ways it is increased or constrained may help in designing more effective systems for managing state-owned enterprises.

Notes

1. Williamson, O. E. 1964. *The Economics of Discretionary Behavior: Management Objectives in a Theory of the Firm*. Englewood Cliffs, NJ: Prentice-Hall.
2. *Steel Nationalization*, Cmnd 2651. London: HMSO, April 1976. Para. 30(a).
3. United Kingdom, Coal Industry Nationalization Act 1946, section 1(1).
4. Canadian Privy Council Officer. 1977. *Crown Corporations: Direction, Control, Accountability*. Ottawa: Supply and Services. Cat. no. CP 32-29/1977.
5. See Kendall, W. 1972. Labour relations. In Holland, S. (Ed.) *The State as Entrepreneur*. London: Weidenfeld and Nicolson.

6. Shonfield, A. 1965. *Modern Capitalism*. London: Oxford University Press, p. 185.
7. Phatak, A. 1969. Governmental interference and management problems of public sector firms. *Annals of Public and Co-operative Economy,* 40(3) (July-September).
8. For a comparable analysis, see Pfeffer, J. & Sallancik, G. R. 1978. *The External Control of Organizations*. New York: Harper and Row.

https://doi.org/10.1142/9789811287510_0013

Chapter 13

Performance Evaluation of State-Owned Enterprises: A Process Perspective*,†

Yair Aharoni

Tel Aviv University, Tel Aviv, Israel

State-Owned Enterprises (SOEs) have become important instruments of social and economic policy in industrialized mixed economies and in developing countries. The use of SOEs as instruments of public policy and the resulting clashes between these enterprises and private firms on the one hand and government and other controllers on the other, are causing concern. Public committees in different countries as well as international organizations have been searching for positive theory for guidance in handling the multitude of problems related to these enterprises. Theoretical models have made important contributions to the formalization of certain problems and the classification of the information needed to solve them. Unfortunately, these theoretical models have had little relevance for the solution of important real problems.

Much of the research on SOEs is concerned with how these enterprises *should* behave, and what should be the product of their operations. Almost no research has been done on why SOEs function as they do. The paucity of knowledge about the operation of SOEs stems both from

*This chapter is reproduced from *Management Science*, Vol. 27, No. 11 (1981).

†All Notes are refereed. Accepted by Arie Y. Lewin; received September 21, 1979. This Note has been with the author 7 months for 2 revisions.

insufficient research effort, and from the concern of researchers with formal structures and products of these organizations and not with management behavior or with decision processes.

The purpose of this paper is to call for research beyond the confines of traditional economics, using the tools of management science to obtain insights into the difficult but salient problems of SOEs.

Keywords: State-owned enterprises; performance evaluation; social control.

Introduction

The share of mixed economies in both developed and developing countries controlled by state-owned enterprises (SOEs) has been on the rise since the thirties and has been accelerating since the end of World War II. In the early 1960s, it appeared that the share of SOEs is declining, at least in Europe. After the energy crisis, however, more enterprises were added to the state-owned list. Today, SOEs account for half or more of total government investment, and in 1978 the international borrowings alone of public sector enterprises amounted to over 30 billion dollars, equal to the total foreign borrowings by central government in that year (*The Economist,* December 30, 1978: p. 41). As international exporters and investors, state-owned enterprises are helping to shape the emerging structure of trade and payments relations in the 1980's. Their presence outside their traditional domain of public utilities and fiscal monopolies is being felt especially in natural resource-based and high technology industries with high barriers to entry, in which private multinational firms have heretofore taken the lead. They are moving into a dominating position in the natural resources field, controlling over 70% of the world oil production, two thirds of non OECD copper output, one third of iron ore and bauxite, etc. As a consequence of government attempts to save declining industries SOEs have begun to increase their importance in senescent industries such as textiles, shipbuilding, steel and auto manufacturing (Keyser & Windle, 1978).

The reasons for establishing public enterprises are varied, ranging from political ideology to the political necessity of saving jobs. Some reasons are peculiar to a certain country. Still all publicly owned enterprises appear to encounter certain common problems. SOEs must meet two apparently contradictory objectives. Being publicly owned, they are expected to pursue various activities in the public interest and at the same time achieve economic goals and generate cash flows in excess of their cash outflows. They have to reconcile business requirements of financial flexibility and prompt reaction to a changing environment with the need to assure public accountability and consistency with social goals, which in many cases, are not prescribed at all. They are also accused of being unfair competitors to private firms, both within the national economy and in the international arena. Indeed, while the State is expected to be an objective and neutral arbiter, the very ownership of enterprises implies that it has partners, competitors and adversaries.

The use of SOEs as instruments of public policy and the resulting clashes between these enterprises and private firms on the one hand and government and other controllers on the other, are causing concern. Public committees in different countries as well as international organizations have been searching for positive theory for guidance in handling the multitude of problems related to these enterprises. Theoretical models have made important contributions to the formalization of certain problems and the classification of the information needed to solve them. Unfortunately, these theoretical models have had little relevance for the solution of important real problems.

Much of the research on SOEs is concerned with how these enterprises *should* behave, and what should be the product of their operations. Almost no research has been done on why SOEs function as they do.[a] The paucity of knowledge about the operation of SOEs stems both from insufficient research effort, and from the concern of researchers with formal structures and products of these organizations and not with management behavior or with decision processes.

The purpose of this paper is to call for research beyond the confines of traditional economics, using the tools of management science to obtain insights into the difficult but salient problems of SOEs.

Multiplicity of Goals and of Principals

Some of the more difficult problems involve the multiplicity of goals and understanding the goal formation process in SOEs. Objectives specify resource utilization and the desired output of an organization at some future time. If objectives are clearly stated, agreed upon and are

[a]For some exceptions see Aharoni (1979), Anastassopolous (1980), Ferrario (1978), and Mazzolini (1979).

quantified, it is possible to evaluate the effectiveness of the enterprise. Normative models for evaluating performance of SOEs have served to define the problem of measuring effectiveness in terms of the required information (Jones & Sakong, 1976; Shepherd, 1978; Turvey, 1971). In the case of SOEs the problems encountered in implementing proposed normative solutions to goal formulation and performance evaluation are complicated not only by problems common to all organizations: uncertainty, high costs of information, (or its unavailability at any price) and difficulties in allocating limited time of executives. In addition to these well-known problems, "the state" is not a person, not even a single organization. The various elected and appointed public officials often perceive the public interest differently. Thus the SOE finds itself contending with conflicting instructions without a clear set of tradeoffs. This problem is further aggravated in countries governed by political coalitions dependent on ambiguity for its survival. Research on SOEs has to consider the problems of multiple goals together with that of multiple principals who attempt to prescribe goals. Indeed devising policies for guiding SOEs and exercising social control over them represent extraordinary difficult problems in an environment suffused with political uncertainty and where rigorous normative criteria become impossible to apply.

Managerial or behavioral theories as developed by Baumol (1959), Simon (1959, 1979), Cyert & March (1963), Marris (1964), or Williamson (1964) provide frameworks for analyzing the firm in terms of multiple goals, decision making processes, relation to the environment etc. In these theories, however, social structures are taken as given. Managers of SOEs, when faced with conflicting direction, become part of the political conflict and bargaining and power relations become important variables. In such a situation the organization resorts to quasi-resolution of conflicts, broad rather than specific definition of problems, or uses logrolling. Open confrontation is avoided although such a confrontation may be needed to solve the conflict and evolve exact guidelines for the enterprise. As a result, managers of SOEs often resort to cooperative strategies for securing social and political support (Zif, 1981).

In a competitive market system, firms are assumed to be dependent only on the market. The only way they can react to the environment is through internal efficiency and the production of useful goods and services to consumers. SOEs clearly do not operate in a neoclassical competitive world. Instead, they are usually large firms in a dominant sector of the economy. Management of these firms have discretion in the choice of strategies, product lines, organizational forms and policies. However, variables such as choice of the domain of activities, technology or physical location are often dictated by government.

Fama (1979), following Jensen & Meckling (1976), views the firm as a "set of contracts" among factors of production, with each factor motivated by its own self interest. In Fama's formulation, separate markets exist for residual risk bearing, for managers and for directors. The discipline imposed by a labor market for managers separate from the one for residual risk bearing, may be sufficient to allow performance evaluation even if ownership is separate from control. Given a competitive labor market for managers, a firm will lose managers if its system is not sensitive to performance and the best are the first to leave.

The construction of an incentive contract to link managers' reward to the achievement of known objectives can theoretically be dealt with in terms of the principal-agent theory. Bergson (1959) proposes such a solution. The theory implicitly assumes that the principal is well-defined and his objectives are clear and well articulated. However, the "agency costs" cannot be conceptually defined in SOEs because the principal is not identifiable. Thus, a contract linking managers' rewards to the achievement of known objectives is unrealistic. SOEs are not usually evaluated by the capital markets. Most SOEs' shares are not traded in the market and their managers often are selected by criteria different from those for selecting private enterprise managers. The measurement of managerial performance in SOEs is much more difficult. As long as the labor market for managers does not operate efficiently, ambitious SOE managers may be able to achieve more discretion than private sector managers. Managers with low tolerance for ambiguity prefer jobs that are highly formulated (Crozier, 1964). Less ambitious managers, faced with conflicting goals and restrictions, may simply choose to defer to governmental constraints. In extreme cases, managers may develop what Phatac (1969) called the "don't rock the boat syndrome", avoiding changes that may alienate any powerful group. Thus redundant workers are not dismissed, erring staff are not disciplined, obsolete plants continue to operate and necessary organizational changes are not made.

Separating Social, Political and Economic Goals

Governments in some countries have attempted to solve such problems by separating economic from social goals, by compensating the enterprise for the economic losses incurred in the pursuit of government mandated social objectives. The NORA Committee in France (1967) recommended that government should give its SOEs more autonomy on matters of tactics and operations and provide them better direction on select strategic issues. It further recommended that French SOEs should be run as commercial enterprises and be financially compensated for any social burdens that may be placed on them by government. In Britain several white papers and reports stressed the need for allowing the nationalized industries to pursue basic economic objectives. In addition investment criteria and financial objectives were imposed as principal devices of economic control of nationalized industries (National Economic Development Office, 1976; White Paper, 1961; Gran Bretagna, 1967; Great Britain Treasury, 1978). In Israel a public committee which proposed the state-owned corporation law stressed that these corporations should be autonomous, managed by their managers and overseen by a board of directors who serve as trustees of the corporation and not as representatives of the government (Hebrew University of Jerusalem, 1970). The proposal also recognized the need to set goals for SOEs congruent with the national interest.

In Sweden the Riksdäg (Swedish parliament) established a single state holding company, the Statsföretag, which would be responsible for most state-owned companies (Statforetag). Statsföretag was set up to emphasize the distinction between general economic policies pursued by government departments and the responsibility of the state in its position as owner of the state joint stock companies. Similar ideas were suggested in Canada (Privy Council Office, 1977).

The concept of separating economic goals from social and political goals has several advantages. Costs of social policies are properly recorded, such policies become available for public scrutiny, the national interest is determined through the public policy process and the management of SOEs have knowledge of the criteria used to judge their stewardship. In actual practice, the dividing line between social and economic goals is not easy to draw, and it is extremely difficult to calculate social costs. When exogenous economic conditions change, the SOE finds that it must renegotiate its agreement with the government. Further, managerial behavior may be influenced by the perception that, in the final analysis, the firm will not be allowed to default. Moreover, when government is composed of an uneasy coalition of disparate elements it is likely to avoid any explicit direction of SOEs and resort to informal influence attempts.

It is clear that the research needs to focus on the relationship between management, directors, government officials and the legislative body. Such research should attempt to answer two broad questions: (1) what are the variables explaining differences in behavior among SOEs?, (2) what adaptations in institutional arrangements, decision rules, organization design and other parameters can improve the performance of these enterprises?

Research on Social Control

Organizations, whose goals cannot be connected operationally with actions, often judge decisions against subgoals that can be so connected. When a problem arises, organizations tend to search for satisfactory solution to the problem as they perceive it. Under these conditions, well articulated in the writings of Simon (1959, 1979) and others, a theory that purports to describe the real world must be able to model the internal processes of the organization. Further, responses to environmental events and pressures depend on the specific decision process that the firm employs. The decision process, in turn, is stipulated to be, at least partially, a function of institutional and legal arrangements that prescribe the roles of the various participants. Therefore research on processes seems more promising than concentrating on the product of the decisions and the ideal measure of performance. The problems perceived by decision makers, the alternatives they weigh, and the consequences they foresee, all depend to a large degree on the social system within which they operate, and on the definition of their role and are not defined once and for all. As Stafford Beer (1959) has stated, normal human behavior consists of what he terms "ubiquitous feedback" or continual referral to problems that led to these results. This produces a continuing series of checks that often lead to a redefinition of the problem.

To consider the decision maker as sitting in an ivory tower, devoting all his time, energy and thought to a deliberate, orderly process of planning and search is a very misleading notion. People in organizations act continuously, making many choices under pressure of time, and unable to respond to every stimulus. The forces leading somebody in the organization to focus attention on certain problems are, therefore, of crucial importance. To the extent that these hypotheses are correct, the outcome of any decision process can be partially controlled by a different design of the roles of different actors. In the specific case of SOEs, changes in the design of the social control system are a possible avenue for changing managerial behavior.

The following are some illustrative ideas involving re-design of the social control system. Managers of SOEs usually attempt to maintain discretionary control over funds generated by operations within the enterprise as a means for maintaining autonomy. Therefore they will tend to accumulate such funds and minimize dividend payout. To allow the government to overrule the board of directors and increase the dividends paid by a wholly owned SOE; the statutes in most countries would have to be changed.

Changes in institutional arrangements can also be effective in influencing the decision making process itself by specifying the participants in the process. Thus, the decisions of state-owned enterprise might differ depending on whether the directors of the enterprise are civil servants of independently elected businessmen. Prescription of what information must be generated by the enterprise before specific decisions can be made can also influence the outcome of decisions. For example, the enterprise might be required to present detailed budgets as a prerequisite for approval of financial or operating plans.

The institution of a third party comprehensive audit as a necessary part of a social control system may clarify possible tradeoffs among objectives. Comprehensive management audits are not restricted to financial transactions. They involve an extended examination and appraisal of the propriety of objectives and of the methods used; the effectiveness of the enterprise in stating objectives and in attaining them, and finally, the efficiency of performance, as measured by the benefits received and the resources utilized. Such audits have been tried by different state auditing organs such as the General Accounting Office in the United States, the Cour des Comptes in France, the Auditor General in Canada and the State Controller in Israel.

Compulsory comprehensive audit of a state-owned enterprise cannot create agreed objectives, but they aid in determining the propriety of objectives actually pursued, recognizing that the perspective of a third party auditor is not necessarily the right one. The audit, however, can result in public disclosure and debate of the actual goals of the enterprise. Independent auditors are also important in making other agents of the state accountable for goals they attempt to pursue.

To be sure, institutionalizing comprehensive audits has some disadvantages. It is costly and diverts managers attention from managing the enterprise. In addition. SOEs may be reluctant to reveal commercial information, since full disclosure places them at a comparative disadvantage *vis* a *vis* their private counterparts. At the same time, the potential of an audit creates an audit anticipation effect (Churchill, 1962) possibly forestalling the pursuit of objectives that management (or the government) perceive to be improper. To be sure, in a parliamentary regime, comprehensive audits may be less effective since the government in power also controls the parliament. In general, comprehensive auditing will be less effective where democratic institutions are less powerful and less diffused, and where checks and balances in the political systems are not adhered to.

Allowing the registration and trading of SOE shares in a capital market, by distributing shares to taxpayers presents another means for achieving social control. If shares of SOEs were to be traded, individuals could optimize the allocation of their risk. SOE risks would be shared by all taxpayers, who maintain a portfolio of securities according to their risk preferences. In addition, capital market trading may increase both accountability and efficiency and reduce the tendency to use SOEs for illegitimate political gains. On the other hand, there might be an undesirable distribution effect (e.g., foreign entrepreneurs may buy the majority of the shares, or the rich might be able to gain control of the firm). Some insights into the problem could be gained from a comparative research of SOE behavior in countries where shares of these enterprises are actively traded, as in the Federal Republic of Germany, with countries where such trading is not permitted. The management of relations between SOEs and government is only one side of the problem. Another is the relationships between state-owned and investor-owned firms. In a mixed economy, the taxpayer expects vigilance on the use of public funds. At the same time, SOEs compete with private enterprises in the capital markets for investment funds and elsewhere for other inputs (e.g., government contracts). Therefore, the complex ways by which public largesse are granted directly or indirectly as well as their uses must be made transparent, enabling public inspection.

Conclusion

There are many difficulties in establishing the "proper" relationships between SOEs, other organs of the state and private enterprises.

The problem of setting goals for SOEs remains largely unresolved. As long as we do not have a theory of the state, as long as we do not know what are the legitimate objectives and tradeoffs, there is no way to arrive at a normative answer as to whether the performance of certain enterprise is "socially desirable".

The complex relationships between the SOE and its environment cannot be solved by an "optimal contract", since the optimality characteristics are ill-defined. Different agents of the state, including the managers of the enterprises and their controllers as well as other constituents, negotiate continually on goals. Even if the problem of goal reconciliation could be solved, there are difficulties in monitoring behavior, controlling the ongoing relationships between SOEs management and other agents of the state and the degree of discrimination between SOEs and private enterprises. In real life situations, it is impossible to foresee in advance all the decisions to be faced. In a world of uncertainty many situations arise in which judgment must be used. Should the enterprise sign a long term contract with a supplier? Should the arms industry of a country A sell tanks to country B? Should a subsidiary be established in a foreign country? In all these cases, the decision making process can be influenced, even though the outcomes are not dictated.

A better understanding of the decision making processes can lead to the design of different processes contingent upon the type of decision to be reached or the type of enterprise in which the decision is being made. A modification of behavior and performance can be achieved by prescribing changes in: (1) the structure in which the activities take place; (2) the participants in the process, their role and their power to veto decisions; (3) the types of information participants should receive before a decision is made; (4) the interactions among various participants.

The degree to which decision processes can be changed depends on the political structure and its ability to adapt itself. It is hoped that the theoretical problems related to SOEs will be explored by more researchers, interested in questions of organization design.[b]

---

[b]A draft of this paper was written while the author was Thomas Henry Carroll-Ford Foundation Visiting Professor of Business Administration, at the Harvard Business School.

The help and encouragement of Arie Y. Lewin and the comments of anonymous reviewers is gratefully acknowledged.

References

Aharoni, Y. 1979. *State Owned Enterprises in Israel and Abroad.* Tel Aviv: Gomeh (Hebrew).

Aharoni, Y. 1981. Managerial discretion in state-owned enterprises. In Aharoni, Y. & Vernon, R. (Eds.) *State-Owned Enterprises in Western Economies*. London: Croom Helm.

Anastassopolous, J. 1980. *La Strategic des Entreprises Publiques*. Paris: Dalluz.

Beer, S. 1959. *Cybernetics and Management.* New York: Wiley.

Baumol, W. 1959. *Business Behavior, Value and Growth.* New York: Macmillan.

Bergson, A. 1978. Managerial risks and rewards in public enterprises. *Journal of Comparative Economics*, 2: 211–225.

Churchill, N. 1962. The effects of an audit. Doctoral dissertation. University of Michigan. A summary of the relevant material is available in Churchill, N. C. & Cooper, W. W. 1964. Effects of auditing records. In Cooper, W. W., Leavitt, H. J. & Shelley, M. W. (Eds.) *New Perspective in Organizational Research.* New York: Wiley, pp. 250–275.

Crozier, M. 1964. *The Bureaucratic Phenomenon.* Chicago, IL: University of Chicago Press.

Cyert, R. & March, J. 1963. *A Behavioral Theory of the Firm*. Englewood Cliffs, NJ: Prentice-Hall.

Fama, E. (1979). Agency Problems and the Theory of the Firm. Working Paper No. CRSP WP 20, Center for Research in Security Prices, Graduate School of Business. University of Chicago, July 1979.

Ferrario, F. 1978. Strategic Management in State Enterprises. Unpublished doctoral thesis. Harvard Business School.

Groupe de Travail du Comtté Interministeriel des Enterprises Publiques, Simon Nova, Chairman. 1967. *Rapport sur les Enterprises Publiques*, La Documentation Française. Paris, April 1967.

Hebrew University of Jerusalem, Institute for Legislative Research and Comparative Law. 1970. *Report of the Committee for the Preparation of a Government Corporation Bill.*

Jensen, M. & Meckling, W. 1976. Theory of the firm: Managerial behavior, agency costs and ownership structure. *Journal of Financial Economics*, 3: 305–330.

Jones, L. P. & Sakong, II. 1976. *A Social Accounting Development for Public Enterprises.* Seoul: Korea Development Institute Working Paper.

Keyser, W. & Windle, R. (Eds.). 1978. *Public Enterprise in the EEC*, 7 Vols. Sitjthoff and Noordkoff.

Marris, R. 1964. *The Economic Theory of Managerial Capitalism.* New York: Free Press of Glencoe.

Mazzolini, R. 1979. *Government Controlled Enterprise.* London: Wiley.

National Economic Development Office. 1976. *A Study of U.K. Nationalized Industries.* London: H. M. Stationery Office.

Phatak, A. 1969. Governmental interference and management problems of public sector firms. *Annals of Public and Cooperative Economics*, 40(3), 337–350.

Privy Council Office. 1977. *Crown Corporations, Direction-Control-Accountability, Government of Canada Proposals.* Ottawa: Privy Council Office.

Shepherd, W. G. 1978. *Public Enterprise: Economic Analysis of Theory and Practice.* Lexington, MA: Lexington Books.

Simon, H. 1959. Theories of decision making in economics and behavioral science. *American Economic Review*, 49: 253–288.

Simon, H. A. 1979. Rational decision making in business organizations. *American Economic Review*, 69: 495–513.

Statforetag, A. B. *Policy for the Statsforetag Group.*

Turvey, R. 1971. *Economic Analysis and Public Enterprise.* George Allen and Unwin: London.

White Paper. 1961. The Financial and Economic Obligations of the Nationalized Industries, Cmnd. 1337. H. H. Stationary Office, April 1961.

Gran Bretagna. 1967. Nationalized Industries: A Review of Economic and Financial Objectives, Cmnd. 3437, H. M. Stationary Office, November 1967.

Great Britain Treasury, The Nationalized Industries, Cmnd. 7131, March, 1978.

Williamson, O. E. 1964. *The Economics of Discretionary Behavior: Management Objectives in a Theory of a Firm.* Englewood Cliffs, NJ: Prentice-Hall.

https://doi.org/10.1142/9789811287510_0014

Chapter 14

State-Owned Enterprise: An Agent Without a Principal*

Yair Aharoni†

Tel Aviv University, Tel Aviv, Israel

State-owned enterprises (SOEs) comprise a large and rapidly growing sector of the economy in the majority of countries in the world today. They have been established to achieve a broad array of public policy purposes in very diverse political and economic systems. Typically, they account for half or more of total government investment, and in 1978 the international borrowings alone of public-sector enterprises amounted to more than $30 billion, equal to the total foreign borrowings by central governments in the past year.[1] As international exporters, importers, and investors, SOEs are helping to shape the emerging structure of trade and payments relations in the 1980s. Their presence outside their traditional domain of public utilities is being felt especially in natural-resource-based and modem high-technology industries with high barriers to entry, in which private multinational firms have heretofore taken the lead. They are moving into a dominating position also in senescent industries such as

*This chapter is reproduced from *Public Enterprise in Less Developed Countries*, pp. 67–76 (1982). Cambridge University Press.

†The help of Ravi Ramamurti, my research assistant at the Harvard Graduate School of Business Administration, and that of anonymous reviewers is gratefully acknowledged.

textiles, shipbuilding, and steel, where the government moved in to save present firms from going under.

Yet despite the proliferation of SOEs since World War II, we actually know very little about the way they are managed. One reason for this lack of knowledge may be the tendency of economic theory to assume a perfect-market economy, in which firms passively transfer inputs procured in a perfect market into output sold in similar markets. Until recently, little attention has been paid to the problems and cost involved in managing an enterprise. By the same token, early socialist theoreticians saw the nationalization of production facilities as a way to achieve some equity and reduce "exploitation". They, too, however, did not pay much attention to the problem of managing the enterprises once nationalized. Rather they assumed — naively as it turned out — that "society will be transformed into a huge organization for cooperative production" in which everyone will work in accordance with the national plan.[2]

In the real world, firms do not operate in a neoclassical competitive environment. Rather, they have certain size and are managed hierarchically; the managers operate under uncertainty, and the information collected is costly.

Uncertainty cannot be fully eliminated by the use of contingency contracts. Under these conditions, the management of the firm has discretion in the choice of strategies, product lines, organizational forms, and policies. They are guided not by an internalized need to achieve a prescribed plan but by other motivations. Thus, managers may use their discretion to expand their staff or to achieve slack or on-the-job leisure.[3] One cannot assume that all decision makers in the economy are working together to achieve identical goals. Therefore, the relationships between managers and the state officials controlling them, as well as the negative and positive incentives to managers, are of crucial importance.

One way to look at the relationships between managers and owners of firms is in the terms of the principal-agent theory. An agency relationship exists when one party (the agent) acts on behalf of another (the principal). The two parties have unequal interests but may have an incentive to cooperate. Contractual arrangements are sought that will induce an agent to behave as if he was maximizing the welfare of the principal. Most analyses of agency relationships assume that the agent can choose a line of action that, together with exogenous events, determines the payoff. The principal is assumed to be unable to change the payoff.

The relationships between owners and managers of business firms are examples of agency relationships. Managers are contracted to act on behalf of (private or public) shareholders. However, as in all agency relationships, the manager is assumed to act to maximize his own interests. Therefore, a "perfect" contract would structure the manager's incentives to correspond exactly to those of the shareholders. In real life situations, no contract is expected to meet this standard, and agency costs are more than the costs specified in the contract.

What are these additional costs? First, there are certain costs of detecting decisions incongruent with the shareholders' interests. The higher the costs of monitoring managers' behavior, the larger their discretion. In real life, monitoring costs are high because the principal (shareholder) does not have an independent source of information. In addition, under uncertainty, optimal decision making depends on the risk preferences of managers and shareholders, which may not be identical. Moreover, to avoid replacement costs, shareholders may allow managers a certain amount of discretion.[4]

All these types of agency costs — distinct managers' interests, monitoring and detection costs, replacement costs — as well as such environmental variables as uncertainty about strategy, are likely to apply to SOEs. However, the agency costs cannot be conceptually defined in SOEs because the principal is not identifiable. The notion that the government or the minister is the principal and that the enterprise is the agent is misleading. Rather, the populace as a whole is the principal, with a variety of agents acting on its behalf. These agents include various government ministers, members of parliament, managers of firms, and so on. All these agents are in fact a coalition — a group working together who share *some,* but not all, goals. SOE shares are not traded in the market, and the populace does not have an effective voice in their direction and control. As state ownership does not necessarily imply social ownership, the mechanism of goal formulation is an important one. A case can be made that SOE management has as legitimate a claim to the participation in the goal formulation on behalf of the principal as do the other agents. The multiple and often ill-defined objectives make performance measurement almost impossible. As a result, the market may police SOE managers much less than in the case of private enterprise.

These problems of social ownership are developed in sections "Shareholders without Shares" and "Legitimacy of Goals and Strategies". In section "Comprehensive Audit", an independent of multiple legitimate claimants to the goal-specification function.

Shareholders without Shares

Private firms are owned by individuals who may buy or sell ownership rights at some price. SOEs are ultimately owned by all citizens of a country and are financed from the general pool of funds mobilized by the government through taxes or other means. However, the SOE "shareholders" do not hold any shares that can be traded in the market, and no market mechanism allows them to signal their views on the performance of the enterprise, nor can they take part in a proxy fight for a take-over bid. Therefore, the citizens of the country do not have even the minimal influence enjoyed by shareholders of a modem corporation.

The state is not a person, not even a single organization. It acts through a variety of ministers, legislators, and civil servants, who are themselves agents of the general public. These different agents invariably see their mission as different from one another. Thus, different objectives are sought by different government ministries, and interorganizational conflicts are normal phenomena. These conflicts affect the process of SOE goal specifications. A government official concerned with foreign affairs may see the reduction of the state's dependence on imported technology as a prime goal and therefore seek an increase in the SOE research and development budget. The minister of labor may see the state's role as maximizing employment and thus favor more labor-intensive procedures for the SOE. The finance minister, viewing himself as "the shareholder", may want the firm to pay higher dividends. Yet another minister, whose agency buys the firm's output, may seek to reduce its prices. These competing representatives cannot be considered *the* principal of the firm whose interests are well defined. Consequently, no "perfect" contract can structure managers' incentives so that their interests will match the principal's goals. These goals are rarely, if ever, stated explicitly and tradeoffs among them are not agreed. Thus, different agents give the enterprise conflicting, parallel commands, which turn SOEs into hybrids, expected to achieve both traditional economic goals in the marketplace and all sorts of social goals: help for the poor, increased employment, a redistribution of income, development of laggard regions, and so on. They are also expected to achieve political goals such as the avoidance of perceived domination by foreign multinationals, developing of new technologies, and enhancement of the glory of the state. Several agents seek to resolve the ambiguity of goals in ways that suit them best. Goal conflicts among state agents are sometimes "solved" by formally assigning two or more of these objectives to an SOE. At other times, conflicting commands are faced by SOEs because several external agents of society, rightly or wrongly, view SOEs as legitimate tools for achieving overall national goals. Thus, the principal (the populace) is represented by a loose coalition of agents: sponsoring minister, the treasury, the civil servants, other ministers, and the parliament. Their decisions are influenced by all sorts of interest groups — consumers, labor unions, and others — all of which claim at least some right to participate in the process of goal formulation. Even in countries with a decentralized framework of control, there is a continuous flow of ex ante intervention in various decisions.

Can the principal be assumed to be a collective term for a coalition of ministers, interest groups, civil servants, trade unions, and parliament members? Even such an assumption does not seem to hold, as SOE managers often try to influence the process of goal specification, resist the imposition of certain goals in many different ways, and claim the right to participate in the formulation of goals.

Legitimacy of Goals and Strategies

There are three major explanations for the ability of SOE managers to resist certain goals imposed on them by various government agencies. The first is the difference between managers' self-interest and that of other state agents. This is by now a well-theorized phenomenon in both large diffused ownership corporations and SOEs. The notion that professional managers single-mindedly operate the firm to maximize profits has long been rejected. It was replaced by "behavioral" or "managerial" theories.[5] This difference in self-interests is also at the root of the agent — principal problem and the view of the firm as a set of contracts.[6]

Second, SOE managers can afford to resist certain goals because it is difficult to measure their performance. In a private firm, managerial performance is scrutinized by the board of directors, which in turn is viewed as a market-induced institution. In an SOE, managerial performance cannot be gauged, because of the many conflicting and ill-defined objectives. Moreover, in many countries, the control structure is not clearly defined, and the board cannot discipline or replace a manager, at least not without a lengthy negotiation with a sponsoring minister and other agents. Therefore, although a market for the services of managers does exist,[7] and although managers might be dismissed, the policing of managers is much more difficult. In such a situation, ambitious managers may be able to achieve more discretion than private-sector managers. Less ambitious managers faced with conflicting goals and restrictions, may simply choose to defer to governmental constraints. In extreme cases, managers may develop what Phatak called the "don't rock the boat syndrome".[8] With this approach, managers avoid changes that may alienate any powerful groups: Redundant workers are not dismissed, erring staff are not disciplined, no obsolete plant is closed, and no organizational changes are made. In short, managers simply develop apathy.

Third and most important, managers consider themselves to be the trustees of the "real" interest of the state at least as much as the government employees. Managers sometimes bring to their job the same set of values and ideologies that belong to the rest of the business world. As they see it, the intervention of various government ministries to achieve non-economic goals is an encroachment on their prerogatives as the trustees of the economic interests of the firm. SOE managers would probably argue that if the government, for social reasons, wants an enterprise to deviate from its economic mission, it should compensate it for the economic losses incurred. Such a point of view has been presented independently by public committees on SOEs in different countries.[9]

Managers of large corporations accept the legitimacy of the shareholders' interests, although they may not always actually pursue those interests. SOE managers may question the legitimacy of demands from government, not only because they try to maximize their own utility but because they perceive the "real" goals of the amorphous principal — the state — to be different. Further, many of them maintain that operational efficiency requires that decisions on objectives and strategy be made within the enterprise itself. In here lies the major difference between SOEs and large private corporations with diffused ownership. SOE management feels it has as legitimate a claim to goal specification as other agents. The government may require the SOE to avoid price increases to combat inflation, to procure locally made and more expensive goods or to maintain the size of its labor force to secure employment, or to pursue certain objectives perceived as important in achieving a short-term political gain. In all these cases, managers may have different perceptions of the legitimate role of the enterprise. They see it as their legitimate right — even their duty to the "real" interest of the state — to try to evade the issue or even fight openly against such a request. They would thus attempt to avoid the order, get around it, or procrastinate. In certain cases, managers may even bring "their" cases before the public by leaking information to the press or by applying to the president or prime minister to appeal a sponsoring minister's decision.

In summary, the behavior of an SOE cannot be explained within the principal-agent theory. Rather, an SOE should be viewed not only as a set of contracts among factors of production but as a coalition of the managers, the board of directors, government ministers, civil servants, parliament members, and others. The principal of the property-rights theory and the classical theory of the firm does not exist. Instead, there are different members of a coalition who share the belief that its survival should be maintained by the continuation of the enterprise.

The actual outcome and degree of discretion managers enjoy in their operations seem to be the result of a fight for power among the various agents of the state. Managers of SOEs seem to spend more time than their private-sector counterparts in managing the environment and aiming at co-opting the controlling agencies or assuring their allegiance. The outcome of this fight for power, that is, the actual strategic choices made, can be predicted only in terms of contingency theory. Although it is beyond the scope of this chapter to propose such a contingency theory, a few examples may be helpful.

The ability of an SOE manager to choose the strategy he prefers and the objectives he sees as most relevant is a joint function of his personality, the legal and institutional environment in which he operates, and the time and expertise of those monitoring him. In general, experience shows that the bigger the firm is, the more independent it is of the government (by generating its own funds), the more technical the information needed to operate the enterprise, and the more expertise concentrated in management at the firm level, the more management can dictate goals. In addition, management enjoys more discretion in its strategic choices when it operates internationally (by being at least partially outside the domain of government control), has a large number of customers and product lines, has a greater freedom to choose its customers, product lines, and suppliers. Finally, the degree of goal congruency is a crucial variable. The more legitimate are the demands of government agencies in the eyes of the manager, the more he will abide by them. I have discussed these points extensively in another publication.[10] Here it is enough to note that the real problem is to define the legitimate role of different state organs and the dimensions of social controls. In practice, these dimensions are ill defined, and conflicts on goals constantly occur.

Even in the rare case in which goals are explicitly stated, they eventually are modified in the daily operations of the enterprise through numerous managerial decisions once the enterprise is established. The lack of performance measurement makes it difficult to monitor these changes. In addition, actual monitoring systems used by different government controllers often lead to distortion.

The complex relationships between the SOE and its environment cannot be solved by an "optimal contract", because the optimality characteristics are ill defined. Different agents of the state, including the managers of the enterprise and their controllers as well as other constituents, look for ways to reach some quasi resolution of conflicts, often by ill-defining the objectives of the enterprise or by official requirements to achieve multiple and conflicting goals.

Lack of agreement on goals seems to be at the root of many difficulties pointed out by studies of SOEs. In the public-administration literature, the problem is referred to as "the accountability vs. autonomy" issue: SOEs are said to need "enough" autonomy to run their business operations without having to face the rigid difficulties inherent in the bureaucratic structure of government. At the same time, it is felt that an SOE should be accountable to government and parliament, and the latter should dictate its goals. Yet, the balance between "autonomy" and "accountability" has never been satisfactorily struck. The preceding analysis shows that this is no accident. The way the coalition of forces is structured bars the definition of precise goals. Even in less complex situations, as pointed out by Cyert and March, a quasi resolution of conflicts is a way of life.[11] However, even though conflicts cannot always be solved, they can be brought into the open to force decision makers to be confronted with several concrete choices. As there is no one principal but several tiers of agents, these agents can be forced to argue on choices to be made — and therefore implicitly on the goals — if independent "goal audit" is introduced, embodied in a broader comprehensive audit, as an integral part of the institutional design. Note that because goals are formulated as a result of interaction in a coalition, different institutional designs may change membership in the coalition and the relative power of different coalition members.

Comprehensive Audit

The term *comprehensive audit* is used here in the sense suggested by Churchill and Cooper.[12] In comprehensive audit, the process of objective appraisal is extended to all aspects of management. The auditor is not necessarily a CPA, nor does he stop at the accounting attest function. Comprehensive audits are not restricted to financial transaction: They are extended to an examination and appraisal of the propriety of the objectives pursued and the methods used, effectiveness in stating objectives and in attaining them, and finally, the efficiency of performance as measured by the benefits received and the resources utilized.

Comprehensive auditing is done by a third party — someone whose interests are not identical with those who are audited or with the government ministry sponsoring the enterprise. The auditors are also agents who may have their own views about the "proper" objectives to be pursued. Also, the development of a comprehensive, audit scheme requires a considerable amount of skill. However, comprehensive audit is a major step in assuring that SOEs are accountable along socially relevant dimensions. In doing so, questions of goals pursued and the "right" objectives are put on the agenda of a public debate once the results of the audit are published.

Comprehensive audits have been tried by different state auditing organs — the General Accounting Office in the United States, the Cour des Comptes in France, the Auditor General in Canada, and the State Controller in Israel are some examples. In all these cases, it seems that such an audit helps to alleviate the lack of a principal. The audits by themselves, of course, cannot create agreed objectives. Different individuals continue to hold different points of view about the propriety of the objectives pursued, but the publication of comprehensive reports brings the conflict to the surface. It also helps in discussing the propriety of objectives actually pursued. This is an important development in an area where agreement on objectives is difficult to obtain and their achievement difficult to control. Needless to say, the impact of the report is largely a result of its general availability to the public. A report presented to management, and to it alone, will not have such an impact.

It might be noted that the existence of the audit creates an audit-anticipation effect.[13] Objectives that management, or the government, feels are improper in the eyes of the public will not be pursued in the first place. The very anticipation of an audit changes the behavior of those that expect to be audited.

To be sure, the institutional mechanism of comprehensive audit is not free of side effects: It costs money and requires managers to divert their energies from managing the enterprise to answering requests for audit.

In addition, SOEs may be reluctant to reveal commercial information, as full disclosure puts them in a position of comparative disadvantage by allowing them less commercial secrecy than their private counterparts. Finally, in a parliamentary regime, as the government controls the parliament, state comprehensive audits may be less effective than one might wish. For that matter, state comprehensive auditing may be even less effective in regimes where democratic institutions are less powerful and less diffused, and where checks and balances in the political systems are not adhered to. In fact, in some such regimes, the government may not allow such audit to be carried out in the first place.

A variation of a "goal audit" may be one in which the government decides on the objectives of each enterprise at the time of creation and on an internal governmental body that reports directly to the board of directors and the government as a whole rather than to a specific sponsoring ministry without publishing the results. This may result in a redefinition or clarification of goals as the avoidance of publicity may reduce the resistance of the ruling coalition to such an audit. However, it may also reduce its effectiveness, as publicity is important in deciding on SOE objectives and priorities while keeping some modicum of freedom.

Conclusions

The agency-costs theory cannot be applied directly to the measurement of the costs of managing SOEs. By the same token, Williamson's definition of discretion does not apply.[14] Both the agent-principal theory and the Williamson hypothesis about discretion assume a clear objective and an identifiable principal. Therefore, Williamson can measure the size of discretion, at least conceptually, as the difference between the maximizing of the welfare of the principal and the actual behavior of the agent plus the cost of the contract. The major problem faced by organizational designers in planning the institutional relationships between SOE management and its constituents is that they somehow have to face the issue of a precise definition of the goals of the state in the establishment and operation of the firm.

The problem of setting goals for SOEs is to a large extent insoluble. As long as we do not have a theory of the state, as long as we do not know what the legitimate objectives of such enterprises are, how they are decided, and who decides on both objectives and trade-offs, there is no way to give a normative answer to whether or not the performance of a certain enterprise is "socially desirable". Yet individuals have a feeling of what is legitimate and what seems to be in the public interest. Therefore, an independent audit of goals and objectives, at least under some conditions, may make the problem recognizable and thus partially solvable. At the very least, the decisions of management and other state agents may be subjected periodically to public scrutiny and subsequent adjustment. Without an open system of goals statement and auditing, state ownership may degenerate into a shift of power to a new managerial or bureaucratic class instead of achieving socially desirable objectives.

Notes

1. Public Sector Enterprise: A State in the Market. *The Economist,* December 30, 1978, p. 41.
2. Burkharin, N. L. & Preobrazhensky, E. 1969. *The ABC of Communism.* London: Penguin, p. 114 (English translation of 1920 Russian original).
3. Williamson, O. E. 1964. *The Economics of Discretionary Behavior: Management Objectives in a Theory of the Firm.* Englewood Cliffs, NJ: Prentice-Hall, pp. 49–52.
4. For examples of optimal literature, see Harris, M. & Raviv, A. 1978. Some results on incentive contracts. *American Economic Review*, 68 (March): 20–30; Harris, M. & Raviv, A. 1979. Optimal incentive contracts with imperfect information. *Journal of Economic Theory*, 20 (April): 231–259; Holmstrom, B. 1979. Moral hazard and observability. *Bell Journal of Economics*, 10 (Spring): 74–91; and Shavell, S. 1979. Risk sharing and incentives in the principal and agent relationship. *Bell Journal of Economics*, 10 (Spring): 55–73.
5. For a discussion of these theories, see Baumol, W. 1959. *Business Behavior: Value and Growth.* New York: Macmillan; Simon, H. 1959. Theories of decision making in economics and behavioral science. *American Economic Review*, 49 (June): 253–288; Cyert, R. & March, J. 1963. *A Behavioral Theory of the Finn.* Englewood Cliffs, NJ: Prentice-Hall; Marris, R. 1964. *The Economic Theory of Managerial Capitalism.* New York: Free Press; and Williamson (1964), *Op. cit.*
6. Two well-known examples are Alchian, A. & Demsetz, H. 1971. Production, information costs, and economic organization. *American Economic Review* 62 (December): 777–795; and Jensen, M. &

Meckling, W. 1976. Theory of the firm: Managerial behavior, agency costs and ownership structure. *Journal of Financial Economics*, 3 (October): 305–360.

7. Fama, E. 1980. Agency problems and the theory of the firm. *Journal of Political Economics*, 88 (April): 288–307.
8. Phatak, A. 1969. Governmental interference and management problems of public sector firms. *Annals of Public and Cooperative Economy*, 40 (July-September).
9. Some well-known examples are the Nora Committee report in France (*Rapport sur les entreprises publique* [Paris: La Documentation fran-gaise, April 1967]); the white paper on nationalized industries in the United Kingdom (*Nationalized Industries: A Review of Economic and Financial Objectives* [London: HMSO, 1967], Commnd. 3437); the Israeli Government Companies Law 5737–1978 (*Sefer Ho Chukkim* 770 [1978]: 163); the Statsforetag law in Sweden; and Canada's privy council report on crown corporations (*Crown Corporations: Direction, Control, Accountability: Government of Canada's Proposals* [Ottawa: Privy Council Office, 1977]).
10. See Aharoni, Y. 1981. Managerial discretion. In Aharoni, Y. & Vernon, R. (Eds.) *State-Owned Enterprise in the Western Economies.* London: Croom Helm, pp. 184–193.
11. Cyert & March, *Behavioral Theory of the Firm.*
12. Churchill, N. & Cooper, W. Comprehensive auditing. Paper Presented at Meeting of Institute of Chartered Accountants of Ontario, Ottawa, June 12, 1978.
13. See Churchill, N. 1962. The Effects of an Audit. Ph.D dissertation, University of Michigan. A summary of the relevant material is available in Cooper, W. W., Leavitt, H. J. & Shelley, M. W. (Eds.) Churchill, N. C. & Cooper, W. W. 1964. Effects of auditing records. In *New Perspectives in Organizational Research.* New York: Wiley, pp. 250–275.
14. Williamson (1964), *Op. cit.*

https://doi.org/10.1142/9789811287510_0015

Chapter 15

Can the Manager's Mind Be Nationalized?*

Yair Aharoni and Ran Lachman

Tel Aviv University, Tel Aviv, Israel

Abstract

The "raison d'être" of nationalization of enterprises is usually the achievement of national and collective goals. Adherence to such goals by the executives of the publicly owned enterprises is a key to their achievement. Yet, in many cases, the executive's adherence to public sector goals is taken for granted. This study examines the existence of expected differences in goal perceptions and attitudes among top executives of industrial enterprises affiliated with the public and private sectors in Israel. Almost no differences were found between the perceptions of these two groups of executives. The lack of differences indicates that mere affiliation with nationalized enterprises does not secure "nationalization" of the executives' goal commitments and goal pursuit, and that the achievement of the nationalization objectives may be hindered.

*This chapter is reproduced from *Organization Studies*, Vol. 3, No. 1, pp. 33–46 (1982).

Introduction

The central question addressed in this study is whether or not mere affiliation with publicly owned enterprises (POEs) is sufficient to motivate the adherence and commitment of executives to goals and objectives sought by the architects of these enterprises. This study compares the attitudes towards ultimate goals and the functional preferences of chief executives of publicly owned industrial organizations with those of their counterparts in private industrial firms.

Organizations are viewed as systems of cooperative action directed towards the pursuit of a set of common goals. These common or ultimate goals legitimize the existence of organizations. However, it is also well recognized that the people in organizations have personal goals which are not necessarily congruent with organizational goals.

Organizations may undertake the achievement of multiple goals, emanating from members of a coalition powerful enough to force the organization to attend to these goals (Cyert & March, 1963). In publicly owned enterprises executives are important members of that ruling coalition. They may or may not have a sense of personal commitment to the goals sought by the establishers of the enterprise, and may or may not be induced to achieve these goals. Thus, whether achieved through a sense of personal commitment or through organizational inducement, some degree of congruence between executives' own goals and their perception of the organizational ultimate goals, is required for the achievement of organizational goals.

In the discussion of the pros and cons of public ownership of enterprises, and the achievement of public goals through nationalization, these enterprises are usually treated as uniform organizational units, attempting to maximize the achievement of their prescribed goals. The managers who coordinate and direct the pursuit of organizational goals are either ignored or implicitly assumed to be totally committed to these organizational goals. However, organizations are not monolithic entities, and managers have a strong impact on the organizational goals actually pursued, either through their interpretations of the goals in a way that reflects their own values, needs, and beliefs, or through the formation of coalitions that influence organizational goal setting (Cyert & March, 1963; Zaleznik, 1970; Buchanan, 1974; Wamsley & Zald, 1976; Katz & Kahn, 1978; Pfeffer & Salanicik, 1978; Simon, 1979). Some authors have even found that the values of the managerial elite are better predictors of organizational goals than are the structural variables of the organization (Hage & Dewar, 1973), or have claimed that the values of the managerial elite members are actually the organizational policy (Guth & Tagiuri, 1965). Since managers' values and orientations are not unrelated to the way they manage, the adherence of the chief executives in the nationalized sector to its "raison d'être" ought not to be taken for granted. It may influence the pursuit and achievement of the objectives sought by the nationalization. Private sector ideology maintains that private firms operating in a free market economy are the most effective means for performing economic functions. For this reason profit maximization, which is the ultimate goal of these enterprises, is legitimized. On the other hand, the ideology of public ownership of business organizations justifies it as a means for pursuing national and social goals that would not have been achieved under private ownership. Publicly owned enterprises are legitimized because they supply services for which society prefers social to individual choice, or political to market allocation.

These differences in the ultimate goals and objectives set for organizations affiliated with the two sectors are assumed by many to find expression in the ways organizations are managed, in their source of capital, in their relationships with government, in the status and role of their workers vis-a-vis management (Simon, 1957; Blau & Scott, 1962; Rainey *et al.*, 1976; Wamsley & Zald, 1976; Kamens, 1977). For example, public enterprises are assumed to be more susceptible to politicization than private ones because of the nature of their relations with high authority (Walsh, 1978; Zaleznik, 1979), their exposure to public scrutiny (Bower, 1977; Nigro & Nigro, 1977); and their political or parliamentary accountability (Self, 1977). It is also argued that publicly owned enterprises are more immune to bankruptcy than private enterprises (Walters & Monsen, 1979; Vernon, 1980) or that their attitude towards risk should be different (Arrow & Lind, 1970).

Some writers, however, do not accept this view on different grounds. In their opinion, managers have their own set of operational goals; that is, management is a universal process irrespective of differences in organizational ultimate goals. For example, Levitt (1973) argues for the existence of a universal and general process of management both in public and private bureaucracies. The culture of bureaucracies, the aspiration to power, and the reactions to external pressure are the same. Murray (1975), who explores some of the comparisons made between management in the two sectors, concludes that the differences found in value systems lie more in emphasis than in substance. The public sector emphasizes political values to a higher degree than the private sector, which puts a greater emphasis on economic values. But in terms of procedural issues, there are no differences between managers of the two sectors.

As pointed out by several writers, the divergence of views and empirical findings about the existence of differences between organizations of the two sectors may be a result of unclear definitions of "the public sector" (Smith, 1975; Rainey *et al.*, 1976). In fact, various studies include different types of organizations in the category "public sector". For example, they equate public sector with governmental administrative branches or agencies and thus compare administrative organizations with competitive business firms. Variations in goals or behavior are then attributed to differences in the goal orientations of the sectors, while in fact such divergences may be explained by differences in the nature, technology, and type of product of the organizations. To avoid such comparison problems, this study is limited to organizations of the same type (manufacturing organizations only) and to executives of a similar position level (chief executive officers). Organizational size was also controlled.

The study was done in Israel which is a "mixed" economy, basically composed of three major ownership categories — the government, the Histadrut, and the private sector. The Histadrut includes the federation of trade unions, production and consumer cooperatives, collective settlements, a vast network of welfare services, and centrally owned holding companies of economic enterprises. Reference in this study is made only to the latter section, that is, the centrally owned holding companies. At the time of the study the government, the Histadrut, and the private sector constituted about 20, 20, and 60 percent, respectively, of the Israeli gross national product. As contended by its leaders, the Histadrut-controlled corporations are similar in their collectivistic and national goal orientations to the orientations of the government sector (Lavon, 1960; Daniel, 1976). Therefore, from the point of view of goal orientation, the Histadrut and the state-owned sectors can be collapsed together as a public sector with strong national and social goal orientation, as opposed to the profit and market orientation of the private sector.

Hypotheses

The basic proposition of this study is that differences in the ideology and ultimate goals of the two sectors will be reflected in the minds of the managers affiliated with the respective sectors. The proposition is examined on two levels: (a) *the attitudinal level,* which includes perceptions and behavioral preferences related to sector objectives; and (b) *the functional level,* which includes perception of relations with environment and behavior related to a national goal.

More specifically the hypotheses are:

A. Executives of the two sectors differ:
   a_1: in agreement with statements about the sectors; and
   a_2: in expressed behavioral preferences.
B. Executives of the two sectors differ in their:
   b_1: perception of the influence of environmental elements on their autonomy; and
   b_2: pursuit of a national goal.

Research Method

The study is based on a secondary analysis of data which is part of a large data set collected in Spring 1970 (Aharoni, 1970). A questionnaire which dealt with topics related to managerial functions and organizational factors was completed by trained interviewers.

This study has, of course, some weaknesses inherent in the analysis of secondary data, primarily collected for other purposes (Hyman, 1971). The main problem is the lack of control over the variables included in the data and the way they are measured. One has to design research on the basis of whatever is available. As a result, some of the measures used here are rather crude and may be insensitive to some of the fine differences in the phenomena being measured. Nevertheless, these measures seem to capture the main differences in the phenomena and yield results which though not conclusive are suggestive. The issues examined here ought to be further investigated using more precise and established measures, particularly of goal commitments and orientations.

The Sample

The study population was defined as general managers of industrial firms in Israel which in 1969 had more than 100 employees. The firm, therefore, was taken as the sampling unit and the person who was acting as the chief executive officer of the firm at the time of the study was taken as a respondent. According to the Israeli Bureau of Statistics, there were 302 industrial firms that met this criterion. The intention was to interview all the general managers of these firms, but only 141 were actually interviewed. Of the remaining 16, 138 refused to be interviewed, 14 were abroad, and 14 did not complete the questionnaire. In addition, 15 firms were found to have less than 100 employees, and 10 had been purchased by others or gone out of business. The rest could not be located (wrong names, wrong addresses, etc.) or were not included for various other reasons. The firms represent a wide range of industries from metal and chemical processing to electrical and electronic products to food and textile industries. Textile and food firms each constituted 20 percent of the sample; firms in the metal industry constituted 7 percent of the sample; the remaining industries were represented by two to five firms each. The size distribution of the firms ranged from 100 to 26,000 employees; the median was 245 employees and the mode was 160 employees.

This is not a probability sample, but since it includes about half of the sampling frame, and the proportion of public to private firms (30 percent and 70 percent, respectively) is similar to their proportions in the Israeli economy at the time of the study (40 percent and 60 percent), it can be assumed that conclusions drawn on a probability sample would not have been substantially different.

Respondents

For ten firms, from the sample of 141, there was not sufficient information about shareholding and thus they were omitted from the analysis. As a result, the group studied included 91 male executives from the private sector and 40 from the public sector. In the two groups the executives, who held similar positions in the same type of organization, were found to have approximately the same age and education: about one-third (35 percent in the public group and 34 percent in the private) were under 48-years-old and about one-third (33 percent and 35 percent, respectively) were over 55-years-old. In the two groups similar proportions of executives had more than a high-school education (40 percent in the public group and 43 percent in the private). Therefore, the two groups of executives were found to be similar not only in their organizational attributes (rank, industry, and size distribution), but also in their personal background.

Definition of Variables

Public and private sectors

Public sector was defined as those industrial firms in which either the government or the Histadrut held the majority of voting shares. The rest of the firms were classified as private sector. The grouping together of government and Histadrut enterprises into one public sector is not only ideologically but also empirically justified. No differences between the two groups were found when comparing them on relevant variables.

Perception of sector goals

Sector goals were defined as a set of directives, values, and ultimate objectives that justify the distinctive roles of any organization or, in this case, of each sector (Parsons, 1956). The executives' perception of these goals was examined by two kinds of measures: agreement with attitudinal statements, and expressed behavioral preferences in hypothetical situations. The first measure comprised nine attitudinal statements selected from a pool of items focusing on two ideological issues: public sector intervention in the free market and determination of efficiency by economic market forces. The selection was based on considerations of content and face validity of items and on their interitem reliability (Cronbach's reliability coefficient for the nine items is $\alpha = 0.77$). Responses to these statements ranged from "strong agreement" (score of 1) to "strong disagreement" (score of 4). Behavioral preferences were elicited which pertain to three legitimizing goals of the public sector: investment in developing regions of the country, increase of exports, and contribution to national goals.

Perception of managerial function

Managers' autonomy from intra- and extraorganizational pressures and influences was the main measure of the managerial function. The respondents were asked to rate both the influence and the desired influence of 13 environmental elements on their autonomy in decision making. Answers ranged from "very strong influence" (score of 1) to "no influence" (score of 15).

Results

Attitudinal level

The first hypothesis was tested using the two kinds of measures mentioned above: acceptance of statements supporting the legitimacy of the sectors or rejection of statements negating it (a_1); and expressed behavioral preferences in hypothetical situations (a_2). Hypothesis a_1 was only partially supported. Responses to the nine statements (Table 1) show that, as expected, on six of the nine statements significant differences were

Table 1. Evaluative and normative perceptions of the sectors.

Item	Sector	Group Mean	S.D.	*t*-value	d.f.	P
1. The Histadrut ought to strive to increase its share in the economy	Public	1.9	0.72	–2.47	125	0.01
	Private	2.3	0.89			
2. Public ownership of firms ought to be decreased because of, inefficiency red tape, and stagnation	Public	2.7	0.54	5.4	125	0.001
	Private	2.0	0.67			
3. Government support of business firms should be eliminated even if it will bring down many firms	Public	2.4	0.69	0.61	124	n.s.
	Private	2.35	0.71			
4. The fact that the Histadrut is an employer as well as a workers' representative creates a paradox that mutilates its role	Public	2.8	0.73	4.8	125	0.001
	Private	2.1	0.69			
5. Government intervention in capital markets is exorbitant	Public	2.6	0.54	3.6	118	0.001
	Private	2.2	0.65			
6. Without government support most of the business concerns in Israel would collapse	Public	2.6	0.59	0.57	123	n.s.
	Private	2.5	0.62			
7. The government does not show concern about industrial research	Public	2.14	0.73	–0.11	116	n.s.
	Private	2.15	0.57			
8. Private sector firms are more efficient than public sector ones	Public	2.7	0.56	6.6	125	0.001
	Private	1.9	0.62			
9. Management in the Histadrut is influenced by political considerations more than by economic ones	Public	2.1	0.65	2.09	57	0.04*
	Private	1.86	0.50			

Note: *Separate variance estimate.

found in the mean attitude scores of groups. However, no differences were found between the groups on three items (3, 6, and 7). Although these three items concern market intervention by the government, private sector managers did not feel differently than public sector managers. The same results were found when organization size was controlled. To examine whether or not there is some underlying structure in the relations between the items, they were factor analyzed. The principal factor method with varimax rotation was used, forcing a two-factor solution. The results show that all six items for which differences between the executive groups were found loaded highly on the principal factor. The items on which no differences were found, do not load on it (Table 2). An examination of the content of the six items of the first factor suggests that these statements may be interpreted as threatening the legitimacy of one of the sectors. For example, the statement favoring the expansion of the public sector may be seen as a threat to the private sector. On the other hand, the three items for which no differences were found do not express such rivalry: they present

Table 2. Varimax rotated factor matrix of nine perception items ($N = 109$).

Items	Factor I*	Factor II
1. Private sector firms are more efficient than public sector ones	0.91	—
2. Public ownership of firms ought to be decreased because of inefficiency, red tape, and stagnation	0.69	—
3. The Histadrut ought to strive to increase its share in the economy	−0.68	—
4. The fact that the Histadrut is an employer as well as a workers' representative creates a paradox that mutilates its role	0.57	0.49
5. Management in the Histadrut is influenced by political considerations more than by economic ones	0.50	0.37
6. Government intervention in capital markets is exorbitant	0.40	—
7. The government does not show concern about industrial research	—	0.66
8. Without government support, most of the business concerns in Israel would collapse	—	—
9. Government support of business firms should be eliminated even if it will bring down many firms	—	—
Variance accounted for	83%	17%

Note: *Factor loadings under 0.35 are not included.

government as a benefactor to both sectors. For example, the elimination of government support may affect firms in both sectors in the same way, and both may benefit to the same extent from government investment in research. Thus, factor I may be conceptualized as a legitimacy threatening factor, and factor II as a residual factor. An interpretation of these results may be that the differences between private and public sector executives are revealed when one of the sectors, its functioning, or its role, is perceived as threatened. The public sector executives then defend that sector's position as their responses to the six items (Table 1) show (low score indicates agreement with the statement). When no such threat, or rivalry between the sectors, is present, sector affiliation does not seem to be related to differences in orientation.

Next, hypothesis a_2 about the executives' preferences for pursuing legitimizing goals was tested. Investment in underdeveloped regions in Israel was one of the major objectives for public ownership of industrial firms at the time of the study. Therefore, executives were asked about their preference to invest in underdeveloped regions as opposed to investing in the central industrial region (based on a scale of 1 = always to 7 = never). There was no significant difference between the mean response of the public (3.7) and that of the private (4.2) sector groups ($t = 0.93$, n.s.).

Another important national goal has been the increase of exports. As a test of the executives preferences regarding exports, they were asked how they would have acted in a hypothetical situation. Assuming that their firm could sell all its products in the local market with a 25 percent profit rate, the executives had to indicate what proportion of products they would prefer to sell abroad (a) with the same rate of profit as in the local market or (b) with less profit. No significant differences were found between the preferences of the executives of the two groups: when the profit rates were the same, the mean proportion of exports for the public group was 61 percent (S.D. = 32) and for the private group 56 percent (S.D. = 29). When profits on sales abroad were indicated to be lower than in local markets (20 percent vs. 25 percent), the mean was 41 percent for the public group and 44 percent for the private one. Even when the profit rates abroad were much lower (15 percent, 10 percent, and 5 percent vs. 25 percent in local markets) about 70 percent of the executives in each group still indicated similar readiness to export part of their products. For a 5 percent profit rate abroad, the mean proportion of exports from total sales indicated was 13 percent for the public sector and 18 percent for the private sector ($t = -1.3$, d.f. = 73, n.s.).

Executives were also asked whether they would prefer: (a) to manage a firm that contributes to the nation but is less profitable (score 1) or (b) a firm that maximizes profits (score 2). No difference was found: the mean response for the public group is 1.3 and that for the private group 1.4.

All these findings indicate that the executives of the two sectors did not differ either in their attitude towards the national goals of increasing exports or investing in developing regions, or in their preference to manage a firm that contributes to the nation. Thus, hypothesis a_2 is rejected.

Functional level

The second hypothesis states that there are differences between executives of the two sectors on the managerial-functional level. Two aspects were examined in testing hypothesis b_1 (1) perception of environmental influence on managers' autonomy in decision making; and (2) perception of how much such influence managers would like to be subject to.

Perception of environmental influence

The chief executives were asked about the amount of influence certain environmental elements (both internal and external) have on their freedom to make decisions. The results (Table 3) indicate that the two managers' groups perceive their autonomy from environmental influences in basically the same way.

Table 3. The influence of environmental elements on managerial autonomy (high score = low influence).

	Mean of Public Group	Mean of Private Group	*t*-value	d.f.	Significance
"Internal" Elements					
Workers	7.1	6.8		107	n.s.
Workers' Union	7.2	7.4		102	n.s.
Board of Directors	3.6	5.6	2.57	93	$p < 0.02$
"External" Elements					
Banks	9.0	7.2		109	n.s.

(Continued)

Table 3. (*Continued*)

	Mean of Public Group	Mean of Private Group	*t*-value	d.f.	Significance
Ministry of Finance	8.3	8.2		108	n.s.
Ministry of Trade and Commerce	9.0	6.8	2.25	111	$p < 0.05$
Investment Bureau	10.2	9.1		99	n.s.
Clients	4.2	4.5		115	n.s.
Suppliers	7.7	7.7		108	n.s.
Competitors	7.0	6.4		112	n.s.
Histadrut	6.2	7.7		108	n.s.
Shareholders	5.1	6.2		103	n.s.
Public Opinion	7.9	7.8		107	n.s.

Hypothesis b_1 therefore, is not supported. Executives of the two sectors do not see differently their managerial autonomy vis-à-vis their environment. Significant differences in perception were found in only two out of the 13 elements presented to respondents: the influences of the Board of Directors and the Ministry of Trade and Commerce. These two elements are unrelated and do not form a coherent pattern; thus they need not be interpreted.

Desired environmental influences

Chief executives were next asked how much influence they ideally would like these environmental elements to have on their freedom to make decisions. Again, the findings do not support the hypothesis: there are practically no differences between executives of the two groups as regards the amount of influence from environmental elements which they are willing to accept (Table 4). It is interesting to note that chief executives in the two groups were most willing to accept the influence of the same three elements: the Board of Directors, customers, and shareholders.

It can be concluded that in terms of the functional orientations towards both internal and external environment influences there are basically no differences between managers in the two sectors, either when the orientation is expressed by perceived influences or when it is expressed by desired influences.

Table 4. The influence of environmental elements the executives are willing to accept $N = 123$ (high score = low acceptability).

	Mean of Public Group	Mean of Private Group	*t*-test Value	d.f.	*p*
"Internal" Elements					
Workers	7.0	7.5			n.s.
Workers' Union	9.9	9.2			n.s.
Board of Directors	4.3	5.4			n.s.
"External" Elements					
Banks	10.9	9.7			n.s.
Ministry of Finance	10.5	9.8			n.s.
Ministry of Trade and Commerce	9.1	9.3			n.s.
Investment Bureau	10.6	9.7			n.s.
Clients	5.4	5.25			n.s.
Suppliers	10.2	10.0			n.s.
Competitors	7.9	8.5			n.s.
Histadrut	8.4	10.1			n.s.
Shareholders	6.1	6.1			n.s.
Public Opinion	9.1	7.2			n.s.

National goal

In addition to the previously described hypothetical behavioral preferences, the executives' functional involvement in export was taken as a measure of pursuing a national objective (hypothesis b_2). The executives were asked about the actual exports of their organizations and their own attitudes towards exports. Only a small percentage of the executives in both sectors responded that they did not export at all (17.5 percent in the public sector and 23 percent in the private sector). All others reported to be engaged in exports and their past and anticipated rates of increase in exports were similar (Table 5).

Responses on these functional levels indicate that the ideology of the sector does not affect the executives' perceptions of the managerial-functional level examined. Executives in the public sector perceive their functional relations with the organizational environment in the same way private sector executives do, without any preference for the so-called "sector relevant" segments. Hypothesis B is thus rejected.

Table 5. Attitudes and export practices in private and public sectors.

	Public		Private				
	Mean	S.D.	Mean	S.D.	*t*-value	d.f.	*p*
1. On a yearly average, what was the rate of increase in export over the last five years?	23.8%	(182)	28.7%	(117)	0.30	101	n.s.
2. What is the anticipated rate of increase in exports for the next three years?	21.2%	(135.5)	27.2%	(91)	0.74	102	n.s.
3. How satisfied are you with the volume of exports?	2.5*	(0.89)	2.2	(0.89)	1.23	99	n.s.
4. How satisfied are you with the increase in exports over the past five years?	2.1*	(0.61)	2.1	(0.74)	0.17	123	n.s.

Note: *Answers ranged from 1 (definitely satisfied) to 4 (definitely dissatisfied).

Summary and Conclusions

The basic proposition of this study was that executives pursue the ultimate goals of their organizations. Assuming that the public (or nationalized enterprises) have ultimate goals different from the goals of private sector enterprises, it was hypothesized that executives of nationalized enterprises will perceive their goals and their functioning differently from their colleagues in private sector enterprises.

However, the hypotheses were rejected, except for a! which was partially supported in that hypothesized differences were found on some of the items but not on others. As suggested by the factor analysis of these items, executives express attitudes supportive of their sector only when its legitimacy is threatened, that is, its goals or functions are challenged or rivalry between the sectors is expressed. On all other goal perceptions or more concrete functional questions, no differences were found. The findings suggest that, except for the threat to legitimacy, the views of top executives on the socioeconomic environment of their organizations cannot be differentiated based on their affiliation with one sector or another. Even "public" environmental organs, such as ministries, trade unions, or public opinion, were not perceived to have more influence on public sector executives than on their private sector colleagues. Thus the assumptions that public enterprises are more susceptible to influence from higher political authorities (Walsh, 1978; Zaleznik, 1979) or to public scrutiny (Bower, 1977; Nigro & Nigro, 1977) are not supported here, at least as far as the executives' perceptions are concerned. All this may suggest that the nationalization of physical assets and resources does not necessarily secure the cooperation of the executives or guarantee the achievement of a sector's objectives. This conclusion is not unique to the Israeli case. Several studies of the history of state-owned enterprises suggest that at least some managers of public enterprises demonstrated concern for economic efficiency and aggressive growth (Dorstein, 1976). The history of ENI, the Italian Oil Company (Votaw, 1964), or that of Renault, the French car manufacturer, show clear signs of such behavior. Some managers have also been known to attempt to enhance their autonomy and to criticize government's encroachment of goals other than economic ones (NEDO, 1976).

The findings of this study support the claim that management is a general process irrespective of the type of organization or its goals (Long, 1954; Levitt, 1973; Sherman, 1966; Murray, 1975). The undifferentiated managerial orientation, be it in terms of "management class" or "general process of management", may justify and perhaps legitimize executives' uniformity in operations and management practices. It seems, however, that executives still have to turn to the sector's ultimate goals to justify the unique role and legitimacy of the organization. The legitimacy of existence, which has not been discussed by the advocates of "general process" theory, may be the point of difference between executives who on the functional level seem to be undifferentiated. Since the existence of a general process of management may have important ramifications for the nationalized public sector and its ability to achieve its goals, further research is needed. At this point it may be suggested that to the extent that the executives' perceptions affect the goal-related decisions which they make, little difference may be expected between public and privately owned enterprises. Different mechanisms are needed to control and increase the consistency between the goals prescribed for the public sector and those pursued by management.

The findings also have implications for recently heard claims about the expansion of state-owned enterprises into international markets, sometimes despite government policy (Mazzolini, 1979). At least in Israel, the orientations towards export of public sector executives are similar to those of their private sector counterparts. If indeed state-owned enterprises receive more subsidies and preferential economic terms, these might be used to induce them to expand into local as well as international markets.

In summary, this study was designed to learn about one aspect of the functioning of state-owned enterprises: the goal perception of their executives. Being a secondary analysis of existing data, it has limitations which ought to be borne in mind. Nonetheless, this analysis does yield some suggestive results. At least among Israeli top executives, goal-oriented behavior does not seem to be governed automatically by the prescribed goals of the sectors. The study of state-owned enterprises should, therefore, take into account not only their prescribed goals and official control structures, but also the perceptions and goal orientations of their managers. Much more attention should be devoted to understanding managerial behavior, and to the mechanisms by which greater consistency can be achieved between the declared ultimate goals of a sector and their execution by managers affiliated with the sector.

Acknowledgment

This study is part of the State-Owned Enterprises Research Program carried out at the Israel Institute of Business Research, Faculty of Management, Tel Aviv University. We wish to thank Derek Pugh for his helpful comments on this article.

References

Aharoni, Y. 1970. The Israeli manager. Research Report, Faculty of Management, Tel Aviv University, limited circulation (In Hebrew).

Arrow, K. J. & Linde, R. L. 1970. Uncertainty and the evaluation of public investment decisions. *American Economic Review*, 60: 364–378.

Blau, P. & R. Scott. 1962. *Formal Organizations.* San Francisco: Chandler.

Bower, J. 1977. Effective public management. *Harvard Business Review*, 131–140.

Buchanan, B. 1974. Government, managers, business executives and organizational commitment. *Public Administration Review*, 339–347.

Cyert, R. M. & March, J. G. 1963. *A Behavioral Theory of the Firm.* Englewood Cliffs, NJ: Prentice-Hall.

Daniel, A. 1976. *Labor Enterprise in Israel*, Vol. 1. Jerusalem: Academic Press.

Dornstein, M. 1976. Managerial theories of social responsibility and goal orientation of top level managers in state-owned enterprises. *The Journal of Behavioral Economics*, 5(2): 65–92.

Guth, W. D. & Taguiri, R. 1965. Personal values and corporate strategy. *Harvard Business Review*, 123–132.

Hage, J. & Dewar, R. 1973. Elite values vs. organizational structure in predicting innovation. *Administrative Science Quarterly*, 18(3): 279–290.

Hyman, H. 1971. *Secondary Analysis of Sample Survey.* New York: Wiley.

Kamens, D. H. 1977. Legitimizing myths and educational organizations: The relationship between organizational ideology and formal structure. *American Sociological Review*, 42: 208–219.

Katz, D. & Kahn, R. L. 1978. *The Social Psychology of Organizations* (2nd edn.). New York: Wiley.

Lavon, P. 1960. *Values and Changes in the Labor Economy.* Tel Aviv: Messilot (In Hebrew).

Levitt, T. 1973. *The Third Sector, New Tactics for a Responsive Society.* New York: American Management.

Long, N. 1954. Public policy and administration: The goals of rationality and responsibility. *Public Administration Review*, 14: 22.

Murray, M. 1975. Comparing public and private management: An exploratory essay. *Public Administration Review*, 35: 364.

National Economic Development Office (NEDO). 1976. A study of UK nationalized industries: Their role in the economy and control in the future. A report to the Government. London: NEDO.

Nigro, F. & Nigro, L. 1977. *Modern Public Administration* (4th edn.). New York: Harper and Row.

Pfeffer, J. & Salancik, G. R. 1978. *The External Control of Organizations.* New York: Harper and Row.

Rainey, H., Backoff, R. & Levine, C. 1976. Comparing public and private organizations. *Public Administration Review*, 36: 233–244.

Self, P. 1977. *Administrative Theory and Politics* (2nd edn.). London: Allen and Unwin.

Sherman, H. 1966. *It All Depends: A Pragmatic Approach to Organizations.* University: University of Alabama Press.

Simon, H. A. 1957. *Administrative Behavior* (2nd edn.). New York: Macmillan.

Simon, H. A. 1979. Rational decision-making in business organizations. *American Economic Review*, 69(4): 493–513.

Smith, B. (Ed.). 1975. *The New Political Economy: The Public Use of the Private Sector.* New York: Halsted.

Vernon, R. 1981. Introduction. In Aharoni, Y. & Vernon, R. (Eds.) *The State in Business*. London: Croom Helm.

Votaw, D. 1964. *The Six Legged Dog.* Berkeley: Institute of Business and Economic Research.

Walsh, A. H. 1978. *The Public's Business: The Politics and Practice of Government Corporations.* Cambridge, MA: MIT Press.

Walters, K. & Monsen, J. 1979. State-owned enterprises abroad: New competitive threat. *Harvard Business Review*, 160–170.

Wamsley, L. G. & Zald, M. N. 1976. *The Political Economy of Public Organizations.* Bloomington, Indiana: Indiana University Press.

Zaleznik, A. 1970. Power and politics in organizational life. *Harvard Business Review*, 49–56.

Zaleznik, A. 1979. Power and leadership in state-owned enterprises. Paper Delivered at a Conference on State-Owned Enterprises in Industrialized Countries, Harvard University, Graduate School of Business Administration, 26–28 March.

Small Firms and Countries in the Global Economy

https://doi.org/10.1142/9789811287510_0016

Chapter 16

The Role of Small Firms in an Interdependent World*

Yair Aharoni

The Leon Recanati Graduate School of Business Administration, Tel Aviv University, Tel Aviv, Israel

Fuqua School of Business, Duke University, Durham, NC 27706, USA

Abstract

Global is often used synonymously with big and giant. A global industry is often characterized as one in which only a few giant multinational enterprises can survive, the enterprises themselves engaging in cross-subsidizing and/or exchange of threats. In fact, however, industries in which the same product is sold all over the world may be very fragmented, as in the case of the watch industry. In many other cases, small or medium-sized firms have been able to become significant global players, by dominating a niche, for example. These firms became global in order to survive in an increasingly interdependent world.

Since most firms in the world are small or medium sized, it is important to understand what are the major necessary conditions for successful

*This chapter is reproduced from *Strategies for Players in a Larger World: The Effect of Regulatory and Information Changes*, pp. 11–32, Emerald.

global operations of small firms. On the basis of a comprehensive research study, this paper lists these necessary conditions. The first is shown to be the identification of a product and a market in a non-global industry, namely one in which more than a small number of giant firms can operate, not only on the basis of economies of scale. In that specific industry, the small firm must dominate a niche, employing a focus strategy. It should maintain flexible systems, allowing fast response time. It should develop learning ability from the different parts of its organization. The paper will also give several examples of successful global strategy of small and medium-sized firms in different industries. Finally, the paper analyzes the necessary entry strategies, distinguishing between entry as a subcontractor or OEM and entry on one's own brand name.

Introduction

Small firms play a major role in most economies of the world. In the United States, almost half of the work force is employed by firms with fewer than 500 employees and 88.4 percent of US firms employ less than 20 persons. (*The Economist*, March, 5, 1988: pp. 69–70). A survey conducted for the Small Business Administration shows that fully 37% of US companies with less than 500 employees are exporting overseas, and that one quarter of all exporting companies, or more than 16,000 firms, employ fewer than 100 people (Rosen, 1990). In smaller countries, a larger percent of the work force is employed by small firms. It is also claimed that small firms create more new employment opportunities than large ones (e.g., Gray, 1989, but see Johnson, 1989).

Despite its salience, attempts to develop widely applicable theories of small business were not always successful. In fact, even a rigorous definition of "small business" has turned out to be difficult. Clearly, however, small business firms are important, and exist side-by-side with much larger corporations.

Since World War II, international trade has increased dramatically, and foreign direct investments (FDI) have proliferated. Traded goods, money, information, labor, and services have all leaped over national boundaries and markets for more and more goods and services are now global in structure. Domestic producers who had enjoyed the luxury of a highly protected home market find themselves facing a direct competition of foreign, much larger, multinational enterprises (MNEs), benefiting from better reputation and lower costs resulting from economies of scale and of scope as well as a global scanning system for cheaper and better sources of labor, vendors, materials, parts and subassemblies. At the same time, in many industries power has been shifted from manufacturers to giant distribution chains of mass merchandisers. Accelerated technological diffusion, integration of capital markets, reduced information and transportation costs, liberalization of trade barriers — all combined to increase the extent and intensity of global interdependence.

In 1965, Marshall McLuhan posited that advances in transportation and telecommunications technologies were drawing the people of the world closer together. The world, he suggested, was on its way to become a "global village". In 1983, Ted Levitt predicted that technology "drives the world toward a converging communality", customer needs are becoming homogenized and MNEs will cease to adapt their products and practices in each country. According to Ohmae (1985, 1990), Japan, the United States and Western Europe are becoming fairly homogeneous and firms must gain share in all parts of this triad in order to survive.

These developments are often seen as giving increasing preference in the market place to the giant global firm over its small-sized competitor. Finance experts draw attention to the growing trend for mergers and acquisitions. By the latter part of the 1990's, predicts Bossidi, vice chairman of the board of General Electric, "there may well be fewer than 25 mega-corporations in the world... The medium-to-large-size generalists... won't be around anymore" (p. 10). Since Elinder (1961), international marketers have wrestled with questions of the degree to which products and marketing methods could be globally standardized. A lively debate enfolded on the degree of inevitability of the transformation of competition to a global rivalry.

Can a small business survive in a globally interdependent world? If so, how? In a frictionless world, all firms are atomistic in size. Competition works to direct resources to any uses achieving high returns, and thus wipes out any persistent unequal returns. One possible result of globalization should be the reduction of abnormal returns. If high returns came about because of government's imposed impediments to resource flows, globalization will wipe out these returns. A possibility of a different sort is that giant MNEs, pursuing global strategy, will create insurmountable barriers to entry that will put an end to small business even in domestic competition, let alone in exports and international production through FDI.

This paper explores ways by which a small business can compete effectively not only in the domestic economy but mainly outside its own national borders. The paper makes a distinction between small business unit and a small corporation. The paper starts with certain clarifications on the scope of the study. It then shortly analyzes the forces leading to a global structure. It then enumerates the bases for competitive advantage, comparing industrial organization and strategy theoretical findings. The next section analyzes the role of a small firm in a domestic setting. Entry strategies are discussed next. In the final section, certain speculations are offered on the role of information, collaboration and risk sharing.

Scope

Several points must be clarified. First, unfortunately, the term "firm" is ambiguous, and is used in at least two meanings. One meaning is an autonomous, independently operated, and homogeneous business unit. Another is in the legal sense of a corporation. This ambiguity has been a major source of confusion that is important to avoid. Therefore, we shall use the term business or business unit (BU) rather than a firm, and the term "company" or "corporation" for a legal, often diversified, entity.

Second, an assumption of the paper is that the small BUs operate in a developed environment and enjoy access to an adequate infrastructure such as telephones, roads transportation, market information facilities, fax and so on. It is well recognized that the infrastructure is extremely inadequate in many developing nations and the lack of such services inhibits corporations from competing in the world market, but these issues are left for another paper.

Finally, the subject of analysis is the small firm, whatever is the size of the domestic market. Foreign trade is relatively less crucial in a large economy than in a small one. A small country must export a very large percent of its GDP so that it will be able to import many of its essential needs and maintain operating efficiency. A small country would also find it more difficult to nurture giant business: Because of the limited size of the domestic market, such a business must be an MNE and only very few small countries are a home country to giant MNEs. The reasons for this phenomenon are not very clear (see Agmon & Kindleberger, 1977). If only large corporations export from a small country, there will be a high level of concentration in exports and too little diversification of the export fields, increasing risks. The country may become too dependent on the large exporting corporations for the standard of living of the population. A small country may therefore prefer to rely on many small exporting corporations rather than a few dominant ones. A small country may also choose to diversify its portfolio for risk spreading reasons and this consideration may preclude investments in certain industries [if economies of scale are significant and minimum efficient scale of a plant means that a very large per cent of the work force should work in one business, being engaged in such a business increases the portfolio risk. It also often means a very high concentration of the labor force in certain skills]. These problems, however, are beyond the scope of this paper.

Background: The globalization of markets

The transportation revolution of the mid-nineteenth century created the beginning of multinational competition. The communication and information revolution created the global competition of today. The forces leading to globalized structure of competition has been articulated by many scholars, (e.g., Hout *et al.*, 1982; Leontiades, 1985) and provoked a lively debate on the degree of inevitability of this transformation of world competition as well as on its causes (see e.g., Davidson, 1982; Fayerweather, 1982; Levitt, 1983; Buzzell, 1968; Quelch and Hoff, 1986; Wind *et al.*, 1973; Douglas & Wind, 1987; Yip, 1989). The need to achieve lower costs and to amortize high fixed cost of research and development, design, production, marketing and services is very often cited as reasons to globalization. Clearly, globalization became possible because of advances in telecommunications and information. Today, technology and information flow quickly across national boundaries. Markets for products develop almost simultaneously around the world. In some cases, globalization is claimed to be inevitable also because customers' needs are becoming homogenized, and people are willing to sacrifice first preferences in product features, design and functions in order to pay a lower price for a second best (Levitt, 1983).

In global industry, by definition, the relevant structure that determines behavior and competitive advantage is a worldwide one, or at least one covering the major developed markets of the world. Strategic positioning of the competitors in major national markets is fundamentally affected by their overall global positions. Firms in global industries often cross-subsidize different markets to achieve market share or threaten a competitor (Hamel & Prahalad, 1985; Prahalad & Doz, 1987). This requires huge investments in core technologies, building and maintaining global infrastructure, daunting expenditures for advertising and massive investments in sales force and distribution systems and cost reduction by international sourcing. It also requires ability to acquire, maintain and deploy large-size physical and human resources. Therefore, it is often assumed that only a handful of giant corporations can compete in a global industry. Many of these giants gradually shift from managing their subsidiaries as a multidomestic portfolio, in which each subsidiary enjoys a high degree of autonomy, to a globally integrated structure, designed to capture the linkages among countries, or to transnational learning organization (Bartlett & Ghoshal, 1989).

Transactions at arm's length were replaced or superseded by transactions within hierarchically structured MNEs or by long-term contracts. Between 1966 and 1975 the majority-owned affiliates of US corporations located in foreign countries originated about one third of US imports (Hellenier, 1981). By 1987, imports associated with MNEs accounted for 41 percent of US imports. MNEs accounted for 72 percent of total US merchandise imports (Whichard, 1989). The largest 500 MNEs in 1981 controlled over 80 percent of FDI and their sales were equal to over 50 percent of the world traded output (Stopford & Dunning, 1983). Since 1983, FDI outflow zoomed, fueled by the greater realization that global expansion is necessary for competitive advantage. European and Japanese MNEs invested in the United States. US FDI in Japan and in Europe has also increased by about 20 percent p.a. and the total US FDI position abroad grew from $226 billion in 1981 to $327 billion in 1988 (Scholl, 1989). Service operations are also increasingly offered by global firms (Dunning, 1989).

To be able to compete, firms must enjoy competitive advantage. The firm-specific advantages have been investigated in the context of a theory of MNE, emphasizing the advantages of internalizing transactions (e.g., Caves, 1971, 1982; Buckley & Casson, 1985; Dunning 1977, 1981, 1988; Krugman, 1970; Rugman, 1981, 1986). Economic theory, however, has been slow in reconciling trade theory with the reality of MNEs operations, the literature on MNEs paid limited attention to competitive strategy, and those interested in strategy largely ignored the multinational dimension.

Recently, an evolving literature on global strategy attempts to combine these different strands (Ghoshal, 1987). Most researchers concentrated their attention on the giant, global MNEs. The impact of global forces on small companies have been almost totally neglected.

To be sure, a small business can compete if it is sheltered from competition, e.g., by high barriers against imports. Import barriers may be imposed by government, but can also be a result of high transportation costs (for example in the case of cement or building materials). They may be derived from the need for proximity to the markets (milk, ice cream and other perishables), from difficulties in transporting the product or because of the importance of local service (industrial cranes or repairs). The ensuing sections of this paper discuss non-sheltered BUs, producing world traded products and services. We shall investigate the possible ways a small business can compete in the interdependent world market.

Bases for Competitive Advantage in a World Market

To find out the means by which small business can compete, the possible sources of sustainable competitive advantage in the international marketplace must be cataloged. One such source is the presence of a fertile climate for certain crops or the existence of certain minerals used as raw materials. The BU gains a cost advantage derived from accessibility to low-cost raw materials sources. A cost based advantage could also be the availability of skilled workers earning low wages. Indeed, in a growing number of fields, competitive advantage lies with low cost Far Eastern producers. Prices for many products have been falling and the low-end of the market has become a commodity business. Small BUs from developed countries with higher wage levels are unable to compete successfully in such markets. For example, in low-priced denim jeans, wage labor costs are the major competitive factor. This is because the most labor-intensive part of the cost structure, cutting and assembly, is also the most significant. The importance of wage rates gives lower labor-cost suppliers from South East Asian countries like South Korea and more recently Indonesia at least a 30% cost advantage over European producers in low-priced denim jeans. A large MNE can compete by sourcing from these countries.

Competitive advantage could be a result of an innovation or specific knowledge or skills. The invention of a safe method to ship elemental bromine in bulk gave the Israeli based Dead Sea Bromine a significant technological lead over competitors who still had to ship in small containers. A very efficient process technology derived from the need in a small market to change products frequently allowed an Israeli food manufacturer to export soups in relatively small quantities, selling them as private brands of medium-sized supermarkets chains.

Competitive advantage could also be based on the ability to realize a price premium. Such a premium can be achieved by tailoring basic equipment or software to customers' specific needs, by offering a special product quality or unique capabilities, or more convenient distribution or better service, or creation of a brand name. More generally, a price premium may be possible because of higher quality, better design innovation, better and faster service, prompt delivery, as well as special relations with customers. In all these cases, the product may be more expensive, but if the BU can command a higher price it may still have a competitive advantage. If BUs focus and specialize in a certain product they are able to develop firm-specific advantages and nurture them into competitive advantages in the global market Thus, if a BU specializes in the hard metals business, or in a specialized water planting device used in the desert, it may dominate the world market, even though it is not large. There are many segments of sophisticated products with a high R&D component that small BUs can compete, To be sure, product life cycles are being shortened by rapid changes in technology. The more expensive (and indivisible) the development costs of a certain project, the higher the portfolio risk for a small corporation, that cannot spread costs and risks over a large production base.

Price premium can also be achieved by having an advantage in marketing. In high-priced denim jeans, South East Asian countries still have a significant advantage in spinning, weaving, and finishing. But they face a major cost disadvantage in marketing and distribution, which account for a much more significant portion of total costs in high priced jeans. Marketing and distribution of high-quality jeans are more expensive because of the larger cost of advertising, promotion, and selling through specialized outlets versus mass chain stores. The clothing industry includes also businesses that provide design capabilities and subcontract the manufacturing, allowing corporations such as Liz Claiborne, Anne Klein or Yves Saint Laurent very clear advantage. The industry also includes firms such as Benneton, offering design skills and integrative worldwide strategy. Similar examples can be shown in other industries e.g., Nike in sports shoes. Small businesses may not be able to compete when large expenditures for the establishment of a brand name are needed — unless they establish strategic alliances or collaborate with other businesses, sharing the brand name. The cost of achieving a price premium varies in different parts of the value chain. Having an advantage in design takes much less resources than achieving advantage in marketing.

Firm size, competitive advantage and industry characteristics

It is generally assumed in economic and strategy literature that large firms enjoy a competitive advantage over small ones, because they command more resources, because they can control a higher market share, because they can ride the experience curve faster, because they enjoy strong bargaining power with suppliers and customers. They can also make more mistakes without being wiped out. Indeed, several research studies in economics (Shepherd, 1972; Gale, 1972; Imel & Helmberger, 1971) demonstrated a significant positive association between firm size and profits. This association was assumed to show a causal relationships between firm's size and profitability. A plethora of studies have also shown the importance of market share as a determinant of profitability. Of course, for the studies to show unambiguous results, the distinction between "business" and diversified "firm" must be scrupulously observed.

Any observation of the profits of various firms in the same industry would show significant variance in returns of real life firms in a given industry. Persistent high profits, unless they are explained away as an accounting error, must be accounted for as a result of some competitive advantage — or a consequence of a strategy. For quite a long time, industrial organization (IO) economists believed that the so-called abnormal profits could be fully explained by tacit collusion or other monopoly behavior, allowing economies of scale or brand loyalty through advertising. Further, firms were assumed to have created barriers to entry. Most of the higher barriers to entry are associated with large corporations and are considered to be the properties of collection of firms, called industry. However, *in* several industries, e.g., real estate, some firms enjoy what an IO economist would see as persistent windfall profits, which cannot be explained by predation, monopoly, collusion or deterrence. Instead, these firms have some specific assets that allow them to get high rent. Of course, for the profits to be persistent, these assets must be induplicable.

Industry is generally defined according to the standard industrial classification conventions. These conventions, while important and useful for many applications, are not always very helpful in defining the basis for a possible sustainable competitive advantage. Strategy, in contrast, emphasizes the unique endowments and actions of individual businesses.

Strategy research shows that the key factors of success in each and every industry are changing with industry evolution and the configuration of a firm's value chain is a dynamic process. At the emerging stage of an industry, technology is a key factor of success. A small business can start with a brilliant product development and achieve rapid growth once the start up phase has been passed. Customers may doubt the ability of a tiny company to meet delivery dates and after sale service demands, but may be attracted by the new features. At the maturing stage of the industry cost considerations become dominant and scale may be more important. Small BUs may not be able to compete at this stage, certainly when markets are homogeneous, standardized and large.

Industries can also be cataloged according to the number of rivals. In fragmented industries no dominant competitor exists. The industry is populated by a large number of small and medium-sized corporations. No business has a significant market share and can strongly influence the industry outcome (Porter, 1980: p. 191). In some of these industries, entry and exit are relatively easy and the turnover of the businesses is very high.

These industries are also characterized by absence of economies of scale or even by diseconomies of scale, high transportation costs, and high product diversity. An industry can also be fragmented because it is new or emerging, and no one firm found the way to dominate the market.

In a global industry, competition in a given geographic area is influenced by the worldwide position of the competitors. In such industries, most firms compete by scale and volume. Competitive advantages could be access to sources of cheaper raw materials; economies of scale in production that extend beyond the size of a national market; benefits from reduced costs resulting from a global scale of activities; ability to amortize high fixed costs on a global scale. Small businesses cannot achieve competitive advantage unless they identify and target a very specific niche.

In a fragmented industry, a single competitor may sometimes be able to achieve dominance if it can standardize the products or components of the products and achieve economies of scale in manufacturing, distribution, or service. In most cases competitors can achieve higher value added in fragmented industries by specialization in product type, segment, customer type or geographic areas.

The small business in a domestic setting

A widely held view is that the right prescription for a small business in a domestic market is to avoid direct competition against the much larger giants. This avoidance is possible in one of several ways. The first is to concentrate activities in fragmented industries.

A second prescription is to pursue a niche strategy (Buzzell & Gale, 1979; Abell & Hammond, 1979) concentrating in those niches that are of no or little interest to the giant enterprises, for example by customization to individual users who are willing and able to pay a premium rather than accept a more standardized version. A niche can be defined along any of three dimensions: customer, product or technology (Abell & Hammond, 1979). To operate successfully in a niche, the BU is expected to *specialize* and to *focus.*

A third possible strategy for a small BU is to take higher risks. Small BUs arc often equated with entrepreneurial behavior in the Schumpeterian sense. These firms may gain competitive advantage e.g., by gaining first mover advantages. In researching such a strategy, one has to look for special managerial characteristics such as need for achievement (McClelland, 1965) or other personality attributes.

Fiegenbaum & Karnani (1991) proposed a competitive advantage of a different sort. Small firms, they demonstrate, enjoy much higher level of output flexibility than their large competitors. Small business is more vulnerable to changes in the environment. It does, not possess enough resources to control the environment but must be able to adjust to any turbulence.

In a seminal paper, Sheshinski & Dreze (1976) demonstrated that when demand fluctuates, the number of firms sustained in competitive equilibrium is increased and each firm produces less on the average with fluctuations than without (1976: 738). Mills & Schumann (1985) extended these results to a model involving asymmetric firms. They demonstrated that under competitive equilibrium, assuming fluctuating demand, firms of diverse size can coexist in the industry. This diversity is a result of a tradeoff between static cost efficiency and volume flexibility. Large size is less of an advantage in an environment characterized by fluctuating demand than in a stable environment. Small firms' competitive advantage comes from their ability to vary output volume quickly.

While these researchers emphasize output flexibility, there are also other sources of flexibility that can allow small BUs not only to survive but even to command abnormal profits. Flexibility can be internal — e.g., by short internal communication lines because of greater interaction among departments and must lower agency costs because of the high motivation than in the large corporations (Woo, 1983, 1987). Such organizational flexibility also allow much faster response to changes in consumer tastes or environmental conditions. In a small business is much easier to identify the person responsible for changes and build the reward system accordingly.

Product life cycles accelerate as technology and fashion evolve rapidly. If the scale of R&D required to design and build a new product is very large when the time between generations contract, a small BU can find it difficult to continue. In many cases, however, a small BU can gain advantage by maintaining a close link with customers — in particular if the number of customers is not very large. Further, fast response time to alter a product, build a sales network or develop a service organization is essential to build and maintain competitive advantage.

A fifth possibility is that the BU is a satellite unit, dependent on either a single corporation or a group of large corporations in an industry. These BUs may supply a large department store private brand goods, or are part of what Kuno (1984) termed "Quasi integration" — being long-term suppliers to large corporations, as in the Kanban system. Kuno (1984) notes that a Japanese car manufacturer buys 75 percent of the parts from outside quasi-integrated suppliers. Under long-term contracts, small BUs are sheltered by the large corporation to which they supply their output, thus reducing significantly marketing costs. Satellite units may also be able to reduce risks. A variant to dependence on one large buyer is the creation of strategic alliance, or the establishment of a network of small businesses — to reduce training costs, to mitigate marketing expenditures, or to allow the scale needed to create and sustain a brand name.

Sixth, small businesses may be based on a major innovation, and may grow to be large businesses at a latter stage. If an entrepreneur starts a new business, it would be small at the beginning but may grow to be large. Sony was established in 1946 by two partners but grew to a billion dollar diversified company. Likewise, Hewlett Packard, Apple and a score of other firms became corporate giants. Of course, many more small corporations never made it, or went bankrupt when the first idea was not enough to sustain a competitive advantage.

Most research findings and stipulations on small businesses assume, at least implicitly, uninational markets. As pointed out above, however, one characteristics of the 1980's is the proliferation of global operations and of global industries. A small business must be able to compete in its domestic economy against giant MNEs intruders attempting to enter this market. It may also be able to compete by exporting to other markets, by licensing or through FDI. We move to discuss the role of a small BU in an increasingly interactive global economy.

The small BU in a global market

In the world markets, as in the domestic market, competitive advantage can be gained as a result of either a cost advantage or a price premium. A business can enjoy an advantage either because it sells a product for the same price as its competitors but has lower costs or because it is able to charge for its products or services a higher price than its competitors.

As in the domestic market, small business can be successful in exporting on their own when they *focus* on and dominate specific market niches which are appropriate to their capabilities. Being small in world terms, even if they are technologically capable of entering large markets they cannot survive there over the long term. They can, however, dominate a niche. A major problem of this strategy is the limitations it imposes on the ability of the BU to grow. If the segment ("niche") grows fast, it may attract larger competitors. In many cases, the technology becomes widely available, reducing significantly the barriers to entry. The pioneer business may lose its business to larger competitors or at least find it difficult to maintain market position. Long-term advantage may depend on continued innovation. If the niche does not grow, the BU does not grow too — unless it diversifies to more businesses, with all the coordination and control problems this strategy entails. If the niche grows big, it will attract large competitors that can bring massive cash, R&D, marketing and managerial resources to the business, making the life of the small BU difficult.

The ability to focus is a necessary but not a sufficient condition. To be successful, small exporting BUs must choose a small number of segments in which they intend (and pursue relentlessly) to establish strength in world terms. At the same time, this specialization must not involve very high costs of establishing infrastructure in terms of the R&D costs, the build up of distribution system or the creation and maintenance of worldwide service capabilities. The giant global corporations have a huge advantage in their ability to amortize staggering R&D costs in the face of a very brief product life cycle. The core technologies used by small business must be also different enough so that they are not part of those served by the large global business or the market must be small enough so that the giants will not be attracted into the field. Since the small business cannot sustain large sales force, this means the size of a typical transaction must be large, either because of high cost per unit production or due to selling the production OEM or to a large distributor on a private brand bases. Small business are at their best when they sell to a small number of sophisticated customers who buy quality, or those needing frequent changes, or a specialized product.

Diamonds are an example of a product with very low transportation costs, very little economies of scale in diamond cutting, and relatively little need to the heavy investment in global infrastructure that makes an industry dominated by global firms: there is no need for heavy R&D outlays, nor the requirement if heavy investments in after sale servicing facilities or the need for large capital outlays for machinery.

Diamond cutting and polishing is an example of a business dominated by small business, in which a few small countries, notably Belgium and Israel (but also India), have been able to maintain a significant presence in world trade through a very large number of extremely small companies. (Raw diamonds, however, are controlled by a worldwide syndicate).

The fundamental challenge for many small BUs is that of creating competitive advantage in spite of substantial cost disadvantages with respect of labor, materials and capital and mainly in marketing costs. To do that, one needs to achieve price premium. If the price premium consumers are willing to pay for better performance or exclusivity exceeds the cost of producing the extra quality or performance, then a strategic competitive advantage is gained. Consumers may be willing to pay a premium for products with heavy creative contents, or where design can be the basis for product differentiation or where outstanding manufacturing quality results in products that perform better, are more reliable, or have unique features. Price premium is also paid for high flexibility, innovation, quick delivery and fast response to customers' needs.

An example of achieving price premium by focusing on specific needs is specialty fertilizer business that sells for up to 40 percent price premium over an equivalent nutrient quantity of a conventional fertilizer. In certain farming applications, producers are willing to pay such a premium.

Small business often takes too long getting to market and once in market does not grow fast enough. Even world leading technology is not sufficient for success if full scale marketing effort is not launched — and this effort may be beyond the means of the small business. Teece (1986) has demonstrated that many small firms offering a good product failed because they missed the complementary assets. One means by which businesses can get these assets is by being a part of a strategic alliance or a satellite to a giant corporation.

Minimum efficient scale (MES) is different in different parts of the value chain. Generally, MES in manufacturing is much smaller than that prevailing in marketing. The establishment and maintenance of a brand name is a very costly business. A network of after sale services must be large and therefore costly. In almost all cases, a small business cannot hope to compete in the world markets unless it establishes and fosters close, collaborative relationships with key customers or other corporations in the foreign markets while at the same time selecting specific segments in which it can be strong in world terms on a continuing basis. A small business may have an excellent product but must have some means for the customers to know about it. It must also develop scanning mechanisms to learn about future customer's needs. A major problem of a small business is thus the cost of acquisition and dissemination of information. The small business also faces high risks. Both problems can be solved by being part of a larger portfolio. The portfolio may be based on ownership or on other collaborative arrangements.

Small BU and small corporation

Note the important distinction between small BUs and small corporations. Small BUs may continue to operate in the world as a part of a general portfolio of unit sizes — depending on the need for flexibility and the size of the world market. These small BUs may be acquired by large, diversified firms. One example of the type of products that allows a small business to compete in an interdependent world environment is that of Dexter corporation. The 1978 long range planning plan states:

Most of the products produced by Dexter are classified as specialty materials, rather than commodities, because they are formulated or designed to perform a specific, vital function in the manufacturing process of Dexter customers or in their end products. These specialty materials are not sold in the high volumes normally associated with commodity business.

Dexter specialty materials require high degree of technical service on an individual customer basis. The value of these specialty materials stems not just from their raw materials composition, but from the results and performance they achieve in actual use.

Dexter is divided into 26 strategic business segments, each one of which is quite small but very specialized. One example is non-woven paper for tea bags. Another is liquid epoxy coating.

Large corporations have advantages that small ones do not possess. It is easier for large corporations to fund new business or revive faltering ones from the earnings of healthy business units. Large corporations attract skilled labor easier than small ones. A large corporation can realize economies of scope across businesses in costs like R&D, marketing, or advertising. One major advantage of a large corporation is its ability to reduce the risk by diversification. For small businesses the means of spreading risks are very important. The large corporation can consist of a portfolio of small BUs but other means of risk spreading are possible.

Clearly, small BUs can operate in an interdependent global system as an integral part of a large, diversified corporation. Small BUs can also operate as satellites of larger corporations supplying parts, selling OEM, or developing private label goods. One possibility, therefore, is that the world is moving toward a concentration in the number of corporations, but these corporations would allow small BUs to maintain their autonomy. The large corporation may concentrate on financial decisions, provide access to markets, decide on new avenues for R&D, or maintain quality control to assure the prospective customer that certain standards of reliability are maintained.

Small corporations can of course continue to exist in the non-tradable parts of a national market, in particular in fragmented industries. Small corporations can also continue to operate if the national government protects the domestic market from foreign competition. Even in these cases, successful small corporations find themselves enmeshed in competition with large MNEs. Unless they join the MNEs, they must find the means to compete against them. Therefore, the small corporation must have a sustainable competitive advantage against a giant MNE: The MNE can get over many of the national barriers by FDI, including the acquisition of the domestic small business. In a global industry, even a government cannot afford the size of funding needed to sustain an inefficient firm. In fact, some governments made a concerted effort to attract MNEs as a means to enhance economic growth and access to export markets. Ireland, Singapore, Taiwan, Scotland, Puerto Rico and to a lesser extent Portugal, Greece and Spain governments have developed sophisticated packages of inducements to attract FDI to accelerate exports. MNEs may acquire local corporations, making them part of a globally integrated network (see Goodman, 1987).

Indeed, MNEs account for about one third of the exports of the NICs in general. In Singapore this share exceeds 90 percent (UNCTC, 1988: pp. 154–155). In the 1980's, Singapore and Ireland each attempted to develop a strong indigenous export sector to reduce the high dependence on foreign MNEs. In doing so, they learned that if a country opts for more involvement of MNEs, it also accepts the risk that it would have much less control of its economic destiny. Strong reliance on subsidiaries of MNEs left the country little autonomy when the MNEs chose not to increase their level of involvement in the economy. Issues of the relations between a giant MNE and a host countries are beyond the scope of this paper (see e.g., Bennett & Sharpe, 1988; UNCTC, 1988).

In lieu of relying on MNEs to build or acquire subsidiaries, a country may help local firms to gain access to the global firm. In return for a large government order, say engines for the air force, the global corporations may agree to develop domestic vendors for its procurement requirements, promising to use its best efforts or even agreeing to commit itself for a certain amount of domestic purchases. Since business strategy is generally based on a stream of resource commitments, once the MNE familiarized itself with the possibilities of using a certain vendor it may often continue working with that vendor, (provided it received good quality product, prompt delivery, and acceptable quality) even after the offset agreement is finished.

Whether the different parts of the MNE are subsidiaries whose activities are internalized into the system, or independent subcontractors, totally dependent on the MNE for orders, the MNEs (and the mass merchandisers) seem to have become the pivotal actors in the global economy. These MNEs may be less able to adapt nimbly to changes than the small corporations, but may develop quasi-integration relations with the small businesses. The only other alternative for the small corporations is to develop risk sharing mechanisms on new products and markets. They can also foster collaboration in R&D and in marketing. Thus, a large MNE has an enormous advantage because of its ability to spend large sums of money for advertising, but a large number of autonomous business corporations can unite in one brand name. This is the case today with regard to New Zealand kiwi growers or Danish furniture. Small corporations can also combine their purchasing power in procuring certain goods through a shared corporation. Pharmacies in Israel use this method. Many other methods of collaboration are possible.

Collaboration and Risk Sharing

If small businesses do not operate under the umbrella of a larger MNE, it must develop other means to scan the environment and to be known to customers. The future means of collaboration and risk sharing are not very clear, but some speculations may be relevant.

Relations among individuals may be based on various forms. One is a hierarchy, in which those at the top enjoy a legitimate right to tell those subordinate to them what to do and the subordinates accept this authority. A voluminous literature in organization theory tells us when will these conditions hold. It is generally assumed that within a company, property rights of owners would allow these owners to give directions to their agents. To the extent that those supposed to obey do not, shirking for example, one faces an agency cost problem. Since the seminal work of Coase (1937) in economics, following early work on the nature of the firm (e.g., Kaldor, 1934; Robinson, 1931, 1934), it is generally accepted that a firm may be more efficient than the market transactions if market imperfections generate transaction costs that are higher than the cost of coordinating the activities by internalizing the transaction under common ownership. Transaction costs were defined by Arrow (1969: p. 48) as “the costs of running the economic system”. Williamson (1981: p. 1544) extended this to include comparative costs of planning, executing and monitoring task competition under alternative institutional frameworks. Principal-agent theory proposes a design of optimal contracts to allow the principal to evaluate and control the behavior of an agent. (For a summary of the organizational implications, see Eisenhardt, 1989; Levinthal, 1988). The principal, of course, does not possess perfect information. There may also be asymmetry of risk preferences and goal incongruence between principal and agent.

In the second half of the 1980's, researchers have noticed an increasing number of coalitions among manufacturing MNEs, including those competing in the same field (Hergert & Morris, 1988; Mariti & Smiley, 1983; Root, 1988; Auster, 1987; Contractor & Lorange, 1988; Mowery, 1988; Link & Bauer, 1989). Firms preferred coalitions to attempts to grow alone, realizing that no one company possesses the resources to always expand on its own. It thus looks for "strategic alliances" to acquire the capabilities it lacks, rather than developing the skills internally or acquiring them in market transactions (Hamel *et al.*, 1989). Many of these strategic alliances were disbanded (Harrigan, 1985, 1988). Critics (e.g., Reich & Mankin, 1986) feared strategic alliances were too short sighted, creating future competitors. There were also studies of hybrid organizational arrangements (Powell, 1987). The major problem identified for these cooperative ventures was their long-term viability. All are, after all, prone to be broken by one party, if that party sees its long-term goals — for instance, learning about some area in which its partner is strong — achieved.

Long-term contracts between parties — e.g., a supplier of an intermediate good and the producer of the final good — can reduce the costs of continual renegotiation. These long-term contracts, too, may not be honored. Therefore, vertical integration may be preferable. Thus, when the assets have no alternative use the buyer and the seller would enjoy bilateral monopoly power. Under this condition of asset specificity, Williamson (1985) argued, vertical integration would be preferred to legal enforcement of contracts to eliminate the risk of becoming hostage to the buyer (or to the supplier).

Clearly, if independent individuals trusted each other they could achieve long-term cooperation without the need for a common ownership structure or even the need for legal enforcement. To be sure, trust is not the same as an agreement. One agent may trust another but still would feel that he should receive a larger pie or that the priorities proposed by the other party are wrong. Therefore, if the sequence of work done is of an important nature, someone will have to be the final arbiter. The source of power to achieve this status is of importance in understanding the structure of the firms. One can be the final arbiter because of specific expertise, or because of ownership rights. In some cases, ambiguity of control can be perceived as a means to engineer trust. Buckley & Casson (1988) argue that a 50:50 joint venture is purposely ambiguous in terms of control in order to engineer a spirit of cooperation.

Developments in information technologies may allow much more collaboration among small business units, instead of ownership relations in a large corporation. The brand name of a large corporation is often an assurance for the consumer that a certain high level of quality is maintained. Yet reduced costs of information may mean that consumers could have much more information available at their fingertips. Thus, one advantage of an international hotel system is the reservation system allowing each and every customer an easy access for reservation plus an assurance of certain standards. Even today, each hotel in the system can be independently owned, sharing information and quality assurance services. In the future a complete and up to date data base may be developed of all hotels (and, for that matter, restaurants and other services) in the world and each one of us could access the data base from a PC, making immediate reservations through pooled telephone lines. In short, new developments in information technologies should allow many forms of collaboration and networking to achieve certain advantages without losing the identity, flexibility, and risk taking characteristics of the small business unit.

Conclusion

Small corporations obviously face a growing disadvantage *vis-a-vis* the large MNEs, and this disadvantage is growing the more integrated markets become. In a closely integrated world, very large investments must be made to develop low-cost sourcing, to nurture an effective international distribution or servicing system or to run an efficient and integrated network. Small corporations may not only lack the cash. Their management team may be stretched very thin by international expansion. Inexperience in global operations and the lack of marketing expertise may jeopardize their operations. Moreover, cross subsidization and economies of scope may rule out the possibility of success in picking narrow segments with smaller resource commitment and relatively less managerial complexity. Competition in mature markets is often based on cost as much as on performance. Unfortunately, small corporations find it much harder than large ones to ride the experience curve to a cost advantage.

Many small companies have grown accustomed to production in the hothouse environment of the domestic protected market. They have not adequately recognized the importance of analyzing the environment and market awareness, and making the product compatible with clients' needs. Many development engineers believe it is enough to make technological breakthroughs — without examining the market and its willingness to accept those products.

A small business may encounter great difficulties if it tries to expand rapidly so as to retain a large market share in a growing market. Fortunately for the small business the experience curve is less crucial in a fragmented industry, or where specialization is important.

If firms do not become large enough to compete with the world industrial giants at product maturity, they must rely primarily on finding market niches that, because of their limited scope, do not justify the large companies' investments in marketing efforts.

Small business units may be successful in the international arena if they follow the CS^2F^3 strategy: customization, small number of transactions (either because of few large clients or selling private brand to a large distributor), superior service, focus, fast response and flexibility. Those who look at industries rather than unique properties of successful strategy might add a fourth "F": fragmented industry. Yet even in the most global of industries one can find specialty needs that small BUs can cater to.

It is important to distinguish between small business units, that can be part of a large or even a giant MNE, and small corporations. In order to boost sales and profits, small corporations should attempt to increase their exports. The major factor inhibiting participation in foreign markets is the scale required in marketing and after sale services. Therefore, small corporations may opt for collaborative relations with large MNEs or OEM. Alternatively, they should collaborate through strategic alliances or different risk sharing arrangements — either on their own or with government's help.

References

Abell, D. F. & Hammond, J. S. 1979. *Strategic Market Planning*. Englewood Cliffs, NJ: Prentice-Hall.

Agmon, J. & Kindleberger, C. 1977. *Multinationals from Small Countries*. Cambridge, MA: MIT Press.

Arrow, K. 1969. The organization of economic activity: Issues pertaining to the choice of market vs. nonmarket allocation. In U.S. Joint Economic Committee, The Analysis and Evaluation of Public Expenditure: The PBS System, Government Printing Office, Washington, DC.

Auster, E. R. 1987. International corporate linkages: Dynamic forms in changing environments. *Columbia Journal of World Business*, (Summer): 3–6.

Bartlett, C. & Ghoshal, S. 1989. *Managing across Borders: The Transnational Solution*. Boston, MA: Harvard University Business School Press.

Bossidi, L. A. 1989. Globalization: It's already here. *Credit Magazine* (September-October): 10–12.

Buckley, P. J. & Casson, M. 1985. *The Economic Theory of the Multinational Enterprise*. London: MacMillan.

Buckley, P. J. & Casson, M. 1988. A theory of cooperation in international business. In Contractor, F. & Lorange, P. (Eds.) *Cooperative Strategies in International Business*. Lexington, MA: Lexington Books.

Buzzell, R. 1968. Can you standardize multinational marketing? *Harvard Business Review*, (November-December): 102–113.

Buzzell, R. D. & Gale, B. T. 1987. *The PIMS Principle*. New York, NY: The Free Press.

Caves, R. E. 1971. International corporations: The industrial economics of foreign investment. Economica, 38: 1–27.

Caves, R. E. 1982. *Multinational Enterprise and Economic Analysis*. Cambridge and New York: Cambridge University Press.

Coase, R. H. 1937. The nature of the firm. *Economica* (New Series), 4: 386–405.

Contractor, F. & Lorange, P. (Eds.). 1988. *Cooperative Strategies in International Business*. Lexington, MA: Lexington Books.

Davidson, W. H. 1982. *Global Strategic Management*. New York, NY: Wiley.

The Dexter Corporation. 1979. Harvard Business School Case Number 379–112.

Douglas, S. P. & Wind, Y. 1987. The myth of globalization. *Columbia Journal of World Business*, 22(4) (Winter): 19–29.

Dunning, J. H. 1977. Trade, location and economic activity and the MNE: A search for an eclectic approach. In Ohlin, B., *et al.* (Eds.) *The International Allocation of Economic Activity Proceedings of a Nobel Symposium Held in Stockholm*. London: MacMillan.

Dunning, J. H. 1981. *International Production and the Multinational Enterprise*. London: George Allen and Unwin.

Dunning, J. H. 1988. The eclectic paradigm of international production: A restatement and some possible extensions. *Journal of International Business Studies*, 19(1) (Spring): 1–31.

Dunning, J. H. 1989. Transnational Corporations and the Growth of Services: Some Conceptual and Theoretical Issues, UNCTC Current Studies, Series A, No. 9, March.

Eizenhardt, K. M. 1989. Agency theory: An assessment and review. *Academy of Management Review*, 14(1) (January): 57–74.

Elinder, E. 1961. How international can advertising be? International Advertiser (December): 12–16.

Fayerweather, J. 1982. *International Business Strategy and Administration*. Cambridge, MA: Ballinger.

Fiegenbaum, A. & Karnani, A. 1991. Output flexibility — A competitive advantage for small firms. *Strategic Management Journal*, 12: 101–114.

Gale, B. 1972. Market share and rate of return. *Review of Economics and Statistics*, 54: 412–423.

Ghoshal, S. 1987. Global strategy: An organizing framework. *Strategic Management Journal*, 8: 425–440.

Goodman, L. W. 1987. *Small Nations, Giant Firms*. New York, NY: Holmes and Meier.

Gray, T. A. 1989. Let small business do what it does best — Create jobs. *Journal of Labor Research*, 10 (Winter): 73–81.

Hamel, G., Doz, Y. L. & Prahalad, C. K. 1989. Collaborate with your competitors — And win. *Harvard Business Review*, (January-February): 133–139.

Hamel, G. & Prahalad, C. K. 1985. Do you really have a global strategy?" *Harvard Business Review* (July-August): 139–148.

Harrigan, K. R. 1985. *Strategies for Joint Ventures*. Lexington, MA: Lexington Books.

Harrigan, K. R. 1988. Strategic alliances and partner asymmetries. In Contractor, F. & Lorange, P. (Eds.) *Cooperative Strategies in International Business*. Lexington, MA: Lexington Books.

Hellenier, G. K. 1981. Intra-firm trade and the developing countries: An assessment of the data. In Murray, R. (Ed.) *Multinationals beyond the Market*. New York, NY: John Wiley and Sons, pp. 31–57.

Hergert, M. & Morris, D. 1988. Trends in international collaborative agreements. In Contractor, F. & Lorange, P. (Eds.) *Cooperative Strategies in International Business*. Lexington, MA: Lexington Books.

Hout, T., Porter, M. E. & Rudden, E. 1982. How global companies win out. *Harvard Business Review*, (September-October): 98–108.

Imel, B. & Helmberger, P. 1971. Estimation of structure-profit relationships with application to the food processing sector. *American Economic Review*, (September): 614–627.

Johnson, P. 1989. Employment change in the small establishment sector in UK manufacturing. *Applied Economics*, 21 (February): 251–260.

Kaldor, N. 1934. The equilibrium of the firm. *Economic Journal*, 44: 60–76.

Krugman, P. 1970. The new theories of international trade and the multinational corporation. In Kindleberger, C. P. (Ed.) *The International Corporation.* Cambridge, MA: MIT Press.

Kuno, T. 1984. *Strategy and Structure of Japanese Enterprises*. Armonck, NY: Sharpe.

Leontiades, J. C. 1985. *Multinational Corporate Strategy*. Lexington, MA: Lexington Books.

Levinthal, D. 1988. A survey of agency models in organization. *Journal of Economic Behavior and Organization*, 9: 153–185.

Levitt, T. 1983. The globalization of markets. *Harvard Business Review*, (September-October): 92–102.

Link, A. N. & Bauer, L. L. 1989. *Cooperative Research in U.S. Manufacturing.* Lexington, MA: Lexington Books.

Mariti, P. & Smiley, R. H. 1983. Cooperative agreements and the organization of the industry. *Journal of Industrial Economics*, 31(4) (June): 437–451.

McClelland, D. 1965. Achievement and entrepreneurship: A longitudinal study. *Journal of Personality and Social Psychology*, 1: 389–397.

McLuhan, M. 1965. *Understanding Media: The Extensions of Men.* New York, NY: McGraw Hill.

Mills, D. & Schumann, L. 1985. Industry structure with fluctuating demand. *American Economic Review*, 75(4): 758–767.

Mowery, D. C. (Ed.). 1988. *International Collaborative Ventures in U.S. Manufacturing*. Cambridge, MA: Ballinger.

Ohmae, K. 1985. *Triad Power: The Coming Shape of Global Competition.* New York, NY: Free Press.

Ohmae, K. 1990. *The Borderless World: Power and Strategy in the Interlinked Economy*. New York, NY: Harper Business.

Porter, M. E. 1980. *Competitive Strategy*. New York, NY: Free Press.

Powell, W. W. 1987. Hybrid organizational arrangements: New form or transitional development? *California Management Review*, 30(1) (Fall): 67–87.

Prahalad, C. K. & Doz, Y. L. 1987. *The Multinational Mission: Balancing Local Demands and Global Vision.* New York, NY: Free Press.

Quelch, J. A. & Hoff, E. J. 1986. Customizing global marketing. *Harvard Business Review*, (May-June): 59–68.

Reich, R. B. & Mankin, E. D. 1986. Joint ventures with Japan give away our future. *Harvard Business Review*, (March-April): 78–86.

Robinson, E. A. G. 1931. *The Structure of Competitive Industry*. London: Nisbet.

Robinson, E. A. G. 1934. The problem of management and the size of the firm. *Economic Journal*, 44: 242–257.

Root, F. R. 1988. Some taxonomies of international cooperative arrangements. In Contractor, F. & Lorange, P. (Eds.) *Cooperative Strategies in International Business*. Lexington, MA: Lexington Books.

Rosen, M. D. 1990. EC '92: A guide for the small company. *Sales and Marketing Management*, 142(11): 96–106.

Rugman, A. M. 1981. *Inside the Multinationals: The Economics of Internal Markets*. London: Croom Helm; New York, NY: Columbia University Press.

Rugman, A. M. 1986. New theories of the multinational enterprise: An assessment of internalization theory. *Bulletin of Economic Research*, 38(2) (May): 101–118.

Scholl, R. B. 1989. The international investment position of the United States in 1988. *Survey of Current Business*, 69(6) (June): 41–49.

Shepherd, W. G. 1972. The elements of market structure. *Review of Economics and Statistics*, 54: 25–37.

Sheshinski, E. & Dreze, J. 1976. Demand fluctuations, capacity utilization, and cost. *American Economic Review*, 66(5): 731–742.

Stopford, J. M. & Dunning, J. H. 1983. *Multinationals: Company Performance and Global Trends*. London: MacMillan.

Tecce, D. 1986. Profiting from technological innovation: Implications for integration, collaboration, licensing, and public policy. *Research Policy*, 15: 285–305.

United Nations Center on Transnational Corporations (UNCTC). 1988. *Transnational Corporations in World Development: Trends and Prospects*. New York, NY: United Nations.

Whichard, O. G. 1989. U.S. multinational companies: Operations in 1987. *Survey of Current Business*, 69(6) (June): 27–39.

Williamson, O. E. 1981. The modern corporation: Origin, evolution, attitudes. *Journal of Economic Literature*, 19(4) (December): 1537–1568.

Williamson, O. E. 1985. *The Economic Institutions of Capitalism*. New York, NY: MacMillan, Free Press.

Wind, Y., Douglas, S. P. & Perlmutter, H. V. 1973. Guidelines for developing international marketing strategies. *Journal of Marketing*, 37 (April): 14–23.

Woo, C. 1983. Evaluation of the strategies and performance of low ROI market share leaders. *Strategic Management Journal*, 4: 123–135.

Woo, C. 1987. Path analysis of the relationship between market share, business level conduct and risk. *Strategic Management Journal*, 8: 149–160.

World Bank, 1990. World Development Report, Washington, DC.

Yip, G. 1989. Global strategy... in a world of nations? *Sloan Management Review*, (Fall): 29–41.

https://doi.org/10.1142/9789811287510_0017

Chapter 17

How Small Firms Can Achieve Competitive Advantage in an Interdependent World*

Yair Aharoni

Tel Aviv University, Tel Aviv, Israel

Small firms play a larger role in the economy than is often realized. Close to 90 percent of American firms employ fewer than twenty persons, and almost half the work force is employed by companies with fewer than 500 employees. In smaller countries, an even larger percentage of the work force is employed by small firms. More important, these smaller organizations are creating the new employment opportunities, not their bigger, better-known counterparts. The number of these firms that have cast their eyes beyond the domestic market may come as a surprise: A survey conducted for the Small Business Administration showed that 37 percent of the U.S. firms with fewer than 500 employees are exporting overseas, and that one quarter of all exporting companies, or more than 16,000, employ fewer than 100 people.

Since World War II, international trade has increased dramatically, and foreign direct investments (FDIs) have proliferated. Traded goods, money, information, labor, and services have all leaped over national boundaries and markets. Domestic producers who had enjoyed the luxury of a highly protected home market find themselves facing direct

*This chapter is reproduced from *Small Firms in Global Competition* (1994), Oxford University Press.

competition from foreign-owned, much larger, multinational enterprises (MNEs), with better reputations and lower costs, resulting from economies of scale and of scope, as well as global scanning systems for cheaper and better sources of labor, vendors, materials, parts, and subassemblies. Accelerated technological diffusion, integration of capital markets, reduced information and transportation costs, and liberalization of trade barriers have all combined to increase the extent and intensity of global interdependence. At the same time, in many industries power has shifted from manufacturers to giant distribution chains of mass merchandisers.

These trends are often seen as giving preference in the future global market to the giant firm, reducing the future role of small business or even questioning its ability to survive in a globally interdependent world. I propose to explore some ways in which a small business can compete effectively not only in the domestic economy, but also internationally.

Several points must be clarified. First, unfortunately, the term *firm* is ambiguous and is used in at least two meanings. One is for an autonomous, independently operated, and homogeneous business unit. Another is in the legal sense of a corporation. To avoid such an ambiguity, I shall use the term *business* or *business unit* (BU) for the first sense, and the term *company* or *corporation* for a legal, often diversified, entity.

Second, the small business units must operate in a developed environment and enjoy adequate infrastructure, such as telephones, roads, transportation, market information facilities, fax, and so on. The infrastructure is inadequate in many developing nations, and the lack of such services inhibits corporations there from competing in the world market.

Finally, the subject of analysis is the small business (and I am not offering a rigorous definition of "small") without regard to the size of the domestic market.

Background: The Globalization of Markets

The transportation revolution of the mid-19th century created the beginning of multinational competition. The communication and information revolution created the global competition we see today. Technology and information flow quickly across national boundaries. Markets for products develop almost simultaneously around the world. The need to achieve lower costs and to amortize the high fixed costs of research and development, design, production, marketing, and services is often cited as a reason to globalize. Ted Levitt argues as well that globalization is inevitable because customers' needs are becoming homogenized, and people are willing to sacrifice their first preferences in product features, design, and functions in order to pay a lower price for their second choice.

In a global industry, by definition, the relevant structure that determines behavior and competitive advantage is a worldwide one, or at least one covering the major developed markets of the world. Strategic positioning of the competitors in major national markets is fundamentally affected by their overall global positions. Therefore, firms in global industries may cross-subsidize different markets in order to achieve market share or to threaten a competitor. A major player in a global industry must build and maintain global infrastructure. This requires daunting expenditures for advertising, massive investments in sales force and distribution systems, and cost reduction by international sourcing. It also requires the ability to acquire, maintain, and deploy large-scale physical and human resources. Therefore, it is assumed, only a handful of giant corporations can compete in a global industry.

Most researchers have concentrated their attentions on the giant MNEs, neglecting the impact of global forces on small businesses. But there are small business units — not sheltered by government protection — prospering in the international marketplace and enjoying competitive advantage. Here is a look at some possible strategies.

Bases for Competitive Advantage in a World Market

There are several sources of sustainable competitive advantage. The first is the presence of a fertile climate for certain crops or the existence of certain minerals. The business unit gains a cost advantage from the accessibility of low-cost raw materials. A second is the availability of skilled workers earning low wages. For example, in low-priced denim jeans, wage labor costs are the major competitive factor, because the most labor-intensive part of the cost structure — cutting and assembly — is also the most significant. Low-cost labor suppliers from countries such as Hong Kong and South Korea have at least a 30 percent cost advantage over European producers. Large MNEs compete by sourcing from the low-cost countries.

Competitive advantage can be the result of an innovation, or of specific knowledge or skills. The invention of a safe method to ship elemental bromine in bulk gave the Israeli-based firm Dead Sea Bromine a significant technological lead over competitors who still had to ship in small containers. A very efficient process technology derived from the need to change products frequently in a small market allowed an Israeli food manufacturer to export soups in relatively small quantities, selling them as private brands to medium-sized supermarket chains.

Innovation may also allow business to realize a price premium. Price premium can also be achieved by tailoring basic equipment or software to a customer's specific needs, by offering a special product quality or unique capabilities, by supplying more convenient distribution or better service, or by creation of a brand name. More generally, a price premium may be possible because of higher quality, better design innovation, better and faster service, prompt delivery, as well as special relations with customers.

If a small BU focuses and specializes in a sophisticated product for which world demand is limited, it is able to develop firm-specific advantages and to nurture them into globally competitive advantages. Thus, if a BU focuses on the hard metals business, or on a specialized water planting device used where water is scarce and costly, it may dominate the world market — without being a giant — and be competitive.

Price premium can also be achieved by having an advantage in marketing. Hong Kong and South Korea still have a significant advantage in the labor-intensive production of high-priced denim jeans. But they face a major cost disadvantage in marketing and distribution, which account for a much more significant portion of total costs because of the larger outlay for advertising, promotion, and selling through specialized outlets (versus department stores). The clothing industry also includes businesses that specialize in design and subcontract the manufacturing, which gives corporations such as Liz Claiborne, Anne Klein, and Yves Saint Laurent their advantage. Benneton has design skills and an integrative worldwide strategy. Nike offers the same in sport shoes.

Small businesses may not be able to compete when large expenditures for the establishment of a brand name are needed unless they establish strategic alliances. And they must choose carefully when looking for a base for a price premium: The cost of achieving this varies in different parts of the value chain. An advantage in design, for example, takes fewer resources than an advantage in marketing.

Firm Size, Competitive Advantage, and Industry Characteristics

It is generally assumed in economic and strategic literature that large firms enjoy a competitive advantage over small ones because they command more resources, they can control a higher market share, they can ride the experience curve faster, they enjoy strong bargaining power with suppliers and customers, and they can make more mistakes without going belly up. Indeed, several research studies have demonstrated a significant positive association between firm size and profits — from which the researchers concluded there was a causal relationship between size and profitability. A plethora of studies have also shown the importance of market share as a determinant of profitability.

Any observation of the profits of various firms in the same industry would show significant differences. Persistent high profits, unless they are explained by an accounting error, must be the result of some competitive advantage, or the consequence of a strategy. For quite a long time, industrial organization economists believed that so-called abnormal profits could be fully explained by tacit collusion or other monopoly behavior, allowing for economies of scale, brand loyalties through advertising, and barriers to entry. Most of the higher barriers to entry are associated with large corporations and are considered to be the property of a particular collection of firms called an industry. However, in several industries, such as real estate, some firms enjoy what an economist would see as persistent windfall profits that cannot be explained by predation, monopoly, collusion, or deterrence. Instead, these firms have some specific — and induplicable — assets that allow them to get high rent.

Strategy theory may be more useful in defining the basis for competitive advantage. Studies show that the key factors of success in each and every industry change as the industry evolves. At the emerging stage of an industry, technology is a key factor of success. A small business can start with a brilliant product, develop it, and achieve rapid growth once the start-up phase has passed. Customers may doubt the ability of a tiny company to meet delivery dates and after-sale service demands, but they may be attracted by the new features. As the industry matures, cost considerations become dominant, and scale may be more important. Small BUs may not be able to compete at this stage, especially when markets are homogeneous, standardized, and large.

Industries may also be viewed according to the number of rivals. In fragmented industries, no dominant competitor exists. Since the industry is populated by a large number of small and medium-sized corporations, no business has a significant market share, and none can strongly influence the industry outcome. Entry and exit from the industry may be relatively easy, and the turnover high. These industries are characterized by absence of economies of scale, or even by diseconomies of scales, high transportation costs, and high product diversity.

In a fragmented industry, a single competitor may be able to achieve dominance if it can standardize the products or components of the products and achieve economies of scale in manufacturing, distribution, or service. Competitors may also achieve higher value-added by specialization in product type, segment, customer type, or geographic areas.

The Small Business in a Domestic Setting

A widely held view is that the right prescription for a small business in a domestic market is to avoid direct competition against the giants. This is possible in one of several ways. The first is to concentrate activities in fragmented industries.

The second is to pursue a niche strategy, concentrating in those niches that are of little or no interest to the giants — for example, by customizing to individual users who are willing and able to pay a premium rather than accept the standard version.

A third possible strategy for small BUs is to take high risks. In researching such a strategy, one has to look for special managerial characteristics, such as what David McClelland has described as the need for achievement, or other personality attributes.

Fourth, small firms also enjoy a much higher level of output flexibility than their large competitors; conversely, they are more vulnerable to changes in the environment. Large size is less of an advantage in an environment characterized by fluctuating demand than in a stable environment. Other sources of flexibility allow small BUs not only to survive but even to command abnormal profits. Short internal communication lines, for example, allow much faster response to changes in customer tastes or environmental conditions. And in a small business it is much easier to identify the person responsible for changes and build the reward system accordingly.

A fifth possibility is that the BU is a satellite unit, dependent on either a single corporation or a group of large corporations in an industry. For example, the BU may supply a large department store private brand or be a long-term supplier to a large corporation, as in the Kanban system. Toyahiro Kuno notes that a Japanese car manufacturer buys 75 percent of its parts from outside quasi-integrated suppliers. Long-term contracts shelter small BUs from risk and significantly reduce marketing costs. A variant of this strategic choice is the creation of a strategic alliance or a network of small businesses, to reduce training costs, to mitigate marketing expenditures, or to allow the scale needed to create and sustain a brand name.

Finally, a small business may be based on a major innovation and may grow to be a large business at a later stage. Sony was established by two partners in 1946 and is now a multibillion dollar diversified company. The same is true of Hewlett Packard, Apple, and a score of other firms. Of course, many more small corporations never made it or went bankrupt when the first idea was not enough to sustain a competitive advantage.

One characteristic of the 1980s, as noted, is the proliferation of global operations and global industries. This means that a small business must be able to compete in its domestic economy against giant MNEs — intruders attempting to penetrate the market. It may also choose to compete by exporting to other markets, by licensing, or through foreign direct investment.

The Small BU in a Global Market

In the world markets, as in the domestic market, competitive advantage can be gained as a result of either lower costs or a price premium. Small businesses (in world terms) can be successful when they focus on and dominate specific market niches.

There are several problems with the niche strategy, however. One is the limitation imposed on growth of the BU. If the niche does not grow, neither does the BU, unless it diversifies to other businesses, with all the coordination and control problems that entails. If the niche grows too fast, however, it will attract large competitors with massive cash outlays and extensive marketing and managerial resources. Then, too, if the technology becomes widely available, barriers to entry are reduced, and the pioneer business may find it difficult to maintain market position.

Hence, the ability to focus is a necessary but not sufficient condition for success. A small exporting BU must choose a small number of segments in which it intends to establish strength — and pursue that strength relentlessly. This specialization must not involve high research and development costs, an expensive distribution system, or the creation and maintenance of worldwide service capabilities. The giant MNEs have a clear advantage in their ability to amortize staggering R&D costs in the face of a brief product life cycle.

The core technologies used by the small business must be different enough so that they are not part of those used by giants, or the market must be small enough so that the giants will not be attracted. Since the small business cannot sustain a large sales force, the size of a typical transaction must be large, either because of a high cost per unit or because the sale is made to a large distributor on a private brand basis. Small businesses are at their best when they sell to a small number of sophisticated customers who buy quality, or to customers who need frequent changes or a specialized product and are willing to pay a price premium.

Diamonds are an example of a product with low transportation costs, little economy of scale in processing, and no need for cash outlays for R&D, for servicing, or for heavy machinery. And diamond cutting and polishing is in fact dominated by small businesses — a few small countries, notably Belgium and Israel (but also India and the USSR), have been able to maintain a significant presence in world trade through a very large number of extremely small companies. (Raw diamonds, however, are controlled by a worldwide syndicate.)

Small businesses often take too long getting a product to market, and once in the market do not grow fast enough. Even world-leading technology is not sufficient for success unless a full-scale marketing effort is launched, and this effort may be beyond the means of a small business. A small business must also develop scanning mechanisms to learn about future customers' needs. And a small business faces high risks. These problems can be solved by being part of a larger portfolio, based either on ownership or some other collaborative arrangement.

The Small BU and the Small Corporation

There is an important distinction between small BUs and small corporations. A small BU may be acquired by a large, diversified firm but still retain its character and autonomy, depending on the need for flexibility and the size of the world market. One example is Dexter Corporation. Its 1978 long-range plan states:

> Most of the products produced by Dexter are classified as specialty materials, rather than commodities, because they are formulated or designed to perform a specific, vital function in the manufacturing process of Dexter customers or in their end products. These specialty materials are not sold in the high volumes normally associated with commodity business.

> Dexter specialty materials require a high degree of technical service on an individual customer basis. The value of these specialty materials stems not just from their raw materials composition, but from the results and performance they achieve in actual use.

Dexter is divided into twenty-six strategic business segments, each one of which is quite small and very specialized. One BU produces non-woven paper for tea bags; another, liquid epoxy coating.

Large corporations indeed have advantages that small ones do not possess. It is easier for large corporations to fund new businesses or revive faltering ones from the earnings of healthy business units. It is easier to attract skilled labor and to realize economies of scope across businesses in costs like R&D, marketing, or advertising. A major advantage is the ability to reduce risk by diversification. For small businesses, the means of spreading risks are very important. A large corporation can consist of a portfolio of small BUs, but other means of risk spreading are possible.

One possibility, therefore, is that the world is moving toward a concentration in the number of corporations, but these corporations would allow small BUs to maintain their autonomy. The large corporation may concentrate on financial decisions, provide access to markets, decide on new avenues for R&D, and maintain quality control to assure the prospective customer that certain standards of reliability are maintained.

Small corporations can of course continue to exist in fragmented industries. They can also continue to operate if the national government protects the domestic market from foreign competition. Even in these cases, successful small corporations find themselves enmeshed in competition with large MNEs. Unless they join the MNEs, they must find the means — the competitive advantage — to compete against them.

The government of a country may wish to help local firms gain access to a global giant. In return for a large government order, say engines for the air force, the MNE might agree to develop domestic vendors for its procurement requirements, promising to use its best efforts or even agreeing to commit itself for a certain amount in domestic purchases. Since business strategy is generally based on a stream of resource commitments, once the MNE familiarized itself with a certain vendor, it might continue working with that vendor (provided it received good quality products and prompt delivery) even after the offset agreement ended.

Other than becoming a part of an MNE, or an independent contractor dependent on an MNE for orders, the only alternative for the small corporation is to develop risk-sharing mechanisms on new products and markets, and to foster collaboration in R&D and marketing. A number of autonomous corporations can unite in one brand name, as is the case with regard to New Zealand kiwi growers or Danish furniture makers. Small corporations can also combine their purchasing power in procuring certain goods through a shared corporation. Pharmacies in Israel use this method.

Collaboration and Risk Sharing

If a small BU does not operate under the umbrella of a larger MNE, it must develop other means to scan the environment and be known to customers. The future means of collaboration and risk sharing are not very clear, but some speculations may be relevant.

Developments in information technologies may allow more collaboration among small BUs, obviating the need for ownership relations as part of a large corporation. For example, one advantage of an international hotel system is in reservations — customers have easy access plus an assurance of certain standards. Each hotel can be independently owned, sharing information and quality control. In the future, a data base may be developed of all hotels in the world (and restaurants and other services, for that matter), which anyone could access from a personal computer, making immediate reservations through pooled telephone lines. Further developments should allow many forms of collaboration and networking to achieve certain advantages of large corporations without losing the identity, flexibility, and risk-taking characteristics of the small business unit.

Conclusion

Small corporations obviously face a disadvantage vis-a-vis the large MNEs, and this disadvantage is growing as markets become more integrated. Large investments are required to develop low-cost sourcing, to nurture an effective international distribution or servicing system, or to run an efficient and integrated network. Small corporations may not only lack the cash, but their management team may be stretched thin by international expansion. Inexperience in global operations and the lack of marketing expertise may jeopardize their operations. Moreover, cross-subsidization and economies of scope across the business units of MNEs may make it more difficult for small corporations to successfully pick a narrow segment of the market requiring a smaller resource commitment and less managerial complexity. Competition in mature markets is often based on cost as much as performance, and small corporations find it much harder than large ones to ride the experience curve to a cost advantage.

Many small companies have grown in the hothouse environment of a protected domestic market and have not adequately recognized the importance of analyzing the market and making the product compatible with the client's needs. Development engineers too often believe that it is enough to make technological breakthroughs, without ascertaining the willingness of the customer to accept the new products.

A small business may encounter difficulties if it tries to expand rapidly in order to retain a dominant share of a growing market. Fortunately, the experience curve is less crucial in a fragmented industry, or where specialization is important.

If a corporation does not become large enough to compete with the world industrial giants at product maturity, it must hope to find a market niche that, because of its limited scope, does not justify a giant's investment in marketing efforts.

Small BUs may be successful in the international arena if they follow the CS^2F strategy: Customization, Small number of transactions (either because of few large clients or selling a private brand to a large distributor), Superior service, Focus, Fast response, and Flexibility. Those who look at industries rather than at the unique properties of successful strategy might add a fourth F: Fragmented industry. Yet even in the most global of industries, one can find specialty needs that small BUs can cater to.

Small corporations (as distinct from small BUs, which can be part of a large corporation) should attempt to boost exports. The major factor keeping them from foreign markets is the scale required in marketing and after-sale services. Therefore, they may opt for collaborative relations with giants, or with other small corporations through strategic alliances or risk-sharing arrangements, either on their own or with government help.

References

Kuno, T. 1984. *Strategy and Structure of Japanese Enterprises*. Armonk, NY: Sharpe.

McClelland, D. 1965. Achievement and entrepreneurship: A longitudinal study. *Journal of Personality and Social Psychology*, 1(4): 389–392.

https://doi.org/10.1142/9789811287510_0018

Chapter 18

Globalization and the Small, Open Economy*

Yair Aharoni

Tel Aviv University, Tel Aviv, Israel

Introduction

The world is increasingly characterized by the disappearance of economic borders. Investment is no longer geographically constrained; industry is far more global in its orientation; the growing sophistication of information technology facilitates global operations and individual customers are becoming more global in orientation. As pointed out by Levitt (1983) customer needs and interests are becoming increasingly homogeneous worldwide. Further, even though people around the world may have different preferences in product features, functions, design and the like, they are willing to lower these preferences for lower prices at high quality. Firms can capture substantial economies of scale in production and more so in marketing by catering to global markets. In addition, fast developments in information technology allow firms to mass-produce items geared to different preferences, so consumers do not need to lower their preferences to purchase from global firms.

At the same time, customers are linked to the same source of global information, and can communicate extremely cheaply. Friedman (1999)

*This chapter is reproduced from *FDI, International Trade and the Economics of Peacemaking* (2000), College of Management, Rishon Le Zion.

quotes the Economist pointing out that a three minutes call from New York to London (in 1996 dollars) cost $300 in 1930. Today, it costs practically zero on the Internet. Customers also can watch news as it happens on global TV networks such as BBC or CNN.

Globalization has become a buzzword. As trade barriers fall and mergers and alliances across borders proliferate, the line between foreign and domestic firms becomes increasingly blurred. Most studies of globalization have focused on giant multinationals. Global is often assumed to be synonymous with "giant". Economic units (and firms) have been assumed to need economies of scale. The nation state was also assumed to be too small a unit to survive. It was assumed that several states would merge into a large economic union. It should be remembered that nations and nationalism is a phenomenon of the 19th century (except England and France) with history as a nation-state originating from the Hundred Years' War (1337–1453). In the Middle Ages the obligations of a peasant were to a landholding hierarchy. Germany was unified to one nation only in 1871, and Italy was not one nation but several kingdoms, unified in mid nineteen century.

As early as 1969, Charles Kindleberger of MIT claimed that "the nation state is just about through as an economic unit". Drucker points out that there were talks on the sovereignty much before the end of 1918. Indeed, West European countries attempted to increase their political and economic ties and created the European Economic Community and then the European Union. North America created NAFTA and Latin American countries joined into the MERCOSUR. Other countries — in Latin America, in Asia and in other parts of the world, also signed regional agreements of cooperation. The onslaught of a global economy seemed to be followed by an amalgamation of states into larger United States of Europe or similar organizations. Globalization was assumed to imply the amalgamation of giant multinationals that can roam the world and "have the technological means and strategic vision to burst old limits — of time, space, national boundaries, language, custom and ideology" (Barnet & Cavanagh, 1994: p. 14). These global giants "are undermining the effectiveness of national governments to carry out essential policies on behalf of their people (Barnet & Cavanagh, 1994: p. 19). The expansion of globalization since the end of the cold war was seen by some scholars as a reason for the small nation states to become obsolete. Thus, Kenichi Ohmae claims the end of the nation state. According to him:

> "Traditional nation states have become unnatural, even impossible, business units in a global economy...nation states have already lost their role

> as meaningful units of participation in the global economy of today's borderless world. The global economy punishes twinging (sic.) countries by diverting investment and information elsewhere . . . . . . the nation state is increasingly a nostalgic fiction. . . . . . the nation state has rapidly become an unnatural, even dysfunctional, unit in terms of which to think about or to organize economic activity. . . . In the borderless world, the key factors for success depend increasingly on universal, not local, conditions. . . . . . For nation states and especially for their leaders, the primary issue remains protection — of territory, of resources, of jobs, of industries, even of ideology". (Ohmae, 1995: p. 10, 12, 13, 42, 68, 79)

It is certainly true that political leaders of the nation state, and certainly those of the very small nation state, face major restrictions on their freedom of action. Governments are severely punished by global market forces if they attempt to maintain an artificially high rate of exchange for their currencies. Countries are vulnerable to what their political leaders may perceive as unfair attacks of financial speculators. At the World Bank meeting in Hong Kong in September 1997 Dr. Mahathir Mohamad, the Prime Minister of Malaysia, coined the global financial markets as "a jungle of ferocious beasts". He blasted the "Great Powers" of financiers such as George Soros of forcing Asian countries to open their economies to global speculators. He took to task Soros personally as being the ominous squeeze behind the Asian crisis. He accused the financiers of trying to manipulate the currencies to destroy the Asian countries as competitors. Soros in his 1998 book claims he was actually a net purchaser of Malaysian Rupiah at the time of the Asian crisis. More important, the financial markets are global and no one person, firm or government can change this fact. If a government is considered as having inappropriate economic policies, the market reacts and the currency of that country may deteriorate in value. Countries are also more constrained than they were in the past in protecting certain firms or certain industries.

Yet, despite gloomy predictions on the death of the nation state under conditions of growing globalization, many small countries prosper and their rates of growth per capita is not lower than that of the larger states. Moreover, the prediction that the nation state is dead or that states will merge or create large and populous federations turned out to be false. In fact, the number of countries has more than doubled in the last three decades of the twentieth century, rising from 96 in 1960 to 192 in 1998. At the same time, the number of countries with fewer than 1 million people has almost tripled, growing from 15 to 43 (World Development

Report, 1999–2000: p. 45). The resistance of colonial people to foreign occupation has terminated the European empires in Africa and Asia. Ethnic and communal conflicts in countries such as India or in Sub-Saharan Africa resulted in the division of areas into different states. One result of the demise of Communism was that the USSR could not hold together and de-merged into several independent states. Yugoslavia, too, was split into several ethnic states. Thus, small nations seem to survive and even prosper despite, or perhaps because of, globalization.

This paper analyzes the conditions under which small states operate in the global village. It points out the opportunities available under globalization as well as the policy implications for governments. Its major conclusion is that — rather than making the small nation state obsolete — globalization created opportunities for growth and prosperity for citizens of small states. This conclusion is true as long as the different nations cooperate. If one assumes war among nations the basic notions of globalization do not hold. Thus a country may decide to continue the operations of inefficient farms to make sure it would have agricultural supplies in case of siege. A nation may also prefer domestic ownership of strategic industries or financial institutions because of security considerations. These issues are beyond the scope of the paper.

Some Characteristics of a Small Country

Small countries may be defined according to a variety of parameters e.g., size of land or size of population. In this paper small countries are defined in terms of the size of population. The size of the country is not necessarily correlated with its wealth per capita or even its wealth. China, the most populous country in the world, with more than 1,250,000,000 inhabitants in 1999, is a relatively poor country in terms of GNP per capita. Switzerland, with 7 million inhabitants, enjoys GNP per capita 53 times larger than that of China.

Small countries are by definition more dependent on foreign trade. Japan is often perceived as a country for which export is a major engine for growth. Yet, with a population of 126 million in 1998 its exports as a percent of GNP was 11.7 percent, almost identical to that of the United States (11.8 percent). On the other hand, for a small country like Costa Rica, exports in 1997 were 45.7 percent of GNP; for Switzerland the ratio was 42.4 percent and for Norway — 41.6 (Table 1).

Table 1. GNP characteristics of large and small nations.

Country	Pop. Millions 1998	GNP Per Capita $ 1998	GNP at PPP* 1998 $	Rank	Average Annual % Growth in GDP 1980–1990	1990–1998	Export % of GNP 1997
Large							
Brazil	166	4,570	6,160	88	2.7	3.3	7.9
China	1,239	750	3,220	129	10.2	11.1	22.3
India	980	430	1,700	163	5.8	6.1	10.5
Indonesia	204	680	2,790	141	6.1	5.8	45.7
Japan	126	32,380	23,180	14	4.0	1.3	11.7
Nigeria	121	300	820	199	1.6	2.6	43.9
US	270	29,340	29,340	3	3.0	2.9	11.8
Small							
(a) *Industrial Market Economies*							
Austria	8	26,850	22,740	16	2.2	2.0	40.6
Belgium	10	25,380	23,480	12	2.0	1.6	71.6
Denmark	5	33,260	23,830	11	2.3	2.8	36.1
Finland	5	24,110	20,270	23	3.3	2.0	38.8
Ireland	4	18,340	18,340	30	3.2	7.5	91.0
Israel	6	15,940	17,310	33	3.5	5.4	31.8
New Zealand	4	14,700	15,840	40	1.8	3.2	32.7
Norway	4	34,330	24,290	8	2.8	3.9	41.6
Switzerland	7	40,080	26,620	7	2.0	0.4	42.4
(b) *Middle Income*							
Bolivia	8	1,000	2,820	140	−0.2	4.2	17.2
Costa Rica	4	2,780	6,620	86	3.0	3.7	45.7
El Salvador	6	1,850	2,850	139	0.2	5.3	24.2
Jamaica	3	1,680	3,210	130	2.0	0.1	74.2
Mauritania:	3	410	1,660	165	1.8	4.2	40.7
Paraguay	5	1,760	3,650	117	2.5	2.8	47.2

(*Continued*)

Table 1. (*Continued*)

Country	Pop. Millions 1998	GNP Per Capita $ 1998	GNP at PPP* 1998 $	Rank	Average Annual % Growth in GDP 1980–1990	1990–1998	Export % of GNP 1997
(c) *Low Income*							
Benin	6	380	1,250	182	2.9	4.6	22.7
Burundi	7	140	620	207	4.4	−3.2	10.6
Central African Rep.	3	300	1,290	181	3.7	4.6	15.9
Chad	7	230	–	–	1.4	1.5	17.1
Senegal	9	530	1,710	162	3.1	3.0	26.7
Siena Leone	5	140	390	210	0.3	−4.7	13.0

Note: *PPP = Purchasing Power Parity.
Source: World Development Report (1999/2000).

The degree of openness of a country may be defined as its total trade (both imports and exports) as a percent of GNP. Table 2 clearly demonstrates that small countries are much more dependent on trade than large countries. This phenomenon can be understood intuitively: small countries do not possess within their borders all the goods their citizens want, and all the raw materials and components its industry needs. Therefore must import more. To finance the relatively large imports, they have to export. To be sure, size is only one of the factors affecting the size of foreign trade and the degree of openness.

Moreover, trade among countries is only one form of interdependence. Much of the trade is carried out within multinational firms and international production is of great importance. Moreover, foreign direct investment embodies a package of assets, of which trade is only one. Other important characteristics of multinationals are the access they allow to markets as well as to technologies and to other forms of knowledge.

There are also other forms of interdependence among countries such as strategic alliances, or technology transfer, In today's world, competition is based more often than not on knowledge and knowledge transfer is increasingly a major source of creating and sustaining competitive advantage. Therefore, when one considers the ability of small countries to

Table 2. Degree of openness among very small, small and large countries in 1995.

Group of Countries	Number of Countries	Percentage of Total	Trade (Exports plus Imports) as a % of GNP	Unweighted Average Level of Trade as a % of GNP
Very Small Countries *(pop. 1–5 million)*	*41*	36	40–160	91
Developing	24	58	40–145	90
Restructuring	11	27	58–160	90
High-Income	6	15	62–139	97
		100		
Small Countries *(pop. 5–16 million)*	46	40	17–27	75
Developing	28	61	17–132	58
Restructuring	8	17	46–228	100
High-Income	10	22	64–297	102
		100		
Large Countries *(pop. 30 million or more)*	27	24	15–90	44
Developing	18	67	15–90	43
Restructuring	2	7	44–53	49
High-Income	7	26	17–71	44
		100		
Total Number of Countries	114			

Source: Dominick Salvatore, *The Economic Performance of Small Versus Large Nations*, p. 32.

survive in a global system, it is important to gauge not only the ability to trade, but also to maintain headquarters of multinationals.

Salvatore (1997) examined the economic performance of small versus large countries in terms of both level and growth of real per capita income, levels of investments and degrees of openness. He concludes that more open countries have grown faster than those with inward-oriented policies. He points out that:

> *a small size is somewhat of an economic disadvantage, but only for developing countries... The same is generally true for rates of growth in per*

> *capita income. On the other hand, large countries are generally less open than small countries and much less open than very small countries... Finally, size does not seem to make much of a difference in the economic performance of high-income economies* (Salvatore, 1997: pp. 39–40).

Table 3 summarizes some of Salvatore's findings. The findings about developed countries may be explained by the importance of technology in stimulating development and as an engine of economic growth and

Table 3. Growth of PPP* per capita income in very small, small and large countries between 1985 and 1995.

Group of Countries	Number of Countries	Percentage of Total	Range of Growth Rates	Unweighted Average Growth
Very Small Countries *(pop.* 1–5 *million)*	39	34	−15.1 to 6.2	−1.0
Developing	24	62	−5.8 to 6.0	0.6
Restructuring	9	23	−15.1 to 2.7	−7.1
High-Income	6	15	−3.5 to 6.2	1.8
		100		
Small Countries *(pop.* 5–16 *million)*	46	40	−7.0 to *6.1*	−1.2
Developing	28	61	7.0 to 6.1	−0.5
Restructuring	8	17	−17.0 to −1.0	−7.4
High-Income	10	22	−0.2 to 4.8	1.8
		100		
Large Countries *(pop.* 30 *million or more*)	29	26	−*8.5* to 8.4	*1.1*
Developing	19	66	−8.5 to 8.4	1.9
Restructuring	3	10	−9.2 to −0.4	−4.9
High-Income	7	24	0.4 to 2.9	1.7
		100		
Total Number of Countries	114			

Note: *PPP = Purchasing Power Parity.

Source: Dominick Salvatore, *The Economic Performance of Small Versus Large Nations*, p. 28.

structural change. Developing countries are latecomers that have to catch up with technological leaders. Finland, for example, has undergone a major structural change. The country moved from reliance on raw materials to a knowledge-based production and it enjoyed a high rate of growth in GNP per capita. Its share of high-tech products in total exports (20 percent) is among the highest among the industrialized countries. The ratio of R&D to GNP is about 3 percent — the second highest among European Union. The country is today one of the leading producers of information and communications technology with a mobile phones penetration of 65 percent — the highest in the world. (Ali Yrkko *et al.*, 2000). The remainder of this paper concentrates on strategic options of developed small market economies.

Before the globalization era, links among countries were not as seamless as they are today. First, a significant part of any country's GNP consisted of non-tradable goods and mainly services. Certainly, government services are not traded in the market and so are goods for which the transportation costs make trade prohibitive. The advance of new technologies and of telecommunications and computers, allowed many services previously perceived as non-tradable to become subject to the rigor of world competition. As one example, auditing and consulting are now dominated by the Big Five accounting firms. Even medical services or university studies are now offered across national borders through Internet and by other means of remote control. Second, and perhaps more important, nations attempted to protect their domestic industries by so-called import substitution policies. World trade was hampered by the imposition of quotas or high customs duties. Domestic firms could operate under the umbrella of protection from foreign more efficient competitors. Indeed, several decades ago, firms were able to compete because the government maintained a policy of protecting these firms against foreign competition. The above is not meant to imply that protectionism is over. The days in which Admiral Perry sailed into Tokyo Bay in 1854 to force the Japanese government at gunpoint to keep tariffs below 5 percent for 50 years may be over. Yet there are many pressures to protect industries because of hopes to maintain employment and existing sources of national wealth from whittling away. There are calls for "fair trade" or "managed trade" — both a euphemism for protection, (for many examples see e.g., Bovard, 1991). Yet in comparison to the past, trade is freer.

Another characteristic of many closed economies is that some firms grew to become large conglomerates (and were even able to export based on marginal cost considerations). In many cases, the capital market was extremely underdeveloped and the large companies relied on an internal capital market: Excess cash flew from cash creating divisions to finance investments in other divisions. Further, the large firms developed a strong political clout and were thus able to get heavily subsidized finance from a government eager to achieve growth and development. Essentially, the large domestic conglomerate became a substitute to the operation of the capital market. Its board of directors closely monitored the management. In some small countries, the availability of a relative low cost capital allowed such firms to grow and prosper. Governments also attempted to increase foreign trade by imposing buy back and offset conditions on large imports. They also protected domestic production. Based on such protection, some firms could export based on marginal costs.

With time, the disadvantages of this system became apparent. Most economists would agree with the World Development Report (1987: p. 85) assertion that "the economic performance of the of the outward-oriented economies has been broadly superior to that of the inward-oriented economies in almost all respects". Such a strategy is even less effective and more costly in a small country with a limited size of the domestic market. In addition, the managerial and political problems of large conglomerates in small countries became apparent. First, a major strategic error of management can create a major shock wave to the total economy. Since the country is small, a very large firm is a major part of its GNP and a significant provider of employment. Second, the very size of such a firm makes it a major political player in the country and blurs the distinction between economics and politics. Finally, the system inhibits competition, with all the known ramifications of monopolistic behavior. Risk reduction considerations call for diversification and the encouragement of a large number of independent firms.

Independently, scholars in finance argued that conglomerates, or highly diversified companies, are traded in the capital market at a discount. In other words, the theoretical break-up value of a conglomerate was posited to be higher than its value as one diversified firm. If the multiple businesses of a conglomerate were floated in the market as independent firms, the sum of their value would by greater than the value of the conglomerate itself. Certain empirical evidence has also pointed out that many mergers destroyed value for the shareholders rather than creating it. Further, it was shown that more focused companies enjoy higher price/earnings ratios than conglomerates. All these studies, based on theoretical views on investor portfolios, diversification and risk, pointed out to the superiority of an open capital market rather than internal allocation of resources within a conglomerate (See e.g., Markides, 1996; Montgomery, 1994).

Today it is standard knowledge that an open economy is much more efficient than a close one. It is widely accepted that all domestic firms must face competition not only locally but also from foreign competitors and that the consumers are much better off if firms face both domestic and foreign competition. To be sure, trade unions sometimes attempt to block foreign competition, in particular when it comes from countries employing extremely low cost labor. It is often claimed that this type of competition is unfair, particularly when it comes from countries employing children at conditions unacceptable under Western developed countries' norms. Other interest groups often call for so called "fair trade" rather than free trade. The military establishment may also press for reliance on domestic sources in the supply of major weapons. These are, of course, important considerations. Yet, the accepted norm has become one of free trade, open borders and reduction if not elimination of an increased number of barriers to trade. It is also generally accepted that autarky is impossible and even not desirable. Further, import substitution policies are much less feasible in small countries with a limited size of the market. More and more political leaders preach for a free trade among nations. A small nation must become a global player. The government could protect firms as long as it controlled imports, but as a country is becoming an integral part of the world economy, facing much more competition from large multinationals, the government's ability to help inefficient sectors of the economy is being curtailed. This is particularly important in small countries, where the ratio of exports to GNP has been growing.

Of course, nations rarely trade. Firms do the trading. These firms can rarely achieve economies of scale based on sales within the borders of a small country alone. The size of the market is much too small to allow such economies of scale. The firm may achieve scale by diversification into related and unrelated fields. A famous example of that strategy are the Chaebols in South Korea. As already discussed, this strategy may not cause the most efficient allocation of resources. Therefore, to achieve scale, the firm must export, or acquire subsidiaries beyond the borders of the country.

In the globalization era, firms can and do develop competitive strengths unrelated to the location advantage of their home countries. This is true not only for firms with international experience but also for the newcomers facing a different environment. Location factors were important several decades ago, and certainly in Ricardo's or Alfred Marshall's time. They are much less relevant today, at the age of the Internet and fax. Today, knowledge is the most important means of creating value. We shift from an economy of goods to an economy of ideas and of knowledge. In such an economy, the firm is portrayed as a solution to the fundamental problem of information processing (e.g., Alchian & Demsetz, 1972; Casson, 1997). Moreover a firm may acquire and gain a competitive advantage by the acquisition of knowledge and by its transfer within the organization. Kogut & Zander (1992, 1993) proposed that multinational enterprises are able to transfer knowledge that cannot be fully codified economically through "a set of higher order organizing principles". Gupta & Govindarajan (1991, 1993) posit that the degree of interdependence of subsidiaries depends on how much of the knowledge they require is held within the subsidiary, how much is received from other subsidiaries or other parts of the firm and how much they supply to other parts. It is thus important to understand where is the knowledge generated and how is it transferred.

Moreover, a multinational may create new knowledge in host countries' subsidiaries, not in the home country. This is obvious in cases in which a multinational creates an R&D center in the Silicon Valley or any other knowledge center. It is possible also when an accounting firm concentrates some of its experts in a certain location or when all the consultants share and transfer knowledge by e-mail. In these cases the knowledge is not generated nor is it necessarily accumulated at headquarters. The ability of a MNE to transfer knowledge across many countries and cultures within the organization has become the major component of the firm-specific advantage of these firms. These firms have not only become a powerful repository of knowledge but mainly an effective agent of the creation of new knowledge and the transfer of existing one.

Developing the Economy of a Small Country

Given this short analysis, what are the options of a small, developed country with an open economy in search for the best means and organizing devices to develop its economy? There are three separate issues to be analyzed. First, what are the available sources of competitive advantage for the firms in a small country. Second, what is the optimal organization of firms in terms of the distribution of firms by their size? Third, does ownership of the firm matter? Competitive advantage is essential to be able to compete. If only a few firms can compete worldwide, the degree of risk to the country is very high. In many cases, these considerations mean that a viable option for a firm is to be acquired by a multinational. This often raises nationalistic feelings. These three issues are discussed below.

To compete in world markets, a firm must enjoy some unique competitive advantage. Competitive advantage can be gained either as a result of cost advantage or a price premium. A firm may enjoy cost advantage and therefore a competitive edge. Alternatively, it may be able to command higher prices in the market than its competitors and thus — a competitive advantage.

A firm is much better off if it can achieve price premium. Price premium may be a result of a superior quality, unique design, specific knowledge accumulated in the firm and so on. Note that price premium must be gained in the market place. In reality, therefore, it is not enough to have a superior product. The product must be marketed, sold and reach a paying customer. The marketing costs may be quite high. In fact, the high cost of marketing may be a major constrain for a small firm. As one example, such a firm would find the costs of reaching final consumers globally prohibitive. It would have to sell its products to a multinational, or on a private brand basis, or to find other means to optimize the marketing costs.

Some of the options (that are not mutually exclusive) for the organization of firms with a clear competitive advantage are:

1. Reliance on a clear cost advantage in one or more raw material or an agricultural product. In a business driven largely by raw material costs, the presence of oil or minerals or fertile climate for certain crops can allow cost advantage. Thus, the exports of some states are based on cost advantage because of the availability of oil, copper, diamonds etc. or because of cost advantages in producing dairy products, coffee, bananas or other agricultural products. In most cases, the reliance on cost advantage means very little diversification of exports with all the risks such a policy curtails. It also often mean that one large firm does all or a significant part of the export. Thus, fuels, minerals and metals are more than 95 percent of total merchandise

exports in Algeria, Iraq, Iran, Kuwait, Nigeria, Saudi Arabia, and United Arab Emirates. Tin is more than 80 percent of total exports in Bolivia and copper comprises the majority of Chile's exports.

In any one country, one encounters heterogeneous firms with asymmetric abilities to compete. Large firms account for a major parts of exports in many small countries. The reduction of the concentration of exports is a major policy goal of a small country.

2. A possible source of cost advantage is a low level of wages. Competitive advantage may be concentrated in a distinct part of the value chain, e.g., when a country is basing its exports on having extremely low cost of labor. This alternative usually means that the country attracts large foreign multinationals that produce the labor-intensive parts in the country. Under this alternative, the country produces and exports parts and components, often to other subsidiaries of the same multinational. The World Development Report of 1999/2000 contains interesting and pertinent data on the share of parts and components in exports of manufacturing in several developing countries. In Nicaragua, for example, this percentage was 24.6 and in Singapore −21.7 percent. However, by definition the necessity to maintain low wages means that it is extremely difficult to achieve an increase in the standard of living. The government may find itself forced to devalue the currency to maintain the advantage of low wages. Moreover, firms in low wage countries tend to be owned and controlled by global multinationals. Alternatively, the multinationals may be the sole buyers of the domestic firm's production. The ownership issue of the firms in the country is a delicate political issue.
3. Firms may achieve worldwide dominance because of first mover advantages exploited fast or some unique core competence. These firms can achieve scale economies on a worldwide basis. Empirical evidence demonstrates that although most giant multinationals have their headquarters in large developed countries such as the United States, small countries can be the home base of giant multinationals. Some examples are Nestle, the food manufacturer from Switzerland as well as several insurance companies and pharmaceutical firms based in that country; Lego from Denmark, Royal Dutch Shell and Philips from the Netherlands and Acer from Taiwan. While these firms maintain their headquarters in the small country they achieve scale by having the world as their oyster. As one example, Nestle's production in Switzerland is less than two percent of its total

worldwide production and sales (communication with the company). In the case of Nokia, local sales are less than two and a half percent of total sales (Ali Yrkko *et al.*, 2000: p. 41). Acer's sales in Taiwan are also negligible and more than two thirds of sales are in the United States and Europe (Acer, 1999).

4. Diversified domestic firms, exporting on the margin with strength based on large size achieved by domination in the domestic market. This option assumes that the capital market is underdeveloped. It is based, at least at the beginning, on strong protection of the domestic market. With globalization, such a conglomerate may or may not have created sustainable world competitive advantages to be able to compete against the onslaught of imports. Often, these conglomerates are becoming a burden on the economy, and use their political clout to continue their operations. Other firms, able to tap the worldwide capital markets, are a much more efficient alternative. In a globalization era, these firms must restructure, as Nokia did. The roots of this firm go back to 1865. At that time it was a forest industry enterprise. In the 1980s it had no less than eleven business lines, including rubber, forest, cable and electronics. Since then, the firm changed itself, focusing on telecommunications and increasing significantly foreign production. At the same time, it has divested all other core competence businesses (Ali Yrkko *et al.*, 2000: pp. 36–37).

   In global markets with diminishing barriers to inter-country trading, successful firms can sell globally and can produce their goods wherever this production is most efficient. Therefore, the size of the country is no more a constraint on the size of the firm. A successful firm from a small country can produce everywhere and sell globally. Note that from the country's point of view, it is much better of when the giant multinational produces and markets in many countries. When domestic production is dominated by one or two giant multinationals, these firms become a dominant force in that economy. Any strategic error of such a firm may have devastating results for the country.

5. Thus, we are left with the last possible theoretical alternative: an economy based on a large number of relatively small firms exporting directly. It is often thought that this is not a viable option since only giant multinationals will be able to survive in the seamless global market place. Mr. Bossidy, then vice chairman of the board of General Electric, predicted in 1989 that:

> *Globalization is transforming the landscape of world trade.... By the latter part of the 1990s there may well be fewer than 25 mega corporations in the world, about equally divided among United States, European and Far Eastern companies.... The medium-to-large-size generalists, serving a limited geographic market and without a specific niche, won't be around anymore* (Bossidy, 1989: p. 10).

In fact, the number of small multinationals is mushrooming. The United Nations data bank shows about 40,000 such firms worldwide. Moreover the number of such multinationals has tripled between the 1970s and the 1990s. With the advance of Internet and electronic commerce, more small firms can become multinationals and compete effectively in world markets. Despite earlier predictions, large firms do not dominate most economic fields, and small firms show high level of resilience, not only in the domestic economy but also in the world market place. Let us turn therefore to the strategies available to small firms.

Strategies Available to Small Firms in a Global Marketplace

Can small firms survive in a global market place or are they doomed to be acquired by a giant multinational? Indeed in some industries one can observe a wave of mergers and acquisitions that shrink the number of firms and increase concentration. One example is the automobile manufacturing industry: Volvo was acquired by Ford Motor Company. Saab — by General Motors. Volkswagen acquired, among others, Seat in Spain, Skoda in the Czech Republic and the British Rolls Royce. BMW acquired Rover (and sold it later to a group of British venture capitalists). Another example is the airline industry, in which — apparently only because of government regulation — we see less mergers but a very large number of strategic alliances and code sharing agreements. Seristo (2000) notes that "In the 1990s the number of alliances grew steadily each year... In 1990 the industry sources listed 172 alliances... there were a total of 513 airline alliances among 204 airlines in mid 1999, with an increase of 40 percent over the year 1997 "(Seristo, 2000: pp. 259–260). In general, alliances are motivated by the desire to achieve risk sharing, scale economies, access to markets, access to technology and market convergence. In the airline case the two main drivers were thought to be the search for more market power and for lower operating costs. Alliances were motivated also by the fact that mergers and acquisitions were tightly controlled and foreign ownership — restricted by governments. Yet, there are small airlines operating in the global market and there are many small firms offering the large car manufacturers parts or components. Indeed, even in large countries small firms employ more employees together than the very large firms and they play an important role in innovation than their better known large counterparts. Small and midsize firms can develop a unique advantage in the global market place.

By definition, small firms can rarely achieve export success based on scale. If they do, they — by definition — become giant firms. Of course, small firms cannot compete head on against the giants. Small firms must develop firm specific advantage by:

- Focusing on a well-defined segment — avoid direct competition. This means concentration of activities in fragmented industries.
- Specialization in innovative ways to meet specific customer needs.
- Large transaction size to reduce marketing costs.
- High level of flexibility allowing fast reaction to changes in economic and technological conditions.
- Fast response to market needs.
- Superior service.
- Customization-offering a customized product or service to those customers willing to pay a premium for such a product or a service.

The reason such strategies are feasible is precisely that the world has become global. The constraint on financing — caused by the lack of development of financial markets — is disappearing because firms can tap capital markets not only domestically but also abroad. The feasible access to global capital markets means that small firms are not dependent on domestic sources of funds. These firms do not need necessarily to be a part of a large domestic conglomerate or of a giant multinational to be able to get financing. In addition, the number of venture capitalists, willing and able to finance start ups, has mushroomed.

The marketing problem is a major constraint, however, for those firms that do not choose to take the risks necessary in order to grow and become a giant firm. An alternative, mentioned above, is to use a niche strategy. Niche, by definition, is of a limited size. Small firms are able to dominate a niche or a relatively small global business segment. Once such firms are successful in achieving a large market share in a specific niche they face a problem: if the niche is growing fast it may attract the attention of large firms. If it is not, the firm must identify, successfully enter and then manage multiple niches. It is also theoretically possible to start with a very limited niche, grow to a larger niche and so on. This theoretical possibility is in reality an onerous task.

Another possibility is to reduce marketing costs. One means of doing so is to sell on a private brand basis, or to sell all. the production to a large multinational that will carry out the marketing or use other OEM. It is also possible to have a limited number of clients each with a large size of transaction. The need of proximity to the market is often a major constraint for small firms, limited in resources, while a firm may start activities by exporting, it would soon need to establish subsidiaries in the major markets, in order to supply after sale services. Because of the marketing costs, a small firm is unlikely to reach successfully a big consumers market on its own. It is better off catering to a small number of customers seeking high-ticket items. In any case, the market segment should be defined to achieve dominance.

Ownership

In a globalized world, firms can grow beyond the limits of the size of the nation. Firms are virtual entities, totally unrelated to the nation. Does it matter if a firm is owned by foreigners? Many economists would agree with Lall (1995) that foreign investment should be encouraged. It is believed that foreign multinationals would give domestic firm an export boost by allowing access to international trading networks.

Still, when a domestic firm is acquired by foreigners, certain citizens feel that such a firm ceased to be a domestic firm. Foreign ownership is seen as wrong, yet in many industries such moves are inevitable. When economies of scale are of importance, the industry becomes globally concentrated. A single major pharmaceutical development project may cost more than $300 million and thus needs a critical mass of global sales, achieved only by the large global players. Of course, domestic firms may operate in a certain niche but may also be acquired by a large firm. This may mean that ownership will be foreign. However, local citizens can also invest their savings in other countries in order to diversify their portfolio. Further, it is rare for private individuals to acquire a firm.

Most acquisitions of domestic firms are carried out by foreign multinationals. General Motors acquired Saab, not an individual family. General Motors itself may be perceived as an American firm. Certainly, it can be also seen as a firm without any national identity.

More than seventy years after the appearance of Berle and Means' seminal work in 1932, the question of ownership seems to be moot. Today even top management of multinationals does not come from one country, and the CEO of a US firm may be a German citizen. As long as peaceful global markets operate, the ownership does not seem to be an important issue. Of course, if one assumes that countries may be at war with each other, ownership does become an important issue, more so in so called strategic industries.

Robert Reich claimed in *The Work of Nations* (1992) that what matters is employment. For him, a Japanese owned firm in the United States is much more important to the country than an American firm producing (and thus creating employment) in another country. He claimed Honda in the United States is more important to the US than Ford in Asia.

In the globalization era, the major asset of a firm may be hypothesized to be its accumulated knowledge. A firm may be seen as a depository and a creator of knowledge. As long as the specific knowledge of the firm is stored in the minds (and the computers) of citizens of the country, the location of activities or their ownership may be of much less significance than it received today. Saab remains a Saab and the knowledge accumulated to make it the unique car it is remains even though ownership of the firm changed. It might get more knowledge from the accumulated knowledge of the owner. All in all, ownership of firms is — or could be — distributed among thousands of shareholders from different countries. Then owners rarely control the firm.

Some Policy Implications

A small country, by definition, is limited by its size. Therefore, the only way such a country may sustain large firms is by encouraging firms operating within its border to move some of the operations abroad. Firms are thus better off if they think globally from their start. If firms tap their capital in the global markets, one constraint of small size disappears. Thus, 125 firms in tiny Israel are listed in NASDAQ or New York Stock Exchange. If firms own producing and marketing subsidiaries abroad — another constraint of small size is being diminished. If a firm is acquired by another firm from another country and becomes a subsidiary of that firm — this is another way to avoid the problem of size. In the market place, the most efficient and innovative firms will be those who will own the others.

Parenthetically, an optimal policy for a small country is to allow the investors in the country to diversify their portfolio by investing abroad and encourage local firms to tap capital abroad. Such a policy reduces significantly the risk to the country.

Risk considerations mean that a government would not want the country to be dependent on one crop, or one conglomerate or one product. Otherwise, the whole country can face a disaster because of nature (such as draught) or because of a strategic error of one company. Thus, the Dairy Board of New Zealand accounts for more than 20 percent of the country's exports. Nokia accounts for about 60 percent of Helsinki stock exchange market capitalization. It also accounts for 20 percent of Finland's exports and 3 percent of its GNP (Ali Yrkko *et al.*, 2000). The most optimal policy for a small country, therefore, is to diversify into a large number of small firms, many of which would be global players. Hopefully, a few of these firms would grow in size and become large multinationals.

If all of the economic resources of a small country are controlled by one or even a few large diversified conglomerates, there is a high probability that the firms might have an undue control not only on the economy of the country but also on its political system. Countries are much better off if their economy is diversified in different economic branches and if in each one of these branches competition prevails. The government is much better of if the inhabitants of the country are encouraged to diversify their investments globally; if they do not invest disproportional sums in a large domestic firm. The country is better off if its production resources and mainly its labor is employed by many firms rather than by one large one. Finally, the country is better off if any of its larger firms diversify their operations geographically rather than concentrate the production in one country.

If a government encourages competition — not only locally but by letting local firms face global competition. If the policies of the government are designed to prevent monopolies, cartels and domestic conglomerates. If it encourages open borders and diminishes any constrain on the free movements of goods, services and factors of production as well as deregulation — then the country will flourish economically. The economic performance of outward oriented strategy "has been broadly superior to that of the inward-oriented economies in almost all respects" (World Development Report, 1987: p. 85). This conclusion is even more straightforward for small countries with a limited domestic market.

To be sure, countries must maintain social cohesion. Government is expected to help the poor. It is also expected to reduce income differences among groups and to attempt increasing the level of income to more regions. Yet social cohesion is too often misinterpreted to mean that government should subsidize ailing firms, letting them or even forcing them to continue their operations to maintain employment. It cannot be overstressed that this is a major mistaken policy. Best managed firms have learnt that they should shrink or exit from low return businesses and invest aggressively in high return business. This same logic applies to the country.

Conclusions

Any economy can be thought of as a portfolio of firms and markets. Economic policy cannot be properly studied nor prescribed without a thorough understanding of how competition varies by industry and how microeconomics of business firms changes over time.

In some industries economies of scale are paramount, and global industries prevail. A small country can achieve long-term growth and rising living standards only if its firms are competitive in terms of the world market. Small firms (and small countries) will find it extremely difficult, say, to produce car engines or passenger airplanes. It may, of course, produce components. On the other hand diamond cutting is an extremely fragmented industry. Small firms can be successful in exporting on their own when they focus on and dominate specific market niches which are appropriate to their capabilities. The ability to focus is a necessary but not a sufficient condition. To be successful, small exporting firms must choose a small number of segments in which they pursue relentlessly to establish strength in world terms. Fortunately, new information technologies create many opportunities for small firms from small countries to dominate globally. Small countries are in a better economic position today than they were several decades ago. Globalization allows these countries to take advantage of the best available world resources in finance and technology.

If small countries choose to encourage integration of the domestic firms in the global economy there is no reason for them not to flourish and prosper. Size of the nation is not a major constraint in a globally integrated world, where firms can tap money in different capital markets, produce in different countries using division of labor within the firm by concentrating labor intensive activities in low wages countries and research and development — where scientists are available. Marketing activities can be spread in different countries, in proximity to the customers.

Of course we have implicitly assumed up to now that all countries of the world bow to the rules of free trade and free markets. While the barriers to free trade are increasingly reduced, they still exist in many areas. One notable example is agricultural products. The Dairy Board of New Zealand operates in close to sixty countries with the milk powder business run from Singapore, the butter — from the United Kingdom and the cheese — from Australia. In this line of business, it says, only 6 percent of the world dairy market is freely tradable (and the dairy board market share in the tradable part is 32 percent). The more countries cooperate to achieve a regime of free movement of all factors of production, as well as information, technology, and investment, the higher is the probability to increase standard of living in the small as well as the large countries of the world.

References

Acer Inc.: Taiwan's Rampaging Dragon. 1999. Harvard Business School case number April 9-399-019.

Alchian, A. & Demsetz, H. 1972. Production, information costs and economic organization. *American Economic Review*, 62: 777–795.

Ali-Yrkko, J., Paija, L., Reilly, C. & Yla-Anttila, P. 2000. *Nokia: A Big Company in a Small Country*. Talousieto Oy.

Barnet, R. J. & Cavanagh, J. 1994. *Global Dreams Imperial Corporations and the New World Order*. New York: Touctone.

Berle, A. & Means, G. 1932. *The Modern Corporation and Private Property.*

Bossidy, L. A. 1989. Globalization: It's already here. *Credit Magazine* (September–October): 10–12.

Bovard, J. 1991. *The Fair Trade Fraud.* New York: St. Martin's Press.

Casson, M. 1997. *Information and Organization: A New Perspective on the Theory of the Firm.* Oxford: Clarendon Press.

Drucker, P. F. 1999. *Management Challenges for the 21 Century.* Jordan Hill, Oxford: Butterworth-Heinemann, p. 56 (Hebrew Translation).

Friedman, T. L. 1999. *The Lexus and the Olive Tree Understanding Globalization.* New York: Farrar, Straus, Giroux.

Gupta, A. K. & Govindarajan, V. 1993. Coalignment between knowledge flows patterns and strategic systems and processes within MNC's. In Lorange, P., Chakravarthy, B., Roos, J. & Van de Ven, A. (Eds.) *Implementing Strategic Processes: Change, Learning and Co-operation.* Oxford: Blackwell, pp. 329–346.

Kogut, B. & Zander U. 1992. Knowledge of the firm, combinative capabilities and the replication of technology. *Organization Science*, 3: 383–387.

Kogut, B. & Zander U. 1993. Knowledge of the firm and the evolutionary theory of the multinational corporation. *Journal of International Business*, 24: 625–645.

Lail, S. 1995. Employment and foreign investment: Policy options for developing countries. *International Labour Review*, 134(4–5): 521–540.

Levitt, T. 1983. The globalization of markets. *Harvard Business Review* (September–October): 92–102.

Markides, C. 1996. *Diversification, Refocusing and Economic Performance.* Cambridge, MA: MIT Press.

Montgomery, C. A. 1994. Corporate diversification. *Journal of Economic Perspectives*, 8: 163–178.

Ohmae, K. 1995. *The End of the Nation State: The Rise of Regional Economies.* New York: The Free Press.

Reich, R. 1992. *The Work of Nations: Preparing Ourselves for 21st Century Capitalism.* New York: Vintage Books.

Salvatore Dominick. 1997. The economic performance of small versus large nations in small states: New challenges and opportunities. *Development and International Cooperation*, 8(24–25): 21–42.

Seristo, H. 2000. International alliances in service business the case of the airline industry. In Aharoni, Y. & Nahum, L. (Eds.) *The Globalization of Services Some Implications for Theory and Practice.* Routledge Studies in International Business and the World Economy. London and New York: Routledge, pp. 258–283.

Soros, G. (1998). *The Crisis of Global Capitalism Open Society Endangered.* New York: Public Affairs.

World Development Report-of different issues.

https://doi.org/10.1142/9789811287510_0019

Chapter 19

Israeli Multinationals: Competing from a Small Open Economy*

Yair Aharoni

Tel Aviv University, Tel Aviv, Israel

Orthodox IB theory initially depicted MNEs as giant firms based in large, developed home markets. The headquarters of these MNEs transfer technology, management know-how, and capital from the home country to their various subsidiaries. Only much later did some researchers recognize that an MNE could be a knowledge seeker in addition to being a knowledge creator. Established MNEs endeavor to augment their knowledge by getting access to foreign-created knowledge, for example by acquisition of foreign firms. The MNE participates in various kinds of localized knowledge simultaneously (Rugman & Verbeke, 2001). The acquired knowledge is then transferred from one subsidiary to another or even to headquarters.

Today, established MNEs actively search outside the firm for technologies, ideas, and products. Procter and Gamble, for example, expects half of its future products to be based on technologies and concepts it will acquire from third parties (on the process see, for example, Huston & Sakkab, 2006). They acquire new technology rather than transferring existing technologies.

*This chapter is reproduced from *Emerging Multinationals in Emerging Markets*, pp. 352–396 (2009), Cambridge University Press.

Porter's (1990a, 1990b, 1998) "demand conditions" are a major part of his "diamond". Firms must have a large home base in order to develop the skills to operate an MNE and to prosper. MNEs possess FSAs that are transferred to a network of subsidiaries in other locations. FDIs, therefore, are assumed to flow from large, developed economies to other developed economies as well as to less developed ones. Recognizing the benefits of FDI to the domestic economy, nations compete intensely with each other to get MNEs to locate value-added activities within their borders.

Far less attention has been paid — at least until recently — to the possibility of encouraging domestic firms in emerging economies to transform into MNEs. In fact, in many economies, foreign exchange controls and other governmental restrictions made the creation of home-based MNEs difficult if not impossible.

Based on Canadian experience, Rugman & Verbeke (1993) pointed out that firms may draw on the strengths of the "diamond" of more than one nation, leading to the development of "double diamond" or even "multiple diamond" perspectives. Such perspectives appear useful mainly when firms from a small, open economy are analyzed (Van den Bulcke & Verbeke, 2001). Israel clearly demonstrates that a large home market is not a prerequisite for creating MNEs. On the contrary, the tiny size of the home market is a major incentive for Israeli firms to become multinationals by catering to much larger foreign markets. In some cases, the move abroad came after the possibilities available in the domestic market were exhausted, but in other cases, the firms sold 100 percent of their output outside Israel. All in all, by 2007, a few hundred Israeli firms had become successful MNEs, with several emerging as global, Israel-based powerhouses.

These outliers can serve as role models for other Israeli firms as well as for managers in other small countries. At the same time, these cases challenge mainstream IB theories, which are mostly based on studies of the world's largest MNEs. While it is true that the largest MNEs account for 90 percent of the world's FDI stock, IB theory must also be able to explain the internationalization of firms from small, open economies, which present different challenges than large economies.

Globalization is often cast as a vehicle by which large firms crush hapless small firms — and small countries. In discussing the case of Israel, this chapter seeks to show that seamless global operations enhance rather than negate the options available to prosperous small nations. As long as the policies of the government in the small country create the proper environment for local entrepreneurs, firms may thrive in global markets if they make the right strategic choices and are managed well.

They may not possess the capabilities to build global consumer brands, but they can thrive by dominating well-differentiated niches.

To be sure, neither competing in large foreign markets nor integrating globally is easy. Indeed, many Israeli firms failed in their attempts to become MNEs, even when they had innovative technologies, because they lacked expertise in marketing, or in managing growth processes. Others succumbed to acquisitions by large European or US-based MNEs. Our focus here is on those that overcame these odds to become Israel-based MNEs.

We identify two types of Israeli MNES: those going abroad only after exploiting the possibilities of the domestic market and those "born global", that started out as multinationals. The first type can be found in most economic sectors, with the exception of public utilities. The second is limited to a few high-tech sectors, such as electronics, telecommunications, and software.

This chapter starts with a brief background on Israel, emphasizing the changes in its economic policies since 1985. The next section describes key changes in the country's business elite. The new macroeconomic environment and the new attitudes of managers were necessary but not sufficient for the creation of Israeli multinationals. The following section demonstrates the key drivers for the success of Israeli MNEs through a detailed case study of the largest of these firms, Teva Pharmaceutical Industries Ltd. A more comprehensive picture of all outward FDIs, comparing their magnitude to other small countries, is then presented. The next section presents a case study of Check Point Software Technologies Ltd, one of Israel's most interesting "born global" MNEs. Based on the above, the following section proposes some hypotheses about the ingredients of a successful strategy for the creation of Israeli MNEs. The section that follows raises some public policy issues. The chapter concludes with possible lessons, generalizations, and suggestions for further research.

Israel — The Country and Its Economy[1]

Israel is a tiny economy with very few natural resources within its borders. Like other small countries, it attempts to define and maintain for itself a place in a world that is becoming increasingly globally integrated. It is one of the few modern states founded by a migration of settlers, forging new institutions in territories perceived to be uninhabited.

---

[1]A part of this section is condensed from Aharoni (1991) and Aharoni (1992).

The return of Jews to their homeland started in 1882, when 20,000 Jews lived in Eretz Israel (Palestine). At that time, the area was rife with swamps and eroded by generations of neglect; there was no electricity; roads were extremely poor. In less than a generation, a group of dreamers worked diligently to form a new nation, to restore a virtually dead language, to create some of the finest universities in the world, and to establish a network of political and economic institutions.

Israel has encouraged Jews to return to their homeland and assisted them in doing so. An "ingathering of the exiles" was one of the highest priorities. In 1948, when the state was proclaimed after Eretz Israel was partitioned, there was a Jewish population of 650,000. From 1948 to 1951, 686,739 new immigrants, 76.4 percent of them from Asia and Africa, doubled that population. The burden of absorbing them resulted in the rationing of food and other essentials.

In 2007 the Jewish population was about 6 million out of a total population of 7.2 million. In the 1990s, the influx of about 1 million Jews from the former Soviet Union included over 10,000 scientists and engineers, augmenting Israel's educational and technical advantages.

The founding fathers of Israel preached a return to agricultural work as a counterpart to the occupational structure of Jews in the Diaspora. These dreams were expected to be achievable by the sheer willpower of the pioneers. Economic laws, it was believed, could be ignored as irrelevant. Instead, reality was mystified and sacrifices were expected. The obstinate devotion of hard-working pioneers, combined with a massive capital flow, turned the land to a mosaic of green; world records were set for milk production; economic growth was rapid.

In the first decade of Israel's existence, GNP tripled; it doubled in the second decade. Until 1972 GNP per capita growth averaged 5.2 percent annually. The first development plan for agriculture (presented in 1950) saw agriculture as a source of employment to 26 percent of all employed. The number of employees in agriculture steadily dwindled — and a large percentage of them are now foreign workers. The weight of agriculture in the business sector in 2006 was a mere 2.6 percent.

Israel is unique among new societies in that it developed on the basis of socialist principles and was created by immigrants from Eastern Europe, not by settlers from Britain or Western Europe. Later, Israel was to be unique because it moved from the dominance of socialist thinking to a strategic alliance with the United States. Its institutions keep modifying their shape as society undergoes metamorphoses.

Israel is also unique in the magnitude of foreign unilateral transfers it received, allowing a high rate of capital formation. The government tapped large sources of capital and therefore could decide on the allocation of that capital. Another unique factor has been the heavy burden of defense expenditures on the economy (peaking at 27.4 percent of GNP in the period 1974–1980). Israel has been vulnerable to military and terrorist attacks. As a result, it has found it necessary to devote a high proportion of resources to defense, to maintain a qualitative military edge over its potential enemies. Another result of the "hostile neighborhood" was that almost all large MNEs refused to defy the Arab boycott and to invest in Israel.

Defense needs created major leverage for developing science-based industries, to ensure a reliable supply of military-related goods. The government established (and owned) Israel Military Industries, Israel Aircraft Industries (1953)[2] and Rafael[3] — the Hebrew acronym of the Armaments Development Authority. The Ministry of Defense traded only with its own firms.[4] In 1967, France imposed an embargo on military-related supplies to Israel. One result was an expansion of the budgets for military research and development. Another result was that these funds were no longer granted only to SOEs.

The need for security was coupled with two other requirements, dictated by the basic values of the state's leaders. The first was the super importance of mutual aid both to existing citizens and to new immigrants, which resulted in the forging of a welfare state. The second need stemmed from a utopian view of the superiority of collective decision making, versus what was perceived as the wild pursuit of private gains.

The combination of these three factors with the gloomy realities of a less developed country reinforced the belief that the state alone could achieve security, social goals, and accelerated economic growth. These beliefs led to a very high level of involvement of government as well as

---

[2]It provides maintenance and rebuilding services for aircraft, and produces military and executive planes, weapons and missile systems, satellites, and electronic and radar-based combat systems. It is Israel's largest enterprise and its biggest exporter.

[3]It also developed and manufactured air-to-air missiles, sea-based missiles and other weapon systems.

[4]One exception was a communications and batteries firm, Tadiran, of which it sold 50 percent to General Telephone and Electronics. In 1966 the Ministry agreed to acquire a 50 percent share in Elbit (military electronics).

of Histadrut (the General Federation of Labor) and the Jewish Agency in ownership of economic units.

They established — sometimes separately, often jointly — many relatively large enterprises financed heavily from public sources. In the 1960s, the government or the Histadrut owned 45 percent of all large industrial plants. Virtually all economic activities were controlled, regulated, and directed by the various authorities. A national authority owned almost all land, leasing such lands for limited periods. Water was allocated by another authority. Importers needed a license. So did those wishing to buy foreign exchange. Bank credit was regulated and the government granted subsidized rates of interest to preferred recipients.

The government protected domestic production, restricting imports through quotas or sky-high tariffs. Most output was subject to price controls. It also subsidized exports. All sources of funds, including pensions, as well as the allocation of these funds, were tightly controlled and were distributed at the discretion of civil servants and politicians.

Since the government fully controlled the capital market, a public offering of shares was not feasible. New entrepreneurs had to present their business plans to the government and/or financial institutions — most of which were also controlled by the government or the Histadrut. Finally, perhaps because of the long reign of ideology, Israelis were told they should be ashamed for wanting to consume more, and that preferring cheaper imports to locally made goods was irresponsible. Outward FDI was certainly not encouraged. Very few firms received foreign exchange allocations for this purpose.

In 1973, Israel was caught by surprise, attacked by Egypt and Syria. Further, the high growth rate in economic activity that had characterized Israel until 1972 came to a halt. One reason was the rise of oil prices. Another was that many Israeli firms were not yet ready to face competition in the world market and achieve export-led growth.

By the 1970s the majority of Israelis were of Asian and African origin. They perceived themselves as deprived persons. They saw the Labor Party elite as an arrogant, intolerant, and paternalistic establishment. The Labor government was toppled in 1977 after several decades of Israel living under the rule of a single, socialist party.

A coalition of right-wing parties formed the government, declared a full liberalization of the economy, and abolished some of the controls on foreign exchange. The country suffered at the time from rampant inflation that at its height reached a level of more than 400 percent per annum. The net external debt reached 80 percent of GDP. It was widely agreed that drastic steps were called for and that the economy had to be reformed.

In 1985, a unity government accepted a stabilization plan proposed by several senior Israeli economists. These economists, trained in Chicago School theory, moved the economy toward liberalization. The plan has been very successful. Since then politicians have been much more willing to accept economists' proposals.

Between 1985 and 1994, major reforms were carried out in the capital markets, the money markets, the foreign exchange markets, the labor market, and in the role of the public sector. Average annual public spending was reduced from 1980–1984 to 1994–1998 by not less than 21 percent of GDP, money transferred from the public to the private sector. The government also increased purchases from the private sector, abolishing its own operations. Foreign exchange controls were totally abolished in 1988 and today there are no restrictions even on institutional investors. Import restrictions were abolished. Tax laws were changed, equalizing the tax consequences of various activities at home and abroad. Corporate taxes were reduced from 61% in 1987 to 45%, then to 36% in 1990 and to 31% in 2006.

The government significantly reduced its control of all sources of funds, the allocation of capital, and the determination of yields. Thus, the allocation of so-called directed credit went down from 65% of total credit in 1983 to 3% in 1998.

A series of reforms reduced the hold of monopolies. In 2005 the ports and the refineries were divided into several firms and were privatized, the telephone company was privatized, and a partial pension reform was implemented. Free trade agreements were signed with both the EU (1989) and the United States (1995) and imports from low-cost countries such as China, Turkey, Mexico, and Poland were allowed with no need for an import license and with much-reduced tariffs.

Another result of the 1985 plan was that many firms — used to protection from imports, a strictly regulated environment, and focused more on good relations with the government rather than efficiency in the marketplace — went bankrupt. A wave of acquisitions consolidated many industries. SOEs were privatized. Privatizations reduced the share of the SOE sector in manufacturing from 27% in 1985 to 10% in 1993. Histadrut-owned enterprises, most of which were characterized by bloated labor forces, were sold to private investors. The share of Histadrut in net product that had gone up from 10% in 1948 to 17.9% in 1953 and 23.0% in 1960 dwindled to 14% in 1993 and to almost zero by 2004.

Entrepreneurs who could achieve results in the marketplace replaced many of the older generation of businesspeople. The Law for the Encouragement of Industrial Research and Development was passed in 1985. Since then, the Office of the Chief Scientist at the Ministry of Industry and Trade has helped to fund innovative projects. Also in 1985, the first Israeli venture capital firm was established. Today, over 100 venture capital firms operate in Israel.

Between 1985 and 2007, a revolution took place in terms of the openness of the economy, foreign currency supervision, budgetary policy, and competition policy. On March 16, 2007, the OECD's Ministerial Council meeting approved a decision to open accession discussions with Israel. Israel's GNP per capita in 2006 was $19,900. The OECD average was $33,400, that of the Euro countries $33,500 and the United States $43,000. Inflation was — 0.1% in Israel compared with 2.1% in the United States and 2.3% in the EU.

Israel is still classified by the Institute of International Finance and by Morgan Stanley as an emerging economy. UNCTAD, on the other hand, classifies Israel as a developed economy. Today, Israel's high-tech industry promotes itself to investors as an alternative to Silicon Valley. The industry is carefully watched by venture capitalists, and dozens of Israeli technology companies have been sold to overseas buyers.

By 1982, Israel counted 300 high-tech firms, of which 122 employed 49 employees or fewer, 67 had 50–99 employees, and 111 employed 100 or more. All in all, these were very small firms. It was estimated at that time that about two thirds of the development engineers in Israel, directly or indirectly, served defense-related needs.

In 1987, the government decided to stop the development of an Israeli jet fighter, the Lavi. Israel Aviation had to fire a large number of skilled engineers with experience in cutting-edge technologies, who were then absorbed into the civilian marketplace. Advanced technologies that were originally developed for military purposes were later used to develop commercial products for civilian use. Thousands of visionaries formed start-up companies, some of which later became successful high-tech MNEs.

By 2004, 33% of Israeli manufacturing exports were in electronics and only 3.6% in textiles (Bank of Israel, Annual report for 2006: p. 60). Information, Communication, and Technology firms (ICT) are classified as trade and services; ICT product was 16.8% of business product in 2006 while the OECD average was 9% (Bank of Israel, 2006: p. 74). Because of the limited size of the domestic market, the share of exports in the output is very large: 57% in 2006, 72% in information technology alone (p. 74).

By 2000, Israel's share of the US and European high-tech market was 1.4%. That share went down as a result of a recession but by February 2007 was up again to about 1.3%. Israeli companies are developers of advanced technologies, enjoying top-notch human resources and government support for corporate R&D and manufacturing facilities. Since 1991, the Technological Incubators Program has provided comprehensive support to new ventures.

Israel still suffers threats to its very existence, resulting in a high level of uncertainty and many swings — for example, in the number of incoming tourists. The country is also far from its markets, unable to sell to its immediate neighbors. This problem is alleviated somewhat by the widespread use of the Internet as a means of quick communication and, more recently, the use of video conferencing. It is still not easily solved.

The New Managers

Another change that came gradually was in the recruitment, education, and tendencies of Israeli managers. In the 1960s managers in the state sector were political appointees, as were managers in the Histadrut sector. There was a strong belief in the superiority of egalitarian society. To avoid a class system, managerial jobs in the Histadrut were rotated. The private sector consisted of a large number of small enterprises, managed by several families of the owners. Those who attempted to grow faced the constraint of the small size of the market. Once competing firms were acquired, the only way to grow internally was to expand into other economic activities. Indeed, holding companies or conglomerates controlled jobs in many parts of the Israeli economy. Each one of these holding companies had a financial institution that allowed it to finance the operations of the various firms related to it. With time, the founders retired. Civil servants and former Army officers were major sources of recruitment of managers in addition to the children or the sons-in-law of the owners.

During the sixties, almost all Israeli entrepreneurs were institutional rather than individualistic, working for the increased power and the glory of their sector and for the expansion of the size of the firms they managed. The managers of these firms also had very cordial relations with government officials and politicians. Personal contacts were deemed essential for business success: the success of the firms they headed depended more on governmental decisions than on their success in managing the firm or finding the right strategy in the marketplace. Firms were shielded from competition. Private entrepreneurs found it extremely difficult to establish new ventures.

A few renegades were encouraged and aided by a major private conglomerate in Israel: DBIC (Discount Bank Investment Company). Its manager was Dr. Augusto Levi, who recruited Dan Tolkowski after he retired in 1958 from his position as Commanding Officer of the Israeli Air Force. Mr. Tolkowsky recognized the need to modernize Israeli industry. The firm he managed helped in the financing and management of several visionaries who demonstrated tenacity and fortitude in getting things done against the odds.

One such company was Iscar, a producer of precision carbide cutting tools, founded in 1952; DBIC became a partner in 1961. Another — Elron (1962) — was the first Israeli start-up in electronics devices. In 1966, Elbit was established to utilize the accumulated know-how of Rafael and Elron in computers. Another joint venture of Elron was Elscint (1969), specializing in CAT scan, and later MRI, technology. DBIC also established Scientific Technology, which became Scitex (1968), focusing on computerized preprinting (Sherman, 1988; Levav, 1998).[5]

[5]Iscar was founded in 1952 by Stef Wertheimer. DBIC acquired the shares of a partner of the small knives producer in 1961. Since then the firm has grown. It also established a separate firm to produce jet engine blades. Elron was founded by Uzia Galil to manufacture electronic devices. Initial funding of $160,000 was received from DBIC and from a venture capital fund owned by Laurence and David Rockefeller. The Rockefellers sold their shares to DBIC in 1966 because they decided to pull out of Europe. Efi Arazi returned to Israel after the 1967 war. His first firm provided computerized printing solutions to the textile industry. He then moved to preprinting. The founders were also the managers of these firms. In 1966 Elbit became a joint venture of Elron and the Ministry of Defense. In 1970, the ministry sold its share to Control Data Corporation. In 1969 Avraham Suhami, with Elron, founded Elscint. Initially the firm sold nuclear physics lab equipment but moved to nuclear scanners with medical applications. Other firms were not part of DBIC. ECI Telecom was established in 1957. It produced military products. It moved to civilian products only in the 1980s. In 1968 Morris Kahan, who immigrated from South Africa, formed the Aurek group with ITT, after the partners won a tender from the Ministry of

These firms were the buds of the high-tech industry of Israel and a few of them were its first "born globals". They focused on knowledge creation rather than knowledge acquisition. They targeted the competitive international markets, not the protected domestic one. They believed they could invent better products and overcome any problem.

As Stef Wertheimer said: "an Israeli can succeed in anything he does. He has to succeed because there is no way back to Hitler" (Levav, 1998: p. 151). These pioneers were often naive but also full of enthusiasm. They were innovators but were cutting milk teeth on production and lacked any marketing proficiency. In quite a few cases, the innovators did not even make the most cursory market survey before they spent time and money on their inventions.

A few of these pioneers were employed by US firms and started the new businesses as a means to return home. Arazi, for one, was able to convince the US firm he worked for to start a subsidiary in Israel for him. In 1974, Intel agreed to open its first development center outside the United States to retain the services of Dov Froman who decided to return to Israel (Breznitz, 2007: p. 195). Benny Landa, the founder of Indigo and an innovator in ink-cased electric photography, came from Canada. To date, Israeli expatriates who worked for global US-based MNEs have tended to form bridges between Israeli firms and firms in Silicon Valley. Many managers in the high-tech firms rotate between Israel and the United States.

The vast majority of Israeli managers today hold an MBA from one of dozens of business schools operating in the country. Many of these managers are engineers; some are economists. These managers were trained to appreciate well-thought-out business plans and clear strategic vision, to think strategically, to value marketing and — above all — profits.

A significant percentage of Israel's business elite may accurately be called part of the "global elite", independent of the government and regulations. They did not inherit their wealth; they created it, tapping venture capital funds, offering IPOs on NASDAQ or in Europe. In the process of getting the funds, they did not need to ask for permissions, licenses, or foreign exchange allocations.

Communications to publish a Yellow Pages telephone directory. Kahan acquired ITT's shares in Aurek in 1973. In 1970 Aurek won a tender to publish telephone directories and formed a subsidiary to set up the computing system for the project. This became Amdocs.

I have studied for decades the structure and conduct of Israeli business firms. These studies show a major revolution (Aharoni, 1976, 2007) in the composition of the business elite, the sources of their recruitment, and their relationships with the political elite. A major reason for the change seems to have been that entrepreneurs today are not dependent on government or on holding companies or Israeli banks. Managers in high-tech firms today are judged by their ability to achieve business results, not by contacts in government or with the old business elite.

Even in regulated enterprises, the level of dependency seems much lower than it was several decades ago. All in all, the business elite are no longer composed of managers relying on the government for help. The new managers look for success by competing in the global market. They value personal success, but at the same time are very much committed to creating a successful country, and to the values of that country.

These managers, scientists, and engineers could easily find lucrative jobs in other countries. They are, however, firmly committed to living in Israel and building the state. One reason, perhaps, is memories of the holocaust: after the loss of a third of the world's Jewish population, Israelis value the security of having their own country to protect them.

The new breed of Israeli business leaders learned that if they wanted the firms they led to grow they had to go abroad, designing and implementing strategies that made them competitive MNEs in world markets.[6] All in all, perhaps the greatest CSA of Israel today is the culture of its residents. It places a premium on entrepreneurship and risk taking. This is manifested in the thousands of start-ups, created by Israelis who left more stable jobs.

Compulsory military service, moreover, creates comradeships that carry over into teamwork in business and informal networks, enhancing mutual learning. Many managers of born globals were pilots, or served in the intelligence corps.

In addition, close-knit communities are created as a result of the small size of the country. There is in the national culture an innate stubbornness, resilience, a strong ability to improvise, the creative drive of a polyglot

---

[6] Several decades ago, I observed that "small countries like Israel produce an exportable surplus of educated, middle-class members of the work force who cannot be absorbed at home. One means of allowing them to keep their national identity and to work abroad is to use them in multinational corporations based in the small country" (Agmon and Kindleberger, 1977: p. xiii).

people, but also impatience with, and a lack of respect for, other cultures. Within this culture it was possible to develop FSAs but also clusters of firms that helped each other and learned from each other's experiences.

One Successful Example — Teva Pharmaceutical Industries

The most successful Israeli multinational has been Teva Pharmaceutical Industries Ltd. Its story is a fine example of success but also of the problems and tribulations of establishing and operating a multinational enterprise from a tiny country such as Israel.

Teva's roots can be traced back to 1901, when three businessmen — Chaim Salomon, Moshe Gutel Levin, and Yitschak Asher Elstein — established in Jerusalem a wholesale drug distributor named after them (SLE) that imported drugs and sold them in the local market.

One result of the Nazi's ascent to power in Germany was that many Jews fled; some emigrated to Palestine. Many of the new immigrants were highly educated and a few of them had experience in the pharmaceutical industry. They established several small cottage plants to produce drugs under license. One of these plants was named Teva ("nature" in Hebrew). These plants flourished during World War II because they became suppliers to the British army. Immediately after the war, the newly created Arab League initiated a boycott against any business operating in the Jewish part of Palestine (and, since 1948, any business dealing with Israel). Large pharmaceutical firms, reluctant to invest in Israel, licensed domestic firms to produce their drugs for the local market.

About twenty small family-owned firms served this domestic market, each with annual sales of about $1 million. In the 1950s, SLE acquired one of these firms (Assia). Eli Hurvitz, who married Dalia Solomon, started working at Assia while pursuing evening studies for a bachelor's degree in economics. By 1962 Hurvitz was CEO. His early strategic vision was to become the market leader in Israel by consolidating the industry. He thus acquired Zori in 1963. Teva, which has been publicly listed on the Tel Aviv Stock Exchange since 1951, was acquired in 1968. The three firms merged in 1976 into Teva Pharmaceutical Industries Ltd., with Hurvitz as the CEO.

Teva became the largest pharmaceutical firm in Israel, producing under license drugs and fine chemicals for the domestic market, with annual sales of $28 million. In 1980 Teva acquired the second largest pharmaceutical firm, Ikapharm, which ran a US Food and Drug Administration (FDA) approved plant, and Plantex, a leading producer of active pharmaceutical ingredients.

Koor Industries, the largest Israeli conglomerate controlled by the Histadrut's Hevrat Ovdim, owned both these firms. Both lost money, and Koor proposed to sell them to Teva for 20 percent of Teva's shares. In addition, Koor loaned Teva IL60 million for ten years. Migada, a manufacturer of disposable medical equipment, was acquired in 1984 and Abic, a major drug manufacturer, in September 1988.

Teva became dominant in the small home market. Clearly, however, the opportunity for further domestic growth was extremely limited. Teva started to export to Africa, but this market was also quite small.

In the early 1980s Hurvitz hired Dr. Joseph Aleksandrowicz to start a strategic planning process, an unheard-of move in Israel at the time. Aleksandrowicz organized a program of seminars for the top executives of the firm to which he invited professors of business administration from Israel and abroad. In one of these sessions, Hurvitz noted that Teva with its diversity of products, technologies, know-how and management should become a billion dollar company.

The reason it was not was that it operated in Israel. The limited size of the Israeli market was a barrier to further expansion, so it would have to enter a large Western market. Entering Europe meant registering each drug seventeen times compared to one time in the United States (Stauber, 2001: p. 33).

In 1982 Teva registered American Depository Receipts on NASDAQ. By 1985, sales revenues were $88 million. In 1985, together with W. R. Grace, a major US conglomerate, Teva acquired Lemon, a small $20 million US arm of a German company, to access the then-embryonic US generic drug market. Once a foothold was established, the company's market share and sales steadily grew. Teva became a bi-national company.

In 1989 the firm and two banks bought out Koor's ownership stake in Teva. In 1990 W. R. Grace sold its Lemon shares to Teva. Hurvitz built an internal team to evaluate acquisitions and the firm gained a reputation for its success in targeting candidates for acquisition, and integrating them quickly and successfully.

By 2007, Teva had become the number one pharmaceutical company in the US in terms of the number of prescriptions written for all drugs, as well as for generics in particular (Teva Pharmaceutical Industries Ltd., 2007: p. 9). Since 1985, Teva has executed fourteen transactions for over $12 billion. By 1993, Teva's sales were $502 million. It passed the billion dollar mark in 2000. By 2002, when Hurvitz retired as CEO and became Chairman of the Board, sales were $2.519 billion and Teva was one of the three top providers of generic drugs in the United States, Canada, the Netherlands, Hungary, France, and the UK. The company continues to grow at an annual growth rate of sales of 20 percent (and more than that on the profit side) both organically and through acquisitions, doubling its sales volume every four years.

Sicor was acquired for $3.4 billion in 2003, not only expanding the company's geographic sphere, but also moving into selling injectable liquid products direct to hospitals. In 2005 Ivax was acquired for $7.4 billion, giving access to a very strong first-to-file Paragraph IV[7] pipeline in the United States and to markets in Eastern Europe and Latin America.

By 2006, 60 percent of the company was owned by mutual funds and institutions. Teva's sales in 2006 were $8.4 billion. Its headquarters is in Israel with subsidiaries in over fifty countries. Its by-laws dictate that the CEO must reside in Israel. By now it is a global leader in generic drugs and an active pharmaceutical ingredients manufacturer in Europe and North America.

Hurvitz also aspired to leverage Israeli science. The huge investment required for in-house R&D and regulatory approval of a new drug (estimated at $1 billion) was beyond Teva's reach. It did develop, register, produce, and market molecules discovered by Israeli researchers — for example, at the Weizman Institute of Science. (Compaxone for multiple sclerosis, for example, registered in the US in 1996. In 2005, Compaxone's sales were $1.2 billion, 12% of Teva's global sales. Compaxone continued to grow by about 22% in 2006.)

Given the limited population of prescribing physicians, the marketing costs are relatively low. Teva had partnered with Sanofi-Aventis to manage the marketing of the drug. Teva also developed Azilect for treating Parkinson's disease, approved by the EU (2005) and the United States (2006). Teva has in the pipeline several other innovative drugs, and some analysts are concerned that this might be too much for Teva's research budget and its limited experience in bringing drugs to market.

[7] A certification standard of the FDA.

Teva is perhaps the best example of a very successful global firm with a home base in Israel. It eschewed the traditional conglomerate model, choosing instead a highly focused approach embraced by later generations of successful Israeli companies. It was able to keep a low-cost mentality and to integrate acquired firms into its culture, creating and maintaining synergies.

The company bred a class of professional managers and scientists never before seen in the country. It served as a bridge from Israeli science to the market and has been an important source of talent and capital for the growing biotechnology sector. With an increasing portfolio of innovative drugs, Teva has to manage quite diverse operations under one roof. It also faces increased competition from new low-cost players — for example, from India — eager to follow Teva's success and increase their own market share.

Outward FDI from Israel: Facts and Figures

Outward FDI from Israel is a relatively new phenomenon. A few MNEs emerged in the 1960s; the majority did not survive. A few more started in the 1980s[8] and in the past two decades their numbers have increased. MNEs became possible as a result of major reforms in government policies leading to structural changes, a key change in the composition of the Israeli business elite, major changes in global conditions — detailed by Williamson and Zeng in Chapter 5 in this volume — and of course the strategies and management processes of the firms themselves.

Teva is the largest of the Israeli multinationals, but only one of more than 150 such firms. Teva is also one example of a firm that internationalized only after it could not continue to grow in the local market, behaving as one would expect based on theory. Other firms in traditional fields went abroad only after they faced limits to growth in the domestic market.

[8] In 1981 brothers Zohar and Yehuda Zisappel formed the RAD group which became one of Israel's high-tech leaders. Many start-ups were formed under RAD's auspices, several of which became MNEs. In 1983 Efrat was founded to develop computerized voice mail. The partners concurrently registered Comverse as the US parent. After a decade of difficulties the firm became a world leader in its niche. In the same year, Indigo developed its digital printer. In 1985, Amdocs was founded to provide billing services to an American firm. In 2006, its revenues were $2.48 billion. It has development centers in Israel, India, the United States, Cyprus, and Brazil.

Some examples of relatively large Israeli traditional multinationals, in addition to Teva, are:

Israel Chemicals, a producer of potash, phosphate rock, magnesium and bromide, raw materials available in or near the Dead Sea. The firm was state owned and at that time its managers had a hard time convincing government bureaucrats that foreign exchange should be allocated to it to purchase a subsidiary to jump tariffs in its exports to Europe.[9] It has been privatized and is now operating in Europe, North America, Latin America, and China. It also maintains global marketing and logistics facilities. It is the only resource-based Israeli MNE. Its global sales from July 2006 to June 2007 were about $4 billion.

Makhteshim-Agan Industries Ltd. (MAI), the result of a merger of the two Israeli producers of crop protection products. Today, MAI is the world's leading manufacturer and distributor of off-patent crop and non-crop protection products. MAI ranks among a handful of the world's largest manufacturers of crop protection chemicals, with subsidiaries in Latin America and Europe. Its global sales from July 2006 to June 2007 were $2.25 billion.

Iscar, a producer of precision carbide cutting tools for hard metal cutting and engine blades. It owns manufacturing facilities in France, Germany, Italy, the Netherlands (established in 1962 to service the German market), Spain, Switzerland, Turkey, and the UK, as well as in the United States, South Korea, Brazil, and Argentina. Being privately owned, the firm does not publish financial information. Globally, it is the second largest producer in its industry, up from number ten twenty years ago. In 2006, Berkshire Hathaway acquired 80 percent of Iscar's shares (but not of the blades firm).[10]

Delta Galil, a global provider of private label apparel, with factories in Jordan, Egypt, Turkey, Thailand, Romania, and Central America, producing ladies' intimate apparel, socks, men's underwear and leisure apparel for the UK and US markets, with global sales of $706.7 million in 2006.

Netafim, an example of a firm that turned Israel's disadvantage into a FSA. Israel suffers from a chronic shortage of water. Netafim invented

[9] In one case in the 1960s the firm asked for a foreign exchange allocation to acquire an Italian manufacturing firm for $10 million. Management believed this acquisition would allow a major expansion. The Minister of Finance refused.

[10] See Letter to Shareholders, 2006, Berkshire Hathaway, p. 4.

drip irrigation to preserve scarce water resources and increase crop yields. Today, Netafim leverages cutting-edge core drip irrigation technologies to provide end-to-end solutions for biofuel energy, turn-key greenhouse projects, wastewater management, and advanced crop management and monitoring systems. With over 2,000 employees, 14 manufacturing facilities in 11 countries, more than 30 subsidiaries and a distribution presence in 110 countries Netafim's global sales are more than $400 million.

Other firms were able to exploit FSAs developed in the domestic market in foreign operations. Thus, Bank Hapoalim, the largest Israeli bank, acquired banks in Turkey and in the United States; Bank Leumi established a bank in Romania.

Other examples are Ormat, an innovator and producer of solar, geo-thermic, and other alternative energy equipment (with twenty-two plants abroad), Elite in coffee, Electra in white appliances, Elbit in military electronics, Israel Aerospace Industries (which in September 2007 opened a wholly owned subsidiary of its international subsidiary to produce unmanned aerial vehicles in Mississippi), and 'Dor Alon and Delek in gasoline distribution.

By 2007, most large firms in Israel in most economic sectors, acutely aware of the limited growth opportunities in the domestic market, had attempted to expand through foreign operations. An insurance company (Phoenix) acquired a Romanian insurance firm, and many real estate developers and construction firms expanded to Eastern Europe, Russia, India, and the United States.

Among the largest twenty-five firms traded on the Tel Aviv Stock Exchange 58 percent of the revenues in 2006 came from operations outside Israel. The highest percentage of foreign operations was in the chemical industry (93%), followed by electronics (81%), holding companies (80%), real estate (67%), and food (40%). At the bottom were banks (11%), insurance (4%), and communications (0%) (Globes, 2007 May: p. 30).

Needless to say, firms must develop the proper strategy and avail themselves of the proper managerial talent, creating the capabilities to compete in foreign countries. Israel Chemicals bases its competitive advantage on the availability of raw materials in Israel. Others rely on unique knowledge — in agricultural products, for example — or on the availability of human resources with deep knowledge of the language and the culture of target countries. Because of immigration, one can find in Israel a bank manager who speaks Romanian, a construction engineer fluent in Hungarian, and so on.[11]

Since the 1960s, the internationalization processes of firms have been the topic of widespread research. Several researchers (e.g., Johanson & Vahlne, 1977, 1990; Bilkey, 1978; Cavusgil, 1980) have emphasized the gradual and sequential nature of the decision making process. A firm is assumed to build a stable domestic position before starting international activities.

Since the 1990s, these views have been challenged. Zander & Zander (1997) followed a hundred years of Alfa Laval. They criticized the idea of evolutionary determinism, pointing out that Alfa Laval's growth shows an oscillating rather than a linear pattern of development.

Others have demonstrated that many firms now do not develop their international activities in incremental stages. Rather, they start international activities, entering very distant markets, right from their birth. Such firms have been labeled "international new ventures" (Oviatt & McDougall, 1994), "high-technology start-ups" (Jolly *et al.*, 1992), and "born global" (McKinsey & Co., 1993; Rennie, 1993; Knight & Cavusgil, 1996; Madsen & Servais, 1997). The explanation for this new sequence of internationalization of firms is claimed to be more global market conditions, new developments in transportation and communications technologies, and the rising number of people with international experience (Oviatt & McDougall, 1994, 1997).

Indeed, many high-tech Israeli firms are born global (Almor, 2000). Israel is widely acknowledged to be a technological innovator (Breznitz, 2006). Israeli entrepreneurs have been successful in creating and managing science-based firms in IT, Internet applications, and telecommunications, as well as in medically related areas (e.g., Medinol, founded in 1992).[12] They develop products solely for international markets, based on niches that have not been developed by larger firms in other countries.

---

[11] As one example, Ossem, one of the largest food manufacturers in Israel, chose to partner with the giant Nestle. In 2007, it built its first plant abroad. It produced an Israeli innovation, vegetarian frozen entrees, in the Czech Republic, in the same city from which the grandfather of Ossem's owners had operated a pasta factory.

[12] Medinol is expert in the field of stenting and the inventor of the flexible closed cell stent design. Medinol owns patents relating to both stent design and stent manufacturing. Medinol invented breakthrough technology based on etching as opposed to the traditional

A combination of an ample reservoir of trained personnel, advanced research and development facilities, government incentives, and access to the US and European markets has made Israel a good base for science-based industry (Avnimelech & Tuebal, 2004; de Fontenay & Carmel, 2004). R&D in areas such as plant and animal propagation helped create a large farm-export industry.

By the 1970s, Israel's R&D prowess had rapidly expanded out of the agricultural and military spheres into expertise in software, semiconductors, medical equipment electronics and communications, and then into biotechnology and advanced materials.

Moreover, as the result of a report from a public commission of scientists (submitted in 1968) the government created an Office of the Chief Scientist (OCS) in the Ministry of Trade and Industry to help finance R&D programs in manufacturing industries, albeit on a small scale (Breznitz, 2007: pp. 50–57). Today grants by the OCS cover between 30% and 66% of total development costs. The OCS also aids start-ups via its Technological Incubators Program, providing institutional support in infrastructure, financing, and business networking.

OCS receives royalties from successful alumni. It also coordinates several bilateral R&D programs. The first of these, established in 1977, is the Israel-US Bi-National Industrial Research and Development Foundation (BIRD F). It was designed to enable Israeli start-ups to form strategic partnerships with large American firms. Others are foundations with Canada, Singapore, Great Britain, and Europe. Currently, with the increase in scope of venture capital firms and the ability to link with global financial markets (Avnimelech & Teubal, 2005) these foundations are relatively less important.

As already pointed out, Elron was the first Israeli start-up, established already in 1961. At that time high tech in Israel was carried out within the state-owned defense enterprises that did not want to compromise their monopoly position on defense orders. Some Israeli firms produced under foreign license but very little interaction existed between research carried out in universities and the operations of manufacturing industries.

Without access to defense orders, the fledgling new ventures did not have any market within Israel. They had to sell all of their production in

---

laser cut method. Stents for both coronary and peripheral applications were exclusively distributed by Boston Scientific Corporation between 1995 and 2002.

foreign markets. But they did not have any knowledge of marketing. One way to get an international marketing base was through tie-ins with foreign partners, but this route left the most important ingredients of survival in the hands of others.

Firms that tried this route faced many problems, from clashes of interest to clashes of culture, to strategy shifts on the part of foreign partners.[13] Even a small change in direction of a giant partner could create an untenable situation for the smaller Israeli partner, inhibiting its growth and leaving it exposed and vulnerable.

Further, markets and customers were changing very fast and these rapid changes challenged many assumptions. A major lesson was that one must be near the market, and therefore essential marketing should not be predicated solely on arrangements with foreign partners.

Scitex was the first to establish a marketing subsidiary in the United States and then a European subsidiary headquarters in 1974 in Brussels. Uzia Galil advocated the "two-legged industrial animal". To be successful, a firm should have operations based in Israel but also maintain a subsidiary or sometimes a parent in the United States, thus becoming bi-national.[14] The firms should develop their own expertise in R&D, production, and marketing. Clearly, it would be futile to develop products of the "me too" category since the tiny Israeli firms could not compete head on with industrial giants. Instead, the firms had to develop products with unique advantages, looking for applications that others either could not address or had overlooked.

In the 1970s, Scitex and Elscint were the two flagships of Israeli high tech, and both were early born globals. Scitex stunned the printing

[13]Thus, Scitex started as Scientific Technology by building a computer-based design system for the textile industry. The marketing was to be done by a textile firm in North Carolina that invested $250,000 in seed money. Alas, the firm was more interested in owning the only working machine than in selling more machines. Arazi had to renegotiate and to pay dearly (Levav, 1998: pp. 119–121). Thereafter, he vowed to have his own marketing subsidiary.

Monsanto was forced to retrench and pulled out of a joint venture; Xerox took over SDS, inhibiting the growth of the joint venture SDS had carved out with Elbit. (Elbit developed and produced the first mini computer.)

[14]Thus, when Fibronics International was created in 1978 to exploit the new field of fiber optics, the firm was established as a US firm functioning through an Israeli subsidiary. Many other examples of bi-national firms followed.

industry in 1979 by introducing the computer-based turnkey Response color prepress system. It served a labor intensive and costly niche. By 1984 its sales were $104 million. It also developed a sister product line to be used in the mapping industry. It then moved to other niches in the pre-printing industry. Some products were successful. Others were not.

By February 1992, Scitex's share of the worldwide color prepress market was estimated to be 45 percent. In 1995, with the advent of desktop publishing on PCs, Scitex's costly machines became too expensive for most publishers. In 2000, Creo acquired Scitex graphic arts operations. In 2004, Eastman Kodak acquired Creo. Efi Arazi left Scitex in 1988, creating a new firm called EFI (Electronic for Imaging) in California.

Elscint, managed by Avraham Suhani, introduced its CAT scanner in 1974. Each scanner was sold for around $500,000. It gambled on new products such as MRI and ultrasound. The world market for computer tomography was estimated at $660 million in the early 1980s with an annual growth rate of 15 percent. Elscint established marketing centers in the United States, Canada, Belgium, France, Germany, Holland, Italy, Sweden, Switzerland, the UK, Brazil, Mexico, South America, and Australia. It had to maintain adequate, comprehensive, and timely after-sales service centers. Its sales were $140 million. In MRI, Elscint produced its own magnets at a wholly owned subsidiary in Oxford, UK. In December 1983 it acquired certain parts of Xonics Medical System, but in February 1984 Xonics filed for Chapter 11 reorganization. Further, changes in health policy in the United States resulted in heavy losses in 1984. Suhami left and the firm went through a difficult restructuring.

Frederick P. Adler, a New York investment banker and venture capitalist, demonstrated that it was possible to raise capital on NASDAQ. Israeli firms could go public in the United States to solve the chronic need for more capital. In 1972 he launched an IPO with Elscint,[15] underwritten by Hambrecht & Quist, and Bache & Co. He later floated the shares of other firms, too, among them Scitex and Elron.

The new generation of Israeli high-tech firms tapped capital from venture capital funds, from NASDAQ, and from Europe. The firms are often incorporated in the United States, they maintain marketing and sales offices outside Israel, produce components in Asia, but maintain some core R&D and managerial decision making in Israel.

---

[15]Elscint was also the first firm to be allowed to issue its own common stock and get tax concessions. Other firms followed.

Between 1990 and 1996 fifty-six Israeli firms issued stock on NASDAQ, raising $18,155 million. Since then the number has more than doubled. In 2005, with the registration of Ituran, Israel became the second country after the United States in terms of the number of firms registered on NASDAQ (seventy-one firms). Canada moved to third place with sixty-eight firms. NASDAQ created a listing of seventy-three Israeli companies called ISRQ with combined capitalization of $50 billion. The daily quote in the Israeli press of Israeli shares in New York includes 116 firms, and 60 more firms appear on European stock exchanges: London, (AIM) Amsterdam, Brussels, Zurich, and Frankfurt.

One reason for the gap in figures is that a relatively large number of Israeli-based firms are incorporated in the United States and therefore are officially US — not Israeli — firms. Others were incorporated in Holland (e.g., Indigo, a major producer of digital printing machines). Many of these born globals grew quite substantially.[16] In addition to Israeli firms officially incorporated in the United States, there were Israelis less interested in maintaining ties to the motherland. They moved to other countries (mainly the United States) and founded firms there. Some of them built quite an empire, but, of course, those are not considered Israeli multinationals.

Table 1 provides some statistics from the World Investment Report (UNCTAD, 2006) on Israeli overseas FDIs for the years 2002–2005. In 2006, outward FDIs from Israel surged. Balance of payments figures show an increase in the investments of Israeli residents abroad (including portfolio investments) from $4.3 billion in 2001 to $4.6 billion in 2002, $7.8 billion in 2003, $13.5 billion in 2004, $18.5 billion in 2005, and $32.1 billion in 2006 (Bank of Israel, 2006: p. 248). These figures are underestimates since they do not include firms registered outside Israel.

Giant multinationals such as Hewlett Packard, Cisco, Lucent Technologies, and San Disk acquired many of the very successful firms. The number of these acquisitions and the dollar value of the transactions

---

[16]Some examples are: Check Point Software Technologies with annual sales of $605.5 million; Nice, which offered comprehensive performance management and interaction analytics solutions, with annual sales of $437.7 million; Amdocs, a billing and customer care provider, with annual sales of $2.48 billion; Orbotech, a supplier of automated optical inspection systems, with annual sales of $416.5 million; and Comverse, a software company, with annual sales of $1.12 billion (all data pertain to calendar year 2006 or fiscal year 2006–07).

Table 1. Statistics on Israeli outward FDIs.

	2002	2003	2004	2005
Greenfield investments abroad-number	39	39	58	54
Number of MNEs for which parent is an Israeli firm			154	
Bilateral Investment Treaties (BIT)				36
Double Taxation Agreements (DDT)				44
Cross border investments purchases (millions of dollars)		1,357	4,003	1,446
Cross border M&A — number of deals		13	29	29
FDI outflows ($ millions)		2,064	4,543	2,492

Source: UNCTAD (2006).

Table 2. Acquisitions of Israeli high-tech firms by foreign multinationals.

Year	Number of Transactions	Value ($ thousands)
2000	64	6,882
2001	29	483
2002	63	21,452
2003	59	1,083
2004	61	1,811
2005	70	2,678
2006	76	10,584

Source: Israel Venture Capital. www.ivc-online.com.

for the years 2000–2006 are shown in Table 2. Such acquisitions continued into 2007.[17]

It is useful to compare Israel to other small countries. Finland is of interest: its economy is also based to a large extent on high-tech firms. Figure 1 demonstrates that as of 2005 the share of inward FDI to the total

[17]Thus, Spansion Inc. acquired Saifun Semiconductors Ltd., a producer of nonvolatile memory, for $370 million in cash and shares; Spansion was the only customer of Saifun. ICAP, the largest inter-bank broker, acquired Triana (maker of software for banks), for $247 million. And Goldman Sachs acquired a block of shares in Mobileye, which made control systems for vehicles, based on an enterprise value of $600 million.

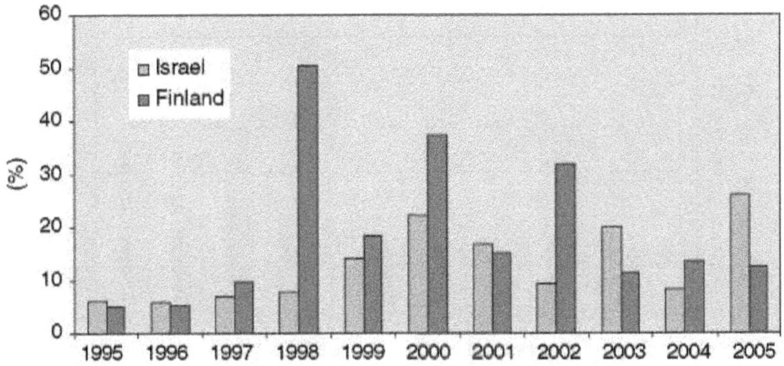

Figure 1. FDI share in total capital stock, Israel vs. Finland.

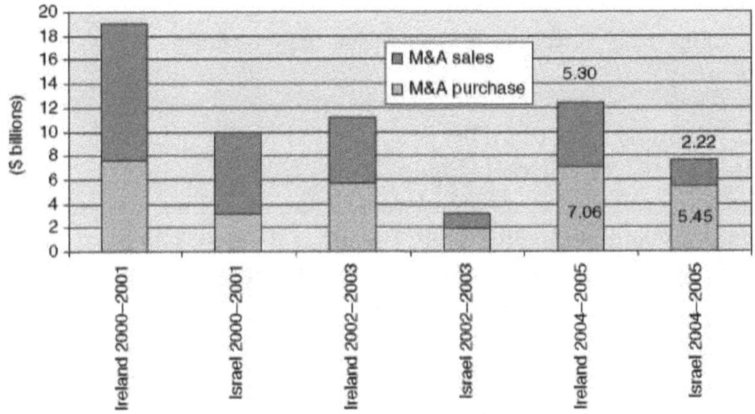

Figure 2. M&As, Israel vs. Ireland, various years.

capital stock in the economy peaked at 26% for Israel but was only 12.3% for Finland.

World M&As surged in 2000 to $1.1 trillion and sank to a mere $296 million in 2003, jumping again to $716 billion in 2005. Figure 2 presents data comparing cross border M&As in Israel and in Ireland. In the figure, M&A sales refer to M&As by foreign firms in the respective economies. M&A purchases are M&As by Israeli/Irish firms. The impact of the bubble can be seen to be much stronger in Israel: the figures for 2002–2003 show a sharp decline compared to 2000–2001. However, the improvement in 2004–2005 is also much faster in Israel compared to Ireland. Ireland was able to attract many MNEs. As a result, most of its

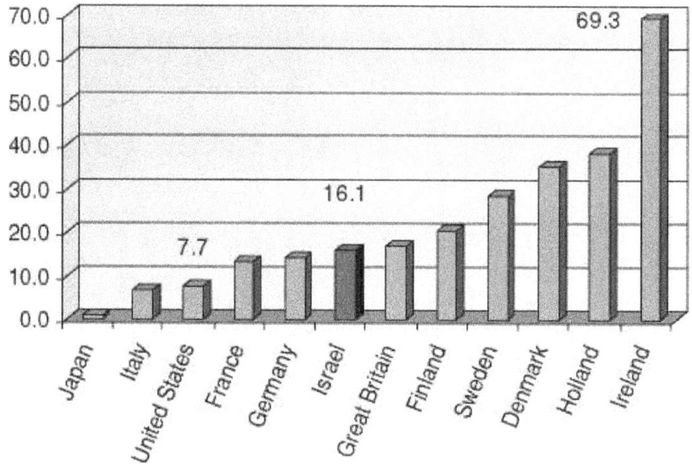

Figure 3. Percentage of GDP accounted for by foreign MNEs.

economy (almost 70% of GDP) is accounted for by operations of MNEs, compared to 16.1% in Israel (Figure 3).

The Bank of Israel compared Israel to nations with a comparable level of technology and per capita GNP: Poland, Slovenia, Hungary, the Czech Republic, Singapore, South Korea, Portugal, and Spain (the "comparison group"). The long-range average (1998–2005) of inward FDI in Israel is 3% of GNP compared to 5.2% in the comparison group. Clearly Israel lagged behind in this respect. The reasons may be distance, the lack of natural resources, or the geopolitical situation. In 2006 inward FDIs were 10.8% of GNP and the percentage of inward FDI in Israel from all developing nations increased to 6% from a long-term average of 3% (Bank of Israel, 2006: p. 270). Of course these figures may be a result of one or two large investments. The inward FDIs in start-up firms have been much more consistent, with investment of about $0.8 billion per annum. Outward FDI as a percentage of GNP for the period 1998–2005 was 1.6% in Israel but 2.5% in the "comparison group". However, Israeli shares have been growing fast since 2001 and in 2006 were 8.5% (Bank of Israel, 2006: p. 274).

In 2006 Israel's population represented 0.1% of world population. It produced 0.25% of world gross product, but was responsible for 1.02% of world M&As and its share in the US and European high-tech markets was about 1.3% (UNCTAD, 2006; Bank of Israel, 2007: p. 10). Several firms achieved very interesting innovations that could lead to another Teva.

Unfortunately, many entrepreneurs are tempted to be acquired by a giant MNE instead of following the torturous road leading to becoming a large MNE themselves. Certainly, the long road from a start-up to an IPO to becoming at least a billion dollar company is full of hazards, obstacles, and stumbling blocks; it is quite tempting to take "the bird in hand".[18]

The initial success of a start-up means domination of a well-defined niche, but the limited size of the niche may constrain further growth. The firm is also often dependent on a very small customer base — sometimes only one (e.g., a retailer). If the firm moves to larger niches or more diversified geographic markets it increases the risk of failure. Quite often, success necessitates heavy investments in an after-sales service network. Again, the firm may decide to give up its independence and be acquired by a giant that can supply such crucial resources. Thus, Indigo, a producer of digital printing machines, was sold to Hewlett Packard when faced with spending large sums to create and maintain an after-sales service network. Both managers and venture capitalists have strong incentives to exit.

A Case Study of a Successful Born Global

Check Point Software Technologies Ltd. is a leader in global network security software. Gil Schwed, Shlomo Kramer, and Marius Nacht, three young programmers, who met in the Israeli army, founded the company in 1993. They recognized the growth of the Internet and saw that a major impediment to this growth would be the fear of hackers. Thus, they focused on Internet security, inventing technology that enabled the creation of Internet firewalls, thereby creating a new market. On June 28, 1996, Check Point launched an initial public offering on NASDAQ. At that time, the firm employed about forty people and its annual revenues were $34.6 million. By 2000 sales had grown to $425.3 million, and a

[18]Mirabilis is one example; the four young entrepreneurs who created ICQ, the first online instant messaging service, sold the firm quite early to AOL, receiving among themselves $406 million. Another example is that of Orni Petrushka and Rafi Gidron, who founded Scorpio Communications and sold it to US Robotics in 1996. In 1998, they founded Chromatis Networks and sold it two years later to Lucent Technologies for Lucent stock valued at $4.8 billion. Chromatis' flagship product, Metropolis MSX, integrated data, voice, and video services on metropolitan networks. In August 2001, after the dot-com bubble burst in the United States, Lucent dropped Chromatis' product line and fired all its employees. As Lucent's share price plunged, the value of the Chromatis sale to its Israeli owners also plunged: to $590 million.

year later the workforce had grown to 1,568, half of whom were employed outside Israel. Its revenues thus grew at an average rate of 50 percent per annum and the company leveraged its leadership position in Internet security. See Figure 4 for financial results. From 1998 to 2000, the firm adapted its organization to global operations. Check Point's focus is on IT security with an extensive portfolio of security solutions. In 2007, the company enjoys dominant market share in these markets. Extending the power of the Check Point solution is its Open Platform for Security, the industry's framework. Check Point solutions are sold, integrated, and serviced by a network of OEM partners, distributors, VARs, systems and network integrators, and Internet Service Providers. Its customers include 100 percent of Fortune 100 companies.

Check Point's development centers are located in Israel and in Belarus. It has offices in Redwood City, California, and in the Dallas, Texas, area. Gil Shwed has been CEO since the firm started. He was inducted into the highly respected CRN Industry Hall of Fame, honored for his work as an early firewall pioneer and for diversifying Check Point into data security. The company has received numerous industry recognitions and awards.

An integral ingredient of the firm's strategy has been reliance on internal growth, avoiding acquisitions, even though the firm had a mountain of cash at its disposal ($900 million by the end of 2006).

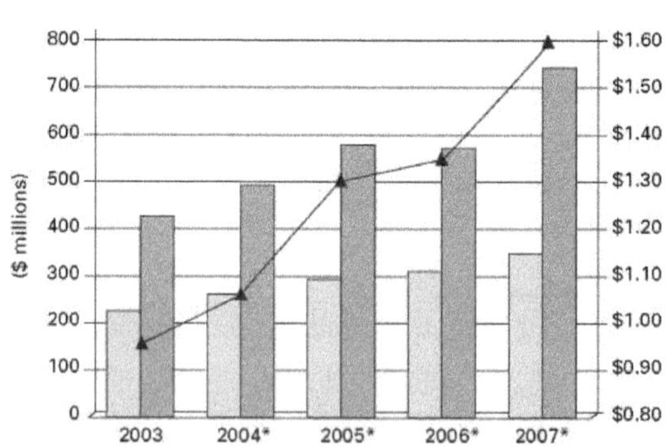

□ Net income □ Revenues A Earnings per share

Figure 4. Check Point: Annual financial results, 2003–2007.

Note: *Presented in non-GAAP format. Financials exclude amortization of intangible assets, acquisition-related expenses, and stock-based compensation.

The firm's few acquisitions included SofaWare Technologies, founded in 1999 in Ramat-Gan, Israel. SofaWare's embedded software powers Internet security appliances, DSL and Wi-Fi routers, as well as broadband modems. It also bought Zone Labs, a security software company, in 2004.

In October, 2005, Check Point announced an agreement to acquire Sourcefire, the developers of Snort, for $225 million. The deal was expected to close by the first quarter, 2006, but Check Point notified the Securities and Exchange Commission in February that the deal was on hold pending approval under the 1988 Exon-Florio provision of the (US) Defense Production Act of 1950, which gives the president the ability to suspend or prohibit a foreign acquisition, merger, or takeover of a US corporation that threatens national security.

It turned out that both the FBI and the Department of Defense objected to the acquisition on security grounds. The deal had been under scrutiny by the CFIUS (Committee on Foreign Investment in the United States), a panel made up of representatives from a dozen government agencies tasked with investigating foreign investments in US companies that could affect national security. According to SecurityFocus, "the process fell afoul of international politics following the public outcry over the failure of CFIUS to further investigate a proposed deal that would have given a Middle Eastern company (United Arab Emirates-based Dubai World Ports) control over six major US ports" (lEMOS, 2006).

The Dubai World Ports deal eventually fell to political pressure. Further investigation by CFIUS into Check Point's proposed purchase of Sourcefire was announced the following day. The decision on Check Point's acquisition of Sourcefire would have been due by March 30. Check Point's decision to pull out of the process was considered an acknowledgment that CFIUS would deny permission for the acquisition. Companies commonly pull out of a pending acquisition before CFIUS renders its judgment.

Of the fourteen cases that have not had approval after further investigation, only one has actually been denied. The companies that had proposed the merger, according to the report published by Congressional Research Service, withdrew the thirteen other deals.[19]

---

[19]The failure of Check Point to get approval to acquire Sourcefire for security reasons was seen as an indication that defense-related firms would not be able to acquire firms in the United States. Yair Shamir, Chairman of the Board of Israel Aerospace Industries (IAI), had a vision of increasing military-related items from 20% of IAI's sales in the US to 40%

Check Point is facing increasing competition from Sisco, Juniper, and Microsoft's Vista operating system. In early 2007, Check Point announced that it had acquired Protect Data AB (PROT.ST) and Pointsec Mobile Technologies AB of Sweden. Pointsec is a provider of mobile device security. Check Point also announced in early 2007 that it had acquired NFR Security, a threat prevention and intrusion prevention company, creators of the Network Flight Recorder, touted as a tamper-proof architecture and tool kit for building network traffic analysis and statistical event records.

According to Mr. Schwed, an Israel-based global firm must capitalize on indigenous advantages: the initiative, fast adaptation to changing conditions, efficiency, and dedication that are Israeli traits (Globes, 2004, December). The major challenge, according to him, is to bridge between the Israeli culture and other cultures. Seeing the world as having the same culture is wrong and would not work. It is imperative to mold a uniform organizational culture for the firm despite the different national cultures. According to Schwed, Israel has an advantage in the development of excellent new products (Globes, 2005, May 18). It must find ways to market the products and to install them. It is also important to satisfy existing customers' demands while at the same time making better and improved products.

Some Lessons from the Israeli Experience

What are some of the lessons from the experience of Israeli firms? First and foremost, in a global arena a firm from a small country does not need to cater to the domestic market. For almost any firm, world markets are wide open and these firms can sell in the large countries. Moreover, a firm from a small country can (and perhaps should) develop a global supply chain, allowing each country to specialize in the part of the product or service for which it enjoys a comparative advantage. There are still many exceptions — for example, in security-related business or in airlines.

Second, the capability of a tiny country such as Israel to produce wealth depends on the extent to which it can create new resources or assets based on technological capacity, management knowledge, and

---

or 50%. He noted, "We shall not acquire any firm in the US until we shall be sure the Administration would not oppose" (Globes, 2007, October 9–10, p. 10).

organizational competence. Unlike Russia or South Africa, the advantage of almost all Israeli-based MNEs is the creation of new assets, not the use of God-given natural resources. These created assets are intangible, mobile, and acknowledge no national borders.

In the 1960s, products were sold for very high prices to a small number of customers. Miniaturization allowed much smaller products and lower transportation costs. Since the 1990s, some products are sold on a tiny compact disk. Note also that it takes several decades before a full transformation of the firms, attitudes, and learning processes take place.

In the global economy there is a new division of labor in which income-generating assets are conceived and designed in developed countries but different parts of them are produced in different locations, creating a global supply chain. This global integration is powered by shrinking costs of transportation and communication and by the widespread use of the World Wide Web. In this world, the quality, energy, resourcefulness, and enterprise of people allow competitive advantage.

Israel has a major advantage in having a relatively large number of scientists. Indeed, Israel is a country of 7 million but has more scientific publications per capita than any other nation, including the United States. Israel has 135 engineers per 10,000 people compared to 85 per 10,000 in the United States. It also enjoys the highest number of medical doctors per capita in the world. Most important, there is a free market for new ideas and also for their financing. The highly educated work force is a major asset in the development of new ideas.

In the 1960s, an entrepreneur with a business plan had to convince the bureaucracy of an industrial development bank, or that of a large conglomerate, of the virtues of an idea to gain access to funds. Today, such an entrepreneur can opt for an IPO on NASDAQ or other equity markets. All in all, a nation can create for itself dynamic competitive advantages in the world markets by a high level of investment in human capital.

Availability of raw materials or cheap labor is not the only means of achieving economic growth or creating home-based MNEs. MNEs can prosper if a nation invests in the creation of new knowledge and skills and if firms are innovative in designing strategies, which introduce to the world economy new products and new processes, differentiated from commodity-like products. To be sure, superior technology is essential but without market knowledge, expertise in distribution, logistics, and management the firm is doomed. It is also possible that Israel will face a short supply of both engineers and managers.

Third, firms from small countries do not enjoy the luxury of growth in the domestic market. In any small country, a firm may first grow by acquiring its competitors. To reach a relatively large size, it must by definition dominate the domestic market. Further growth can only be achieved by diversification — either to other products in the same country or to new geographic areas. If geographic diversification is chosen, the firm may export, but more often it has to take the route of outward FDI. Each of these routes involves certain risks; neither is easy to implement. These firms may try to grow by entering the huge and lucrative US market even before US firms would expand globally or even regionally.

Fourth, almost all Israeli firms are small by world standards. None is among the Fortune 500. Had some firms been huge, they might have had too much political clout and too much impact on the small economy. In this sense, hundreds of small and medium-sized multinationals are preferable to a few giant ones. In a small home market, one firm can easily supply the whole market, thus enjoying monopoly power.

Fifth, the best way to force firms to face competition is to open the economy to foreign competitors and foreign-based MNEs. An Israeli firm faces one of three strategic choices: (1) It can be acquired by a foreign MNE. (2) It can lobby the government to be protected because of national interest, security considerations, or some other political reason. (3) It can become a multinational itself. These characteristics are very common in small countries but are very different in large economies.

Sixth, the firm must enjoy a clear competitive advantage. The advantage must be dynamic, since whatever advantage one has could be copied by other firms in other countries. In Israel, again, such an advantage is based on created assets mainly as a result of having a better-educated labor force, not by relying on cheap labor or natural resources. The created assets have been forged in specific areas in which Israelis had a competitive advantage because of a stock of accumulated knowledge (e.g., data security). The presence of many firms led to positive cluster effects. These cluster effects included professional networks with other Israeli firms as well as with firms founded by Israelis abroad. These effects have been particularly useful in overcoming difficulties of access to markets because of distance from markets and inexperience (de Fontenay and Carmel, 2004).

Achieving sustainable competitive advantage or creating FSAs requires a deep understanding of the environment but also of the strengths and weaknesses of the firm. In this sense, it is important to avoid the dogma of "generic strategies". The environment of the firm shapes performance but does not fully determine results (Aharoni, 1993: p. 31). Industry analysis is crucial, but a firm can also create a new industry or define a well-differentiated segment within an industry. Thus, producing generic drugs is not the same as producing a pharmaceutical industry, and attempts to gain the 180 day US exclusivity advantage is not the same as R&D for a new ethical drug. Most Israeli MNEs created a new industry or carefully carved a well-defined niche within the existing industry. Given Imaging developed the first ingestible video camera that fits inside a pill. Providing a view of the small intestines from the inside, it helps diagnose digestive disorders. Check Point created the market for network security. Amdocs is a leader in integrated customer management of IT. Retalics specializes in retailing applications: Mercury in enterprise testing and performance management solutions. Radvision is the leading provider of products and technologies for unified visual communications over intellectual property and 3G networks. M-Systems created a new market for USB flash disks but did not attempt to create a global brand. They all dominate a well-defined niche.

The conditions for success are very different at different stages of the firm's life. A firm must continuously adapt to a complex set of shifts. In many cases, unique strategic innovations are crucial to attain advantages. Crucial also is the ability to avoid reliance on areas of weaknesses for the specific firm. Israeli firms are generally more creative and more flexible, but they rarely have strengths in mass marketing to the final customer, nor do they possess the scale and the resources to establish a global brand or to erect a global system of after-sales service for equipment. Israeli firms have been extremely successful when focused on a very clear segment, starting with a small segment and growing to a larger one. Even today, some start-ups develop valuable technologies only to discover that their target market is unaware of them.

Several ingredients of the success of Israeli MNEs (not only in high tech) seem to have been the following:

- focus on a well-defined market segment;
- specialization in innovative ways to meet specific customers needs;
- high degree of flexibility allowing fast reaction to changes in economic, political, and technological conditions;
- optimized use of a global value chain;
- fast response to changing market needs;

- offering a superior service or customized products to those willing to pay a premium;
- reduced marketing costs through large transactions to a limited number of well-defined customers;
- ability to identify targets for acquisition and capabilities of integrating the acquired firm to gain synergies.

A more macro lesson of the Israeli experience is that transformation of large communities to new ideals does not seem to hold in the third generation. Israel's pioneers believed community life could and should transform the basic nature of human beings by creating new economic and social arrangements. For these arrangements to work effectively, individuals must sacrifice private interests, placing themselves at the disposal of the community and suppressing their greed.

Israel's experience shows that such a commitment is possible for special reasons and for a limited time. The commitment to live only for nationalistic ideals has waned three generations after the declaration of statehood. To be sure, many Israelis still will not consider living in another country — although for some moving to the United States is a possible alternative to managing an Israeli firm.

Since a very large percentage of Israeli MNEs are born globals, it is possible to offer a few generalizations regarding the characteristics of this new type of multinational. First, the major competence of these firms is in R&D and knowledge, not in production. In fact, production is often outsourced. "Globality from inception is possible because of intangibility of [the] most critical resource — i.e. technological knowledge as well as market knowledge, which does not necessarily require much capital and is not dependent upon scale economies" (Almor, 2000: p. 139).

Second, managers of born globals enjoy an intimate knowledge of foreign markets or at least can rely on a network of persons with such knowledge. Third, the industry and the firms within it enjoy the fruits of a learning curve. As one example, when the first prospectus was prepared to float Elscint, the lawyers had difficulty reconciling the legal and regulatory requirements of both Israel and the United States. Today, after hundreds of IPOs, these lawyers are very knowledgeable regarding legal requirements. Further, other law firms learned too and became proficient in the art of prospectus writing. Learning has been important in many aspects of the creation of a born global.

Fourth, new firms inherit the culture of a founding firm and face fewer difficulties in their early stages. Fifth, one shortcut to growth is acquisitions. Born globals seem to acquire firms for several reasons. One is to reduce competition. Another is to learn, to gain competitive knowledge; another is getting access to related technologies, to new geographical markets, or to related niches.

By definition, a niche is limited in its size. To grow, a firm has to expand to larger niches even though it is likely to encounter fierce competition from giant firms. Unfortunately, in many cases the born globals are acquired before they reach a large size. Indeed, the jury is still out as to the ability of a few dozens Israeli firms to reach the size of Teva. Too many of them are acquired, and venture capital funds tend to prefer exit. Quite a few Israelis think this is normal: the sharks always eat the sardines, not the other way round. Further, the venture capitalists press for exit and the founders of the firm are always tempted to receive the large sums available to them personally in such an exit. From a public policy point of view, it would be much better if the firms continued to grow as Israeli-based multinationals. Perhaps ways should be found to make such a path more attractive to the original entrepreneurs.

A Few Public Policy Issues

Rapid globalization has led to many political concerns. It evokes many issues related to the choices that nations have in pursuing economic development. When domestic firms relocate value-creating activities abroad, many are concerned that the economy loses employment opportunities. This, of course, is a worldwide problem. Managers would claim that they maintain more lucrative jobs by exporting the low skilled ones. Thus the previous manager of Delta Galil argued: "The plants in Jordan and Egypt make it possible to work on management in Israel as well as development, design, and marketing, all the capital intensive activities" (Ha'Aretz, 1999, August 8).

Several US-based MNEs — IBM, Intel, Motorola, Google, and Microsoft, among them — maintain R&D facilities in Israel.[20] It may not

[20] In fact, in 1981 the Israelis developed a cheaper version of the 8086 processor, renamed the 8088. In 2003, an Israeli-designed chip named Banias got a break with Intel's push into the notebook computers and was a part of the Centrino package (Lerner, 2008).

matter to a young Israeli engineer if one of these firms or an Israeli-owned firm employs him or her. Yet others claim that these firms gain resources by using the rarest resource: the ingenuity of the local "brain power", but do not funnel much more into the local economy. Manufacturing facilities, the more massive employers, are built in other, lower-cost, countries, thus not allowing Israel to leverage its major resource (Levav, 1998: p. 168).

Perhaps Israel's policy makers made the wrong choice in vigorously trying to attract such research centers. More generally, studies of the benefits of FDI tend to ignore the possibility that a home-based MNE can confer more benefits than a foreign MNE. The question revolves around both the benefits of the FDI but also the potential alternative uses of scarce human resources such as scientists, innovators, or engineers.

A more specific issue is that Israel (or any small country) is less able than a large country to diversify risks. Indeed, many small countries are dependent on one firm for a majority of the foreign exchange earnings. This is true for countries whose major earnings come from a natural resource such as oil or tin. Moreover, if the country gains a competitive advantage in a certain global industry, this advantage would mean high dependence on one large firm. Such a firm becomes by definition a dominant force in the economy. It may also enjoy a great deal of political power and in some cases it may make the government subservient to its power. This may be true even if the government owns the firm (Aharoni, 1982). Further, the state cannot afford to allow such a firm to go under because of the impact of such a bankruptcy on the whole economy.

The less a country is dependent on one or even a few firms, the better off it is in terms of spreading risk. It is also better off in terms of avoiding or at least reducing the high cost of economic power stemming from concentration of economic activities in the hands of a few firms. Global integration, driven by the advance of electronic commerce, coupled with the shrinking cost of transportation and communications, has enabled even tiny firms to become multinationals. Yet another necessary condition is that these firms should be able to tap capital from foreign stock exchanges or from venture capitalists. In the 1960s, these firms could not have taken off unless the government or an owner of one of a few conglomerates had financed their initial operations. If public policy creates conditions favorable for many firms to seize opportunities available in the global market place, a large number of firms in different industries may produce the country's GNP, avoiding reliance on a handful of firms.

Security is also an important issue. The case of Check Point not being allowed to acquire a US firm for security reasons is one example. Israel, being in a constant state of war, must find policy answers to security considerations related to foreign investments in strategic sectors. Of course, as Robert Reich[21] was the first to point out, there is a world of difference between ownership, management, day-to-day operations, and control. Clearly (whoever owns the firm), local workers would be hired to perform the day-to-day operations. Israelis may even manage the firm.

What matters to Reich is the creation of employment. He claims that Honda in the US is more important to the US than Ford in Asia (Reich, 1990, 1991). Yet, control has its ramifications not only because security-related secrets might be leaked but also because the firm may abruptly decide to cease operations. Even if it continues the R&D, it may not produce in Israel, thus not leveraging the major advantage of innovative engineers and creating less employment than desirable.

In a large, developed country, the question of ownership may seem moot. Ownership is extremely diffuse and top management — who may or may not be citizens or even residents of the country in which the firm is incorporated — make the decisions. A firm may be seen as a depository and a creator of knowledge; its major asset is the accumulated knowledge. Therefore, as long as the knowledge is stored in the minds (and computers) of citizens of the country, ownership may be insignificant, in particular when ownership is distributed among many shareholders from different countries. In Israel, ownership is not yet separated from control.

In a globally integrated world, what is an Israeli multinational enterprise? As shown above, for tax and other reasons, quite a few Israelis register their firms in the United States or in some tax haven country. Israelis found the firm and manage it but it is not incorporated in Israel. Such a firm would not appear in the official statistics as an Israeli outward FDI, but in many ways may be considered an Israeli MNE. Indeed, the press depicts many of these firms as Israeli firms. As already pointed out, the number of Israeli firms traded on NASDAQ as quoted in the Israeli press is 116, not 73. The difference stems from the large number of Israeli-owned firms incorporated outside Israel. Legally, and therefore for

[21] US Secretary of Labor (1993–1997) under President Bill Clinton.

statistical purposes, they are not Israeli.[22] The popular press sometimes gets carried away, counting firms owned by Israelis who long ago left the country and are now US citizens.[23] Perhaps what matters is also the enhanced value added. Strategic decisions made by an Israeli MNE may be more inclined toward enhancing the welfare of the country, or at least allowing Israel right of first refusal.

Conclusions

Israel went through a revolution. In the first three or four decades of its existence it was a state with a strong communal orientation, believing that the individual must serve the public needs, subordinating any individual goals. Economic policies were centered on import substitution and detailed controls of almost all economic activities. The Israeli government protected domestic firms by creating tariff and non-tariff barriers. Successive socialist governments believed in the development of domestically owned industrial infrastructure.

Under these circumstances, it was virtually impossible to create an Israel-based MNE. By 2008, Israel was open to a global world and was much more influenced by American individualism and by liberal economic ideas. The vast welfare state was reduced in scope, SOEs were privatized, and major reforms were carried out in many areas of economic activity. One major result was that business was not dependent any more on the state's resources for its existence. There was a total shift in the

---

[22] Thus, Verint was the world leader in networked video management. It was the provider of choice for fifty-five airports, twenty-five seaports, seven out of every ten US banks, two of the world's five largest retailers, and government organizations around the globe. This leadership was built on an integrated portfolio of networked video solutions for enhancing security and enterprise efficiency. It was started and is still managed by Israelis. World headquarters is in Melville, NY, but the R&D and strategic direction came from Tel Aviv, Israel. The same was true for Comverse, the parent of Verint, and for Amdocs, both Israeli founded and managed.

[23] A case in point is SanDisk, a major producer of flash memory. This US-incorporated firm was founded in 1988 by Dr. Eli Harari, who came from Israel. It had operations in many countries, including a joint venture with Toshiba, and a development center in Israel. In 2006, it acquired a major Israel-based competitor, M-Systems, the inventor of the USB flash drive known as Disk-on-Key, for about $1.55 billion. This acquisition of an Israeli company was registered as inward FDI into Israel despite the acquiring CEO's ties to Israel.

leadership of business enterprises. Many firms were acquired or failed. The Histadrut enterprises were sold, the government enterprises were privatized, and the Israeli currency was fully convertible. The government lifted all restrictions even on institutional investors, ended exchange control, enabled free movement of capital, and signed free-trade agreements with Europe and the United States, opening up its market to imports from any country in the world.

Business schools educated a new generation of managers, who saw new strategic options for Israeli firms. Deregulation and free imports meant heightened competition from foreign MNEs. Business managers awakened to the inevitability of multinational operations. The Bank of Israel noted: "[T]he direct investments are needed to be able to compete in the global market, since they increase the contact to essential resources for global competition such as production systems, financial markets and foreign capital as well as technology and labor force" (Bank of Israel, 2006: p. 274).

When the macroeconomic policy changed, virtually every large firm had to become multinational or be acquired by a foreign MNE. Israel's strength in high tech was bolstered by government support, stemming from the realization that the country lacked much in the way of natural resources and would not want to base competitive advantage on low-cost labor. The government helped by providing funds for R&D, for technological innovation, and for the creation of a local venture capital industry.

By the end of 2006, hundreds of Israeli firms grew by becoming MNEs. Reduced demand in Israel — for example, in construction — combined with the opening of Eastern Europe, helped to encourage outward FDI. At the same time, technology entrepreneurs were lured to the vast US market, starting born global MNEs. These firms used the Internet as a marketing tool. The need to cut costs led to the moving of production to low-labor-cost countries. Many of these firms took the road of greenfield investments, carving their way into the international competitive markets by dominating a niche. They later expanded through M&As. Indeed, it was not easy to attain critical mass by relying only on internal growth. Their major FSAs seem to have been innovation and the flexibility of their management.

The Israeli economy is noted for an increased concentration of capital in the hands of a few individuals and multinationals. Yet many firms blossomed, unrelated to established business elites. Some were very successful and others stumbled. All realized that to grow one had to invest outside the small domestic market. Later, firms faced a choice of a different nature: trying to become a giant or being acquired by giant foreign MNEs. Several firms attempted to become giants but finally succumbed to the lure of being acquired.

Another strategic choice was the degree to which firms should concentrate their investments in Israel or move operations, including possibly headquarters, to other countries. Some firms chose to maintain Israeli headquarters, while others did not. Israeli MNEs also faced the dilemma of whether to create jobs at home or to follow dispassionately the dictates of global market forces. Decisions on these issues seem to have been dependent at least as much on the ideological proclivities and allegiance to Israel of the companies' top management as on economic rationales.

The history of Israel clearly demonstrates that the government of a small country should encourage free trade, investment, and flows of capital, and concentrate on the maintenance of law and order, and on investments in human capital through education. Politically, such a government may opt for distribution policies that enhance social cohesion, prohibit the conversion of natural habitats to urban areas, or achieve any other of a number of cultural and social goals. As long as the country adheres to liberal economic policies, it can prosper, because wealth-creating individuals, who are highly mobile in today's global economy, will relocate elsewhere if the home-country's policies become unfriendly to businesses.

Firms from such a country can become global players. They can remove the shackles of small market size, and finance their operations by access to large global capital markets. Last but not least, much depends on leadership, strategic vision, and the managerial abilities of a very small number of visionaries who lead firms to great success in the global competitive arena. A small country often suffers from a short supply of these individuals.

Researchers can help policy makers from small countries by further examining some of the issues raised above. Thus, what is specific to Israel and what can be generalized to other small countries? Israel is widely acknowledged to be a technological innovator (Breznitz, 2006). Can other countries follow the same route, and if so, how? Further, what should be the policy on security-related enterprises? Should a firm from a small country start as a bi-national, maintaining marketing and pre- and post-sales services facilities in the United States, and R&D at home? How can benefits to the domestic economy be maximized? How are clusters formed, and what are their significant contributions? What are the costs of distance? What is the role of expatriates in allowing access to firms from the homeland?

Decision making in MNEs involves high levels of uncertainty and is based on incomplete information. Unfortunately, many studies assume perfect information and full rationality, thus missing the problems that decision makers face in the real world. These studies also miss the impact of corporate culture. Incorporating behavioral theory, bounded rationality, effects of clusters, cultural impact, and the role of expatriates and their willingness to help their country of origin may allow a better, fuller explanation of the Israeli story, and perhaps thus enhance IB theory.

Acknowledgment

I am very grateful to Pavida Pananond and Peter Williamson for their very constructive comments on an earlier draft of the chapter. The figures were updated when the chapter was submitted in 2007. In 2008 Teva announced its intention to acquire Barr Pharamaceuticals in the US. In September 2008 Iscar acquired Tungaloy Corporation of Japan, a manufacturer of drilling and milling tools, for $1 billion.

References

Agmon, T. & Kindleberger, C. P. 1977. *Multinationals from Small Countries.* MIT Press.

Aharoni, Y. 1976. *Structure and Conduct in Israeli Economy.* Tel Aviv: Gomeh (Hebrew).

Aharoni, Y. 1982. State-owned enterprise: An agent without a principal. In Jones, L. *et al.* (Eds.) *Public Enterprise in Developing Countries*. New York: Cambridge University Press, pp. 67–78.

Aharoni, Y. 1991. *The Israeli Economy Dreams and Realities.* London: Routledge.

Aharoni, Y. 1992. *The Political Economy of Israel.* Tel Aviv: Am Oved (Hebrew).

Aharoni, Y. 1993. From Adam Smith to Schumpeterian global firms. *Research in Global Strategic Management*, 4: 17–39.

Aharoni, Y. 2007. New business elites. In Rafael, E. B. & Steinberg, Y. (Eds.) *New Elites in Israel.* Jerusalem: Bialik Institute (Hebrew).

Almor, T. 2000. Born global: The case of small and medium sized, knowledge-intensive Israeli firms. In Almor, T. & Hashai, N. (Eds.) *FDI, International Trade and the Economics of Peacemaking.* Israel: College of Management of Rishon LeZion, pp. 119–139.

Avnimelech, G. & Teubal, M. 2004. Venture capital-startup coevolution and the emergence and development of Israel's new high technology cluster. *Economics of Innovation and New Technology*, 13: 33–60.

Avnimelech, G. & Teubal, M. 2005. Evolutionary innovation and high tech policy: What can we learn from Israel's targeting of venture capital? STE-WP-25, March.

Bank of Israel. 2006. *Annual Report.*

Bank of Israel. 2007. *Recent Developments in the Economy*, May, p. 10.

Bilkey, W. J. 1978. An attempted integration of the literature on the export behavior of firms. *Journal of International Business Studies*, 9(1): 33–46.

Breznitz, D. 2006. Innovation-based industrial policy in emerging economy? The case of the Israeli IT sector. *Business and Politics*, 8: 1–38.

Breznitz, D. 2007. *Innovation and the State Political Choice and Strategies for Growth in Israel, Taiwan, and Ireland.* New Haven: Yale University Press.

Cavusgil, S. T. 1980. On the internationalization process of firms. *European Research*, 8 (November): 273–281.

de Fontenay, C. & Carmel, E. 2004. Israel's Silicon Wadi: The forces behind cluster formation. In Bresnahan, T., Gambardella, A. & Saxenian, A. (Eds.) *Building High Tech Clusters.* Cambridge: Cambridge University Press.

Globes. 2004. G Magazine (Hebrew). December 2004.

Globes. 2005. G Magazine. May 18, 2005.

Globes. 2007. Financial Consumerism Supplement, p. 30. May 2007.

Globes. 2007. p. 10 (Hebrew). October 9–10, 2007.

Ha'Aretz. 1999. (Hebrew). August 8, 1999.

Huston, L. & Sakkab, N. 2006. Connect and develop: Inside Procter and Gamble's new model for innovation. *Harvard Business Review*, 84(3) (March): 58–69.

Johanson, J. & Vahlne, J.-E. 1977. The internationalization process of the firm: A model of knowledge development and increasing foreign market commitments. *Journal of International Business Studies*, 8: 23–32.

Johanson, J. & Vahlne, J.-E. 1990. The mechanism of internationalization. *International Marketing Review*, 7(4): 11–24.

Jolly, V., Alahuta, M. & Jeannet, J.-P. 1992. Challenging the incumbents: How high technology start-ups compete globally. *Journal of Strategic Change*, 1: 71–82.

Knight, G. & Cavusgil, S. T. 1996. The born global firm: A challenge to traditional internationalization theory. *Advances in International Marketing*, 8: 11–26.

Lemos, R. 2006. Check Point Calls Off Sourcefire Buy. www.securityfocus.com/print/news/11382. March 24.

Lerner, S. 2008. Intel Opens Israeli Plant for Next Generation Chips. Bloomberg.com. July 1.

Levav, A. 1998. *The Birth of Israel's High-Tech.* Tel-Aviv: Zmora-Bitan (Hebrew).

Madsen, T. & Servais, P. 1997. The internationalization of born globals: An evolutionary process? *International Business Review*, 6(6): 561–583.

McKinsey & Co. 1993. *Emerging Exporters. Australia's High Value-Added Manufacturing Exporters.* Melbourne: McKinsey & Co. and the Australian Manufacturing Council.

Oviatt, B. M. & McDougall, P. P. 1994. Toward a theory of international new ventures. *Journal of International Business Studies*, 25: 45–64.

Oviatt, B. M. & McDougall, P. P. 1997. Challenges for internationalization process theory: The case of international new ventures. *Management International Review*, 37(2): 85–99.

Porter, M. 1990a. *The Competitive Advantage of Nations.* New York: Free Press.

Porter, M. 1990b. The competitive advantage of nations. *Harvard Business Review*, 68(2) (March/April).

Porter, M. 1998. *On Competition.* New York: Free Press.

Reich, R. B. 1990. Who is us. *Harvard Business Review*, 68(1) (January-February): 53–65.

Reich, R. B. 1991. *The Work of Nations Preparing Ourselves to 21st Century Capitalism.* New York: Vintage Books.

Rennie, M. W. 1993. Global competitiveness: Born global. *McKinsey Quarterly*, 4: 45–52.

Rugman, A. M. & Verbeke, A. 1993. Foreign subsidiaries and multinational strategic management: An extension and correction of Porter's single diamond framework. *Management International Review*, 33(2): 71–84.

Rugman, A. M. & Verbeke, A. 2001. Subsidiary specific advantages in multinational enterprises. *Strategic Management Journal*, 22(3): 237–250.

Sherman, A. 1988. A dream realized. *Israel Economist.*

Stauber, J. 2001. *From Teva to Check Point.* Tel Aviv: Yedioth Acharonot (Hebrew).

Teva Pharmaceutical Industries Ltd. 2007. Investor Lunch Presentation, Tel Aviv, Israel (August). Available at www.tevapharm.com/pdf/CapitalMarketQ2.pdf.

UNCTAD. 2006. *World Investment Report.*

Van Den Bulcke, D. & Verbeke, A. 2001. *Globalization and the Small Open Economy.* Aldershot, UK: Elgar.

Zander, I. & Zander, U. 1997. The oscillating multinational firm — Alfa Laval in the period 1890–1990. In Bjorkman, I. & Forsgren, M. (Eds.) *The Nature of the International Firm.* Copenhagen Business School Press.

Service Firms in the Global Economy

https://doi.org/10.1142/9789811287510_0020

Chapter 20

The Internationalization Process in Professional Business Service Firms: Some Tentative Conclusions*

Yair Aharoni

Tel Aviv University, Tel Aviv, Israel

Introduction

In 1940, Colin Clark (p. 34) noted that the "economics of tertiary industry remains to be written". Hill, in 1977 (p. 336), found the "complete neglect of services in economic theory is almost incredible given the role of services in contemporary economics". In the 1980s, the neglect is in the process of being redressed but many questions are still unanswered, both when these firms are looked at as black boxes and when the inner operations of the firms are considered.

The participants in the conference all stressed the importance of understanding the distinctions between "goods" and "services". Despite much effort, these distinctions are still not very clear. Many of the services are embodied in goods but are also sold separately. Design activities is one example. A designer may work as an independent. Alternatively, a designer may be an employee of a firm. In the first case, the work will be recorded as a "service", in the second as "goods". This point is repeatedly made by different authors and many attempts have been made to offer

*This chapter is reproduced from *Coalitions and Competition: The Globalization of Professional Business Services*, pp. 280–285, Routledge.

different definitions of services and to draw boundaries between goods and services. Stigler's observation from 1956 that there seems to be "no authoritative consensus on either the boundaries or classification of the services industries' (Stigler, 1956: 47) still holds true. (For a summary of the many definitions and classifications, see Grönroos, 1990: 26–35.) Moreover, the exact definition of a profession still has to be agreed on. Yet it is generally agreed that we live in a service society and that the rules of this society have to be understood.

It is also clear that our knowledge of certain service firms is quite embryonic. Most academic work on services and on their globalization seems to have been done by marketing experts (for early contributions see Wilson, 1972; Kotler & Bloom, 1984) who increasingly emphasize the importance of quality and the need to reduce perceptual gaps between service suppliers and receivers (see Brown *et al.,* 1991; Zeithaml *et al.,* 1991). What emerged from our conference was a montage of a wide variety of issues and points of view. Several participants attempted to look at the phenomenon of services in general. Much less was distilled about the specific forces related to the professional business firm. To some extent, of course, these professional business service (PBS) firms share characteristics with other firms. Indeed, several participants stressed the need to build the theory of the global PBS as an extension of the tested theories they, and others, developed to explain goods-producing multinational enterprises (MNEs). Clearly, for any firm, the advantages of operating beyond national borders must exceed the additional costs of doing so. Therefore the PBS global firm may be seen as a special case of the goods-producing MNE. The global PBS must be able to internalize operations across national borders so that the co-ordination of activities within one operation unit is more efficient than market activities between different ownership units. Indeed, transaction costs economics was used to explain multinational banks (Grubel, 1977; Gray & Gray, 1981).

It is also evident that some service firms followed goods-producing MNEs (on banks, see Channon 1988: Ch. 6). For many PBS firms, the need to serve multinational clients is said to have been a major reason for international expansion. The demand pull also created a perceived necessity to build or acquire subsidiaries abroad to facilitate their firm-specific advantages (FSAs) rather than move persons from headquarters on a temporary assignment. PBS firms may also be perceived as a means to reduce the problem of asymmetric information. The uncertainty as to the outcome of a service transaction entails a preference for firms with a reputation and a proven track record and thus allows these firms to have specific ownership advantages. At the same time, there seems to be very little advantage stemming from economies of scale.

Differences

One difference between other MNEs and PBS firms is that the international expansion of PBS firms is much more strongly influenced by different regulatory and licensing environments. It may well be that one reason for the widespread operations of multinational management consulting firms is the relative lack of such differences in regulation. Moreover, management consultants do not have to be licensed. They can also incorporate, reducing the risk to any individual partner. It may also be that management is perceived as a US-developed craft and a US origin is seen as providing credible quality signals. Thus, heterogeneous regulatory and institutional environments may reduce the ability to achieve FSAs to allow multinational operation. Further, the regulatory environment means that PBS multinational firms face different hurdles from other MNEs in international operations. Whether or not harmonization and mutual recognition will eliminate this problem remains to be seen. Even if they do, one major distinction of PBS firms will remain — that they are totally dependent on the skills of the professionals. A PBS firm enjoys very few economies of scale. The economies of scope it can achieve by producing closely related services are also limited by the ability of professionals to learn from each other and to co-operate. Information technology may make it is easier to reduce the per-unit cost of a service by offering similar services. Still, since the major assets of a PBS walk home every night, much depends on the ability of the firm to recruit, organize, train and motivate professionals. Without such an ability the firm would be unable to signal quality and reputation and thus would not be able to be successful. Whether or not an ownership structure is indispensable or whether different pools of professionals participating in a network is sufficient is a fascinating question for further research. A related question is the degree to which innovation may create FSAs in a PBS. Clearly, a global PBS necessitates the skills of organizational learning, which is stressed for "transnationals" by Bartlett & Ghoshal (1989). Internationalization strategy, as shown by Carman & Langeard (1980), is much riskier for a service firm than for a manufacturer of physical goods. The service firm is allowed a much shorter time for learning and getting used to the new market. It has to start producing its service all at once, maintaining direct contacts with its customers. For a PBS firm, added complications are different licensing arrangements and different regulations.

All told, the discussion in the conference clearly shows that our knowledge of the strategy, structure and means of creating FSAs of an international PBS firm are at the embryonic stage. Much more research effort is needed to allow more definite conclusions on any of the topics discussed in the conference.

Future Research Areas

Four major research areas should be stressed. The first is broadly related to the inner workings of the service firms and organization design issues. How do these firms process information effectively? How is a network managed? How will the characteristics of the PBS firms and the key success factors faced by them affect their choices with regard to ownership and to control. Will the future see more networking, strategic alliances and co-operative ventures arrangements rather than firms connected by ownership ties? A related question is the complex relationships between professional standards, enforced by various professional organizations and the increased possibility of competition. The trade-off between these two is regarded differently not only in different countries and cultures but also by different professional associations.

A second area of research is in the interaction between political and economic issues. The role of government in regulating services has undergone a major revolution recently. The degree to which even more deregulation is possible, or the possibility of mutual recognition as in the EC, has to be researched. More generally, the trade-offs between economic forces leading to a growing demand for globalization and political realities, as well as cultural traditions looking for differences between nations and a different distribution of benefits, must be carefully studied. It is useful to learn also who is regulated: the service activity, the service provider or the movement of the service provider.

A related question is the possibility of an operation of a Gresham law of professional standards. Thus, the Securities and Exchange Commission (SEC) in the USA has maintained very high levels of reporting requirements relative to other countries. Could the globalization of markets mean that firms would tend to register their shares in places where the reporting requirements are the least stringent — followed by growing pressures on government to relax standards? Research should also be related to possibilities of reaching an international agreement on PBS trade, investment and movement of labor.

The impact of data movement issues on new economies of scale and of scope as well as on international trade is a third major area for research. Many service industries tend to enjoy much higher levels of economies of scale. The most extreme example is in restaurants, not in PBSs. Those used to be Ma and Pa operations. Today — with the help of franchising and of computers — they have become huge global firms on a world scale, as in the case of rental cars, hotels or airlines, e.g., with instantaneous guaranteed systems of reservations. Data services accelerated the possibilities of international trade in services. It also made networking a very important organizational means of achieving these advantages.

Fourth, PBS firms depend on highly skilled persons to execute the work. The importance of recruiting, developing, educating and maintaining the loyalty of the professionals who will be supplying the services cannot be overstated. Research on human resource management should allow academics to help managers in achieving better selection methods in recruiting, more efficient training, greater socialization, better career design and higher levels of loyalty. Note that technology is transferred by training efforts. Firms want to ensure that those trained will remain. They also hope to inculcate a similar culture and ways of operation among their many employees in different countries.

It would also be important to try and show how much of the differentiation and firm-specific advantages in the goods sector are in actual fact a result of services embodied in the goods. Much of the goods reputation, after all, is really a result of delivery commitments, information provided to customers, customer support staff and other kinds of services.

With the many changes in technology, one relevant question for research is the degree to which the professional business firm, under constant pressure for lower costs, would move from being a highly customized skill-intensive operation to what Roger Schmenner (1986) called a "service factory" and what Levitt (1972) called the "production line approach" (see also Levitt, 1976). It may well be that globalization of PBS operations is still at an embryonic stage. It is not a necessary condition for success and only a few firms may choose to follow this path. In a global industry, a firm must operate globally in order to survive. In PBSs, most firms are local. There are only a handful of firms that decided to expand globally, because they had to serve multinational clients or owing to an idiosyncratic decision of a top manager. The internationalization of PBS firms was to a great degree demand driven. Firms that had no choice but to follow their clients or lose them were mainly auditing firms, much less so legal services. Indeed, there is a major difference in the degree of concentration of different PBSs. Yet, even in auditing where the concentration is highest, there are many small firms serving domestic markets. Moreover, some international PBS firms serve a specific niche. All in all, PBS firms were rarely able to expand into new areas based on reputation and thus achieve economies of scope. In advertising, for example, the attempts to sell "one-stop shopping" to clients has faltered. Firms are still not sure how to achieve a corporate culture that will dominate diverse professions with different belief systems from different countries but also from different professions. Many firms are still groping for means to cross-refer clients and find it difficult to achieve the level of stability enjoyed by goods-producing MNEs. Unlike goods, professionals can — and sometimes do — walk away from the firm, not infrequently taking clients with them. It is also much more difficult to maintain consistency in service quality.

More research is needed about the reasons for the differences in the magnitude of multinational operations of firms in different PBSs. Why is it that most universities did not become multinationals? What, then, explains the great success of Berlitz all over the globe? Why do auditors and management consultants operate globally while most law firms and all dentists are local? Why are some PBSs (real-estate agents, lawyers) compensated on a basis of commission while others are paid for time? What are the key factors of success for such firms? Are these key factors similar across professions or not?

There are many more interesting research questions that could be added, such as the degree to which some professional services (e.g., engineering design) influence the sourcing of a project, or the applicability of general rules and theories of trade and investment to PBSs. All in all, the globalization of services opens many vistas for important work. Understanding PBS MNEs may also enable us to assess how universal and generally applicable are our theories on the trade and investment in goods.

https://doi.org/10.1142/9789811287510_0021

Chapter 21

The Organization of Global Service MNEs*

Yair Aharoni

Recanati Graduate School of Business Administration, Faculty of Management, Tel Aviv University, Tel Aviv, Israel

Since the seminal work of Chandler (1962), the notion of a linkage between strategy and structure has become widely accepted — that is, if an organization is to implement its strategy most effectively, it needs the appropriate structure and support systems. At the same time, it needs the flexibility to exploit strategic options that arise from environmental changes. However, at least in the short run, a firm cannot easily change its organizational structure, and this may be a major impediment to its ability to change its strategy. In an increasingly globally integrated world, firms attempting to become major players in their industry need to cope with and exploit environmental changes and adjust their organizational structure to create what Bartlett & Ghoshal (1989) termed "transnational" organizations. In other words, firms need to be able simultaneously to achieve local responsiveness, global efficiency, and the creation of knowledge (learning).

Chandler based his conclusions on a study of four of the largest corporations in the United States — General Motors, Dupont, Standard Oil,

---

*This chapter is reproduced from *International Studies of Management & Organization*, Vol. 26, No. 2, pp. 6–23 (1996).

and Sears Roebuck — of which only Sears Roebuck was a service organization. Indeed, much of the literature on both the strategy of multinational firms and organizational structure has emanated from studies of large and powerful manufacturing firms, notwithstanding the ever-increasing importance of large multinational firms in service industries. While some of these service industries have more in common with MNEs producing goods, others are quite different. The purpose of this paper is to explore the effects of globalization on the organizational structures and systems of service firms in general, and professional service firms in particular. The paper postulates certain relationships between key success factors in multinational professional service firms and the structure and systems of these firms. The resulting propositions help provide the basis for a contingency theory of organizational structure and systems.

In the first section, some of the contributions to organization design theory and to organizational taxonomies arc briefly surveyed. In the second section, some of the relevant theories on the organizational structure of multinational enterprises are reviewed. The third section discusses the globalization of services, while the fourth proposes a taxonomy of multinational service firms by the key factors contributing to their success, and it hypothesizes on the implications for organizational design. This analysis is offered as preliminary to devising a contingency theory of organizations for service multinationals, particularly professional service multinationals.

Organizations — Structure and Design

Organization theory is a positive theory focused on understanding organizations. On the basis of its findings, the organization focuses its design on normative solutions, that is, on the optimal means of creating an organization to achieve given goals and missions. Organization theory has moved a long way from the belief prevailing at the beginning of the century in immutable general laws of organization design or in the classical depiction of a "machine" organization. March & Simon (1958) summarized the state of the art as follows: "Much of what we know or believe about organizations is distilled from common sense and from the practical experience of executives. The great bulk of this wisdom and lore has never been subjected to the rigorous scrutiny of scientific methods" (p. 5). Many assertions have since been tested to check whether or not they are supported by the facts. In addition, the importance of such factors as information, motivation, power, conflict, and innovation have been subjected to much scrutiny. Moreover, different theses have also been tested in a variety of national and cultural contents. Thus, Chandler's work was tested by Channon (1973) in Great Britain, Dyas in France, Pavan in Italy, and Thanheiser in Germany — all in 1972 doctoral dissertations at the Harvard Business School.

The organizational structure of the firm has been shown to be a reflection of its operating environment. Lawrence & Lorsch (1967) examined the firm's differentiation and integration characteristics in three industries. By differentiation, they meant orientations toward goals, time, and interpersonal relationships, as well as toward the degree of formality of the structure; by integration, they meant the degree of collaboration among departments working on common projects. They demonstrated that these characteristics depend on the degree of turbulence in the environment: in a highly stable environment, organizations tend to be much more integrated, whereas in a turbulent environment, differentiation becomes more necessary.

In Lawrence & Lorsch's (1967) model, complex tasks are performed through increased task specialization and subsequent coordination. The different needs in different stages in an organizational evolution have also been recognized. Child (1972) called attention to the importance of growth as a means of meeting the aspirations of the participating members of the organization. Kimberly (1976) argued for a dynamic perspective — researching the different stages in the life cycle of organizations — from creation to transformation to maturity and then decline. Pfeffer & Salancik (1978) distinguished between internally generated growth, to achieve individual or organizational goals, and growth based on biological systems limited by constraints and resources. They saw growth as a purposeful response to external constraints. Others stressed uncertainty (Koberg & Ungson, 1987) or size (Slater, 1985; see also Galbraith, 1973; Jurkovich, 1974; Thompson, 1967).

Mintzberg (1979) developed a taxonomy of organizational structures in different categories of organizations — the entrepreneurial, bureaucratic (machine and professional), divisional, adhocracy, and matrix. He suggested that, as organizations grow, they undergo structural changes — from the entrepreneurial to bureaucratic, divisional, and finally matrix structures. An organization can be bureaucratic without being centralized. This happens when professionals are needed because of the complexity of tasks, but the tasks themselves can be perfected through standardized operating programs. The result is the professional bureaucracy structure.

Structural changes, therefore, correspond to both internal requirements and environmental demands. They are contingent on quite a large number of factors. Organizations must change and adapt to internal political conditions, to external changes in the environment, and to technological changes and the opportunities they create. Integration mechanisms are needed to achieve coordination and these needs also depend on situational variables such as the competitive market structure or the stage of the life cycle (Galbraith & Nathanson, 1978). Although empirical research has failed to lend unequivocal support to the hypothesis that strategy follows structure, the implementation of any strategy must be based on a certain structure and on systems, including rewards.

Organizations arc basically information-processing entities, and must match the demand for information processing with the capacity of the firm to do it. The information required depends on the environment, on technology, and on other variables such as size and complexity. Nowadays, firms can create significant competitive advantage on the basis of sophisticated use of information systems. New information technologies are facilitating new forms of organizations and different structures, allowing greater integration across national borders. The increased power of personal computers, for example, is profoundly affecting both structures and systems. Computers have also allowed service firms to achieve both low-cost positions and customized services. All these new developments arc allowing new types of structures, such as the "infinitely flat" organization (Quinn & Paquette, 1990).

New telecommunications capabilities have eroded the boundaries between firms and their suppliers, as well as between geographic territories; and organizations can run borderless networks connected by electronic data interchange (EDI) and electronic mail with very little formal hierarchy. Moreover, in a knowledge-based society, the ability to tap all possible knowledge to achieve the task is crucial. Much of the needed knowledge cannot be maintained in books on standard operating procedures, but is tapped by professionals communicating with each other. Professional workers must be willing to cooperate across tasks, professions, and geography to implement the strategy of the firm. This kind of cooperation has been achieved by professionals such as engineers and consultants. However, when a firm needs to trim its staff, self-preservation, fear, and frustration may lead individuals to be much less cooperative.

The organization of the future is sometimes portrayed in terms of project management and flat structures (e.g., Peters, 1992; Quinn, 1992). This type of structure is perhaps more appropriate to expert organizations such as consulting firms or CNN (Cable News Network), with their prima-donna "star" performers, than to organizations that can standardize their operation to allow a machine bureaucracy as the optimal mode. Indeed, companies such as CNN, EDL, and McKinsey & Co. are organized around many small teams carrying out shifting project assignments. They employ mainly bright, aggressive, though not arrogant, individuals who are unwilling to abide by too many arbitrary rules and standard operating procedures, but are happy to do all it takes to get the job done. These organizations focus on solutions to customers' problems, which they achieve at a much greater speed than the older, hierarchical bureaucracy.

Much in the way of theoretical contributions and empirical evidence is available on the relationships between structure and contextual factors. A survey of the organization theory literature certainly shows a diverse and sometimes inconsistent set of rules related to the organizational structure of firms. In many cases, the number of variables to be taken into account is quite large. Duncan (1979), for example, suggested a decision tree for structures based on three possible dimensions of the environment: complexity, change, and segmentation. Robbins (1990) discusses environmental hostility, positing that greater hostility necessitates greater centralization. Perrow (1967) discussed the impact of technology, while Pugh *et al.* (1969) considered the impact of size. If one combines all these variables with Mintzberg's (1979) basic configurations (simple, functional, divisional, matrix, machine bureaucracy, professional bureaucracy, ad hoc), a very large number of possible combinations emerge. Organization theory guides managers in choosing those configurations that allow fit between the organization and various parameters, such as environment, strategy, size, technology, and management style. These variables may or may not be different in an international context. Bartlett & Ghoshal (1989) in particular stressed the role of overseas operations (as well as the development and diffusion of knowledge) in creating unique configurations for international operations. According to these authors, firms operating in many countries can be based on self-sufficient national units and a decentralized system ("multinational"), on a globally scaled centralized system ("global"), on a hybrid design in which only sources of core competence are centralized and the rest of the operations are decentralized ("international"), or in the transnational mode, in which functions are dispersed across the globe but integrated to achieve competitive advantage, with knowledge being developed in different parts of the system and shared by all of its parts. The transnational design, according to Bartlett & Ghoshal (1989: p. 207), goes beyond the matrix configuration (for somewhat similar configurations, see Habib & Bard, 1991). Integration can be achieved by several means, to be discussed later.

The Organizational Structure of the Multinational Enterprise

The increasing importance of various forms of multinational enterprises spreading their activities across national boundaries has not escaped the attention of academics. A large number of treatises have been written, attempting to explain, inter alia: (1) the reasons for internationalization; (2) the reasons for the various forms of internationalization, such as licensing, joint ventures, strategic alliances, or wholly owned subsidiaries; (3) factors explaining the competitive advantage of a multinational firm vis-a-vis its domestic rivals; (4) the ways multinational enterprises compete with other similar enterprises on a global basis; (5) the organizational structure of the multinational enterprises; (6) the relationships between the multinational enterprise and home and host countries.

Almost all of these works have aimed at explaining the extracting and/or manufacturing multinational enterprises (but see Boddewyn *et al.*, 1986). Until the beginning of the 1980s, it was assumed that services were nontradable. Thus, internationalization has been studied mainly by the Uppsala school and has been viewed as a process in which the enterprise gradually increases its international involvement (see Johanson & Vahlne, 1977, 1993; for a summary, see Luostarincn, 1979; Luostarinen & Welch, 1990).

Three decades of research on multinational firms since the seminal work of Hymer (1976) have led to the conclusion that a multinational firm must have some advantage to offset the additional costs of running its operation, compared with domestic rivals. Different authors have proposed different types of advantages, most of which are assumed to be intangible and firm-specific. In a producing enterprise, most of these advantages are based on scale, specific knowledge, or brand names. John Dunning attempted to combine many of the explanations in his eclectic theory (Dunning, 1977, 1988, 1993), while Ozawa (1979) proposed some differences between US- and Japanese-based multinationals. With time, research evolved from a total reliance on economic factors to a focus on internal issues of firms' operations (Rugman, 1981). It was only toward the end of the 1980s that researchers began to relate to management issues (Bartlett & Ghoshal, 1993; Ghoshal & Westney, 1993; Ghoshal & Nohria, 1989; Hedlund, 1986).

Again, much of this research is not always applicable in attempting to explain why some service-providing firms have become multinational and others have not. Thus, if reputation and brand names are important firm-specific advantages, why was the Harvard Business School unable to exploit these advantages when it tried to build an executive development program in Mt. Pélerin, Switzerland (Aharoni, 1995b)?

In the past decade or two, most studies have stressed the globalization of operations. Within multinational firms, globalization means the increased integration of resources and capabilities, and it can be operationalized by the extent of transfer of these resources within the multinational enterprise (Gupta & Govindarajan, 1994; Kobrin, 1991). The resources crossing borders can be capital, products, or knowledge. In a "transnational" firm, the flows are two-way — from subsidiaries to headquarters and from headquarters to subsidiaries — and they are associated with increasing information flows. Managing international interdependencies is inherently more complex than managing activities within a single nation. Firms must organize to derive, combine, and transfer resources (Ghoshal & Westney, 1993; Leong & Tan, 1993). Thus, international management theory can benefit from the knowledge to be derived not only from economic theory or strategic management analysis but from organization theory too.

Yet very little research has been done on organizational structure. A notable exception is the work of Stopford & Wells (1972), who were the first to show that firms adopt different strategies in different stages of their internationalization; while Egelhoff (1988) stressed information processing. Organizational structure is no longer considered a sufficient explanation of multinational operations, and an understanding of managerial systems and control mechanisms is perceived to be a necessary additional line of inquiry (Bartlett & Ghoshal, 1993; Ghoshal & Westney, 1993; Hedlund, 1986; for a summary of works on coordination mechanisms, see Martinez & Jarrillo, 1989). Organizational structure is nevertheless a major constraint on the strategic flexibility of the MNE. Once a certain structure has been adopted and functions, authority, and operations have been distributed among different units in different countries, any reorganization is both time-consuming and costly. It also often works against a firm's "administrative heritage" (Bartlett & Ghoshal, 1989). Thus, a firm that has enjoyed a long tradition of a multidomestic strategy will have to contend with serious challenges if it is to move swiftly to a global strategy, as the history of firms such as Procter and Gamble or Philips amply demonstrates.

In a multinational enterprise, the key decisions relate to the means of coordination, degree of integration of activities from the home center, and the degree to which authority is dispersed across countries. The giant European (and a few American) multinationals of the pre-World War II era developed a very decentralized structure in which each subsidiary was allowed a great deal of autonomy and maintained its own production, marketing, and even development facilities. Headquarters appointed key personnel, approved major capital expenditures, and received dividends. Each subsidiary was allowed a high degree of differentiation as well as local adaptation. Given the state of the managerial arts and the relatively high costs of transportation and communications, this structure seems to have been the most appropriate for its time.

The US multinationals in the period after World War II were generally much more integrated and centralized, and all new technology and products stemmed from the home country. The greatest strength of these firms was their ability to internalize the transfer of technology and of management skills across national boundaries. The subsidiaries did enjoy a high level of autonomy, but their competitive advantage derived mainly from transfers of technology, know-how, and brand equity from the center. Many of these firms, which Bartlett (1986) called "coordinated federations", lost ground in the 1970s and the 1980s to Japanese competitors that used "centralized hubs" — a very efficient domestic hub and a global, integrated system based on economies of scale in manufacturing at the center, with subsidiaries supplying mainly distribution and service functions, at least initially.

When scale is a key factor of success, global integration turns out to be very effective. Yet, local responsiveness — to the domestic conditions as well as to the different governments — is often required too. Many MNEs advocate both global integration and local responsiveness — what Bartlett (1986: p. 377) termed "the transnational solution". Bartlett believes that, during the 1990s, firms will be forced to achieve both efficiency, through scale and integration, and local responsiveness, through catering to differentiated demands from customers and to pressures from governments for local content as well as other regulations. The simultaneous pursuit of these two requirements (global integration and local responsiveness) is also important in maintaining a high level of innovativeness. This objective may be achieved by using different structures for different parts of the value chain, and often by outsourcing certain activities. Scale economics call for integration, but innovations arc best encouraged by decentralization. The center ceases to be the only source of ideas or new products. In contrast, each national unit is a source of ideas that are shared throughout the whole network, and each may achieve global scale by being the world source of a certain product for the whole system, with different subsidiaries having different roles (Bartlett & Ghoshal, 1986: p. 90). The center, for its part, should foster "supportive organizational norms and values" (Bartlett, 1986: p. 388).

The experience of manufacturing MNEs shows that increasing internationalization may threaten their stability because domestic markets are no longer sheltered from the onslaught of intensified global competition. They are also broadening their global scope in many service industries. The new demands on multinationals have come about because of globalization and because of the enormous advances in information technology. Many firms have achieved advantage by the use of proprietary software. Some were able to achieve "mass customization" (Quelch & Hoff, 1986); others created global networks that made it easier to share information with suppliers as well as customers and across geographical areas. Computers not only allow speed but enable the firm to install intangible assets and to trade in ideas. Only ten years ago, centralized mainframes comprised about three-quarters of all computing power, whereas today the figure is between 1 and 5 percent. Sales of the personal-computer (PC) industry (both hardware and software), by contrast, grew from $2 billion in 1981 to $82 billion in 1990 (Peters, 1992: p. 115). In the new age of modem information technology, firms can build and sustain a competitive advantage based on information systems. This is particularly apparent in services such as reservations systems and frequent flyer (or user) programs of airlines and hotels.

Another anticipated change is a reduction in the importance of scale. The giant diversified firm of two or three decades ago is now trying to shape itself up and reduce its size. In 1954, the first year for which *Fortune* magazine published its "500" ranking, these firms represented 37 percent of US GNP. By 1979, the share was 58 percent. Since then, they have been losing ground in the market. Their share was 42 percent in 1989 and 40 percent in 1991, which is equal to the 1959 figure (Peters, 1992). It is argued that the only way giant firms can survive is by becoming less hierarchical, more decentralized, and organized on the basis of teams carrying out ever-changing projects. In short, manufacturing MNEs will have to learn from service firms. An idea of the corporation of the future that will operate in the borderless world may be seen in the professional business services and the many strategic alliances that already exist today.

Information technologies and other changes have allowed many new forms of organization. The common denominator of all these entities is the form of the organization's various boundaries. The legal boundaries remain the same, as in strategic alliances, so that coordination has to be achieved among legally separate organizations. This active coordination means extensive expansion of the information boundaries and often of management boundaries. Thus, suppliers may be allowed to get into the computer of a firm and supply goods without a specific order. In a network type of activity, the organization must be defined to include all the separate legal entities that comprise the network. The management boundaries are extended to the whole network to ensure coordination. Coordination itself can be achieved through different forms that may or may not be centralized. The *process* of coordination and integration may be formal — developing systems, policies, and standards (Child, 1972); it may be effected through *central processes* — by the direct intervention and actions of an elite group based in a unit designed as headquarters in the management of each separate division (Bartlett & Ghoshal, 1989); or it may be achieved through *socialization.* The latter prevails when the task is unique, integrated, or ambiguous (Ouchi, 1977, 1980). Bartlett & Ghoshal (1993) argue that, in new organizations, each subsidiary is a self-contained unit that is part of a whole. These and other new forms of organization are more prevalent in service firms, particularly in professional service firms.

Globalization of Services

In recent decades, growth in the service sector in most countries has been very impressive, particularly in the operations of global service MNEs, which may or may not have become not only multinational but also global for the same reasons as the manufacturing firms. The accelerating trend of corporate internationalization has put a premium on the ability of service firms to serve their clients uniformly worldwide (Aharoni, 1993c). Financial institutions, accounting firms, law firms, and management consultants have all followed their manufacturing clients abroad. In addition, some leading firms have expanded internationally to create challenging work opportunities. Thus, McKinsey & Co. created its London office in 1959, and by 1990, 63 percent of its income was generated outside the United States. By the 1980s, the belief among service firms that they must follow their clients to other parts of the globe had become pervasive. Moreover, the United States has gone further than any other country in deregulating its airlines, trucking, and telecommunications, compelling these industries to restructure and reengineer to meet competition by undergoing a wrenching overhaul of management systems. US firms also recognized earlier that advantage lay in a lead in brainpower and innovation, and accordingly spent large amounts of money on R&D. Today, of course, the US lead in brainpower is eroding with the increasing level of technological sophistication of firms from other countries.

All service organizations operate in several distinct markets and must satisfy at least three sets of goals: economic goals (profitability, growth), satisfaction goals (of staff, often desiring professional challenges and variety), and client goals. To achieve all or a subset of these goals, some firms opt to become global players, as part of a network of independent entities sharing common services or by managing a single global firm. Of course, the firm must organize its value-creating activities in a way that will help it achieve the greatest degree of success.

Studies of national accounting firms in North America indicate governance structure and primary task as important characteristics (Aharoni, 1993b; Greenwood *et al.*, 1990). Governance structure is based on partnership, with local offices as the principal place of business. Managers return to these offices after a temporary assignment in the top office. Local offices are independent, inter alia, because of professional norms of independence. Tasks are carried out by principal partners helped by associates, in proximity to the client. Greenwood *et al.* (1990) point out that these task characteristics are not amenable to central control. Control is achieved mainly through certain shared norms, agreed standards, and peer review (Aharoni, 1993a, 1993b).

Yip identified certain "globalization drivers" (1992: p. 31) and global "strategy levers" (p. 15) that explain why certain firms (or certain industries) have become global. One group of globalization drivers are those based on market. A second group stems from cost. A third are government globalization drivers, and the fourth are what Yip terms "competitive globalization drivers". Johansson & Yip (1994) found that market and cost drivers were more significant than government or competitive drivers in their sample of manufacturing businesses. This finding may or may not hold for service industries, where government globalization drivers might be more relevant.

Yip (1992: p. 15) also identified five global strategy levers, to measure international strategy on a scale of pure multidomestic to pure global. The global ends are as follows:

- Global market participation: countries are chosen according to their potential contribution to globalization benefits, not only on the basis of their stand-alone attractiveness.
- Global products/services: a standardized core product or service with a minimum of local adaptation or none at all.
- Global location of value-adding activities: the value chain is broken up so that each activity may be conducted in a different country.
- Global marketing: a standard marketing approach is applied around the world, even though not all elements of the marketing mix need be identical.
- Global competitive moves: these are integrated across countries. The same type of move is made in different countries at the same time or in some systematic sequence, or a competitor is attacked in one country in order to drain its resources for another country, or a competitive attack in one country is countered in a different country.

The same levers may be conceptually identified in service industries, though their importance may not be significantly different. In some cases, the levers relate to industries. In others, they relate to firms (an example is Berlitz).

In services, Heskett *et al.* (1990) used the concept of the "strategic service vision" (SSV) to analyze the alignment between target market segments, the service concept, the operating strategy, and the service delivery system. When target market segments are in different countries, the service delivery system is often guided by standard firm practices across countries, as in the case of American Express travelers' checks or McDonald's. Service firms must be able to guarantee standardized quality services across many countries. Clearly, one advantage of a multinational hotel system is that it can promise "no surprises". By contrast, however, some global service firms, notably professional service firms that sell expertise, focus on diagnosis, and the projects they handle are customized and specialized. To address each local market with customized service, some firms find that they have to be much less integrative and to differentiate across market segments. The problem with such a choice is the greatly increased complexity. The decision to serve vastly different customers in different geographic locations fosters a need to develop entirely different strategic service visions with all the added complexity this entails. In the extreme, if the firm is totally differentiated, it may find that it has no communality and therefore no competitive advantage over a domestic firm. It may find it better to use a loose, ephemeral network of professionals who do not share all standard operating procedures or profits worldwide. Even within professional business services, however, there are cases where firms offer less creativity and more standard procedures. Thus, in auditing and information-systems consulting, the firm offers more standardized service. The blend of standardized procedures and customized solutions is different in different professions. The more standardized the elements, the easier the integration, the less complex the structure needed, and the greater the probability of global operations.

Clearly, both the globalization drivers and levers and the key factors of success are different in different types of firms. Some sell expertise, others efficiency, and still others experience. In some types of business, the uncertainty in the mind of the client is very high — sometimes even after the service has been rendered (as in the medical profession). In others, it is not. Some are people-intensive, while others need scale and/or capital. All of these factors may have an impact on the organizational structure. The next section proposes a fuller taxonomy and advances some contingent factors in terms of organization structure.

Propositions on the Structure of Professional Service Multinationals

Professional service firms are different from manufacturing multinationals in several important respects.

First, they are people-intensive and demand minimal investment in fixed assets. In addition, key persons capable of creating value added do not have to work for a particular firm. They can move easily and can also work on their own — in other words, the firm becomes a "voluntary" organization. A corollary of the above is that, in some firms, the most critical assets walk out the door every night and a crucial success factor is the ability to recruit and retain the best and most imaginative talents. These persons have to be carefully nurtured, motivated, and allowed to grow. They have to be trained and retrained and their values reinforced through indoctrination. Incentive systems need to encourage teamwork and cooperation. These factors, though important, are not crucial to success in travel-related business, for example.

In some professional service firms, economies of location are important. That is, it is important to have a branch wherever the multinational clients have branches. Failure to participate in a certain strategic market can undermine global competitiveness. For example, the fact that some European firms were unable to establish a strong base in Japan limited their ability to use economics of scale and reduced their exposure to new innovations; more importantly, it prevented them from creating a hostage for good behavior on the part of their major Japanese rivals. It is hypothesized that this participation is less crucial in some service industries such as auditing than in others such as travelers' checks or airlines.

Professional service firms are marked by a "think versus grind" mentality. Professional business services that offer mainly expertise can leverage the time of senior professionals much less than even other professional service firms, not to mention hotels or restaurants. Their staffing requirements call for getting the best persons or top-percentile graduates from the best schools. Others that deal with familiar, often standard types of problems depend for their success on efficient performance. The "think" expertise type is much more difficult to globalize, and it attracts clients by the reputations of its employees rather than by the firm's name. The more standardized the solution, the greater the importance of integration and of centralization, and the smaller the need for differentiation, the easier it is to offer global services and to enhance the ability of each location to serve clients by drawing on the firm's systems, its accumulated knowledge in databases, and the experience of the whole network.

A related factor is the degree of customization. The success of certain service firms (such as McDonald's) has been largely based on the ability to create standard performance based on routine and repetitious work. It is important to distinguish between routines and standardization. Audit work, for example, is based on routine and repetitious work, but there is a great deal of variability in the different audits performed for firms from different industries.

The degree of importance of information systems (e.g., reservations in hotels or airlines, databases of firms on systems, experience, or skills available within the firm) is another critical factor. The more important and developed the information systems, the easier it is integrate activities, even across national borders.

Another factor is the degree of the client's uncertainty before or even after the service has been rendered. Service firms need to be client-centered. Clients may or may not appreciate the intellectual challenge of a solution or may even be unable to distinguish between competent and outstanding technical work. Often, a large number of contingencies cloud the ability of a client to assess the work (e.g., is a lawyer good even though he or she did not win the case?). One result is that clients focus more on what they perceive as the quality of delivery than on the quality of the work itself. Clients are often shopping for peace of mind, reassurance, trust, or confidence (Aharoni, 1995a). Maister (1993: p. 73) says that, in the medical profession, people look for availability, affability, and ability — in that order. Because of all these considerations, clients often use proxies for quality, one of which is size (Greenwood *et al.*, 1990).

Finally, the higher the uncertainty, the greater the willingness to pay for reputation and brand, and therefore the greater the competitive advantage of those firms that succeed in creating a major integrated global organization.

These variables may be a vector in a matrix that explains firms' decisions to use different structures and systems. In addition, an interim variable that will affect the choice is the form of entry: A firm may opt for a very weak form of a global network such as using correspondents (as in financial institutions), or it may refer the work to a trusted domestic firm; it may decide to create or to join a network of independent firms, as accountants often do; it may choose strategic alliances or joint ventures, or it may acquire or create a wholly owned subsidiary.

Another critical factor in the internationalization success of professional service firms is governance structure. Firms registered as corporations — such as consulting firms — are often organized hierarchically. Many other professional firms are partnerships, with *ad hoc* committee structures and therefore very weak central headquarters. In other words, the legal boundaries of service multinationals tend to be different from their management and information boundaries. In a strategic alliance or a network, overall strategic direction is limited to certain functions agreed upon by all participants through a process of negotiation and consensus building. Successful implementation of the strategy depends on acceptance of the ideas by the different legally autonomous entities. No hierarchical relations exist, at least not formal ones.

In this type of firm, different sets of management skills are needed. The first relates to recruitment — or the way subcontractors, partners, or vendors are chosen. The right choices are crucial to the operational success of the network as a whole. Second, top management has to manage an array of independent persons who are not cogs in the wheels of a corporate hierarchy but a part of an autonomous organization. Since added value comes from knowledge, those with more knowledge will enjoy more power. Third, the network must be flexible and flat: flexibility is important because very often changes cannot be anticipated; flatness is important because, if communications have to go up and down hierarchies, much time is lost. To achieve responsiveness to markets, communications must be unimpeded, and horizontal consultation has to be encouraged. In addition, initiative has to be encouraged or even mandated through a socialization process. Managing such a network is a rather delicate affair, since the system may run out of control.

From the conceptual discussion up to this point, particularly that relating to the very useful differentiation/integration framework, the following rules for organization design in service multinationals appear to emerge.

First, the higher the degree of homogeneity among clients in different countries, the greater is the need for formal standard systems. Therefore, the more a firm serves global clients, the greater the pressures for common standards and centralized coordination and control (see also Brown *et al.* in this issue). Global clients demand service of consistent quality and quick access to the best experts available. These demands increase the need for linkages across different entities, better integration, and more formal processes of coordination.

Second, the more complex and/or diversified the work performed for clients, the greater is the need for experts from across the network and formal integration (Aharoni, 1993a).

Third, the greater the importance of scale, the greater is the tendency of the firm toward integration. Integration is also important when the economics of location are salient or when capital-intensive services are being provided. It is easier when the tasks being performed are repetitive. By contrast, the more expertise and thinking that are needed, and the greater the need for innovation or brain work, the more difficult it becomes to formally enforce standards and the greater the need for differentiation. In the extreme, when the key factors of success are the expertise and superior minds of individuals who tend to resent formal processes (Hinings *et al.*, 1991), integration is almost impossible. The organization will be extremely flat and based on project management. The contradictory pressures for more central control and more independence are the major challenge of the global service firm, in particular, the professional service firm. These firms are also constrained by their administrative heritage, based on an organization of independent partners. Enforcement may be achieved by moral suasion, by appeals to collegial loyalty, by socialization processes, by training, and even by indoctrination, to get what Maister termed "the one-firm firm", or by a constant flow of information and horizontal transfer of knowledge (Aharoni, 1995b).

Fourth, coordination and integration among units are based less on traditional forms of organizational structure such as divisional or formal bureaucracy than on committees designed to achieve coordination in the flow of resources among the different units. These resources are capital, technology, persons, and information.

Fifth, while manufacturing multinationals allocate capital for investment and repatriate dividends, professional service firms hardly move capital across borders. The resources transferred are mainly persons and information, and, to a lesser extent, technology.

Sixth, some professional service firms will increasingly be organized as centralized bureaucracies if they are able significantly to increase the part of their work that is based on experience, with the availability of databases — of both past experience and available skills — a key factor of success. The greater the need for a network of scholars and professionals, the more individualistic they become, and the less central control the firm has over them. To be sure, advances in information technologies allow much more differentiation while, at the same time, tapping into centralized resources. However, old-fashioned centralization is detrimental to the work of the organization.

Seventh, information flows are difficult to manage because of their volume, complexity, and diversity. However, professional norms, as well as rules, roles, and responsibilities, may allow more effective horizontal transfer of knowledge. As one example, university professors devote a significant amount of time learning about the work of others through a word-of-mouth web of relationships. Senior professors spend an inordinate amount of time refereeing papers or writing letters of recommendation for tenure or promotion at other, often remote, universities. This work is not remunerated financially, but is still meticulously carried out because of the commitment to professionalism and excellence. Academics know one another and socialize at conferences, where they receive instant feedback. Thus, the individual reputation stakes are very high (see Aharoni, 1995b).

Eighth, a major difficulty is the means of enforcing priorities for work done by an entity in one country for one in another country. Thus, the audit of a subsidiary of a multinational in a certain country can be of great importance for the auditors in the country where this multinational's headquarters reside.

Finally, bargaining and consensus building among committee members as well as *ad hoc* task forces and individual partners with high status provide alternatives to hierarchical structure.

Although the list of possible propositions connecting the contingency variables and organizational structure is much larger, the major lesson of this paper is that there is a need for much more research on alternatives to structure as a means of achieving coordination and integration.

Conclusions

A firm operating globally must manage the flow of people, information, services, and money across national borders. It must nurture and cultivate distinct competence that will allow it to offer better or more efficient services than the domestic firm, as well as the executive reward system and the systems of coordination and control that will nurture its strategy. Even more than in extractive and manufacturing firms, the success of the global service MNE depends on its ability to gain and to maintain clients. In addition, firms must make sure they are able to recruit and maintain the human and other resources needed to operate in the market of their choice. A major constraint on the globalization of services is the ability to integrate all activities, particularly as most service firms need to have a high degree of local autonomy and flexibility. An important question is what kind of value-adding support does each subsidiary receive from headquarters? Because of the speed of change in the marketplace, on the one hand,

and better information processing on the other, globally operated firms can learn a lot from the way organizations are designed in the investment-banking business (Eccles & Crane, 1988), or in the professional business services or in networks such as CNN or EDL. The new knowledge-based organization in a brain-based economy will have to be organized more like professional service firms or institutions of higher learning, which have traditionally faced a more fickle environment of shifting temporary assignments. This paper proposes some variables that impinge on a contingency theory of organizational design of global service firms.

References

Aharoni, Y. 1993a. Globalization of professional business services. In Aharoni, Y. (Ed.) *Coalitions and Competition: The Globalization of Professional Business Services.* New York: Routledge, pp. 121–142.

Aharoni, Y. 1993b. Ownership, networks and coalitions. In Aharoni, Y. (Ed.) *Coalitions and Competition: The Globalization of Professional Business Services.* New York: Routledge, pp. 121–142.

Aharoni, Y. 1993c. The internationalization process in professional business service firms: Some tentative conclusions. In Aharoni, Y. (Ed.) *Coalitions and Competition: The Globalization of Professional Business Services.* New York: Routledge, pp. 280–285.

Aharoni, Y. 1995a. The role of reputation in global professional business services. Invited Lecture, University of Lausanne, Switzerland.

Aharoni, Y. 1995b. A note on the horizontal movement of knowledge within organizations. Paper Presented at the Conference on the Management of Change in Knowledge Based Organizations, University of Alberta, Canada.

Bartlett, C. 1986. Building and managing the transnational: The new organizational challenge. In Porter, M. E. (Ed.) *Competition in Global Industries.* Boston: Harvard Business School Press.

Bartlett, C. & Ghoshal, S. 1986. Tap your subsidiaries for global reach. *Harvard Business Review*, (November–December): 87–94.

Bartlett, C. & Ghoshal, S. 1989. *Managing across Borders: The Transnational Solution.* Boston: Harvard Business School Press.

Bartlett, C. & Ghoshal, S. 1993. Beyond the M-form: Toward a managerial theory of the firm. *Strategic Management Journal*, 14 (special issue): 23–46.

Boddewyn, J. J., Halbrich, M. B. & Perry, A. C. 1986. Service multinationals: Conceptualization, measurement and theory. *Journal of International Business Studies*, 17(3) (Fall): 41–57.

Brown, J. L., Cooper, D. J., Greenwood, R. & Hinings, C. R. 1996. Strategic alliances within a big-six accounting firm: A case study. *International Studies of Management and Organization*, 26(2) (this issue).

Channon, D. F. 1973. *The Strategy and Structure of British Enterprise.* Boston: Harvard Business School, Division of Research.

Chandler, A. D. 1962. *Strategy and Structure, Chapters in the History of the Industrial Enterprises.* Cambridge, MA: MIT Press.

Child, J. 1972. Organizational structure, environment and performance. *Sociology*, 1–22.

Duncan, R. B. 1979. What is the right organization structure? *Organizational Dynamics* (Winter): 59–79.

Dunning, J. H. 1977. Trade, location of economic activity and the MNE: A search for an eclectic approach. In Ohlin, B., Hesselbom, P. O. & Wijkman, P. M. (Eds.) *The International Allocation of Economic Activity.* New York: Holmes and Meier.

Dunning, J. H. 1988. The eclectic paradigm of international production: A restatement and possible extension. *Journal of International Business Studies*, 19(1): 1–31.

Dunning, J. H. 1993. *Multinational Enterprises and the Global Economy.* Workingham: Addison-Wesley.

Dyas, G. P. 1972. The strategy and structure of French industrial enterprise. Unpublished doctoral dissertation, Harvard Business School.

Eccles, R. G. & Crane, D. B. 1988. *Doing Deals: Investment Banks at Work.* Boston: Harvard Business School Press.

Egelhoff, W. 1988. Strategy and structure in multinational corporations: A revision of the Stopford and Well's model. *Strategic Management Journal*, 9: 1–14.

Galbraith, J. R. 1973. *Designing Complex Organizations.* Reading, MA: Addison-Wesley.

Galbraith, J. R. & Nathanson, D. A. 1978. *Strategic Implementation: The Role of Structure and Process.* St. Paul, MN: West.

Ghoshal, S. & Nohria, N. 1989. Internal differentiation within multinational corporations. *Strategic Management Journal*, 10: 323–337.

Ghoshal, S. & Westney, E. 1993. *Organizational Theory and the Multinational Corporation.* New York: St. Martin's Press.

Greenwood, R., Hinings, B. & Brown, J. 1990. P2 form strategic management: Corporate practice in professional partnerships. *Academy of Management Journal*, 33(4): 725–755.

Gupta, A. K. & Govindarajan, V. 1994. Organizing for knowledge flows within MNCs. *International Business Review*, 3(4): 443–457.

Habib, M. M. & Bard, V. 1991. Strategy, structure and performance of U.S. manufacturing and service MNCs: A comparative analysis. *Strategic Management Journal*, 12: 589–606.

Heskett, J., Sasser, E. & Hart, C. 1990. *Service Breakthroughs: Changing the Rules of the Game.* New York: Free Press.

Hedlund, G. 1986. The hypermodem MNC — Heterarchy? *Human Resource Management*, 24(1): 9–35.

Hickson, D. J., Pugh, D. S. & Pheysey, D. C. 1969. Operations technology and organization structure: An empirical appraisal. *Administrative Science Quarterly*, 14: 378–397.

Hinings, C., Brown, J. & Greenwood, R. 1991. Change in an autonomous professional organization. *Journal of Management Studies*, 28(4): 375–394.

Hymer, S. H. 1976. *The International Operations of National Firms: A Study of Direct Foreign Investment.* Cambridge, MA: MIT Press.

Johanson, J. & Vahlne, J.-E. 1977. The internationalisation process of the firm — A model of knowledge development and increased market commitments. *Journal of International Business Studies*, 8 (Spring-Summer): 23–32.

Johanson, J. & Vahlne, J.-E. 1993. Management of internationalization. In Zan, L., Zambon, S. & Pettigrew, A. M. (Eds.) *Perspectives on Strategic Change.* Hingham, MA: Kluwer Academic Publishers, pp. 43–78.

Johansson, J. K. & Yip, G. S. 1994. Exploiting globalization potential: U.S. and Japanese strategies. *Strategic Management Journal*, 15(8) (October): 579–601.

Jurkovich, R. 1974. A core typology of organizational environments. *Administrative Science Quarterly*, 19(3): 380–394.

Kimberly, J. R. 1976. Organizational size and the structuralist perspective: A review, critique and proposal. *Administrative Science Quarterly*, 571–597.

Koberg, C. S. & Ungson, G. R. 1987. The effects of environmental uncertainty and dependence on organizational structure and performance: A comparative study. *Journal of Management*, 13(4): 725–737.

Kobrin, S. J. 1991. An empirical analysis of the determinants of global integration. *Strategic Management Journal*, 12 (Special issue, summer): 17–31.

Lawrence, P. R. & Lorsch, J. W. 1967. *Organization and Environment.* Boston: Harvard Business School Press.

Leong, S. M. & Tan, C. T. 1993. Managing across borders: An empirical test of Bartlett and Ghoshal's (1989) organizational typology. *Journal of International Business Studies*, 24: 449–464.

Luostarinen, R. 1979. The internationalization of the firm. Helsinki: Helsinki School of Economics.

Luostarinen, R. & Welch, L. S. 1990. Chapter F: International business operations. In *International Business Operations.* Helsinki.

Maister, D. H. 1993. *Managing the Professional Service Firm.* New York: Free Press.

March, J. G. & Simon, H. A. 1958. *Organizations.* New York: Wiley.

Martinez, J. & Jarrillo, C. 1989. The evolution of research on coordination mechanisms in multinational corporation. *Journal of International Business Studies*, 20(3): 489–514.

Mintzberg, H. 1979. *The Structuring of Organizations.* Englewood Cliffs, NJ: Prentice-Hall.

Ouchi, W. 1977. The relationship between organizational structure and organizational control. *Administrative Science Quarterly*, 22: 95–113.

Ouchi, W. 1980. Markets, bureaucracies and clans. *Administrative Science Quarterly*, 25: 129–145.

Ozawa, T. 1979. *Multinationalism: Japanese Style.* Princeton, NJ: Princeton University Press.

Pavan, R. J. 1972. The Strategy and Structure of Italian Enterprise. Unpublished doctoral dissertation, Harvard Business School.

Perrow, C. 1967. A framework for comparative analysis of organizations. *American Sociological Review*, 32: 194–208.

Peters, T. J. 1992. *Liberation Management: Necessary Disorganization for the Nanosecond Nineties.* New York: Knopf.

Pfeffer, J. & Salancik, G. R. 1978. *The External Control of Organizations.* New York: Harper and Row.

Pugh, D. S., Hickson, D. J., Hinings, C. R. & Turner, C. 1969. The context of organization structures. *Administrative Science Quarterly*, 14: 91–114.

Quelch, J. A. & Hoff, E. J. 1986. Customizing global marketing. *Harvard Business Review*, 64(3) (May–June): 59–68.

Quinn, J. B. 1992. *Intelligent Enterprises: A Knowledge and Service Based Paradigm for Industry.* New York: Free Press.

Quinn, J. B. & Paquette, P. C. 1990. Technology in services: Creating organizational revolutions. *Sloan Management Review*, 31(2) (Winter): 67–78.

Robbins, S. P. 1990. *Organization Theory: Structure. Design, and Applications* (3rd edn.) Englewood Cliffs, NJ: Prentice-Hall.

Rugman, A. 1981. *Inside the Multinationals: The Economics of Internal Markets.* New York: Columbia University Press.

Slater, R. O. 1985. Organization size and differentiation. In Bacharach, S. B. & Mitchell, S. M. (Eds.) *Research in the Sociology of Organizations*, Vol. 4. Greenwich, CT: JAI Press, pp. 127–180.

Stopford, J. & Wells, L. H. 1972. *Managing the Multinational Enterprise.* New York: Basic Books.

Thanheiser, H. T. 1972. The Strategy and Structure of German Enterprise. Unpublished doctoral dissertation, Harvard Business School.

Thompson, J. D. 1967. *Organizations in Action.* New York: McGraw-Hill.

Yip, G. S. 1992. *Total Global Strategy: Managing for Worldwide Competitive Advantage.* Englewood Cliffs, NJ: Prentice-Hall.

https://doi.org/10.1142/9789811287510_0022

Chapter 22

The Competitive Potential of Technology-Intensive Industries in Developing Countries*

Yair Aharoni[†] **and Seev Hirsch**[‡,§]

[†]*The Leon Recanati Graduate School of Business Administration, Tel Aviv University, Tel Aviv, Israel*

[‡]*Institute of International Economics and Management, Copenhagen Business School, Frederiksberg, Denmark*

Introduction

The impact of technology on economic development and the interaction between technology, trade and investment policies are among the least understood aspects of the economic development process. Until the 1980's, most research on economic development was based on neoclassical economic assumptions, namely that technological changes come about because of reactions to changes in factor prices, while the firm was treated as a "black box". The discussion revolved around the labor or capital

*This chapter is reproduced from *The World Economy: Challenges of Globalization and Regionalization*, pp. 99–118, Palgrave.

[§]This paper draws upon a larger study commissioned for the United Nations, Transnational Corporations and Management Division, Project on Globalization and Developing Countries, and will appear under the auspices of the United Nations.

intensity of the production techniques — or the "appropriateness" of the technology.[1] Attention was also drawn to the comparison of purchasing "packaged" and "non-packaged" technology (Kaitsos, 1974).

Technology transfer requires a certain degree of technical know-how on the part of the receiving firm, and not all firms are able to use available knowledge (Aharoni, 1991). Factor substitution is not based on well-defined menus that firms can scan (Dahlman & Westphal, 1982). Further, the accumulation of knowledge may change the course taken by the firm by stimulating activities never before imagined. Several case studies published in the 1980's, e.g., Jorge Katz's (1978, 1984) studies of Latin America, Teitel (1981, 1984), Lall (1980, 1981), Westphal (1983), allow a glimpse into the trials and errors of the innovation process.

Available data indicate that transnational corporations (TNCs) control a high share of employment, output and trade in technology-intensive industries and of access to new technologies. TNCs possess firm-specific intangible assets, including outright control of proprietary technological knowledge, and accumulated expertise in the management of international operations. After 1983, global flows of foreign direct investment (FDI) expanded at an unprecedented rate. Even though it grew like a tidal wave, the share of FDI going to developing countries (DC's) declined over time.

We assume that DC's seek to increase their share of world output, employment and trade of technology-intensive products, which has been very small to date. Achieving this goal depends both on macro-environmental, conditions and on the strategy of business organizations. This paper examines the characteristics of high-technology products and of the firms which produce them, focusing on the processes which go on within the firms and their interaction with their domestic and international: environments. It spells out the main conceptual and policy implications of the interrelationship between technology acquisition, FDI and trade.

Section "Technology and Competitive Advantages: Firm Product Characteristics" analyzes the operations of traditional and technology-intensive firms operating in domestic and international markets. It explores their interactions with the input and output markets, and with other economic actors, which interact in the production of internationally competitive and internationally marketable goods and services.

Section "Technology Policy Options — A Conceptual Scheme" outlines a conceptual scheme for evaluating technological development options available to developing countries. It considers market and technology dimensions, technology levels, product characteristics and market orientation, technological infrastructure, and components of technology policies.

Section "Transnational Corporations and Product Characteristics" examines the relationship between TNCs and technology development. The examination shows how TNCs acquire a competitive edge in technology-intensive products. The discussion reviews the different motives of TNC activities and discusses the conflicting and complementary interests of TNCs, their home and host countries.

The concluding section argues that a meaningful expansion of an outward-looking technology-intensive sector is extremely difficult without the involvement of TNCs in the process. The choice is not between TNCs and domestic firms, but rather between foreign-based and home-based TNCs.

Technology and Competitive Advantages: Firm Product Characteristics

Universal and firm-specific inputs

Technology or "Technological capability", as defined by Lall (1990), has entrepreneurial, managerial and technical components. It encompasses the knowledge required to mobilize the human, material and financial resources employed by the firm. It is embodied in the managers, engineers, skilled workers and other employees. Technological knowledge, according to Patel & Pavitt (1987: 60) is often tacit and mostly specific to firms and to particular classes of products and production processes. It takes the form of codified and un-codified operating norms and policies, as well as past investments in process engineering and in product research and development. Technological and other types of knowledge possessed by the firm can be viewed as a distinct firm-specific production factor. From an economic perspective, this knowledge can be viewed as an intangible asset which, like a machine, can be employed to increase the value (or reduce the unit costs) of the firm's output. Like a tangible asset, firm-specific knowledge depreciates over time. Depreciation in this case takes the form of obsolescence. The knowledge possessed by the firm becomes diffused through expiry of patents, reverse engineering and straightforward copying. In time, the products on which it is based and the processes used to manufacture them may get copied by competitors, some of whom may have access to less costly universal production factors.

Acquisition of technological knowledge progresses from the ability to absorb universal technologies embedded in equipment and coded in blueprints, through the ability to absorb, upgrade and license technologies, engage in reverse engineering, adapt processes used by other firms, and manufacture products whose specifications are not in the public domain. Parts of the technical components of firm-specific knowledge can be obtained through licensing, or through contract research. In either case, the knowledge obtained must be actively absorbed by the receiving firm. The process takes time and is cumulative (Cantwell, 1989) and requires building what Carlsson & Eliasson (1991) termed "competent teams". The basic knowledge base which constitutes technological capability remains intact as long as the team which embodies the capability continues to function. The firm attains the highest level of technical knowledge when it acquires the ability to develop its own products, i.e., to manufacture products based on in-house knowledge acquired through its own R&D efforts.

The technological standard of individual firms depends not only on internal decisions and on the level and quality of the country's technological infrastructure. The better the educational system, the research done by universities, the linkages between universities and firms, the diffusion of technical standards, availability of testing facilities and other institutions, the more productive the process of firm-specific knowledge building and the less the cost incurred by the individual firms in the process of creating the required level of their specific knowledge.

Universal and firm-specific outputs

Universal inputs (i.e., skilled and unskilled labor, financial and physical assets) combined with firm-specific knowledge, are employed to manufacture goods and services which may be grouped on the basis of the intensity of the inputs which they contain into Firm-Specific and Universal Products.

Firm-specific products (S-products) contain a significant element of proprietary knowledge — knowledge which is available to the firm and not to its competitors — which imparts unique characteristics to the products, which consequently command a premium price. In contrast, the manufacture of universal products (U-products) does not depend on the possession of proprietary knowledge by the producer. The technology is easily acquired and absorbed, and its possession does not confer a competitive advantage on the firm which possesses it.

Goods cannot be marketed unless they are accompanied by some services, transportation being an obvious example. Unlike goods, services are intangible. They cannot be inventoried and, most important, to render a service, the provider must interact with the user.

In services as in goods we distinguish between universal services (U-services) and firm-specific services (S-services). Universal services — finance, insurance, and transportation — can be acquired in the open markets. Firm-specific services — instruction, installation, repairs, etc. — depend on proprietary knowledge originating with the manufacturer of the goods.

Super computers, numeric control machine tools, medical scanners, telephone exchanges laser equipment and robotics are examples of S-goods associated with S-services. Before a medical scanner can be used, operators must be trained, the scanner must be installed and run in, spares must be supplied and the provision of maintenance services must be assured. These S-services must be provided either directly by the equipment manufacturer or by an organization specifically authorized by the manufacturer to provide them.

Video equipment and personal computers are examples of S-goods whose associated services have become universal. In this case, some services have been embodied in the equipment, which has been designed in such a way as to minimize the need for repair and maintenance. The information required to provide the remaining services has been made public by the manufacturers, thus making it possible for the equipment to be serviced even by persons not specifically authorized to do so by the manufacturer.

Since information is a public good it tends to be diffused over time and become public knowledge, regardless of the intentions of the manufacturer. As S-products mature their associated services become "universalized". Thus, the services associated with cars, household appliances and industrial equipment which started out as S-services, when these products were initially introduced on the market, have become more and more universal, as the relevant information has become diffused (Hirsch, 1989; Hirsch & Meshulach, 1992).

The product characteristics described above influence the organizational modes employed in their manufacture and distribution both within a country's boundaries and internationally. Considering U-products first, recall that the knowledge required for their manufacture and servicing is in the public domain. The production technology is easily available, and can be acquired together with the production equipment which several firms from different countries will be eager to supply. The associated services can be similarly obtained from universal-service providers, firms which specialize in the provision of the service, and which do not depend on outsiders for product-specific knowledge.

S-product industries tend to be dominated by firms characterized by vertical integration where R&D, manufacturing, distribution and servicing are undertaken by organizations owned or controlled by a single firm. The operating modes of U-product firms are likely to be more varied, and unbundling to be more common. Thus, contract research, subcontracting of key components, distribution and servicing by independent agents, are more prevalent in the U-product than in the S-product industries.

International transactions in universal and in specific products

The distinction between goods and services discussed above is particularly germane when we consider international transactions. Marketing across national boundaries requires knowledge of foreign languages, familiarity with more than one legal system and "ways of doing business" in the target markets, as well as dealing with foreign exchange and specialized financial instruments. These activities tend to be more complicated and more costly than marketing in the familiar and close home market, giving rise to an export marketing cost premium. The premium, which increases with both physical and psychic distance (Luostarinen, 1979; Johanson & Vahlne, 1977), is also influenced by the characteristics of the products being traded.

The export cost premium of S-products is, other things being equal, higher than the cost premium associated with U-products. The difference is particularly critical for the specific-service-intensive S-S-products. The knowledge on which the service components of the product is based originates, as was noted above, with the manufacturer of the good. Bearing in mind that the provision of services requires interaction between producer and customer, the knowledge required for the provision of the service must be transferred to an organization which is located close to the latter.

Turning from the firms to the national economy, we note that, typically, there is a significant difference between the industry structure of developing and developed economies, the output of the former being characterized by a high proportion of U-products and a low proportion of S-products (see World Bank, 1992). By the same token, analysis of the trade of different countries will usually reveal that developed economies tend to have a surplus in S-products, while developing economies tend to have a deficit in S-products, financed by a surplus in U-products.

One of the goals of economic development is to change this distribution, and to increase the share of S-products in the industrial output of developing economies. Achievement of this goal requires an increase in the relative number and growth rate of S-product firms, expansion and upgrading of their technological base, production techniques, and marketing capabilities. This transformation cannot be achieved by the efforts and initiatives of business firms alone. They must be accompanied by appropriate public policies.

Technology Policy Options — A Conceptual Scheme

Firms differ widely in their capabilities to efficiently deploy different technologies. These differences vary from one part of the value chain to another. Firms within a certain country are heterogeneous in terms of their capabilities. A specific firm may possess higher levels of skills than another firm. A cluster of firms in a certain area in which related and supporting industries operate may possess some advantages, including demanding buyers with stringent needs (Porter, 1990: 586). The aggregate of firms' capabilities can be viewed in some sense as the national capability. These capabilities are also affected by technology policy, which is based on certain basic choices, which have a market-orientation and technology dimensions.

We distinguish between inward (domestic market) and outward (world market) orientation of firms.

Outward orientation means that the standard against which firms measure their performance and target their policies is the standard adopted by world leaders — in terms of quality, product specifications, delivery practices, service provision and price. Inward market orientation is a characteristic of firms which shelter behind trade barriers which enable them to raise prices, downgrade quality, provide poor services, and generally offer products which cannot compete in the world market with the leaders. Natural barriers are frequently augmented by protectionist policies such as import quotas, prohibitive tariffs, foreign exchange limitations, licensing requirements, discriminatory technical standards, or terms of access to public procurement, "voluntary export restraints", and a myriad of other non-tariff barriers so extensively used in both developed and developing countries.

Note that outward orientation is not synonymous with export orientation, and that similarly, inward orientation is not the same as import replacement. Both terms focus on the nature of the competition and not on the target markets. Thus, while export-oriented firms will generally follow an outward orientation in the sense used here, firms engaged primarily in import replacement will not necessarily be inward oriented. A liberal import policy, for example, may force an import-replacing firm to adopt an outward-oriented technology posture.

Technology levels, product characteristics and market orientation — A macro-view

The relationship between technology levels, product characteristics and market orientation is shown in Table 1. The table shows a 3×2 matrix of the options available to public policy makers when economies are grouped on the basis of the level and complexity of technology which the industrial sector is capable of using, and on the direction of market orientation.[2]

Table 1 distinguishes between the following six cells:

I. Inward-oriented U-U products based on technology absorption.
II. Outward-oriented U-U products based on technology absorption.
III. Inward-oriented S-U products based on technology adaptation.
IV. Outward-oriented S-U products based on technology adaptation.
V. Inward-oriented S-S products based on technology creation.
VI. Outward-oriented S-S products based on technology creation.

Clearly, the two dimensions represent a continuum in reality; the division into two discrete groups is done only for expository purposes.

Different economies will be characterized by different distributions, the position of each country being characterized by the clusters of firms which dominate it. The location of these clusters is in turn determined by

Table 1. Technology level and market orientation.

Technology Level	Low Absorption	Medium Adaptation	High Creation
Products	U-U	S-U	S-S
Inward Orientation	I	III	V
Outward Orientation	II	IV	VI

capabilities of firms, by resource availability, and by history, which includes the outcome of past technology policies. As pointed out by Lall it is the "complex interaction of incentives, endowments, institutions, and technological efforts" (Lall, 1990: 59) that explains the performance of a given country.

In the least developed economies almost all firms are found in the first cell. Firms possess only the technical ability needed to manufacture products labeled in section I as U-products, based on publicly available mature technology for the domestic market. The technical knowledge required for the manufacture of these products is readily available, and is frequently obtainable together with the production equipment. The goal of technology policy of economies in this development stage is to establish their capacity to absorb existing universal (mature) technologies developed elsewhere. Skills needed to market the products internationally are rarely available, and external inputs are also difficult to acquire. A major advantage of countries in cell 1 is likely to be their low labor costs or abundance of certain natural resources.

Firms in the second cell, like those of the first, are U-goods producers. They must, however, be internationally competitive since they compete by definition with world-class firms either in the home market or in third-country markets. The technology level in this case must be higher than that attained in the first cell. The products must be price competitive and conform to a consistent level of quality. Most important, while firms may enjoy government protection in the domestic market, some of them face intense competition in the international arena, increasing the incentive to master better operating methods.[3]

Firms in the second cell concentrate in some cases on one specific portion of the value chain. Thus, they may perform subcontracting work of labor-intensive parts of a product exported to of through TNCs. Firms may be able to export products based on mature technologies with or without the help of the TNCs. Developing countries such as Bangladesh or Pakistan are able to produce such goods as basic textiles or jute goods for local consumption and export.

Based on sustained efforts and learning by trial and error, economies, may be able to upgrade their technological capabilities, still basing themselves on the same low labor cost advantage and moving to cells 3 or 4. Starting with absorption of universal technologies by equipment embodied diffusion, some firms in developing countries moved to learning and absorbing more complex technologies and also to the innovation of new technologies. These firms acquired the necessary knowledge to produce high technology goods, but lacked the capabilities $_{\mathrm{f}}$to market these goods, and in particular the network needed for the supply of pre- and post-sales services. Thus, firms were able to produce electronic components by mastering certain elements of the more complex technologies needed for the production of the components, the fastest way of gaining such mastery being to work with established TNCs.

The third level of technology capability is the highest of all. As knowledge and experience accumulate, firms are able not simply to understand what is needed to use a known technology. They are also able to invent new technologies and supply the services associated with them. Thus, at an earlier stage of its development, the Japanese industry concentrated on technology acquisition, quality improvement, and productivity gains (Abbegglen & Stalk, 1985). Later the Japanese moved to the creation and mastery of advanced technologies. The same has been true for South Korea, where firms were established through transfer of universal technology after building organizations capable of absorbing the technologies (Kang, 1989). Later the firms began to produce variations in the product, increasing innovation by a process of learning and adjustment (Kim, 1980), thus becoming technology-intensive.

Economies that have attained the sixth cell level boast a well-developed technological infrastructure which offers a wide range of services to the business sector. Firms produce world-class S-goods and services developed internally, which compete in the global market place. Firms belonging to this class have well-developed downstream operations which market their output and provide their customers in the home market and in the international markets with the required associated services.

The economy is dominated by technology intensive industries, in which changes in the knowledge base are frequent and are transmitted rapidly to new processes and product specifications. Because of the need to tightly couple scientific knowledge and production, these industries employ a high percent of scientific manpower and spend a high percent of sales revenue on R&D. These firms must take high risks. In a new technology field, the failure rate is extremely high, standardization and volume production are impossible, and the risk that the market will not accept the new product is high.

Technological infrastructure

Technology absorption and technology creation capacities are enhanced by the development of the technological infrastructure, which includes technical schools, colleges, universities and research institutions. These institutions turn out skilled employees, engineers and, in time, scientists who constitute the technological manpower employed by business enterprises. The investment in education is essential to develop cadres of people capable of understanding technology, absorbing and upgrading technology, and ultimately developing new technologies (Aharoni, 1991). In the early phases of development these persons acquire the capacity to engage in effective global scanning and in absorbing and disseminating technologies that originate abroad.

The major market failure in this area is not in transferring inappropriate technology, but in the inability to transfer suitable technologies developed abroad because the potential recipients lack the capabilities necessary to absorb them. Only when educational levels have been raised, and a minimum number of engineers and scientists is available, do the import of technology and its assimilation become technically and economically feasible.

The level of technology capabilities also depends on macro-environmental conditions, including government regulations, the level of patent protection and anti-trust laws, and the characteristics of the physical infrastructure. General macro-economic policies must create an atmosphere amenable to the flourishing of entrepreneurs. Macro-economic policies that encourage savings, achieve stability and facilitate long-term planning in business firms are of utmost importance.

Components of technology policies

Formulation of public technology policy involves difficult choices. Governments surely cannot pick individual winners (Nelson, 1990). Even business firms cannot always make the right technological decisions since, by definition, such decisions are based on incomplete and unreliable information. The choice is not simply between "*laissez faire*" and "picking winners". It must be realized, however, that even a decision to set up a department of computer science in an institution of higher learning and not, say, a department of chemical engineering, reflects a belief about future "winners". In due course, the abundance of computer scientists in relation to chemical engineers will undoubtedly affect the competitive advantage of the economy and the sectorial distribution of business investments.

The need to "bet on winners" may be regarded as the essence of the market economy. The investment decisions of individual business enterprises represent their bets. Inevitably, some bets are successful and others fail. When it is claimed that governments as a rule are not good at picking winners the implication is that governments are not better equipped than entrepreneurs to forecast the outcome. Businessmen, who risk the money of presumably informed investors, as well as their own money, on the one hand, and who stand to make substantial personal gain from successful "winner picking", on the other, are assumed to be better qualified than government bureaucrats, to make these decisions.

It is, however, highly probable that in the absence of an active public policy the business sector will under invest in risky technology-intensive projects. In developing countries, where the risks are high, where the capital markets which elsewhere provide efficient instruments for allocating and sharing risks are often nonexistent, the likelihood of underinvestment in technology-related projects is particularly high. Public policy in this case must substitute for the malfunctioning or non-functioning institutions which in the advanced countries help entrepreneurs with the complicated task of risk taking and risk apportioning. The entry costs into high technology industries such as telecommunications and pharmaceuticals, and medium technology industries such as the automotive, shipbuilding and chemicals industries are extremely high. Consequently there is little doubt that business firms in developing countries will enter these industries only if public policy is sufficiently pervasive to neutralize the high risks and other market failures.

The role of public policy need not be confined to the creation of macro-economic and appropriate environmental conditions, to legal and administrative frameworks, to law enforcement, and the provision of efficient public services. It can be, and often is, much more direct and active, ranging from direct funding of R&D activities, subsidies for capital expenditures and training, public procurement, etc.[4]

Transnational Corporations and Product Characteristics

We have shown that industrial development implies the increase in the share of S-product manufacturer in the economy, and that this in turn requires that firms enhance their capacity to absorb, adapt and improve and ultimately create product and process technologies, and develop an international market orientation. TNCs typically have these capabilities.

Since manufacture of many products is characterized by multiple stages, TNCs can minimize total production costs by sourcing primary and intermediate inputs in the least-cost location. Intra-company sourcing rather than arm's length sourcing will be used when intra-company transactions are less costly, or more reliable in terms of quality, delivery time, etc.

Affiliates of TNCs also engage in marketing, which implies interfacing with customers, product distribution and provision of pre- and post-delivery services. Multi-product TNCs are able to use their marketing affiliates to distribute products manufactured by both domestic and foreign affiliates. Affiliate marketing is superior to marketing by independent distributors when S-S products are involved, i.e., when associated services depend on proprietary knowledge supplied by the product manufacturer. Marketing by independent organizations leads to loss in revenues and market power because it requires sharing of proprietary product information with outsiders.

R&D, which constitutes an important element of firm-specific knowledge creation, will presumably be located mainly near the head office, in close proximity to where the most important strategic decisions are made and where it can be more easily coordinated, controlled and monitored.

TNCs are superior as instruments for conducting international business to alternatives such as exporting or licensing when the transactions in which they engage have the following characteristics: they combine firm-specific knowledge with conventional production factors located in one or more foreign countries, and, furthermore, internalization of some or all of the core activities (R&D, manufacturing, marketing, etc.) is economically superior to arm's length transactions, carried out through the utilization of external markets. These characteristics are spelled out in detail in Dunning's Eclectic Model (Dunning, 1988). They generally conform to what we have labeled S-products, where R&D accounts for a significant share of total costs, where control over the interface between R&D and production is of crucial importance, and where product marketing is frequently associated with services which depend on firm-specific knowledge.

By controlling the most important links in the value chain which extends from R&D through production to distribution and provision of pre- and post-sales services, TNCs not only minimize costs; they also enhance market power in comparison with single-country firms which do not control their downstream operations. This point is particularly relevant to the technology- and service-intensive S-products.

Public policies towards TNCs

While there is no question that TNCs offer an efficient mechanism for expanding the S-products sector, we must examine the extent to which TNCs interests typically coincide or conflict with those of the developing countries.

The motivations behind international investment by TNCs are commonly said to include one or more of the following factors: "resource seeking", "market seeking", and "efficiency seeking" (Dunning, 1988: 13; Stopford & Strange, 1991: 70).

Resource-seeking FDIs are intended to secure access to strategic resources such as oil, iron ore, aluminum and copper ore, in those cases where open market transactions are not considered sufficiently reliable. "Sourcing" is another relatively recent phenomenon associated with resource-seeking. In this case, access is sought to low-cost unskilled or semi-skilled labor needed to perform labor-intensive operations constituting an integral part of a multi-stage manufacturing process.

"Market-seeking" FDI is intended to remove or reduce barriers which hinder access to different markets. Geographic distance and cultural distance are examples of such barriers. Entry barriers may also be erected by governments seeking to protect domestic industries against foreign competition, or to encourage inward FDI. Market-seeking investments need not be limited to the domestic market of the host country (import substitution).

Affiliates created in one country can be used as "export platforms" to serve third-country markets, and even the home country of the TNC in question. Investments in the UK by Japanese automobile manufacturers, for example, are said to be intended to service the entire European Community, of which the host country is a member (Ozawa, 1992).

"Efficiency-seeking" FDI is concerned with the global or regional rationalization of the TNCs' operations. Realization of scale and of scope economies associated with R&D, manufacturing, marketing or even introduction of corporate monitoring and control systems or human resource development, often depend on the ability to closely coordinate some of the activities performed by affiliates located in different countries.

TNC, host country and home country interests

TNCs, as was demonstrated above, constitute a highly efficient mechanism for creating firm-specific knowledge and for transferring this knowledge to different affiliates. TNCs are similarly effective in integrating geographically dispersed and functionally separated markets and operating activities. And yet, both inward and outward FDIs have been traditionally viewed with suspicion and mixed feelings by home-country and host-country policy makers and scholars alike. Many governments, even when they are ideologically committed to the market system, have often sought to restrict and control TNC activities. Apparently there is after all a built-in conflict of interest between states, which seek to maximize the value of the wealth available to local economic agents, and the TNCs, which presumably seek to maximize the wealth of their shareholders.

The conflict may be not only over the distribution of the net value (i.e., profits) created by the TNCs, but also over the location of different activities performed by them, the rate of investment, direction of trade, deployment of local labor and managers, etc. The home government wants high value creating activities to be located within its territory, even when this implies a diminution in total value created by the TNCs, and subsequent loss of income for the TNCs' shareholders or other stakeholders located in third countries (Stopford & Strange, 1991).

Since the bargaining power of the host-country government and other stakeholders is limited by the economic clout of the foreign TNCs, which often enjoy the explicit or implicit backing of their home governments, host-country stakeholders (employees, suppliers, competitors and, of course, governments) inevitably feel that their share of the total value created is unfairly small.

Concluding Remarks

TNCs, by their very existence, diminish the control which governments exercise over their residents. When the agents which effectively control a specific TNC have an economic interest in evading or subverting specific government policies they have access to the mechanisms required to do so. Other objections are based on the notion that home-based TNCs export capital and jobs, and scarce managerial talents. While these claims may be true, it must be recognized that if small economies in general, and DCs in particular, seek to possess internationally competitive S-product industries, the choice is not between domestic firms and TNCs but rather between home-based and foreign-based TNCs. The economy will have to do without some or even most of these industries if TNCs are unacceptable to public policy makers.

Despite the inevitable conflicts between the TNCs and potential host countries over the division of costs and benefits associated with their operations, there is little doubt that there is no substitute for the TNCs' presence in economies seeking to develop an outward-looking S-product sector. Public policy may nevertheless be employed to hasten the process of technology transfer, to reduce the costs of TNC involvement and to increase the benefits retained by the host country.

The above conclusion regarding public policy towards TNCs should not be interpreted as advocating a hands-off policy towards TNCs. Host governments have good reasons not to accord TNCs automatic "national treatment". The terms of entry should be negotiated by the government and not be left to the vagaries of the market. In return for access to the market, to local labor, natural resources and other production factors, TNCs should be made to pay the highest possible price commensurate with their bargaining power.[5] Negotiations should not be limited to capital transfers, to royalties, transfer prices, taxes and to employment. They should involve the technologies to be transferred, the volume and quality of the local contents to be produced, the number and status of expatriate and of local managers, the amount and sophistication of R&D to be performed locally, as well as the volume of exports and the target markets.

An active public policy has an important role in the process of industrial development. That role should not be confined to the creation of macro-economic and appropriate environmental conditions, to legal and administrative frameworks, to law enforcement, and the provision of efficient public services. Even when the environmental conditions are "right" there is no guarantee that the "invisible hand" will bring an outward-looking S-products section into being. The "invisible hand" sought to be helped by public policies which have clear objectives for the economy, and have the means to influence the behavior of business firms in a manner which is consistent with these objectives.[6]

In his well-known book, "*The American Challenge*", about the impact of the American TNCs on the world economy, Servan-Schreiber (1967) concluded that the only effective way for the Europeans to counter the American challenge was to establish their own multinational firms. His advice was in fact heeded, first by the Europeans and later by the Japanese. The "American Challenge" has evaporated in the sense that US-based TNCs do not dominate the technology-intensive sector to the extent that they did in the early post-war years. Developing countries seeking to establish themselves in these industries may have no choice but to follow the same route — establish their own TNCs.

Notes

1. For a review see Cooper (1980), Steward (1979) and Stewart & James (1982).
2. The analysis in section 1 suggests that of the theoretically feasible intermediate stages U-S and S-U, the former represents an empty set.
3. On the incentives created in export oriented situations, see Balassa *et al.* (1982) and Porter (1990).
4. For a detailed review of technology policy in the leading OECD countries, see Ergas (1987). Ergas distinguishes between "mission" oriented technology policies (US, UK, France) and "diffusion" oriented policies (Switzerland, Sweden, Germany).
5. See Teece (1986) and Stopford & Strange (1991) for interesting discussions of the changes in the bargaining power of TNCs and developing countries over time.
6. A growing number of TNCs from developing countries have in fact been established in recent years. For details see Lall (1990), UNCTC (1992a), and The Economist (1991).

References

Abegglen, J. C. & Stalk Jr., G. 1985. *Kaisha, The Japanese Corporation*. New York, NY: Basic Books.

Aharoni, Y. 1991. Education and technology transfer. In Agmon, T. & Von Gilnow, M. A. (Eds.) *Dialectics of Technology Transfer in International Business*. New York: Oxford University Press, pp. 79–102.

Balassa, B. & Associates. 1982. *Development Strategies in Semi-Industrial Economies*. Baltimore, MD: Johns Hopkins.

Cantwell, J. C. 1989. *Technological Innovation and Multinational Corporations*. Oxford: Basil Blackwell.

Carlsson, B. & Eliasson, G. 1991. The nature and importance of economic competence. *IUI Working Paper* #294. Stockholm: IUI.

Cooper, C. 1980. Policy interventions for technological innovation in developing countries. Staff Working Paper No. 441. World Bank, Washington, D.C.

Dahlman, C. J. & Westpahl, G. 1982. *Technology Effort in Industrial Development: An Interpretative Survey of Recent Research*. In Steward, F. & James, J. (Eds.) *The Economies of New Technology in Developed Countries*. London and Colorado: Frances Printer and Westview.

Dunning, J. H. 1988. Chapter 5: The investment development cycle and third world multinationals. In Dunning, J. H. (Ed.) *Explaining International Production*. London: Unwin Hyman, pp. 140–168.

Ergas, H. 1987. Does technology policy matter? In Guile, B. R. & Brooks, H. (Eds.) *Technology and Global Industry: Companies and Nations in the World Economy*. Washington, DC: National Academy Press, pp. 191–245.

Hirsch, S. 1989. Services and service intensity in international trade. *Weltwirtschaftiches Archiv*, 125(1): 45–60.

Hirsch, S. & Meshulach, A. 1992. Towards a Unified Theory of Internationalization. Tel Aviv: The Israel Institute of Business Research, Working Paper No. 1/92 (mimeo).

Johanson, J. & Vahlne, J. E. 1977. The internationalization process of the firm — a model of knowledge development and increasing market commitments. *Journal of International Business Studies*, 8 (Spring/Summer): 23–32.

Kang, T. W. 1989. *Is Korea the Next Japan?* New York: Free Press.

Katz, J. 1978. Technological Change, Economic Development and Intra and Extra Regional Relations in Latin America. IDB/ECLA/UNDP/IDRC Regional Program of Studies on Scientific and Technological Development in Latin America, Working Paper 30. Buenos Aires.

Katz, J. 1984. Technological innovation and dynamic comparative advantage: Further reflections on a comparative case study program. *Journal of Development Economics*, 16(12) (September–October): 13–37.

Kim, L. 1980. Stages of development of industrial technology in a developing country: A model. *Research Policy*, 9: 254–277.

Lall, S. 1980. Developing countries as exporters of technology. *Research Policy*, 9: 24–52.

Lall, S. 1981. Indian technology exports and technological development. *The Annals of the American Academy of Political and Social Science*, 458 (November): 151–162.

Lall, S. 1990. *Building Industrial Competitiveness in Developing Countries*. Paris: Development Center of the Organization for Economic Cooperation and Development.

Luostarinen, R. 1979. Internationalization of the Firm, Acta Academiae Oeconomicae Helsiniesis Series A: 30. Helsinki: The Helsinki School of Economics.

Nelson, R. R. 1990. Capitalism as an engine of progress. *Research Policy* (Netherlands), 19: 193–214.

Ozawa, T. 1992. Cross-investments between Japan and the EC: Income similarity, product variation, and economies of scope. In Cantwell, J. (Ed.) *Multinational Investment in Modem Europe: Strategic Interaction in the integrated Community*. Cheltenham: Edward Elgar Publishing.

Patel, P. & Pavitt, K. 1987. Is Western Europe losing the technological race? *Research Policy* (Netherlands), 16: 59–85.

Porter, M. E. 1990. *The Competitive Advantage of Nations*. New York: The Free Press.

Servan-Schreiber, J. J. 1967. *The American Challenge*. New York: The Atheneum Press.

Stewart, F. 1979. *International Technology Transfer: Issues and Policy Option*. Staff Working Paper. World Bank, Washington, DC.

Stewart, F. & James, J. (Eds.). 1982. *The Economics of New Technology in Developing Countries*. London: Frances Pinter Limited.

Stopford, J. & Strange, S. 1991. *Rival States, Rival Firms; Competition for World Market Shares*. New York: Cambridge University Press.

Teece, D. J. 1986. Profiting from technological innovation. *Research Policy*, 15(6): 286–305.

Teitel, S. 1981. Towards an understanding of technical change in semi-industrialized countries. *Research Policy*, 10(2): 127–147.

Teitel, S. 1984. Technology creation in semi-industrial economies. *Journal of Development Economics*, 6(1/2) (September–October): 39–61.

The Economist. 1991. Survey, Asia's Emerging Economies. November 16, 1991.

UNCTC. 1992. Current Studies No. 18, Series A. *Foreign Direct Investment and Industrial Restructuring in Mexico*. New York: United Nations.

Vaitsos. C. 1974. *Intercountry Income Distribution and Transnational Enterprises*. Oxford: Claredon Press.

Westphal, L. 1983. Empirical justification for infant industry protection. Staff Working Paper No. 445. World Bank, Washington, DC.

World Bank. 1992. *World Development Report*. Washington, DC: World Bank.

Aharoni's Final Academic Presentation

https://doi.org/10.1142/9789811287510_0023

Chapter 23

Internationalization of State-Owned Firms: Do Governments Help or Hinder?*

Yair Aharoni

Tel Aviv University, Tel Aviv, Israel

OK, I am Yair Aharoni. I'm now confined to my apartment because of the coronavirus, so I have prerecorded my contribution to the session.

Ms. Cheng sent me four questions that I should refer to. Here is the first question: Are managers pawns of the politicians who suppress firm internationalization? Or do managers have agency and influence the internationalization process of state-owned firms? The other three questions are about the same idea, in that we compare what happens to management and the government, but we talk about universal government and universal management.

My major point is that, after many years of studying different areas, and mainly state-owned enterprises, I have learned that generalizations are very dangerous, because there's always an exception, and there's always something that is different. So, in a way, it all depends. If we talk about management, yes, ownership is not control. This is something we have known for many decades. We know that managers possess a monopoly on the information. But managers, when they internationalize, have to get the approval of their board of directors and then the question is how

*Transcript of a presentation at the 2020 Academy of International Business Conference.

these directors are elected, how they are selected, and how they are nominated. And this is different because of different reasons in different countries.

And so, my general point is that we should not look for universal solutions but try to find the variables that are different and see what the impact of each one of them is, and that's what I'll do in my contribution shortly.

The first variable is ideology. Different governments are elected and believe in different ideologies. We have communist countries, we have countries in social democratic regimes, and we have liberal countries. Each one of them relates differently to state-owned enterprises and the degree to which state-owned enterprises can do things on their own.

I can use my own country, Israel, as an example. Israel has what is called a Government Cooperation Act of 1975, and according to this act, a state-owned enterprise should behave or consider things the same way as a privately owned enterprise, so there shouldn't be any difference. The only difference is that the government is allowed by special resolution of the whole government to give it special requests, and this resolution has to be approved by the Finance Committee of the Knesset, which is the Israeli Parliament.

So, in Israel, state-owned enterprises are quite independent of the government. The government is interested mainly in getting dividends. And as long as they get the dividends, they don't get into such questions as whether or not the firm will internationalize.

This was not always so. There was a time that we had foreign exchange control, and this gave an enormous dependency. There was a case of an Israeli firm that had an opportunity to buy — to acquire — a subsidiary in Italy and in this way to get access to the Common Market at that time, which is now the European Union, and then get much more export. The Minister of Finance had to approve the foreign exchange to buy the firm and he said, and I quote, "I am not supposed to help Italy but Israel", and refused to allocate the funds. Today, this would not be a problem because they don't exert foreign exchange control and this firm could simply go to the bank and buy US dollars or Euros whatever currency it likes.

But again, one thing that has to be taken into account is the degree of dependency on these kinds of things.

The other major variable is industry. Industries are different in different ways. One way in which industries differ is the degree of importance of this special state enterprise for the country. To me, a very extreme example is Saudi Arabia. Aramco is a state-owned enterprise, and it controls the oil exploration and oil production of the country. And so, for this firm, it is very important to get access to refineries and other means of distribution, and the firm would be willing to internationalize by buying refineries in other countries and so on. I do not think that, in this case, the government will be against it. As a matter of fact, the government may push it to do it.

Then there's the question of high-tech versus low-tech. Firms that are in high technology get access to different technologies by acquiring subsidiaries in different countries that allow them access to the technology. And again, in this case, I think the government would accept such a move and even encourage it.

On the other hand, if there is a firm constructing apartment houses in a certain country, and it wants to do this in other countries, I am less sure that the government will be interested in helping them do it.

There is a very specific kind of variable, which is the reason for public ownership. I just want to give some esoteric examples. Renault, in France, was nationalized because it helped the Nazis during World War II. So, in this kind of reasoning, whether it is internationalized or not is less, I think, important to the government, and it will be less willing to impede such a move. The same is true for airlines today that are in problems because of the coronavirus, and so different country governments are willing to help them by buying shares — and by buying shares, the firms become state-owned enterprises but with less interest of the government to questions that are of interest now to us now, like internationalization.

Another variable is the size of the country. Small countries are very much dependent on exports. And if you are a state-owned enterprise from a small country, you'll do anything to increase exports, including internationalization, acquiring different parts of the value chain, and so on and so forth. And again, in this case, I don't think the government will be very much against it and certainly will not impede this kind of move.

To conclude, I would like to urge all young researchers to study these important topics but to make sure that they avoid the kind of generalizations of assuming that all the governments of the world behave the same way or that all the managers of the world behave the same way, and instead try to find out what are the variables that are important to explain changes among different countries, different governments, and different enterprises.

https://doi.org/10.1142/9789811287510_0024

Chapter 24

Reflection on Yair Aharoni's Presentation

Cheng Li

University of Manitoba, Winnipeg, Canada

When I first invited Professor Yair Aharoni to join my AIB2020 panel, *Internationalization of State-owned Firms*, last November, I did not have much hope since it takes 10 hours on a direct flight from Tel Aviv to Vancouver, where the conference was originally going to be held. The transcontinental flight will make average people think twice before saying "yes" to a one-hour panel discussion, let alone an 89-year-old. Surprisingly, without much delay, Professor Aharoni sent me a brief reply in which he wrote: "In principle, I will be glad to do it". His generosity went beyond anything I had expected.

It was November 26, 2019 when he wrote back, and no one could have detected a slight hint of a pandemic. So, I took the "in principle" as a "yes" and expected the AIB conference to happen as planned. Little did I know that the short phrase "in principle" encapsulates Professor Aharoni's years of wisdom in dealing with the unknown, both in his academic research and in his long-serving tenure as the first dean of the business school at Tel Aviv University. Then came the pandemic, which infected tens of millions of people, killed hundreds of thousands, and forced a lockdown on the entire world. The world has been drastically changed by the pandemic: instead of going to the office, people have started to work from home; large groups of social gatherings have been banned by most of the governments around the world; and digitalization and government order have become pervasive in the media as the pandemic situation evolves. In a world where the outbreak of the pandemic caught everyone off guard, Professor Aharoni has shown the rare quality of being prepared for the unknown and remaining flexible as things develop. Flexibility is a philosophy central to most of his academic work.

Scholarship on the internationalization of state-owned multinationals (SOMNCs) has greatly increased both with China's rise as a major world economy and the avid globalization of multinational firms. However, in the 1980s and 1990s, few scholars focused on this subject, with Professor Aharoni being chief among that exclusive group. Recent changes in our economic reality and shifts in the landscape of international business have since spawned many books and publications in the past decade. While media coverage on SOMNCs — "the Leviathans of global investment" — continues unabated, major themes abounding in the literature are that SOMNCs are less profitable than their private counterparts because political agendas supersede any firm's commercial agendas with respect to profit maximization and that managers of SOMNCs are pawns of their government. The implied assumption in much of these narratives has to do with the neoliberalism doctrine: government interventions destroy business values.

Yair Aharoni's AIB 2020 speech, "Internationalization of State-owned Firms: Do Governments Help or Hinder?", challenged this underlying assumption. Unlike the rigid principle of neoliberalism, which focuses primarily on US firms, Aharoni's ideas blend behavioral elements with economic rigor to offer insights into ownership implications in the global business environment. Throughout his speech, the fundamental question was whether managers are pawns of the politicians who suppress firm internationalization or whether managers have agency and influence the internationalization process of the state-owned firms. The gist of Aharoni's general arguments boils down to this: it all depends. Many other scholars who have conducted in-depth analyses on the internationalization of state-owned MNCs eventually reached the same conclusion. Aharoni's work, from idea generation to completion, is parsimonious, nuanced, and balanced. His argument is impactful because he has gone beyond economics training and analyzed real-life problems in managerial practices across different countries and in multiple sectors.

Aharoni has highlighted four contingencies that influence the role of governments in the internationalization of state-owned firms. First, he points out the importance of the ideology through which SOMNCs are created. SOMNCs have to abide by host country laws and regulations; however, a host country with a democratic political system or liberal beliefs may distrust SOMNCs. For instance, in the United States, it is assumed that SOMNCs prioritize state-orchestrated agendas and aim to achieve foreign governments' political goals. This is a crucial point of departure from much of the existing literature, which has primarily focused on the economics of SOMNCs, as Aharoni has precisely directed scholars' attention toward the ideological clashes often present in the internationalization of state-owned firms.

Aharoni has also importantly drawn attention to the regulatory processes to which SOMNCs are subjected. In particular, if SOMNCs depend on their home governments for regulatory approval in order to invest abroad, they are more likely to behave differently than private MNCs in that managers have little agency in carrying out commercial agendas. On the other hand, if SOMNCs are not subject to regulatory processes in their foreign investments, they are more likely to behave similarly to their private counterparts, and managers of SOMNCs have greater flexibility. His point about how SOMNCs rely on home governments has shed light on an important gap in the current research, which previously implicitly assumed this reliance. In this way, Aharoni invites scholars to carefully reassess this crucial assumption underpinning much of the writing on this topic.

Aharoni has posited the importance of the industries in which SOMNCs are created. Traditionally, the purpose of state-owned firms has been to solve market failures in domestic industries. As a result, state-owned often firms operate in industry contexts that do not require internationalization. Some industries, however, bear strategic significance to home governments, which have grown increasingly more sophisticated in leveraging market power to the advantage of home markets by creating national champions in the global market. Governments can enact industry policies to protect and allow certain firms to benefit from these policies. Institutional support enables MNCs to operate and compete in a global environment and "knowledge-intensive industries characterized by high levels of research and development (R&D) expenditure and advertising expenditure, and by the employment of skilled labor" (Buckley and Casson, 2009: 1563). In contrast, MNCs lack these skills and so do not have the flexibility to compete globally in an effective manner. Therefore, these advantages derived from industry policies and institutional support are relevant to any discussion on state-owned firms' internationalization.

To further seek answers as to whether managers of SOMNCs, as pawns of the government, are or are not instrumental to market success, Aharoni has argued that the reasons why state-owned firms are created matter. If SOMNCs are created for political purposes, managers are more likely to conform to political norms and pressures and are thus less profit-driven. On the other hand, if SOMNCs are created for economic reasons, managers are more likely to be chosen and assessed based on their professional qualifications; consequently, managers of those SOMNCs are more likely to adapt efficiently to market conditions. Aharoni has brought forward a crucial point in unpacking market logic in SOMNCs, which have been traditionally painted with a broad brush.

Aharoni encourages scholars to pay attention to home country characteristics, such as country size. State-owned firms from a small country face more urgency to internationalize than those from a large country. In making his point, Aharoni offers a critical caveat: not all firms are from a home country with a sufficient domestic market to support their operations. Thus, investigating the role of market size is crucial in understanding the internationalization of state-owned firms, which may have nothing to do with the political agenda but everything to do with the domestic market's limited size.

In his speech, Aharoni provided an insightful account of critical contingencies that influence the internationalization of state-owned firms and managers' roles within those SOMNCs. Adapting to Aharoni's insights, future research can clarify and reassess some of the literature's implied assumptions and further develop a more comprehensive framework.

It is my sincere hope that those of us in the academic community can be as accommodating to this kind of adaptation as Professor Aharoni proved to be in his work and, indeed, in his contributions to the AIB 2020 conference. After all, despite being an 89-year-old scholar living in Israel, belonging to the WHO's highest-risk category for susceptibility to the virus, he was not limited by either his existing health conditions or the threat of the pandemic in participating in forums and email threads as frequently as everyone else.

Even when the organizers announced that the in-person AIB conference would be canceled, Aharoni sent a pre-recording of himself within a few days for his virtual participation. In the process, he communicated frequently through emails, trying to ensure that his recording format was compatible with the virtual conference platform and his speech was well connected with other panelists' contributions. As a junior scholar, I am deeply touched by his passion for research and generosity toward budding academics like myself, especially given that he managed to participate in our scholarly discussion at AIB despite his illness and all the chaos brought about by the pandemic. This kind of engagement and generosity will be greatly missed within our community. In a year largely defined by loss, your loss, Yair Aharoni, remains so prominent given the void it has left behind.

Reference

Buckley, P. & Casson, M. 2009. The internalisation theory of the multinational enterprise: A review of the progress of a research agenda after 30 years. *Journal of International Business Studies*, 40: 1563–1580.

Part 3

Recognition and Recollection from AIB Fellows and Other Scholars

https://doi.org/10.1142/9789811287510_0025

Chapter 25

International Colleagues Remember Yair Aharoni

Arie Y. Lewin*, Ravi Ramamurti†, and Elizabeth L. Rose‡

**Duke University, Durham, NC, USA*

†Northeastern University, Boston, MA, USA

‡Indian Institute of Management Udaipur, Udaipur, India

Among the many acknowledgments of Yair Aharoni's contributions to research, education, and practice was his election, in 1990, as a Fellow of the Academy of International Business (AIB). Established in 1959, the AIB is the leading global academic association in the area of international business. The AIB Fellows "are a select group of distinguished scholars who have been recognized for their outstanding contribution to both [the AIB] and the international business field as a whole" (https://www.aib.world/about/aib-fellows/).

Yair remained an active member of the AIB, and the AIB Fellows, until the end of his life. He was well known for his involvement in AIB Fellows events, and his 2020 AIB presentation is transcribed and commented on elsewhere in this volume. Therefore, it is not surprising that there was an outpouring of acknowledgments and remembrances when the news of his death was communicated to the AIB Fellows on August 6th, 2020. The resultant flurry of activity forms much of this section, which includes essays written by AIB Fellows addressing both Yair's deep and extensive contributions to key aspects of international business research and a collection of personal recollections of a fellow.

During his long career, from his Harvard PhD in 1961 to his final AIB presentation in 2020, Yair was well known for challenging conventional thinking about international business; his perspective was driven by a combination of intellectual rigor and his deep connection to policy and managerial practice. He generated seminal insights into many areas, several of which are addressed in AIB Fellows' contributions in this section. Peter Buckley addresses the far-reaching impact — and the enduring relevance — of Yair's 1966 book, *The Foreign Investment Decision Process*, illustrating how this early work created the foundation for much of Yair's later research. Robert Grosse considers Yair's fundamental contributions to two areas of shared interest — internationalization in the service sector and among state-owned enterprises — both of which are topics that are pertinent to the current literature. Louis Wells discusses Yair's work, with a focus on the emphasis on managerial decision-making, from the perspective of having been exposed to Yair's then-recent 1966 book as a doctoral student. Pervez Ghauri describes having been introduced, later in his career, to Yair's work and its nuanced consideration of time in the context of decision-making, while Jeremy Clegg expounds on the insights into the practice of decision-making that Yair gained from his interactions with managers. Raj Aggarwal summarizes Yair's impact on the field of international business for a non-specialist audience. Focusing on methodological issues. Rebecca Piekkari, with honorary Fellow Ingmar Björkman, addresses Yair's resolutely qualitative and case-based approach to research.

These research-oriented pieces are followed by a selection of vignettes representing personal remembrances of Yair from seven AIB Fellows: Mary Yoko Brannen, Farok Contractor, John Daniels, José de la Torre, Steven Kobrin, Arie Lewin, and Mira Wilkins.

This section concludes with contributions from three additional scholars who relate some of their memorable interactions with Yair. Niron Hashai reflects on Yair's strong impact on the international business and strategy research ecosystem in Israel, while Christian Bellak writes of Yair's role as a behavioral scientist and Laszlo Tihanyi discusses some important lessons learned, as a young researcher, from Yair.

https://doi.org/10.1142/9789811287510_0026

Chapter 26

Yair Aharoni's 1966 "The Foreign Investment Decision Process": A Classic Work of International Business Research

Peter J. Buckley

University of Manchester, Manchester, UK

Prologue

For the publication of my 1993 book of readings with Pervez Ghauri (*The Internationalization of the Firm*), I asked Yair Aharoni if I could abridge his classic 1966 book, *The Foreign Investment Decision Process*, as the opening chapter of the book. Naturally, I gave him the right to veto over any possibility that I mangled his classic work. When I sent the abridgment, Yair told me that it was "better than the original". That was kind because the qualities of the abridged chapter entirely derive from the original text.

Foreign Investment as a Behavioral Process

The foreign investment decision is analyzed as a complex social process that is influenced by social relationships both within and outside the firm. Aharoni provides a thick description of individual and organizational behavior over time and demonstrates the crucial effects of managerial perception and uncertainty in the course of the process. A holistic understanding of all the stages in the process is necessary to comprehend the

"FDI decision". Although Aharoni analyses the decision as a succession of stages, he is at pains to point out that, in the real world, these stages are ill-defined and messy. The book emphasizes the importance of "the initiating force" that starts the firm moving toward the decision for an FDI and explains elements that may wrongly be labeled "irrational".

This classic work laid the foundations for the study of FDI decision-making, FDI by smaller firms, and the role of uncertainty in international business decision-making.

In any decision process, Aharoni says, there are five key elements. (1) Any choice made in the organization depends on the social system in which it takes place. (2) The process takes time. (3) Decisions are made under uncertainty. (4) Organizations have goals (note the plural). (5) There are significant constraints on the freedom of action of the decision makers. Each of these elements has profound consequences for the FDI decision process.

For Aharoni, the timing of a foreign investment depends very much on chance stimuli and on the way that management processes convert these stimuli into decisions to invest abroad. The propensity of a firm to invest depends on the strength and frequency of these stimuli to invest. Stimuli may arise from within the firm (perhaps from a self-aggrandizing proposal from a key manager) or from outside (a tariff increase by a foreign government, altering the balance between exporting and FDI). Once an investment project has been formulated, a search is initiated for relevant information. During the search, some members of the search team become committed to the project, largely because of the sunk costs of time and effort they expend. If their appraisal succeeds in correcting the inherent pessimism of top management, then it leads to a decision to invest (Buckley & Casson, 1976).

Aharoni tells the foreign investment story over time, emphasizing the key elements. "Organization and Environment" is the context in which the decision takes place. The routine aspects of the firm's operation, its way of doing things, and its power structure are internal initial conditions for the genesis of the process. The competitive and market structure in which the firm operates also sets the scene for the unfolding drama. Aharoni was certainly ahead of the game in emphasizing the "Time Dimension" of the decision process. FDI is not a point of time, single, snap decision, but it is an unfolding process with stages and subdivisions and not necessarily a single linear sequence. There will be diversions, delays, and failures along the way and the firm will not necessarily behave as a single actor because individual managers and cliques of managers will act in their own self-interest. The final outcome "the foreign investment decision" is only one step in a long sequence of decisions made during the process. We, as observers, and even the decision makers, may not recognize exactly when an irrevocable commitment to FDI was made. "Uncertainty" is a key (possibly **the** key) to Aharoni's analysis. In the book, Aharoni has an excellent discussion of Knightian uncertainty versus "measurable" risk. Tellingly, he notes that uncertainty exists not only with regard to the consequences of alternative decisions but also about the alternatives themselves. The opportunity set is unknown to the protagonists. In view of current analyses of VUCA (Volatility, Uncertainty, Complexity and Ambiguity) in the global economy, this book is clearly a precursor of modern strategy analysis. The conclusion is that projects deemed "too risky", even if there is the possibility of high profits, are ruled out in the early stages of investigation. This observation has been confirmed time and again in subsequent international business research. The "Goals" (noting the plural) of the firm are also key influences on the process. Aharoni observed a multitude of goals and motivations of individual executives in his primary research. The interaction of competing goals within the firm is unresolved by Aharoni and he felt it to be unresolvable. Any business decision is beset by "Constraints". This includes unobtainable information (known unknowns), information that is too costly in management time and money (unknown but expensive knowns), and of course unknown unknowns, the essence of uncertainty. Previous company policies, too, are shrewdly listed as constraints.

The Foreign Investment Decision

There are key stages in the foreign investment decision process: the initiating force or forces, the decision to invest, the creation of commitments during the investigation, and reviews and negotiations. The study concentrates on the firm's first foreign investment and Aharoni gives an enviable and penetrating description and analysis of decision-making under uncertainty leading to the first FDI. He then adds a longer-run final stage that is more concerned with the organizational development of a nascent international firm than with investment decision-making.

Even now, Aharoni's work has profound research relevance. The initiating force deserves more attention than it has subsequently received in extant international business literature. The package of internal (executive interest), external (a powerful outside agent's proposal), and environmental (foreign competition) influences needs to be carefully unpacked, and their significance to be carefully weighted and contextualized. The internal political procedures of persuasion, negotiation, the creation of commitments, bounded rationality in management teams, and the role of hierarchy in decision-making are all at the forefront of current international management research. The bearing of theoretical explanations on the FDI decision is also a vibrant issue (Buckley *et al.*, 2007). The relationship of the short-term decision-making on key events such as (the firm's first) FDI with the longer-term development of an international strategy is still ripe for research development.

Assessment

From the evidence of his case studies, Aharoni suggests that the results conflict with profit-maximizing assumptions. However, the results are broadly consistent with profit maximization under conditions of uncertainty. Aharoni produced a brilliant description of an organized, albeit inefficient, search procedure. The principal inefficiencies are the lack of routine scanning of the environment for profitable investment opportunities and the over-commitment of certain managers to the projects that they are appraising. Both factors are unsurprising, given the small scale and inexperience of the case study companies and their naivety in international investment and given that Aharoni is examining the firms' first foreign investment (Buckley & Casson, 1976).

This book is an outstanding investigation of short-run decision-making under uncertainty. The first four stages of the decision process concentrate on the first foreign investment and to this is added a longer-run organizational development phase, as the firm learns from its first FDI and then moves on to be a truly international firm by adding further subsidiaries and consolidating then into an organizational structure (the international division). A great deal of subsequent work has fleshed out internationalization and globalization strategies, the final stage of Aharoni's process. The short-run decision-making aspect has been formalized by real options analyses, but the achievement of generalizing from case studies has surely never been equaled.

Conclusion

Aharoni's book is justly regarded as a classic. It can be read with profit in today's vastly different global environment. Many aspects of that environment have changed, notably the availability and cost of information, techniques of managing at a distance, digital internationalization, and the political and social background of business. The issues of uncertainty are now multidimensional and decision-making processes are at least as complex as the picture painted by Aharoni. Researchers committed to the furtherance of understanding modern international business and the strategic problems of (particularly startups and small) internationalizing firms should be encouraged to read this book, even 55 years after its original publication.

References

Aharoni, Y. 1966. *The Foreign Investment Decision Process*. Cambridge: Harvard University Press.

Buckley, P. J. & Casson, M. C. 1976. *The Future of the Multinational Enterprise*. London: Macmillan.

Buckley, P. J., Devinney, T. M. & Louviere, J. J. 2007. Do managers behave the way theory suggests? A choice-theoretic examination of foreign direct investment decision-making. *Journal of International Business Studies*, 38(4): 499–518.

Buckley, P. J. & Ghauri, P. N. 1993. (Eds.) *The Internationalization of the Firm: A Reader*. London: International Thomson Business Press.

https://doi.org/10.1142/9789811287510_0027

Chapter 27

Tribute to Yair Aharoni

Robert Grosse

Thunderbird International Business School, Phoenix, AZ, USA

I am very sorry to learn of Yair's death. He was one of my most valued long-distance friends over the years. In the 2000s, he and I interacted frequently at Academy of International Business (AIB) meetings, where he participated in panels and sessions to talk about a number of his interests, which we shared: management of state-owned enterprises, privatization of state-owned enterprises, internationalization of service-sector firms, theories of the multinational enterprise, and of course his path-breaking theme of looking in detail at the foreign (direct) investment decision process. I think that we must have enjoyed dozens of coffee-fueled discussions of things like why privatizations have produced some terrible outcomes in a number of countries (e.g., in Eastern Europe) and much more positive outcomes in others (e.g., in Chile), and how business service companies internationalize on bases that are not all that different from the strategies of "traditional" manufacturing companies. Yair's wide-ranging interests and his careful thought process were extremely insightful and challenging to those who might not analyze things quite so deliberately and incisively. It is funny, but I cannot remember a time when I disagreed with his reasoning; we had different examples in mind for our thinking in many instances, but I could never find fault with his logic — even if it did not support my point of view!

Remembering back to the old days, or perhaps in my case the fairly early days of AIB, I did not know Yair at all except from his PhD thesis and his effort to understand how (big) company managers make decisions to go overseas. His analysis was always held in great esteem by colleagues writing about foreign direct investment, but the person himself was not well known, perhaps outside of his HBS classmates and teachers. This is logical, given his huge commitment to building business education in Israel for many years. It may have been when he went to Duke in the 1990s that he started becoming a regular at AIB annual meetings and becoming much more widely known among our members. And, of course, his analyses of privatizations and service-sector MNEs were pathbreaking when those subjects became hot topics in international business in the 1990s.

What a wonderful colleague and friend. I will miss Yair greatly.

Aharoni on Services Globalization

Yair got involved with the analysis of business services such as accounting/auditing, legal, management consulting, and investment banking at the end of the 1980s and produced several articles and a couple of books on service sector internationalization during the 1990s. He was not the first academic to consider the globalization of services companies, but he did offer a very clear analytical structure for thinking about business services companies and a useful comparison of service-sector MNEs versus manufacturing MNEs.

In his typical dispassionate manner, he points out the following:

1. (Business) services are intangible, while goods are tangible — the classic starting point for analyzing services.
2. Service "quantities" can only be measured by the duration and intensity of the service given to a user.
3. Although services are heterogeneous, in all of them, the customer participates as a productive resource and does not simply receive the service.
4. Services are tradable through three means: "pure" international trade of services sold through the mail or phone or internet, enticing clients to come to the service provider's country to obtain the service, and sending the firm's own employees overseas to serve the client at the client's location.

5. When uncertainty about the business or environment is higher, a client will be more willing to pay for reputation and brand, so multinational service providers are attractive in this context.

Just as in his original work on the foreign investment decision process, Aharoni looks at the international provision of business services in organizational detail, exploring the elements that the customer/client provides, the elements that the multinational service company provides, and how the people involved interact to carry out the production and delivery of the services.

For example, if we consider a McKinsey management consultant dealing with a bank in India, the first question in understanding the situation could be as follows: Why did the bank need outside help, and why did they choose McKinsey? Aharoni points out that some services such as this one require great expertise, which resides in the (quality or knowledge of) the person providing the consulting service. So, evidently, the bank in India wanted some knowledge of the market or the competition or the product array to provide, making the use of an outside source of expertise attractive. They may have chosen McKinsey because of the company's reputation, possibly just proxied by the size of McKinsey and its global scope. Or the particular banker involved may have worked with McKinsey before, or even with a specific consultant at McKinsey. The whole decision-making process is not simple or generic, but rather it is bound up in people and their relationships. And the fact that the service is so differentiated makes it difficult to realize economies of scale in providing it. What management consulting firms can do is develop an internal database of previous clients and services provided, so that any one consultant potentially can take advantage of the firm's own experience, even if he/she was not involved in the previous project(s). Digging into these details, and considering the ways in which services companies can strategize with respect to deploying people, using different organizational structures, and seeking particular types of clients, was Yair's passion and his analytical strength.

As a multinational banker, from my personal experience, I found it somewhat difficult to use Aharoni's perspective because my business includes both retail financial services that may be quite homogeneous and also investment banking services that are more like the management consulting described above. The two are incompatible strategically — but that just means that the organization (bank) needs to separate the two activities into divisions and people that have different skills and relationships. The clarity of Yair's thinking is what can enable the institution to advance in understanding how to compete in more than one business or sector.

He also looked at the question of how to organize a global business services firm. Among other points of differentiation among service firms, he pointed to the "think versus grind" nature of the work. If the client wants an audit of one of its divisions or provision of a fairly standard financial service in different locations, then the provider service firm may operate a more integrated and centrally controlled business and just grind out the service. If the client wants highly differentiated consulting advice or advertising or legal service, then much more original thinking is needed to provide the more idiosyncratic service. In the latter type of market, for very non-standardized services, the global service company will need to operate in a much more decentralized manner, leaving a lot of room for local people to tailor their services to the client's needs.

Note that the logic employed by Aharoni is concerned with the degree of centralized decision-making versus the autonomy of affiliates in different countries. At the time he was writing, most of the big accounting/auditing firms, (US-based) investment banks, and law firms were organized as partnerships, where the local partners might share to some degree in global earnings, but their relations with clients were fairly independent of partners in other countries. Since then, beyond the top three or four in each industry, the firms have, in many instances, become corporations, with outside shareholders. All of the Bulge Bracket investment banks either went public and became traded companies, were acquired by commercial banks, or went bankrupt during the Global Financial Crisis of 2008–2009. Going public enables them to raise funds more easily since their financial statements must be audited by outside accounting firms, and so their business is more financially transparent. Regardless of the ownership structure, the decision-making structure remains very decentralized, since local partners need to make decisions on a daily basis in dealing with both multinational and domestic clients.

Aharoni also points to some of the features that make decentralized organizations more important to the success of some multinational service firms. As already noted, the more non-standardized the service being provided, the more that decentralization is needed. Contrarily, if fairly standardized service is feasible, then tighter home-office control is helpful. And when there is a large benefit to providing the same service in different locations to different clients, then economies of scale also favor centralized decision-making.

The way in which coordination is achieved across affiliates in different countries is often accomplished through committees or teams of people who work together to resolve a particular problem or challenge and then are reassigned to work with different people on other projects as the need arises. A flexible structure is a common need for multinational business service providers (Aharoni, 1996: 19) when client needs are very differentiated.

Altogether, Aharoni paints a detailed picture of the structure and functioning of international professional services companies that directs us to both a better understanding of how they can operate to take best advantage of their people's skills and knowledge and also adapt their "products" to different needs of clients in different industries and countries. His contributions to our understanding of these firms are especially valuable in an era when services have become the dominant type of business around the world, far surpassing manufacturing, agriculture, and mining as sources of employment and of value-added in national income.

Reference

Aharoni, Y. 1996. The organization of global service MNEs. *International Studies of Management and Organization*, 26(2): 6–23.

https://doi.org/10.1142/9789811287510_0028

Chapter 28

Yair Aharoni Memorial

Louis T. Wells

Harvard Business School, Boston, MA, USA

Yair Aharoni belonged to the first generation of students of multinational business at Harvard Business School (HBS); their work eventually led to the large Multinational Enterprise Project directed by Raymond Vernon. The group comprised many faculty and doctoral student researchers that explored a wide range of international business (IB) topics and utilized various methodologies. Yair finished his doctoral degree (DBA) in 1961, two years after Ray arrived at HBS and just before I came to the school for the MBA program; therefore, I just missed knowing him when we were students. In fact, MBA students and DBA candidates rarely mixed anyway. But I discovered, on moving on to the doctoral program, that his thesis and book, *The Foreign Investment Decision Process*, had already appeared on the reading list for the International Business DBA oral exam. I do not remember whether the thesis version was assigned before the book appeared, although I believe it was. I got to know Yair later, at the annual Academy of International Business (AIB) meetings, when he visited HBS, and when he was at Duke. It was always fun to engage in the friendly debates he was bound to initiate. To start them, he would put forth some idea very forcefully, to say the least. But he would listen to counter-arguments, fight back, and eventually adjust his ideas if the target's arguments were good. Anyone who knew Ray, especially in his early days in academia, can understand why Yair and Ray got along so well.

The Foreign Investment Decision Process contributed greatly to our understanding of international business. At the core, it reminded us that decisions are made by human beings, with limited information and based on trust that often came from social and, in the investments on which he concentrated, ethnic ties. The term "bounded rationality" had appeared earlier, but Yair studied in depth how it affected foreign investment decisions and really brought the concept into the IB field. His research certainly influenced my *Third World Multinationals*, as it led me more quickly to recognize the importance of diasporas and family members abroad in determining patterns of trade and, in particular, investment decisions. Further, when I was working with investment promotion agencies much later, I regularly referred their managers to Yair's book. Several ended up building on its implications, directing investment promotion efforts to groups in the rich countries that had ethnic ties to the country trying to attract investment.

Today's doctoral students are rarely encouraged to do the kind of research and writing that Yair did. Instead, they are pushed by their advisors, and later by journal editors, toward quantitative research. Yair's thesis may not have been acceptable at many other schools, even at the time he wrote it. HBS had a tradition of honoring "clinical" research, not just "quantitative" research. In fact, when I was a DBA candidate, I was required to take a course in "clinical" research methodology. That tradition is not nearly as strong today, largely as a result of the market for doctoral degree holders. Today, many university search committees are not interested in candidates who produce the kind of research that Yair did.

Moreover, today's doctoral candidates lean toward write-ups of their research that follow a standard, and usually boring, format: literature review, statement of problem, hypotheses, methodology, statistical tests, conclusions, and, the seemingly inevitable, suggestions for further research. Others have noted that this first book by Yair is very readable. That is likely due in part to the influence of Ray Vernon, who encouraged doctoral students to depart from the standardized structure and produce theses that were written like good books, not mechanistically organized according to some rigid format. Of course, Yair should be credited with following the unusual advice in a very effective way.

The change in what is acceptable research is unfortunate, especially when one looks back at the impact of Yair's first work. It is interview-based, non-quantitative, yet carefully done, and has had a significant impact on the field of international business. Moreover, it is consistent with what Ray described as an important role of business school research: propose ideas based on observations in the field that have been largely ignored by disciplinarians (economists, sociologists, and so on), carry investigation of the observed phenomena far enough to attract the interest of disciplinarians, and let them carry on with perhaps less rich and less multidisciplinary research but with quantitative testing. The endpoint is adjustments to their more structured theories to correspond to new observations from the real world.

We will miss Yair, as well as the kind of research, writing, and fun that he produced.

https://doi.org/10.1142/9789811287510_0029

Chapter 29

A Tribute to Yair Aharoni

Pervez N. Ghauri

University of Birmingham, Birmingham, UK

Back in 1993, when Peter Buckley and I published our first edition of *The Internationalization of the Firm: A Reader*, where we did a chronological review of the development of the international business field, some colleagues pointed out that we had missed Yair Ahroni's work. I had never met Yair at that time and was not familiar with his work. Peter, however, was familiar with his work and knew Yair well. The book was a big success and was soon a must-read for PhD students and younger colleagues in international business. The publisher started talking to us about the next edition after a couple of years and we started thinking about it, also remembering that we had to get Yair's work in the next volume.

We thus contacted Yair (Peter contacted him, to be correct) and wanted to have his seminal work included in the next edition. He was very helpful and gracious and sent us his 1966 book, *The Foreign Investment Decision Process*. If I remember correctly, Peter wrote an abridged piece from Yair's book that was sent to him for his approval and he was very happy with that. This abridged article from his book appeared as the first chapter in the second edition of *The Internationalization of the Firm* in 1999. Many colleagues congratulated us for now presenting the complete picture of the international business field.

I must admit that I was not familiar with his work before that and, from his chapter, I learned a lot about how decisions are made in organizations in general and how foreign investment decisions are made.

He introduced the elements in the decision process while analyzing the decision process for foreign direct investment. He explained that decisions are made within an organization that already has a strategy, procedures, and policies and is composed of individuals each with his/her own goals and ambitions and having relationships with other individuals within and outside the organization. All this influences specific decisions.

Another important element presented was time, in that the decision is spread over a longer time, and not at one point of time, as several smaller decisions have to be made at different times to come to the conclusion of making or rejecting the investment. Uncertainty was the next element, as businesspeople live under uncertainty and are always trying to avoid this uncertainty. They thus make decisions that do not depend upon uncertain future predictions, as they can only take a certain degree of risk. This means that they are mostly working for the avoidance of risk and uncertainty. The next element he introduced was goals. Decision makers are trying to achieve their goals. The goals of different managers and the organization need to come together for a decision to be made. The final element that was presented was constraints, meaning that managers need to investigate a number of variables in the new market that can create hurdles, such as the political environment, the legal system, and the size of the market. To make an investment decision, thus, managers need to know a good deal about the new environment. All these concepts that he introduced have become incorporated into well-known international business theories. His was indeed a pioneering work.

Since then, we have published several editions of that volume, every time reshuffling and revising different chapters and adding new seminal work. The latest one appeared in 2015 under the title *International Business Strategy: Theory and Practice*. Throughout these years however, Yair's article has always been the first chapter, also in this latest volume.

During this process, I came to know Yair very well and we met at least a couple of times every year, in AIB and EIBA conferences and in some specialized conferences. One organized every year by Professor Lars Oxelheim, in Molle, Sweden, was particularly a very good one. This was a very special conference with only invited speakers from the European Commission, the Swedish government, the Central European Bank, and prominent academics. This conference always had a European theme;

however, Yair was often invited as a keynote speaker and a prominent member of the closing panel.

I have many fond memories from that conference and long walks that we had in the Swedish countryside. Professor Oxelheim often compiled a book from the selected papers from Molle conferences and Yair's contribution was always very prominent in these volumes. I worked more closely with Yair when Professor Oxelheim and I compiled a book entitled *European Union and the Race for Foreign Direct Investment in Europe* in 2004. Yair contributed a chapter on the airline industry and pointed out how this industry has escaped the global integration of production and consumption, as airlines were often protected by states as an attribute of sovereignty. He called for a coherent and liberal policy for international air transport. Not long after that, we witnessed the policy of "open skies" and the deregulation of the airline industry that was adopted by most countries.

I came much closer to him after I was elected as an EIBA Fellow in 2008, as Yair was already an EIBA Fellow. He used to advise me on different matters and about how EIBA was run. When I was appointed Treasurer/Secretary to the Fellows, he was very helpful and always had ideas to reform EIBA Fellows meetings and organization. He was particularly concerned with how to keep senior Fellows, who have retired from their universities, active in EIBA and to encourage them to attend EIBA and Fellows' meetings. He was very active in these meetings and had some very good ideas. Many of these ideas were implemented. Later, in 2015, I was also elected as a Fellow of the Academy of International Business. As in the case of EIBA, Yair was already an AIB Fellow and welcomed me with open arms. This was thus another event where we met every year. During all these years, he was very regular in AIB and EIBA and I learnt a lot from him. He will be missed.

https://doi.org/10.1142/9789811287510_0030

Chapter 30

Tribute to Yair Aharoni

Jeremy Clegg

University of Leeds, Leeds, UK

A theme in the body of work of the late Yair Aharoni is that you should not believe what you read. Yair's academic life was a demonstration of this, and of how much we need to keep this in mind, for the vitality of our subject field. One of the aspects of great research that is generally lost to posterity is how the researcher came to develop his or her thinking. In the case of scientific research, you could say "Why is it important, the science is the science?" That may be true if we are talking about the textbook account. But the textbook is not a blueprint, and it is certainly no inspiration to new generations of researchers. New researchers are the ones about whom I worry. The foreshortened distillations of literature encourage them only to aspire to make their contribution to where the gaps appear (or where they are told the gaps are). But that misses the point. The point is that the received account is almost certainly wrong.

Beyond the towering achievements of Yair is his method — and the method is the story. And what a story it is. I will not rehearse here the substance of Yair's work (well, apart from a couple of lapses) as I am sure others will do this wonderfully. Fortunately, Yair, in his writings, has left a legacy also that is a four-dimensional account (with time in it) of how he came to change the way we think about managerial decision-making within international business.

Yair was trained as an economist. This is an excellent education — on what not to believe. The neoclassical economics that has been so influential on our subject field of international business, and the management of it, has given us a two-dimensional view — literally. This is something that Yair was at pains to point out. The diagrams that have shaped the way we think (and the models underlying them) shaped the way we research. In fact, the economists that belong to the age of political economy, and not to the age of the reductionists and formalizers, are those that Yair most resembles. But, today, it is generally not possible to avoid excessive reduction within mainstream economics, so we are fortunate that we have international business within which to do the research that needs to be done to explain the world as it really is.

So, if we do precisely what I have just said we should not do, which is to boil down, Yair's message to new researchers is to be critical of what you read but more than this to think about the human dimension. This necessarily means talking to the practitioners — letting them speak within their own terms of reference and not within categories determined by the researcher alone.

Why we stand in such great need today of Yair's message is precisely because we have diminishing marginal returns (I know, a neoclassical economics concept!) to received theory. We have these diminishing returns because we are extending from known theory, in increments, generally to support the existing way of thinking, because this way publication success lies. Even the journals that proclaim their interest in theory are, in fact, more interested in not deviating too much from the *status quo*. This itself is a very human frailty. What Yair writes is that "reality … is socially and politically constructed rather than objectively determined". These words appear in an AIB *Insights* article from 2013, but they summarize Yair's approach. This simple statement is the guiding principle for research today, as much as it was at the start of Yair's long research career. We are not going to find the answers in a microeconomics text, however advanced, however modern, and however formally expressed. This is why his research is founded upon talking to those who are the actors — the practitioners. Journal editors today are universally exasperated by the poverty of new theoretical insights that have any chance of being useful. The field is dominated by secondary data analysis, and even primary survey data may fail to reveal the insights that Yair's method of "talking to the practitioners" would reveal, certainly without the legwork of doing that talking first.

Another big learning point from Yair's career, for new researchers, is to feel fervently about a problem. If the problem is something that worries the researcher, then this is actually better. All of this does not sound too much like "taking the researcher out of the research". But that is just at the stage of establishing the problem. After that, it is all down to one of the many things that Yair excelled: dispassionate hard graft. That takes time, and time is the one thing of which researchers today really feel deprived. But the message of quality rather than quantity is supreme. Yair was able to combine both, but only because he frontloaded the deep thinking, and carried on thinking all the way through; looking out for the answers, and the results, that did not fit received wisdom and even his own evolving wisdom.

Yair's method sounds like a recipe for disaster — but he did not simply generate "negative results". He did generate negative results — but only for the current way of thinking, as he was ready to supply the answers. And that is what makes the difference as an innovator.

Yair was one of the "first in" to research on state-owned enterprises (SOEs) — firms that are, par excellence, those that do not fit conventional theory within the management of international business. This was anticipated by decades of work that is at the forefront today and in which Yair had continued to be a key actor. It is high risk, but Yair's injunction to those of us in the IB "establishment" is to encourage originality, to make it more rewarding, and to make sure that the stories are told about how the great ideas and the foundations of our subject field came to be established, though they should always be contested. Beyond being a figure whose name is revered for his enduring contribution, Yair's canon has much to impart to new researchers today.

Yair was truly a pioneer in our field, and the vitality today of the research stream that he did so much to kickstart stands as a testament to his seminal work. I feel particularly sorry for junior researchers who will never come to know Yair in person and to interact with him. His faithfulness in attending AIB events meant a lot to us all. I have read the moving tributes by the Fellows of AIB, which span the entire range of recollections, from the originality of his research and its importance for us to this day to the highly personal. We have lost a great man in our field, but he leaves us a wonderful legacy that I hope and believe will continue to be built on for many years to come.

I hope that AIB will encourage our new researchers to continue to learn from Yair. His body of work is extensive and hugely influential.

His approach — the curiosity, the questioning, and the skepticism are his greatest gifts. How will AIB achieve this? One great start is the recently completed *History of the AIB* by Jean Boddewyn and James Goodnow. But that is just the beginning, and the AIB History Project must continue, for the benefit of new researchers, to capture how great innovators such as Yair came to change the way we think and, I hope, the way we research.

https://doi.org/10.1142/9789811287510_0031

Chapter 31

Yair Aharoni: Personal Memories and a Short Tribute

Raj Aggarwal

Kent State University Foundation, Kent, OH, USA

Professor Yair Aharoni was a remarkable individual. I grew up knowing that our goal in life should be to make a positive difference in the world and leave whatever we get involved with in better shape than we found it. While I am unsure if I have done that adequately — in any case that is a judgment for others to make — I have little doubt that Yair made a big difference in the world. I know he did leave it better off. First, he significantly advanced our understanding of perhaps the most important phenomenon of our times — economic globalization. Second, he was a kind and generous individual who greatly influenced the better scholars and others around him. Next, I address these two contentions in greater detail.

Yair Aharoni the Scholar — A Layman's Perspective

There are many excellent scholarly statements and expositions (including some in this volume) about Yair's scholarly contributions. Instead of repeating another version of that, here I add a perspective that is more accessible and provides an example of the importance of Yair's scholarship for the wider world. This version of Yair's scholarly contribution can be read more widely including by non-specialists and by intelligent laymen.[1]

While globalization is an important multidimensional phenomenon, economic globalization seems to be a fundamental driving force for many other dimensions of globalization. The economic globalization phenomena have been around since pre-historic times, ever since groups of humans discovered that they could trade their own goods for more likable goods produced by other not so familiar humans living at a distance (sometimes the traded goods were exotic brides or husbands). Such globalization took a great leap forward once writing and record-keeping were invented. Gopinath (2018: 3) cites a 14th-century Sanskrit anthology from India on the wisdom of taking a tolerant and even an admiring view of people from a distant group. Archaeologists and historians have found evidence of such trading with distant places throughout history. For the last millennia or so, we have seen many waves of globalization with steady growth interrupted by wars, famines, plagues, or other crises during which globalization slows, stops, or even reverses temporarily. The last wave of 19th-century growth in globalization was interrupted by WWI and the crises that preceded it and resumed a few years after the end of WWII. The current wave of growing globalization seems to have hit some headwinds and leveled off after the great recession of 2007–2009.

Economic globalization in this last post-war period (since about 1950) has been greatly facilitated by dramatic multilateral and bilateral reductions in barriers to trade. There are good, logical reasons for economic globalization to grow. Such globalization is driven by its ability to increase worker and consumer satisfaction. Economic analyses have shown clearly that globalization creates new wealth by exploiting specialization and promoting economies of scale. Just by trading and exchanging goods, everyone is better off, and both sides have new wealth to share (although it is not always shared evenly). This creation of new wealth is an essential and powerful driver underlying the relentless and continuing rise of economic globalization.[2]

[1]In this exposition, I have glossed over the specific scholarly contributions by Yair, but I have tried to convey Yair's contributions in very broad terms.

[2]Technology is another force that has also facilitated globalization. For example, the growth of cultural and social globalization has been greatly facilitated by the growth of the technology of video and verbal communications and the associated severe drop in the costs

But, with globalization, people employed in making goods that are now imported will lose jobs while others employed in export sectors will gain jobs, so there are new winners and losers within each country benefitting from international trade. If economic policy is not used to negate or reduce these disparities (using the new wealth created by cross-border business), the political system is likely to be used to oppose globalization. So, much has been written to defend economic globalization (Bhagwati, 2004). Nevertheless, international trade has been a great driver of globalization.

In recent decades, in addition to cross-border trade, an organizational form has become increasingly important for economic globalization. Instead of relying on reduced cross-border barriers, this organizational form overcomes such barriers to optimally arranging multicountry resources to create new wealth and promote economic globalization. Indeed, globalization has been facilitated by the growth of the multinational corporation (MNC), an organization that combines the limited liability of its own (a great financing advantage) with the hierarchical structure of management to engage in global business. This organizational form has been around for a while. Indeed, one of the first limited liability corporations was the East India Company formed in the 16th century to trade between England and India. Similar organizations were formed around the same time to exploit other areas of the globe, e.g., the Dutch East India and the Hudson's Bay companies. While around for a while, this organizational form had not been well understood. Yair significantly advanced our understanding of MNCs.

MNCs are important as many of them have grown to be very large with business operations spread in many countries. They usually develop unique advantages in the form of proprietary sources of cheaper inputs, technology, brand names, and specialized management skills.[3] These

---

of such international communications. Similar cost reductions and the wide availability of international travel have also contributed to the cultural and social globalization. The widespread availability and use of machine translation (e.g., by Google devices) further lower the global cultural and social barriers. Clearly, cultural and social globalization underwritten by communication technologies is important for economic and business globalization.

[3]MNC-based globalization is also facilitated by the changing nature of work. As long as the Internet is available, we can now work from anywhere, including our offices, homes, a beach, or anywhere in the world. Thus, much work can be outsourced to workers almost anywhere in the world. This ability to outsource work to cheaper overseas

advantages and intangible assets give them unique benefits to organize and manage global production and sales. MNCs have now grown very important even in relation to powerful nation-states. For example, they often have the ability to avoid taxes and regulations imposed by any one country (by shifting operations and profits to lower-cost locations). Finally, MNCs are also very important as they now account for a major portion of international trade.

In sum, in modern times, there have been, roughly speaking, two major channels for economic globalization: cross-border trade and cross-border investment (Friedman, 2000). At a time when most economists focused on trade as the channel for economic globalization, Yair focused his and the world's attention on the channel that was less well understood, the multinational corporation (MNC), by shining a strong intellectual light on the nature of foreign direct investment (FDI). By illuminating the nature of FDI and the MNC, Yair became a major contributor to the nascent field of international business (IB). MNCs have grown in importance since Yair's illuminating early work — perhaps partially because of it.

The bottom line is that MNCs are important and major instruments for creating and increasing wealth via globalization. Not only do they account for most FDI flows, but they are also responsible for the largest proportion of internal trade. Because of their size and ability to create wealth, MNCs are now arguably some of the most important economic entities in the world (Dunning, 1993). There are good reasons to believe that MNCs are likely to continue to grow as facilitators of economic globalization.

Scholarship by Yair Aharoni significantly advanced our understanding of MNCs and their ever-growing influence.

---

locations is just in time to serve the consequences of important demographic trends. Birth rates are declining rapidly in the developed countries to below replacement levels while death rates in these countries are declining at the same time, leading to ever-larger proportion of older folks and a decline of working-age people. In contrast, many developing countries have rising portions of young people. It may have some setbacks, but the economic system will eventually find ways to arbitrage worker shortages in the developed countries with a simultaneous surplus of working-age human resource in other countries (Aggarwal, 2011).

Yair Aharoni: The Person

However, in spite of being a giant in the field of international business, in person, he never let on that he was. Unlike many scholars with high standing in the profession, Yair was always friendly, respectful, and helpful to other IB scholars, no matter their prominence or lack thereof. This was also my own experience over the years with Yair. That was his true nature as I confirmed over four decades at the annual meetings of the Academy of International Business (AIB). I found few other people that were as generous and kind as him at those meetings. No doubt, in the future, I will still (mistakenly) continue to expect his friendly greetings as I have over the years when we ran into each other at the annual AIB meetings.

Over the years, I was very fortunate to have him as a friend and mentor. He was not one to give explicit advice and directions, but he was an excellent listener and would react wisely to whatever was on my mind at that point. Advice with a very light touch! Just perfect.

Not only was he a world-class scholar, but he was also a manager and dean. In that sense, I felt that he was experienced in the areas that I considered important for me, both in academics and in executive work in MNCs. Indeed, I gained from his perspectives as a scholar, manager, and dean. For example, in inviting me to contribute to one of his early edited volumes on the MNC, he gave me (a young scholar) a chance to express in print some of my thoughts on the global expansion of Japanese financial service firms (Aggarwal, 1992).

When I became the dean of a largish business school (~70 full-time PhDs and another ~70 staff and part-time and adjunct professors) at a mid-west state university, I found that Yair was one of the few people with whom it was useful to exchange perspectives on various aspects of being a business school dean. For example, we both shared the importance we gave to bringing working executives into the business school, where they can interact with faculty and students (of course, in doing so, it was important to manage expectations on both sides).

As I moved along in my career and years, I realized that Yair was also a great example of a true and dedicated professional. He stayed active all his life even after his multiple, so-called, retirements. Over the years, I had enjoyed serving on many corporate boards (e.g., 24 years in one case and 26 years in another). So, he has been one of my inspirations as, even after my, so-called, retirement, I stay busy — a little bit as an academic but more so now as a business person and as a contributor of time, talent, and treasure to non-profit organizations.

Over the years, I have been grateful for many other kindnesses by Yair. I will miss my colleague, mentor, and friend. Fortunately, I know that I was not the only recipient of Yair's kindness and largesse. So, Yair's passing is indeed a great loss to the IB profession.

References

Aggarwal, R. 2011. Developing a global mindset: Integrating demographics, sustainability, technology, and globalization. *Journal of Teaching International Business*, 22(1): 51–69.

Aggarwal, R. 1992. The global expansion of Japanese financial service firms: Role of domestic economic and regulatory policies. In Aharoni, Y. (Ed.) *Coalitions and Competitions: The Global Expansion of Service Firms*. London: Routledge, pp. 229–252.

Bhagwati, J. 2004. *In Defence of Globalization*. New York: Oxford University Press.

Dunning, J. 1993. *Multinational Enterprises and the Global Economy*. New York: Addison-Wesley.

Friedman, T. 2000. *The Lotus and the Olive Tree*. New York: Anchor Books.

Gopinath, C. 2018. *Globalization*. Cheltenham, UK: Edward Elgar.

https://doi.org/10.1142/9789811287510_0032

Chapter 32

Yair Aharoni: An Abductive Case Researcher

Rebecca Piekkari* **and Ingmar Björkman**†

**Aalto University School of Business, Espoo, Finland*

†Hanken School of Economics, Helsinki, Finland

Introduction

Yair Aharoni was an unorthodox international business (IB) researcher in many respects, but he was particularly fascinated with the case study. While many early IB researchers were trained as economists and tended to consider case study research as descriptive at best, Yair was convinced that the case study allowed researchers to get much closer to reality than what was possible with econometric techniques (Aharoni, 2013: p. 17):

> Had I chosen to study foreign investments through a mail questionnaire, however carefully designed, I would never have been exposed to the rich saga of the real foreign investment decision process and to the way real managers in real firms make decisions. Rather I could have suggested wrong policies... I have always tried to understand the actual behavior of persons within a firm — not how they *should* behave.

It did not take much to convince Yair to contribute to an edited volume on the case study (Piekkari & Welch, 2011). It is this chapter on which the present essay is largely based. Yair outlines his vision about the way to conduct research in IB as follows (Aharoni, 2011: pp. 51–52):

> The task of IB researchers should not be to gather facts and measure how often certain patterns occur, but to appreciate the different constructions and meanings that people place upon their experience. Human behaviour is very complex. Executives do not always maximize profits. They are also family members, belong to different clubs and interest groups and are citizens of a nation — and all of these affiliations impact on our behaviour.

His PhD thesis — which he later revised into a book that became a classic in the IB field (Aharoni, 1966) — was about the way foreign investment decisions were made by US manufacturing firms. He was the first to study these decisions as a process and soon realized that the classical economic theory of capital investment was not helpful to understand the behavior of US manufacturing firms (Aharoni, 2013: pp. 17–18):

> Classical economics-based theory alone is insufficient to understand the complexity of real life. We must incorporate politics, culture and institutions. Only if all of these approaches are woven into our theories may they be helpful for businessmen and for policy makers.

Yair argued for the necessity to recognize that decisions are made under uncertainty within an organizational and social system. He firmly believed that the field of IB would benefit from taking seriously managerial behavior, processes, and politics in its explanatory models. He also had a practical goal — to affect policymakers in order to increase FDI to countries such as Israel.

Benefits of the Case Study as a Research Strategy

As a graduate of Harvard Business School, Yair Aharoni was exposed to the use of cases for both teaching and research purposes (Aharoni, 2011). During his remarkable career, he wrote more than 150 cases, ranging from Israel, the US, and Europe and covering a broad range of industries from manufacturing to services.

He was a highly devoted case researcher because the case method allowed him to penetrate into the ways firms actually behave and to understand the complexity of real-life decision-making as opposed to what managers would like him to think or what economic theory predicts (Aharoni, 2011: p. 41):

> I am deeply convinced that — at least in some of my studies — I would not have understood many business phenomena, or the way decisions are made, had I used any other method.

Yair firmly believed that great "insights are only the result of a careful study of specific cases", not "from a statistical study of a large population of firms in an industry" (Aharoni, 2011: p. 46).

An Abductive Moment

Unlike induction, which begins from data, abductive theorizing starts from previous research. When entering the field, the case researcher already has a set of pre-conceived theoretical expectations. The process of abduction is triggered by a surprising observation in the field that existing theories do not seem to be able to explain. In other words, abduction is the process of providing a theoretical explanation for the unexpected empirical finding. At its best, an abductive moment leads the researcher to redirect the study in searching for an explanation and to develop new theories and concepts — to reconceptualize the phenomenon itself (Tavory & Timmermans, 2014). We believe this is what Yair did.

In his writings, Yair vividly describes how the classical economic theory of capital investments was not able to explain what he was seeing in his empirical cases about the processes leading up to US firms deciding to invest in Israel (Aharoni, 2011: p. 43, italics added):

> I made a list of firms that had considered an investment in Israel. I wrote about 40 case studies on the history of the decisions, both by interviewing managers and by reading files of correspondence and other documents related to the decision. I soon found out that tax incentives did not play the decisive role I had expected them to play. Moreover, the picture emerging from my field research seemed to be one of utterly irrational behaviour and a complete lack of economic logic. *The decision process had very little in common with the classical economic theory of capital investments.* It was necessary to look at the system as a whole, recognizing that

> decisions are made under uncertainty within an organization and a social system. Once I changed the lens what seemed irrational made sense.

The abductive moment described above led Yair to develop a behavioral theory of FDI decision-making. It explains how and why FDI decisions are made, and how and why commitments accumulate. The mismatch between classical economic theory and the "real world" that is captured in the above quotation was upheld over time because researchers had faith in the explanatory power of economic theory, thereby hampering theory development. As Yair (Aharoni, 2011: p. 50) wrote almost 50 years later:

> In my view, these discrepancies are largely a result of clinging onto principles of economic theory, ignoring signals from the real world of real firms that could have been discovered through case study research.

Yair was convinced that case research was a means to correct the discrepancy between theory and the "real" world. Yair was not the first scholar to point out the limitations of classical economic theory. Cyert and March (1963) published the behavioral theory of the firm, which had an important influence on Yair's analysis that was presented in his book published in 1966. Though his findings fit well with many elements of the behavioral theory of the firm, he found the theory lacking in some respects. Basically, Yair argues that the theory pays too little attention to the social context in which FDI decisions are made. Therefore, the framework that he developed "differs somewhat from that suggested by Cyert and March" (Aharoni, 1966: 300).

In the field of IB, Yair was one of the forerunners in the way he used an abductive approach to build a new theory. After theoretical immersion in economics, he exposed himself to the realities facing managers and built novel explanatory models by combining, as well as contrasting, field insights with relevant previous research. Yair's abductive research approach was a great source of inspiration for the second author of this chapter in his doctoral thesis (Björkman, 1989) examining FDI decision-making processes in Finnish corporations.

Importance of Context

In case study research, the basis for generating theoretical explanations of social behavior lies in contextualizing the research phenomenon.

Social and cultural practices and processes cannot be understood without reference to the broader historical, institutional, political, and social forces in which they are embedded. At the same time, understanding context is the very essence of what international business stands for as a field (Welch *et al.*, 2011).

Yair believed that it was important to understand the context and that the case study method was very well suited to produce context-dependent knowledge. Multinationals operate in different contexts, constantly learning and adapting to changes taking place in their environment as well as shaping this environment. Therefore, "[t]o a large extent theory is very much context dependent" (Aharoni, 2011: 49). Yair's findings derived from small countries with limited market size and his work on service firms allowed him to challenge the universality and applicability of existing theories.

Yair did not select typical cases but went for outlier firms that were "operating by different ideas, achieving success by being unique in a certain specific, well-identified" (Aharoni, 2011: 45). He argued that "services provided many 'black swans'" that challenged received wisdom in IB theory (Aharoni, 2011: 47). The in-depth approach that characterizes the case study allowed him to dig deeper into outlier cases. As Yair explains, "what appears to be 'white' often turns out on closer examination to be 'black'" (Aharoni, 2011: 47). He found it rewarding "to look at the unique, the different and the outlier rather than search for central tendencies in a population of MNEs" (Aharoni, 2011: 53). Studying such cases lead to contextually rooted knowledge and also to insights that have more general implications for advancing the field of IB.

Conclusion

Toward the end of his career, Yair Aharoni wrote several papers in which he reflected on what he had learnt (Aharoni, 2011; Aharoni *et al.*, 2011; Aharoni, 2013). He argued persuasively for the value of the case study as a research method and called for a return to case research as an important way forward. He was of the opinion that IB scholars need to gain a better understanding of the changing reality of global business. Recent case studies published on the management of multinational corporations (Ambos *et al.*, 2020; Mees-Buss *et al.*, 2019; Stendahl *et al.*, 2021) in the *Journal of International Business Studies* can be viewed as a tribute to

Yair Aharoni and his great contributions to our understanding of key questions in international business research.

References

Aharoni, Y. 1966. *The Foreign Investment Decision Process*. Boston: Harvard Graduate School of Business Administration.

Aharoni, Y. 2011. My 50 years of case research in international business: The power of outliers and black swans. In Piekkari, R. & Welch, C. (Eds.) *Rethinking the Case Study in International Business and Management Research*. Cheltenham, UK: Edward Elgar, pp. 41–54.

Aharoni, Y. 2013. A few lessons from my long experience in IB research: Opinion/Editorial. *AIB Insights*, 13(4): 17–19.

Aharoni, Y., Tihanyi, L. & Connelly, B. L. 2011. Managerial decision-making in international business: A forty-five-year retrospective. *Journal of World Business*, 46: 135–142.

Ambos, T. C., Fuchs, S. H. & Zimmermann, A. 2020. Managing interrelated tensions in headquarters–subsidiary relationships: The case of a multinational hybrid organization. *Journal of International Business Studies*, 51: 906–932.

Björkman, I. 1989. *Foreign Direct Investments: An Empirical Study of Decision Making in Seven Finnish Firms*. Helsinki: Hanken School of Economics.

Cyert, R. & March, J. G. 1963. *A Behavioral Theory of the Firm*. Englewood Cliffs, NJ: Prentice-Hall.

Mees-Buss, J., Welch, C. & Westney, D. E. 2019. What happened to the transnational? The emergence of the neo-global corporation. *Journal of International Business Studies*, 50: 1513–1543.

Piekkari, R. & Welch, C. (Eds.) 2011. *Rethinking the Case Study in International Business and Management Research*. Cheltenham, UK: Edward Elgar.

Stendahl, E., Schriber, S. & Tippmann, E. 2021. Control changes in multinational corporations: Adjusting control approaches in practice. *Journal of International Business Studies*, 52: 409–431.

Tavory, I. & Timmermans, S. 2014. *Abductive Analysis: Theorizing Qualitative Research*. Chicago: University of Chicago Press.

Welch, C., Piekkari, R., Plakoyiannaki, E. & Paavilainen-Mäntymäki, E. 2011. Theorising from case studies: Towards a pluralist future for international business research. *Journal of International Business Studies*, 42: 740–762.

https://doi.org/10.1142/9789811287510_0033

Chapter 33

Personal Recollections from AIB Fellows

Mary Yoko Brannen, *Copenhagen Business School*

Yair left us much too soon! I remember him from when I was first starting out "on the market", as it were, in IB — single mom of an infant daughter, qualitative researcher, coming out of a non-Ivy League institution. He, together with Oded Shenkar, was so encouraging of Jane Salk and me doing ethnographic work in IB even while we were having the darnedest time getting it published. He, like many in our field, was widely read, a truly cross-disciplinary, open-minded scholar. Perhaps, this was the source behind the ever-present twinkle in his eyes. He will be sorely missed.

Farok Contractor, *Rutgers University*

The Foreign Investment Decision Process (1966) was among the first IB books I read as a PhD student at Wharton. Later, I appreciated Yair's other works, conversations with him, and his gentlemanly comportment.

What is a scholar's contribution worth? Few of us will win a Nobel. But each of us, especially AIB Fellows, adds to the river of human thought. Our contributions may be small compared to the total volume, or flow, of ideas. But they can have a catalytic or leavening influence that makes a difference in the direction of scholarly thought and professional action.

As an early pioneer in IB, Yair Aharoni certainly had such an influence.

John D. Daniels (Deceased), *University of Miami*

I first knew of Yair Aharoni when a fellow PhD student suggested I read *The Foreign Investment Decision Process*, which Yair had just published based on his dissertation. This study not only inspired my own choice of a dissertation topic but also remains in my opinion to be the definitive behavioral explanation of why and where companies invest abroad.

One of my fond memories of Yair was from the University of South Carolina conference in the late 1980s, which nearly all IB scholars attended. After two or three days of discussion on how IB studies should evolve, Yair asked to read a short summary of a meeting from about 10 years before. It showed that we were still talking about the same things without having made any notable progress. Such a response was typical of Yair, who had a way of listening to all viewpoints and then synthesizing a summary response.

I knew Yair professionally at AIB annual meetings for many years before our paths crossed at a non-AIB event in Istanbul. It was there that we came to know each other on a personal basis as he and Ofira joined Letty and me in exploring the city for several days. Afterward, we always sat together at AIB annual Fellows' dinners, the last of which was in Copenhagen. (Unfortunately, they could not get visas for the meeting in Dubai.) We also spent a delightful and informative time together in Tel Aviv.

I shall personally miss Yair. His contributions to the IB field were monumental. He was also an inspiration to be forever inquisitive and gracious in one's comments.

José de la Torre (Deceased), *University of Bologna*

I, too, am deeply saddened by this news. It seems like these days most news is bad, whether at the national or international level, and we keep losing many of the field's early leaders as the tyranny of time weighs on all of us.

I arrived at HBS in 1966, so a few years after Yair had finished his degree and moved back to Israel, but his presence was deeply felt in our program as we all were strongly urged to read his marvelous book, *The Foreign Investment Decision Process*, a wonderful example of how an innovative and deeply practical study could result from a dissertation process. For years afterward, I referred to it in my courses and seminars, particularly with PhD students, and shared many of its conclusions with my classes.

As several of you have mentioned, I thoroughly enjoyed Yair's company at the AIB meetings. Few among us would forget his constant urging the Academy to keep both our annual fees and, most importantly, the conference fees, as low as possible so that everyone could afford it. I visited Yair in Israel on a couple of occasions while living in Europe and, although we never collaborated on a project, we shared many discussions of key topics that concerned us over the years.

In 2010, after having served as External Examiner for the Cyprus International Institute of Management in Nicosia for several years, Yair decided to step down. He then recommended my name to the Institute's leadership as a possible replacement and it was through this process that I stepped into his very large shoes to carry on in this capacity for the next four years. This brought me into contact with several of our members who played a leadership position either on the faculty of CIIM (e.g., Jim Leontiades) or on its Academic Council (e.g., Avi Meshulach and Nakiye Boyacigiller, among others). Throughout my service in this position, I counted on and generously received Yair's advice and counsel as I dealt with and/or met a number of challenges or obstacles in the performance of my duties. Yair was always available and most willing to help.

As Alain said earlier, Yair was one of those rare birds who could fly high in scholarship and also in administration, in practical relevance, and in mentorship. I know it is somewhat unimaginative to say that he will be missed, but in this case, I really mean it. One more bright light from our founding years is extinguished, but there is no doubt that his work and ideas will continue to influence our field for generations.

May he rest in peace.

Stephen J. Kobrin (Deceased), *University of Pennsylvania*

Yair was a curmudgeon in the best sense of the word, typically cutting straight to the point and not putting up with a lot of nonsense. He was always interesting and a good colleague and friend. He was "present at the creation" or just after the creation of the international business (IB) field and his work was important in its development.

His dissertation and further work on the foreign direct investment decision process was novel and a critical step in the development of the IB literature. He was among the first to view the foreign direct investment decision as a managerial process subject to all of the subjectivity and inconsistencies inherent in any managerial process or any human decision process for that matter.

Yair's research was an important factor in the development of the literature on political risk. His conclusion that managers do not formally integrate risk assessments into investment decision-making but both subjectively determine the degree of risk associated with any country or area of the world and then simply avoid areas perceived as risky had three implications which provided a basic framework for the assessment of political risk. First, risk is specific to a given investment and a general statement that a country was "risky" was not useful; second, objective and rigorous means of assessing investment-related risk needed to be developed; and third, formal integration of the risk assessment into investment decision making is necessary.

Yair Aharoni will be sorely missed but not forgotten.

Arie Y. Lewin, *Duke University*

I have been emotionally overwhelmed by the outpouring of memories and recounting of Yair's founding contributions to what became the current field of international business scholarship. When I joined the faculty of the NYU Graduate School of Business' Department of Management in August 1966, Yair was a visiting professor in the accounting department. Professor Lee Seidler recalled, in his note of condolences to Yair's daughter Orna, that he "first met Yair in 1965 when we [Lee and Yair] shared a small, inside office at NYU Graduate School of Business". It was Lee Seidler who introduced Yair and his first wife, Miri, to my wife Anita and me. This was the start of a life-long relationship. At Yair's invitation, I spent my first sabbatical leave, during 1971/1972, at The Leon Recanati School of Business at Tel Aviv University. Although Yair had stepped down as the founding dean of the business school, our major joint project was to plan the Institute of Management Science (TIMS) International

Conference in Tel Aviv, which Yair, Professor Melvin Shakun (NYU), and I organized in June 1973.

However, I had no real knowledge of Yair's seminal contribution to international business, including his famous HBS dissertation and his book, until he visited Duke University in September 1979. Yair was a guest at our house, and he worked for hours on end in our study, drafting his paper that appeared in *Management Science*, "Performance evaluation in state-owned enterprises: A process perspective" (1981, 29(11): 1340–1347). It was during the intense one week of writing this paper that I learned about Yair's PhD dissertation, his book, and his already-extensive work on state-owned enterprises.

Dean Thomas Keller recruited Yair to join the Fuqua School faculty as the J. Paul Sticht Visiting Professor of International Business. Yair joined, in the summer of 1987, a faculty that had voted the previous year not to authorize an IB department. But, by the spring of 1988, Yair had single-handedly convinced the school (basically by visiting every faculty member, one-on-one) to add a new course, entitled "International Environment of Business", to the required core curriculum of the first year of the MBA program. Of course, none of the Fuqua School faculty could teach the course, and it fell on several of us (including me) to sit on Yair's teaching of five sections of the course during the spring of 1989. In spite of this heavy teaching load, Yair found the time to establish the Fuqua School's Center of International Development Research (CIDR) and, in 1992, he became the founding director of the Duke University Center for International Business Education and Research (CIBER). His winning proposal focused on supporting the launch of the Global Executive MBA (GEMBA) Program at Duke, which became a leading global MBA and executive program incorporating remote and in-class teaching, with terms taught on location in India, Latin America, and the UK. As the director of the CIBER, Yair, on several occasions, persuaded faculty to visit or attend IB training programs at some of the best departments (INSEAD, Leeds, Indiana, Thunderbird) and to engage with specialized IB conferences. In my case, he arranged for me to attend a three-week course at HBS, designed and led by Lou Wells.

His 60th birthday celebration was a surprise party at our house, which brought together many of Yair's colleagues from across Duke and the Beth El Synagogue, where he was an active member of the Orthodox community. In the spring of 1995, Yair retired from Duke to return to Israel. Perhaps, my fondest memory of Yair came about after I became the

Editor-in-Chief of *JIBS*. It was a very emotional call. I could sense that Yair felt that his internationalization proselytizing efforts had come full circle and that I had "graduated" as a *bona fide* IB scholar. It made me very proud and reminded me of how he used to reminisce about Ravi Ramamurti and how Ravi had emerged as a true IB scholar.

In my book, Yair was a prince of a fellow and a down-to-earth scholar. I will cherish his memory forever.

Ravi Ramamurti, *Northeastern University*

I had a special bond with Yair and was sorry to get the sad news from his daughter.

Soon after arriving as a doctoral student at HBS in 1977, after working for the government and SOEs in India, I met Yair, who was then a visiting professor there. I was elated to discover that he too was interested in SOEs! Yair was the first person I worked for as an RA. I learned so much from him about SOEs in many countries, especially Israel, which he knew intimately, having served on several boards and government committees. I realized later that one of Yair's great traits was the capacity to use everyday life experiences — including mundane activities such as checking into a hotel or traveling from one city to another — as "data" to confirm or repudiate some theory of management. For Yair, bridging theory and practice was not an abstract idea but a way of life. That's why he had a theory about everything and usually an unconventional one!

When Yair left HBS, I completed my dissertation with Ray Vernon but continued to stay in close touch. He was a mentor, a well-wisher, an advocate, a friend, and a professional guide. He was always telling me to aim higher, not to settle for less than I deserved, and so on! He encouraged me to do things I thought myself totally incapable or undeserving of, from serving on the Farmer dissertation committee to aspiring for a chair or becoming an AIB Fellow!

Yair came home a number of times and loved home-cooked Indian food. Meena and I were thrilled to visit him in Israel with our three children. That was when Niron Hashai and I organized a *festschrift* in his honor at Tel Aviv University. The last time I saw Yair was at the Copenhagen AIB conference. His last email to me was to send good wishes for our youngest son's wedding (postponed by COVID). My reply included a picture of a young Yair (discovered in a pile of old photographs), taken when we were both in Caracas for a conference!

Yair was brilliant, insightful, had a tremendous work ethic, and tremendous zest for life. He was an original thinker and a tenacious debater. For the last few years, his eyesight was failing badly, but he pressed on, as if nothing had changed, still wanting to write more articles. Less well known perhaps are some of Yair's other qualities, such as a deep sense of caring and loyalty to family and friends. For example, he always made it a point to attend my paper/panel sessions, even when other parallel sessions were clearly much better bets! I feel awful having missed Yair's session at this year's virtual AIB — it would not have happened if roles had been reversed.

I will miss Yair, and AIB meetings will not be the same.

Mira Wilkins, *Florida International University*

I first met Yair, probably in late 1964, 1965, or early 1966. We had adjacent offices in the newly opened, just completed Uris Hall at Columbia Business School. Nearby were offices of individuals early involved in AIB: Emile Benoit, Roy Blough, and the younger men, George Simmons (whose DBA was from Indiana University) and Charlie Stewart. Yair and I were the same age (actually I was several months older). We talked often and shared the view that decision-making in large corporations was far from always neat or orderly. Decisions could be explained *ex post* but often not *ex ante*. I also shared his view that talking with key participants in international business was invaluable. I had differences with his arguments but always respected them.

I had forgotten — until I read Lou Wells' tribute — that Yair was a student of Ray Vernon, one more star in the roster of Ray's group at Harvard Business School, so many of whom for years formed a core group within the AIB (think, Lou Wells, the late Bob Stobaugh, the late John Stopford, and Jose de la Torre) and also many others not so well known in the AIB (and not Fellows): Larry Franko, Mike Yoshino, Yoshi Tsurumi, Mark Mason...

I kept in touch with Yair over the decades and saw him at AIB meetings and other occasions. When he was in Miami as a guest of John Daniels, I had lunch with him. He was always a thoughtful person, eager to discuss ideas.

He will be missed.

https://doi.org/10.1142/9789811287510_0034

Chapter 34

Yair Aharoni: His Influence on the Strategy and International Business Areas in Israel and on My Work

Niron Hashai

Arison School of Business, The Interdisciplinary Center, Herzliya, Israel

University of Manchester, Manchester, UK

I came to know Yair Aharoni when I was a PhD student at Tel Aviv University in the late 1990s. My advisor, Seev Hirsch, another international business giant who passed away this year, was a close friend of Yair's, and this has led to many interactions between Yair and me.

Yair was a true "sabra" in terms of his character, in the sense that when you met him it was a "what you see is what you get" experience. In other words, if Yair did not like you, you knew that, but, at the same time, he was the first to congratulate you on an accomplishment.

As a student, I already learned of Yair's vast contribution to the management field in Israel. In 1966, he left The Hebrew University to become the first dean of what is now called the Coller Faculty of Management at Tel Aviv University. This faculty, which has traditionally been the largest and most influential management faculty in Israel, has been shaped largely by the vision of Yair. Indeed, in 2010, Yair won the Israel Prize for his research work in management and also for his contribution to the establishment of this faculty. Yair also contributed a lot to the development of the business school at the College of Management, Academic Studies, where he served as the president.

Throughout the years, Yair was pivotal in building the Faculty of Management at Tel Aviv University and strengthening the international business side of it. In that respect, Yair made tremendous efforts to recruit top strategy and international business scholars to the faculty. The international business group at the Faculty of Management of Tel Aviv University included world-renown stars, such as Tamir Agmon, Seev Hirsch, Oded Shenkar, and Teddy Weinshall. It was a very strong and reputable research-oriented group.

Yair was also extremely instrumental in developing the next generation of strategy and international business scholars in Israel. He participated often in research seminars, where he was always very vocal, believing that giving true feedback in such seminars is instrumental to improving research. In the early 2000s, I participated regularly in a strategy and international business seminar series organized by the late Prof. Avi Fiegenbaum and Prof. Eli Segev. This series was meant to allow junior faculty and PhD students to present their work. Yair's comments in these seminars have been extremely helpful in shaping the work of many Israeli scholars, including myself.

My memories of Yair are not only of a straightforward person who could easily identify weaknesses in research but also of a vivid reader that has never ceased to amaze me with his ability to identify high-quality papers. His experience in that respect, knowing very quickly how to identify top-quality research and dismiss weaker studies was truly an exceptional quality of Yair's.

Looking back at Yair's lifetime as a scholar, it was always clear to me that, to a large extent, he covered a very broad range of strategy and international business areas in his work. Importantly, he was ahead of most scholars in writing about new trends in international business.

Yair, together with Seev Hirsch, was among the first to explore the role of multinationals from small open economies. Specifically, Yair was interested in the drivers and impediments that firms originating from a small open economy such as Israel face when internationalizing. One key impediment was the small home market of such firms that required them to bear costly interactions with end customers in foreign markets, without being able to also build on a home market as "low-hanging fruit".

In a series of works (e.g., Aharoni, 1992, 1994, 2000b, 2009; Aharoni & Hirsch, 1996), Yair demonstrated how fairly small multinationals from small countries, such as Israel, could overcome their inherent scale disadvantages relative to larger multinationals based in large home markets. Among the strategies he identified were the focusing on well-defined segments to avoid direct competition with large incumbents that often preferred to serve mainstream markets, reducing marketing costs by engaging in large transactions, which often means targeting business-to-business (B2B) rather than business-to-customer (B2C) transactions, reacting quickly to customer needs by being technologically flexible, and providing superior pre- and post-sale service. This line of work has contributed vastly to my work on the strategic configuration of small and medium-sized multinationals (Almor & Hashai, 2004) that need to focus on specific market segments and go for B2B rather than B2C transactions in order to compensate for their cost disadvantages.

Yair's seminal book, *The Foreign Investment Decision Process* (Aharoni, 1966), is surely one of the most influential works regarding the decisions of firms to internationalize. In this book, as well as in the following studies (Aharoni, 1993; Aharoni *et al.*, 1978), Yair highlighted the decision to internationalize as a key strategic decision. An important observation that Yair made in this regard is the critical role of a "champion" within the firm who is emotionally invested in the decision to internationalize and who presents compelling arguments for foreign expansion and highlights the negative consequences of not doing so. Without someone fighting this battle, Yair argued, it can be very difficult to persuade key decision-makers to internationalize.

In this respect, Yair identified the complex inter-relationships between changing attitudes, opinions, and social relationships, as well as the role of past experience, present events, and perception of the future as critical factors affecting the decision of a firm to internationalize. This line of work of Yair's has influenced me greatly in my thinking about the processes by which firms internationalize and mainly in the ways gradually internationalizing born global firms expand abroad (Hashai & Almor, 2004), especially their sequencing between the depth (foreign market specific commitment) and breadth of internationalization (the range of foreign markets); see, e.g., Hashai (2011a). This part of Yair's work is still part of my ongoing research on the role of founders in the internationalization of international new ventures (Hashai & Zahra, 2017).

Yair was also greatly interested in the difficulties of supplying services abroad, due to the intensive interaction that is required between the service provider and its customers (Aharoni, 1993; Aharoni & Nachum, 2000). Among the insights from this line of work was recognizing the role of reputation in enabling firms to provide services abroad (Aharoni, 2000a) and recognizing that alliances with local firms may be necessary to build relationships and credibility with customers, suppliers, regulators, and other institutional actors (Aharoni, 1993). In Aharoni (1996), Yair further emphasized that integration and centralization of global operations is an important determinant of the ability of services providers to successfully compete abroad because it allows firm-specific knowledge to be transferred efficiently to foreign subsidiaries. Since efficient knowledge transfer often requires the standardization and automation of firm-specific knowledge, internationalizing services providers must make tough decisions about which parts of their knowledge base to transfer outside the home country, including to strategic partners. Such choices should allow for efficient knowledge transfer without giving away the firm's core competencies or its competitive advantages. This line of work has contributed vastly to my work on the internationalization of high-technology firms that need to absorb and orchestrate costly pre- and post-sales services to their foreign customers (Almor *et al.*, 2006) and my work on service multimerizations (Hashai, 2011b).

To conclude, Yair regularly crossed traditional academic boundaries to study the interplay between firms, markets, bureaucrats, and politicians, frequently in an international setting (Aharoni, 1977, 1981, 1986, 1991). In addition to the above topics, he studied, extensively, state-owned enterprises and their internationalization and explored the relationship between multinationals and home/host governments. I will greatly miss Yair's broad views, deep insights, and academic integrity.

References

Aharoni, Y. 1966. *The Foreign Investment Decision Process*. Cambridge: Harvard University, Graduate School of Business Administration, Division of Research.

Aharoni, Y. 1977. *Markets, Planning and Development*. Cambridge, MA: Ballinger.

Aharoni, Y. 1981. *The No Risk Society*. Chatham, NJ: Chatham House.

Aharoni, Y. 1986. *The Evolution and Management of State-Owned Enterprises*. Cambridge, MA: Ballinger.

Aharoni, Y. 1991. *Israel's Political Economy: The Dreams and the Realities*. London: Routledge.

Aharoni, Y. 1992. The role of small firms in an interdependent world. In Burton, R. M., Obel, B. & Forsyth, J. (Eds.) *Strategies for Players in a Larger World: The Effect of Regulatory and Information Changes*. Amsterdam: Elsevier, pp. 11–32.

Aharoni, Y. 1993. The internationalization process in professional business service firms: Some tentative conclusions. In Aharoni, Y. (Ed.) *Coalitions and Competition: The Globalization of Professional Business Services*. London: Routledge, pp. 280–285.

Aharoni, Y. 1994. How can small firms achieve competitive advantage in an interdependent world? In Agmon, T. & Drobnick, R. (Eds.) *Small Firms in Global Competition*. New York: Oxford University Press, pp. 9–18.

Aharoni, Y. 1996. The organization of global service MNES. *International Studies of Management and Organization*, 26(2): 6–23.

Aharoni, Y. 2000a. The role of reputation in global professional business services. In Aharoni, Y. & Nahum, L. (Eds.) *Globalization of Services: Some Implications for Theory and Practice*. London: Routledge, pp. 125–141.

Aharoni, Y. 2000b. Globalization and the small, open economy. In Almor, T. & Hashai N. (Eds.) *FDI, International Trade and the Economics of Peacemaking: Papers in Honor of Seev Hirsch*. Rishon LeZion, Israel: College of Management Academic Division, pp. 90–116.

Aharoni, Y. 2009. Israeli multinationals: Competing from a small open economy. In Ramamurti, R. & Singh, J. V. (Eds.) *Emerging Multinationals in Emerging Markets*. Cambridge: Cambridge University Press, pp. 352–396.

Aharoni, Y. & Hirsch, S. 1996. The competitive potential of technology-intensive industries in developing countries. In Svetlicic, M. & Singer, H. W. (Eds.) *The World Economy: Challenges of Globalization and Regionalization*. London: Palgrave Macmillan, pp. 99–118.

Aharoni, Y., Maimon, Z. & Segev, E. 1978. Performance and autonomy in organizations: Determining dominant environmental components. *Management Science*, 24(9): 949–959.

Aharoni, Y. & Nachum, L. (Eds.). 2000. *Globalization of Services: Some Implications for Theory and Practice*. London: Routledge.

Almor, T. & Hashai, N. 2004. Competitive advantage and strategic configuration of knowledge-intensive small and medium sized multinationals: A modified resource-based view. *Journal of International Management*, 10: 479–500.

Almor, T., Hashai, N. & Hirsch, S. 2006. The product cycle revisited: Knowledge intensity and firm internationalization. *Management International Review*, 46(5): 507–528.

Hashai, N. 2011a. Sequencing the expansion of geographic scope and foreign operations of "born global" firms. *Journal of International Business Studies*, 42(8): 994–1015.

Hashai, N. 2011b. Global service multinationals from a small open economy: The case of Israeli hi tech services providers. In Ramamurti, R. & Hashai, N. (Eds.) *The Future of Foreign Direct Investment and the Multinational Enterprise*. Bingley, UK: Emerald, pp. 335–356.

Hashai, N. & Almor, T. 2004. Gradually internationalizing born global firms: An oxymoron? *International Business Review*, 13(4): 465–483.

Hashai, N. & Zahra, S. 2017. Founders' prior industry specific and general international experience and the international expansion of new ventures. Academy of International Business Annual Meeting, Dubai.

https://doi.org/10.1142/9789811287510_0035

Chapter 35

Yair Aharoni: Behavioral Scientist

Christian Bellak

University of Business and Economics, Vienna, Austria

In their "Foreword" to Yair's 1966 book, *The Foreign Investment Decision Process*, Professors Raymond A. Bauer, Pearson Hunt, and Raymond Vernon note that "What is needed is not a series of insights but rather a breaking down of barriers by the creation of a new structure of theory". This idea, certainly akin to Thomas S. Kuhn's *Structure of Scientific Revolutions*, which was already in its 6th edition in 1966, struck me when I was a doctoral student and is something you would hardly have heard even 30 years later at my university.

Like many others, I "met" Yair first through one of his writings, in particular his 1966 book, which is based on Yair's doctoral thesis and the underlying fieldwork, which started in 1960. The choice of subject was motivated by the inadequacies of classical theories of investments: "Economic theory does not pretend to mirror reality. It only claims, by a process of simplification, to isolate some significant strands in economic causal sequences, and to describe how these strands operate" (Aharoni, 1966: ix). This led him to conclude that economic theory "therefore is rarely either right or wrong" (Aharoni, 1966: ix). These are insights that are still difficult to grasp for today's students in economics.

While most students are struggling to get a grip on the many theories and new developments in economic theory during their PhD studies, Yair wanted to go much further: "Instead of basing my analysis on the *ceteris paribus* assumption, I tried to grapple with the problem as a whole and identify the *ceteris*" (Aharoni, 1966: ix).

Rather than dismissing traditional theory altogether, as is often done, Yair dissected the theory in a stepwise manner and argued consistently why the *ceteris* was needed. Yair came up with three main issues — (i) scarcity of management time, (ii) cost of information and the commitments involved, and (iii) the cost of organizational effort — which led him to argue that organizations are adapters, rather than maximizers (as assumed in traditional models).

There is no doubt that one of the major developments in today's market economies is the huge increase in the market power of large firms (Phillipon, 2019). This impacts, in important ways, the behavior of large multinational firms or should we say organizations. May they be innovators at the technological frontier, or lazy incumbents; may they be old, established firms or newcomers; may they be active in traditional industries or platform companies; may they serve one-sided or two-sided markets and/or be superstar firms… as is well known, there is a quiet life for firms and managers based on monopoly profits (Hicks, 1935). Organizations as adapters come immediately into mind. While, of course, there are new developments, methodologically as well as in economic theory, over such a long time span, many of these could not have been studied back in the 1960s.

Several years after my first encounter with his 1966 book, I had the chance to meet Yair in person at a workshop I organized in Vienna.[1] Yair's main interest at the time had shifted toward the service sector and the airline industry in particular (Aharoni, 2004), as well as toward topics concerning the role of large MNEs in small countries. I will never forget a fierce discussion between Yair and his close friend Seev Hirsch in one of the panels when they could not have disagreed more on the effects of foreign takeovers in small countries (Hirsch & Almor, 1996). Only minutes later, when we had lunch, they were both chatting and laughing together — you cannot imagine how relieved I felt.

As Yair remarked in a retrospective of his 1966 book, "forty-five years after the publication of *The Foreign Investment Decision Process* (…),

[1] Small Open Economies (SMOPEC) Workshop, Vienna University of Economics and Business, 1996. Participants (in alphabetical order): Yair Aharoni, Ilan Bijoui, Elisabeth Beer, Robert Gärtner, Per Heum, Seev Hirsch, Reijo Luostarinen, Lars Oxelheim, Torben Pedersen, Vitor Simoes, Marjan Svetlicic.

a relatively large segment of international business research continues to leave limited or no room for decision-making on the part of managers" (Aharoni *et al.*, 2011: 135). Behavioral economics still was in an infant stage in the 1960s (Baddeley, 2017) and only really took off in the 1980s. Therefore, Yair's innovative and forward-looking contribution to the field of international business, as well as behavioral economics, must be seen in this context.

Indeed, Professors Raymond A. Bauer, Pearson Hunt, and Raymond Vernon conclude the above-mentioned "Foreword" by saying that "[Dr. Aharoni's] … achievement joins the slowly growing number of studies that will lead us to the integration in behavioral studies that we have been looking for so long". While one could not agree more, it seems that, even by today's standards, we have not achieved the envisaged goal of "breaking down of barriers by the creation of a new structure of theory". Rather, international business theory has continuously developed and integrated behavioral issues and Yair's book remains a key stepping stone in this process until today.

References

Aharoni, Y. 1966. *Foreign Investment Decision Process*. Boston: Harvard Business School.

Aharoni, Y. 2004. The race for FDI in services: The case of the airline industry. In Ghauri, P. N. & Oxelheim, L. (Eds.) *European Union and the Race for Foreign Direct Investment in Europe*. Amsterdam: Elsevier, pp. 381–406.

Aharoni, Y., Tihanyi, L. & Connelly, B. L. 2011. Managerial decision-making in international business: A forty-five-year retrospective. *Journal of World Business*, 46: 135–142.

Baddeley, M. 2017. *Behavioral Economics: A Very Short Introduction*. Oxford: Oxford University Press.

Hicks, J. 1935. Annual survey of economic theory: The theory of monopoly. *Econometrica*, 3: 1–20.

Hirsch, S. & Almor, T. (Eds.) 1996. *Outsiders' Response to European Integration*. Copenhagen: Handelshøjskolens.

Kuhn, T. S. 1962. The structure of scientific revolutions. *International Encyclopedia of Unified Science*, Vol. 2, No. 2. Chicago: University of Chicago Press.

Phillipon, T. 2019. *The Great Reversal: How America Gave up on Free Markets*. Cambridge: Harvard University Press.

https://doi.org/10.1142/9789811287510_0036

Chapter 36

Learning from Yair

Laszlo Tihanyi

Rice University, Houston, TX, USA

I met Yair Aharoni in 1989 when I joined Duke University as a visiting scholar. I arrived in Durham, North Carolina, from Hungary, after defending my doctoral dissertation and completing a six-week-long English course. As a junior faculty member, I received a scholarship from the Soros Foundation to spend a year at any university in the United States that was willing to accept me. I applied to Duke to be able to learn from three leading scholars in my field: Yair Aharoni, Rich Burton, and Arie Lewin. I was thrilled when I received the invitation.

I spent the year at Duke attending classes and reading books and articles that I received from Yair, Rich, and Arie. Since 1989 marked the fall of the Berlin Wall and the collapse of the socialist system in Central and Eastern Europe, Yair and I started out our conversations about state-owned enterprises based on his 1986 book. Yair's analysis of state ownership in *The Evolution and Management of State Owned Enterprises* offered several new insights. It was particularly interesting for me to read about the prevalence of this organizational form in Western economies. His analysis was thorough and balanced. Our conversations over the year shifted to international business based on his 1966 book, *The Foreign Investment Decision Process*. However, it was only a few years later that I appreciated the importance of that book.

I started my doctoral studies at Indiana University a few years later. Marjorie Lyles's seminars and the research collaborations with her and her students helped me better understand the complexities of foreign investment decisions and the role of managers. I updated Yair about my progress during our phone conversations and at the AIB annual meetings. I also taught chapters of his book in my IB doctoral seminars in the following years.

We started to discuss the possibility of a *Journal of World Business* special issue on managerial decision-making in IB in 2006, 40 years after the publication of *The Foreign Investment Decision Process*. Yair, my former doctoral student, Brian Connelly from Auburn University, and I selected seven articles by IB authors from around the world, including Francisco Figueira-de-Lemos, Jan Johanson, Jan-Erik Vahlne, Raymond Mataloni, Mike Kotabe, Crystal Jiang, Janet Murray, Michael Harvey, David Griffith, Tim Kiessling, Miriam Moeller, Bo Bernhard Nielsen, Sabina Nielsen, Pavlos Dimitratos, Andreas Petrou, Emmanuella Plakoyiannaki, Jeffrey Johnson, Tarik Driouchi, and David Bennett. We enjoyed the editing process and the writing of the introduction to the special issue, which was published in 2011.

I feel fortunate to have been able to learn about scholarship from Yair. I realize that I am as old today as he was in 1989 when we first met. Looking at the long list of his accomplishments over the past 30 years motivates me to remain productive as a researcher.

Part 4

Yair Aharoni's Deep Connection to Place

https://doi.org/10.1142/9789811287510_0037

Chapter 37

Yair Aharoni: Academic Entrepreneur, Senior Policy Adviser, and Executive Don

Arie Y. Lewin*, Ravi Ramamurti†, and Elizabeth L. Rose‡

**Duke University, Durham, NC, USA*

†*Northeastern University, Boston, MA, USA*

‡*Indian Institute of Management Udaipur, Udaipur, India*

Yair Aharoni was a native-born Israeli *sabra* (cactus fruit that has a prickly exterior and a soft, sweet interior), typical of Israelis who pride themselves on their can-do attitude, frankness, and shameless audacity. Typical of a *sabra*, Yair, who was born in 1931, joined the Israel Defense Forces (IDF) at the age of 19, serving between 1950 and 1956. He retired with the rank of Captain as head of the Air Force Statistical Branch (1951–1956). While serving in the IDF, Yair earned a Diploma (1955) and an MA from the Tel Aviv University School of Law and Economics (1958). His thesis, entitled "Industrial Democracy Over the Past Half Century", was awarded the Payis Prize for the best thesis.

During his studies for the MA degree, Yair worked at the Israel Institute of Productivity as the head of the cost accounting section and as the head of the training department, in charge of planning courses for different levels of management and consulting on cost accounting methods for various companies in Israel.

Although building the Recanati Business School at Tel Aviv University was always a priority, he had a much broader vision of how the school and the faculty could be involved with growing the management expertise of enterprises in Israel or supporting government development policies. He served on the Board of Directors of several business and non-profit organizations; among them were the largest industrial firms in Israel, including Maalot, The Israel Securities Rating Co. Ltd, and Moritz Tuchler Hitum Ltd. In addition, he served on numerous public committees in Israel, including the Committee on the Enactment of Government Corporation Act.

Yair Aharoni recognized very early that the economic development of Israel, like other small economies, would be constrained by its small domestic market. With his friend and collaborator, Professor Seev Hirsch, he explored the impediments to internationalization faced by companies in small and open economies. The focus of this work was on how domestic companies who aspire to internationalize could overcome their scale disadvantages in order to compete with larger MNEs who had the advantage of being based in much larger home markets. In a series of reports and papers, Aharoni and Hirsch argued for internationalization strategies that were anchored in finding and competing in niche markets, avoiding direct competition with established dominant competitors that were serving mainstream markets, optimizing marketing costs by seeking and focusing on large transactions, and avoiding or minimizing B2C (business-to-customer) transactions and instead focusing on B2B (business-to-business) transactions by honing client-centric custom flexibility. The growth of the Israeli defense industry, which consists of about 150 manufacturers and service providers, is a key example of the success of this line of thinking.

However, Yair's crowning achievement was the founding, in 1966, of the Leon Recanati Graduate School of Business Administration at Tel Aviv University. He served as the dean and the head of the Accounting department through the 1970 academic year. Professor Yair Orgler, in his contribution to this volume, describes Yair's tenacity in creating an independent business school within Tel Aviv University. Accomplishing this meant that Yair had to overcome the resistance of the university's rector, and most of the deans, who did not consider business administration to be a legitimate social science discipline; this was despite the fact that, at that time, the Hebrew University in Jerusalem offered a relatively new graduate business program and the Technion, Israel Institute of Technology in Haifa, offered an Industrial Engineering and Management program. Yair, however, had a strong backer in Dr. George Wise, the president of the university. Dr. Wise convinced the Recanati family to make a large contribution toward the construction of the business school, which led to the approval of the MBA program. The rector and the Academic Senate, however, insisted on affiliating the business school faculty with the social science faculty. Yair, however, was unwavering in arguing — at every opportunity — that the business school should be independent. A compromise was eventually reached such that the faculty of the business school would be affiliated with the Faculty of Social Sciences for a trial period. To gain independent status, the business school would have to recruit a world-class faculty, attract a sufficient number of students, and offer an MBA program characterized by academic rigor. As Professor Orgler describes it, Yair "managed to recruit teachers from top U.S. universities" and designed an MBA program competitive with top US business schools. By the end of the first year, the Tel Aviv University Academic Senate approved stand-alone status for the new business school and its faculty.

After stepping down as dean, Yair devoted his efforts to executive education. He is acknowledged as the farsighted futurist of "business strategy" and top-management development in Israel; see the contributions by Professor Orgler and Avishai Gal. Foremost in this regard was the establishment, in 1973, of the Top Executive Course (TEC) at the Recanati Business School, which he directed from July 1973 to July 1976. TEC offered state-of-the-art seminars and high-level practitioner-oriented courses to senior executives of large firms in Israel who had not had prior academic training. Yair took the direction of top-management development to the next level when, in October 1981, he became the CEO of the Jerusalem Institute of Management (JIM), which had been founded in 1975 at the Hebrew University in Jerusalem as a top-management institute for Israel. Yair's new role coincided with the move of JIM from the Hebrew University, to become affiliated with the Leon Recanati Graduate School of Business Administration at Tel Aviv University.

JIM had been established in 1975 by Harvard Business School faculty, with the support of key industry leaders in Israel. It was the country's first autonomous, stand-alone applied research and top-management development organization, focusing on training for senior managers and board members of the largest public and private enterprises in Israel. As the new CEO of JIM, Yair initiated in-house programs for major companies; many of these programs were taught by Harvard Business School faculty. Early in his tenure, Yair founded the Strategy Club, which initially served senior executives involved with strategic planning and, over time, evolved to become the place for CEOs and company owners "to learn from each other" and exchange ideas ranging from business strategy to internationalization and international business. Yair maintained his participation in Strategy Club meetings until his death. (For more details regarding JIM and the Strategy Club, see the tribute by Avishai Gal.)

Yair's contributions to management education and practice in Israel were foundational and transformative. However, his impact was not confined to his home country. In 1987, Thomas Keller, the founding dean of Duke University's Fuqua School of Business, recruited Yair to lead the internationalization of the faculty. Keller's goal was to accomplish this without creating a standalone international business group. Within a year of his arrival at Duke, Yair had met individually with every faculty member and led the school to adopt a new core course for the MBA on the "International Environment of Business". As part of the mission to internationalize the Fuqua School, Yair applied to the US Department of Education for a grant to support a Center for International Business Education and Research (CIBER). The application was successful, and he was the director of the Duke CIBER from 1992 until 1995, after which he returned to Israel.

Still not ready to retire, Yair became the first rector of the College of Management in Rishon LeZion in 1996. His unique vision was to create and build a degree-granting academic institution to serve qualified students who had not gained admission to the elite universities in Israel; for more details, see Tribute the contribution by Professor Tamar Almor.

The enormous contributions of Yair Aharoni to the state of Israel, with respect to business and management education, were recognized officially in 2010 when he was awarded the nation's highest honor — the Israel Prize — for Management Sciences.

https://doi.org/10.1142/9789811287510_0038

Chapter 38

Professor Yair Aharoni — A Tribute

Yair E. Orgler

Coller School of Management, Tel Aviv University, Tel Aviv, Israel

Yair Aharoni was born in Zichron Ya'akov, Israel, in 1931. He served in the Israel Defense Forces between 1950 and 1956, in various staff and line officer duties. His final position was Head of the Statistical Branch, Israel Air Force, holding the rank of captain. During his military service, he completed his undergraduate studies at the School of Law and Economics, which was later absorbed by Tel Aviv University. The thesis for his subsequent M.A. studies, titled "Industrial Democracy over the Past Half Century", was awarded the Payis Prize in 1957. Keeping up the practice of combining work with academic studies, he headed the cost accounting section and training department of the Israel Institute of Productivity. During those years, he was also socially active in founding the Israel branch of AIESEC and the Association of Graduates in Social Sciences in Israel.

The next step was graduate studies in economics at Harvard University, which culminated in the doctoral program at the Graduate School of Business Administration. The title of his dissertation was "The Decision-Making Process in Foreign Investments" and he received his doctoral degree in 1961. He spent the next three years in Israel and returned to the US for a year-long visiting position at Columbia University. During that time, he traveled frequently to Harvard and worked feverishly on transforming his dissertation into his groundbreaking book,

The Foreign Investment Decision Process, which was translated into Japanese and Spanish. He returned to a lecturer position at Hebrew University and, in mid-1966, joined Tel Aviv University as an associate professor, spending the greater part of his time on the foundation of an independent business school. Later that year, he was appointed the first dean of the Leon Recanati Graduate School of Business Administration.

I met Yair in August 1967, when I was visiting Israel with my wife Rebecca to see our families after the Six-Day War, having been in the US for three years for my graduate studies.

Yair was very enthusiastic about the potential of the Recanati School in a period when academic business education in Israel hardly existed. At that time, there was only one, relatively new, graduate program at the Hebrew University in Jerusalem and an Industrial Engineering and Management program at the Technion, Israel Institute of Technology, in Haifa. Being located in Tel Aviv, Israel's economic and business hub was a great advantage. In addition, the fact that the business school was an independent unit was a major advantage. Being familiar with the American system, it seemed quite natural to me. Only later on did I learn that there had been bitter arguments between the rector and the president concerning this issue, in which Yair played an important role. I will be more specific on this later in this piece.

To sum up the meeting, Yair did his best to convince me that the Recanati School was a much better choice than a position at Hebrew University, which had a worldwide reputation. I explained that I had chosen the position of Senior Economist at the brand new research department of the Federal Deposit Insurance Corporation (FDIC) in Washington DC so that I could devote all my time to research prior to returning to Israel. In addition to being very informative and convincing, Yair was really friendly. When he escorted me to the door, he saw that Rebecca was waiting for me outside. He scolded me for not entering with her. I explained that I thought that it would be unwise to participate together in a job interview.

Shortly afterward, I received a job offer. During the coming months, Yair sent me, like all the new and potential recruits, a short newsletter titled "To our friends in the diaspora". The newsletter contained information about the progress of the school, new hires, new courses, admissions, and so on. In addition, he personally made sure that I got all the necessary information about travel expenses and potential financial assistance upon returning to Israel. In the coming months, I received offers for teaching positions at the Hebrew University and the Technion, but the Recanati School was my first choice. I was scheduled to start teaching in the fall semester of the 1968/9 academic year. However, since I was making good progress in several empirical research projects for which the data were available only at the FDIC, I asked Yair for a one-semester delay and he graciously agreed. Several months later, for the same reason, I asked for another — and last — delay. This time, Yair refused. He wrote me that students had already registered for my two classes and he had nobody to replace me. Grudgingly, I agreed and arrived close to the beginning of the spring semester. To my great disappointment, it turned out that only a handful of students had registered for one class and two for the other, which was consequently canceled. As it turned out, Yair had been aware of the poor registration but said honestly that he was concerned that I would keep delaying my return as several other new recruits were doing. In retrospect, it made homecoming much easier. More important was the sad news that my mother had been diagnosed with cancer that was at an advanced stage. My return in the spring of 1969 enabled me to spend a lot of time with her in her last months. For this, I will ever be grateful to Yair.

Yair made three major contributions to establishing the Recanati Graduate School of Business Administration. The first was approving the independent status of the school in the university. The second was the establishment of the Institute of Business Research in Israel (IBRI), and the third was the formation of a management training program called TEC — Top Executive Courses; these were both integral parts or "subsidiaries" of the business school.

I would like to discuss each of these achievements in more detail but, prior to doing so, it would help describe Yair as an academic leader and entrepreneur. To begin with, he was an avid reader of worldwide academic developments in business and management. However, he was not a straightforward follower of trends but an independent, out-of-the-box thinker. In addition, he was an expert at maneuvering in the dense forest of university politics. For example, one of the tactics he used to get approval from the top academic committee of the university for his unconventional ideas was to raise the ideas time and again until most members got tired of listening to him and he got approval. Finally, he was not an optimizer but a maximizer. I once consulted with him on how to solve a specific organizational problem within certain constraints. He told me that I had to decide first what I wanted to achieve, without regard for the constraints, and then try to remove or circumvent the constraints to the best of my ability. That is what he did in forming the Recanati School and its two subsidiaries.

The establishment of the Recanati School, especially its independent status, was vehemently opposed by the rector and most of the deans. The main reason was that business administration was considered by many as a profession and not a valid, research-based field. Second, it was claimed that it was more important to invest resources in the existing faculties of the young university, which desperately needed them. Third, if at all, the school should be part of the Faculty of Social Sciences, as was the case at Hebrew University in Jerusalem. In this struggle, which lasted for several years, Yair found a strong ally in Dr. George Wise, the president of the university. Dr. Wise convinced the Recanati family to donate a substantial amount for the construction of the school and, finally, MBA studies were approved. The issue of affiliation was not resolved, and Yair was adamant that the school should be independent. After long discussions, a compromise was reached. The school would be affiliated with the Faculty of Social Sciences for a trial period. If it demonstrated a respectable curriculum, high-quality faculty, and solid registration, it would gain independent status.

Yair worked very hard to achieve this goal. He managed to recruit teachers from top US universities like Stanford, Harvard, Chicago, and UCLA. His aim was to have faculty from diverse schools of thought and teaching methodologies. This caused endless discussions at faculty meetings but was fruitful in crystalizing and improving the curriculum. In preparing the program, Yair was assisted primarily by his old-time friend and colleague Seev Hirsch, who also received his doctorate from Harvard and later followed Yair as the second dean of the school. They spent hours on end going over brochures of MBA programs at leading US business schools and selecting the courses most relevant for Israel. In addition, a minimal and efficient administrative staff was hired and the plan for the Recanati building was drafted. Consequently, after a single academic year, the university senate approved a stand-alone status identical to much larger faculties.

As mentioned before, Yair established two "subsidiaries" of the Recanati School: the TEC — Top Executive Courses — and the Institute of Business Research in Israel. The objective of the TEC was to offer high-quality seminars and courses to top executives of large Israeli firms who did not have academic training. At the same time, it provided an additional source of income for faculty members who taught those courses.

Later on, one-year diploma programs for middle management were offered and, today, it also offers short programs for managers from other countries such as China. Thus, it generates income which is used mostly to support research and other needs of the school.

The objective of the Institute of Business Research (IBRI) Israel was to have an independent research facility that would provide funding, especially to young faculty members until they gained sufficient experience for submitting proposals to Israeli and international research funding organizations. Yair solicited donations from large Israeli corporations in order to establish an endowment fund that would be an independent source for funding small research projects and preliminary studies toward the submission of major proposals. The IBRI was organized in the form of a nonprofit corporation. Representatives of the major donors were members of the board, together with faculty members and university officials, while the dean served as chairman. Needless to say, the independent status of the IBRI caused endless conflicts with the university research authority, which took years to settle. Still, it demonstrates Yair's original thinking and persistence in achieving his often unconventional goals.

Upon completing his term as dean in 1970, Yair accepted a visiting position at the Graduate School of Business Administration at Stanford University. From this point onward, he began an international career with numerous lectures at conferences, seminars, and visiting positions at leading universities worldwide. The longest and most productive one was at Duke University. Nevertheless, being a true Zionist, Yair spent most of his time in Israel at Tel Aviv University, part of it jointly with other academic institutions. At the Recanati School, he held the Daniel and Grace Chair in International Business and later the Issachar Haimovic Chair in Business Policy. In the mid-1970s, he served as academic director of TEC. In the 1980s, he was the director and CEO of the Jerusalem Institute of Management (JIM), a top management development institute, and, in the 1990s, he served for five years as rector of the College of Management — Rishon LeZion. Throughout all those years he continued doing research that was published in books and top-level journals. His books are used in many universities worldwide and he presented his articles at numerous conferences. For his scientific research contribution, he received the Landau Prize in 2007.

In 2010, Yair received the highest scientific recognition in our country — the Israel Prize. The prize was awarded in the area of Management and Administrative Science. It was given in recognition of Yair's groundbreaking research performance and seminal contribution to management education in Israel. The judging committee provided lengthy explanations and reasons for granting the prize. Many of them are spelled out in detail in this tribute, including the founding of the first independent graduate business school in Israel, the Institute of Business Research in Israel, and management training programs at all levels. Naturally, his pioneering research on globalization was highlighted. In addition, the committee mentioned the importance of his studies of government-owned corporations and the impact of government regulations on Israeli business. All in all, it is crystal clear why Yair was one of only four to receive the Israel Prize in the area of management and administrative science over more than 60 years.

https://doi.org/10.1142/9789811287510_0039

Chapter 39

My Memory of Yair Aharoni

Jehiel Zif

Tel Aviv University, Tel Aviv, Israel

I met Yair Aharoni for the first time in Boston in, or about, 1971. He was involved with Harvard and I ran a startup company in educational aids. He impressed me with his straight talk, reasonable proposals, and many connections at Harvard. He encouraged me to join the newly established faculty of business administration at Tel Aviv University, where he was the first dean. I expressed interest, but I was not ready to leave what I was doing. A year later, I sold my shares in the company that I was running and decided to return to Israel.

At that time, I accepted Yair's offer and joined the business faculty at Tel Aviv University. In consideration of my educational publications, Yair helped me get a starting position as a senior lecturer. I became involved with academic issues as head of the curriculum committee. Many of the faculty members came from schools that did not use cases for teaching. I had an informal coalition with Yair in promoting and using case teaching.

As the first dean, Yair helped create a very friendly social environment in the school. The faculty members were young and full of energy. As an outcome, we had many social activities, including playing basketball together and holding dancing parties in different homes.

In 1977, I came to Northeastern University in Boston for a two-year sabbatical. Yair was there part of the time, involved with issues of managing public enterprises at the Harvard Institute of International Development. As a result of the interaction with Yair, I joined a group of researchers involved with managing public enterprises and I wrote two papers on the subject. Yair was guest editor of a *Management Science* issue on managing public enterprises, and one of my articles was accepted for that publication. Yair introduced me to Dick Mallon, the director of the Public Enterprise Summer Workshops at the Harvard Institute of International Development. Dick offered me a teaching role in the program. My first summer teaching position in 1978 was extended for 16 more years.

For some reason, during the period of our sabbatical in Boston, Yair needed a place to stay. He stayed with us for about a week to 10 days. I remember that, at the end of this time, Yair invited us to a Chinese restaurant for a departure celebration.

At different times, my wife, Yael, and I met his first wife Nili, his daughter, and later on another daughter whom he and his wife adopted. I remember that Nili showed us her knitting artwork.

Back in Israel, Yair was always active with different initiatives. One of his initiatives was to get funding for improving the management skills of executives in Israel. The program involved a variety of courses, using case studies, for active executives. In a number of these courses that were strategy-oriented, Yair invited me to teach with him.

At Tel Aviv University, Yair was teaching business policy while I was teaching marketing. At some point, there was a need for an additional business policy instructor. I decided to sit in his business policy class and watch his case teaching. I remember his comments about a Harvard case on Marks and Spencer. He suggested that the firm did much better in the UK than in other countries because the owners had the opportunity to personally visit the stores. After watching Yair, I started to teach business policy as well.

In recent years, Yair's vision and hearing deteriorated. He was still coming to the business school quite often. He was willing to read and make comments on a paper that I wrote, even though it was not easy for him. I appreciated his effort on my behalf and his helpful critique.

I will miss Yair as a friend and a colleague.

https://doi.org/10.1142/9789811287510_0040

Chapter 40

Small Countries Creating Global Advantages: A Tribute to Yair Aharoni

Tamar Almor

School for Behavioral Sciences and Psychology at the College of Management, Rishon LeTsiyon, Israel

Yair Aharoni was the leading professor in Israel for Business Policy when I was a student at the Faculty of Management of Tel Aviv University in the 1980s. He was also known for his research in International Business and his knowledge in this field. However, our Hebrew textbooks on "Introduction to Accounting" were written by him as well. In that sense, Yair was a true renaissance man, with an immensely broad basis of knowledge and interest.

Like many of his generation, he grew up together with the State of Israel. Born before the establishment of the State in 1948, he was of the generation of Israelis that fought for the establishment and existence of this small country, which tried and succeeded to survive in a hostile environment. As such, he lived in Israel's history, of which he was an inseparable part. His contributions to the development of Israel's academic achievements, specifically of the Faculty of Management at Tel Aviv University, were significant. As the first Dean of the Faculty, he created the vision that would accompany it for many years. In later years, he was the first Rector of the College of Management, which trailblazed a new type of academic institution, non-subsidized but overseen by the Council of Higher Education (CHE), opening up opportunities for many young

Israelis who wanted to attain academic degrees but were not accepted to the relatively few universities in Israel. Academic institutions like the College of Management provided academic opportunities not only for students but also for young academics seeking to develop an academic career. At that time, the academic environment in Israel was extremely conservative and, for many young women as well as academics from non-Western backgrounds, it was nearly impossible to develop a career in the established universities. Thus, our paths crossed again, at the College of Management, where I was hired as a young Ph.D. and Yair became the Head of this academic institution. During that period, we even shared an office briefly, when we moved into our permanent campus in Rishon LeZion, and rooms were at a premium.

Yair graduated from Harvard University in the early 1960s, where he wrote a groundbreaking study titled "Decision Making Process in Foreign Investments", which was published in 1966 (Aharoni, 1966) and which still is current in its insights and way of thinking. In the early 1990s, when I wrote my Ph.D. thesis on "International Strategic Alliances: A Strategy to Cope with a Changing Environment", I used his work on foreign investment decisions. Even today, his work is still current as it shows that investments are rarely the result of a single, clear-cut decision. In his work, he shows that investment decisions are usually the result of carefully built-up processes, involving not only economic but also particular and human interests. He argued that investment decisions can be the result of one extremely motivated person in the organization who pushes towards a certain investment, even though this may not be the most obvious investment in economic terms.

Studies published during the last 10 years have found that a large portion of the variance in the performance of organizations can be explained by the "CEO effect" (Quigley & Hambrick, 2015). Studies indicate that an individual in an organization, especially in managerial and executive functions, can have a major impact on that organization (Datta *et al.*, 2003; Helfat & Peteraf, 2015). Indeed, in a study we conducted some years ago (Shoham *et al.*, 2017), we found that an individual board member can affect strategic decisions dramatically. In my view, these studies are a direct continuation of Yair's arguments, which showed that investment decisions are frequently driven by interests of individuals in an organization.

During the late 1980s, Yair, together with his friend and colleague, Seev Hirsch, became worried about Israel's economic future. At the time,

Israel was still a very small, closed economy, which was becoming increasingly dependent upon funds supplied by the United States. Yair, together with a team of researchers from Israel and the US, initiated a study which was named "Export-led growth strategy for Israel". The report of the study, which was published in 1987, stated that Israel should make a major effort to reduce its dependence on foreign support and money. Therefore, it was argued, Israel must pursue an export-led growth: "*As Israel is too small to create economies of scale in a wide variety of industries by serving the home market alone, it must invest in export to grow and become prosperous*". The study that was conducted presented Israel's policymakers with four goals (Export-led growth strategy for Israel: 1–2):

1. Increased exports must become a national priority.
2. The strategy and culture of most Israeli firms need to change from import substitute, defense supplier, or raw material developer to focused builder of international competitive advantages.
3. Israelis must learn to market their products better.
4. The uneasy relationship which exists between the Israeli government and Israeli businesses must be modernized; the businesses must be allowed to function more independently.

The report showed that Israel's economy had lost the capacity to grow and increase the standard of living for its citizens. At the time when the report was written, Israel was suffering from a high level of foreign debt, and a large part of its exports was based on natural endowments and agriculture as well as polished diamonds. Moreover, many academics were leaving Israel, creating a brain drain. The team concluded that Israel should improve its value added per employee by introducing higher skill levels into the labor market, among others. The report stated that, to prosper, Israel must achieve growth not only in physical volume but also in the value added per employee of its exports. The study recommended Israel's government to invest in incentives for investment rather than in pure subsidies while focusing on certain industries and policies. It further suggested that Israel's government invest in the export industry and help firms to develop their exports. It suggested that the government establish a conditionally reimbursable loan fund, providing loans for projects which involve entry into risky (R&D) projects and markets for export. It recommended getting the BIRD (Binational Industrial Research and

Development) Foundation involved, which eventually, according to the report, could become self-sustaining after initial capitalization. It also suggested that government increase funding of the Chief Scientist to encourage the development of startup companies and new ventures. The researchers further proposed that Israel should develop a class of licensed venture capital funds in which individuals and corporations could invest.

The report stated: "Startup companies are unlikely to provide the major share of export growth in the next ten years, but they are crucial to Israel's long-term economic development". Little did the researchers know that, 20 years later, Israel would become known as "Startup Nation", attracting policymakers, researchers, and students from around the world who were interested in understanding how Israel underwent this major change from exporting oranges to exporting knowledge-based products and services.

While the report was not the only one written, it did have a major impact on the thinking of Israel's leading politicians and policymakers. During the first part of the 1990s, Israel was inundated with about one million new immigrants from the disintegrating Soviet Union, who were looking to better their economic situation and provide a better future for their children as well as to become part of Israel's society as Jews who were not allowed, for many years, to immigrate to Israel. Thus, Israel's policymakers saw an opportunity to change the country's economic situation. As advised by the researchers, the government established two funds which encouraged venture capitalists to invest in budding high-tech firms by matching their investments and by sharing the upside of the investment and bearing the risk of the downside. Rather than subsidizing high-tech startups, the government created incentives for investments, thereby establishing a totally new industry in Israel, that of venture capital. Today, Israel has one of the leading venture capital industries in the world. The government also invested resources in the Export Institute, which started to assist small Israeli firms to develop their international markets. The Chief Scientist (recently renamed the Israel Innovation Authority) started to fulfill a central function in the development of civilian R&D and provided much-needed support for new R&D projects. The BIRD foundation, as well, started to play an important role in the development of Israel as "Startup Nation" (Almor, 2011, 2014).

In 2000, Yair wrote a chapter in a book created as a tribute to Seev Hirsch (Aharoni, 2000). His chapter was named "Globalization and the Small, Open Economy", in which he discussed strategies for small firms hailing from small, open economies such as Israel. In the conclusion of this chapter, he wrote that, if small countries choose to encourage the integration of domestic firms in the global economy, there is no reason for them not to flourish and succeed. In his view, 13 years after the research report on export-led growth was written, the size of a country was not a major constraint in a globally integrated world. He stated that, by concentrating on research and development in countries where scientists are available, such as in Israel, and by focusing on global market niches, a country could become increasingly prosperous.

Indeed, examining Israel's economic figures in 2019, about 80% of the country's total civilian export was based on knowledge-intensive products and services. Israel's GDP per capita PPP grew from about US$12,600 in 1990 to nearly US$42,000 in 2019, topping the growth of most OECD countries during this period. In addition, it reduced its debt from over 90% in the 1990s to about 60% in 2019.

By implementing many of the recommendations from the research report, Israel's policymakers created an economically strong country, based on knowledge-intensive industries. Israel has been able to attract major investments from many global high-tech companies, hundreds of whom have established R&D centers in Israel, many of them acquiring local new ventures and startups. All of this is supported by a vibrant venture capital industry. There is no doubt in my mind that Yair Aharoni, as well as Seev Hirsch, by presenting their views on international business, business strategy, and policymaking to academics, politicians, business leaders, and others over the years, are part of the reason that Israel's economy is so successful today. Yair's vision, that small open economies, such as Israel, can develop global competitive advantages, thereby creating economic growth and quality of life for its citizens, became a reality during his lifetime.

His sharp analysis of complex economic situations has certainly impacted the understanding of thousands of students who took his classes over the years and who subsequently became business and policy leaders. His contribution to the academic development of International Business and Business Strategy remains and still forms the basis for future research.

References

Aharoni, Y. 1966. *The Foreign Investment Decision Process*. Cambridge: Harvard University Press.

Aharoni, Y. 2000. Globalization and the small, open economy. In Almor, T. & Hashai, N. (Eds.) *FDI, International Trade and the Economics of Peace Making: A Tribute to Seev Hirsch.* School of Business Administration, The College of Management, Rishon LeZion, Israel, pp. 90–116.

Almor, T. 2011. Dancing as fast as they can: Israeli high-tech firms and the great recession of 2008. *Thunderbird International Business Review*, 53(2): 195–208.

Almor, T. 2014. Israel start-up nation: Creating technology based, international new ventures. *EIBAzine*, 14: 14–18.

Datta, D. K., Rajagopalan, N. & Zhang, Y. 2003. New CEO openness to change and strategic persistence: The moderating role of industry characteristics. *British Journal of Management*, 14(2): 101–114.

Export-led growth strategy for Israel: Final report. 1987. JIM (Jerusalem Institute of Management).

Helfat, C. E. & Peteraf, M. A. 2015. Managerial cognitive capabilities and the microfoundations of dynamic capabilities. *Strategic Management Journal*, 36(6), 831–850.

Quigley, T. J. & Hambrick, D. C. 2015. Has the "CEO effect" increased in recent decades? A new explanation for the great rise in America's attention to corporate leaders. *Strategic Management Journal*, 36: 821–830.

Shoham, A., Almor, T., Lee, S. M. & Ahammad, M. 2017. Encouraging environmental sustainability through gender: A micro-foundational approach using linguistic gender marking. *Journal of Organizational Behavior*, 38(9): 1356–1379.

https://doi.org/10.1142/9789811287510_0041

Chapter 41

Some Memories and Reflections on and of Yair Aharoni

David M. Brock

Ben Gurion University, Beersheba, Israel

I met Yair for the first time in the late 1980s at a small synagogue we both attended in Durham, North Carolina. At the time, he was a visiting Professor at Duke, and I was a doctoral student and teaching at North Carolina State University. While we shared some academic interests, my memories from those years are that we did not get into specific research topics but rather discussed other issues of mutual interest. Some years later, while at the University of Auckland, my own research interests gravitated toward international business and professional service firms, and it was then that I noticed the prominence of the "Aharoni" name in both these literatures. I renewed contact with Yair, we reconnected, and we began working on several projects.

Initially, he wrote a chapter (Aharoni, 1999) in the Brock, Powell, and Hinings (1999) edited book on changes in professional organization. A decade later, we collaborated on editing a special issue of the *Journal of International Management* on "50 years of IB research". My favorite project with Yair was a paper entitled "Ricardo Had No Internet", presented at the 2008 AIB meetings in Milan — and I have reproduced some excerpts in the second half of this essay. He was a founding member of the *Journal of Professions and Organization* editorial board, and his work is still regularly cited in recent work on the professional service sector (e.g., Boussebaa & Faulconbridge, 2019; Skjølsvik *et al.*, 2017). He had a passion for ideas, theories, and principles and continued to contribute to these scholarly fields to the extent that his health permitted, way into his retirement.

The "Old School"

My sadness in hearing of Yair's passing, and reflecting on who he was, is very much tied to nostalgia for the "old school" generation where one's values were less likely to be eclipsed by expedience. Two brief stories illustrate these values.

The first story took place in the 1970s when Yair was visiting UC Berkeley. In those days, there was very little red tape involved in visiting scholars obtaining a "green card" (permanent residence) in the United States, and Yair was advised that this status would save him the trouble of having to apply for visas each time he visited. Yair said that he very much understood the advantages that a green card would bestow, but yet he felt that permanent residence in the US would contain an element of turning his back on Israel — and his values did not allow him to be comfortable with that status.

The other anecdote took place in the past decade. Yair was asked to write a letter of recommendation for a promotion/tenure committee that was evaluating a junior faculty member. Knowing (as we all do) that these letters take considerable time and effort, one of the people involved offered to prepare a draft of a letter for Yair's approval. However, Yair turned down the request with a few succinct words that very much encapsulate the "old school" approach: "Yair Aharoni writes his own letters!"

As mentioned earlier, Yair and I presented a paper at the 2008 Milan AIB conference, which very much encapsulated his critique of, and his recommendations for the betterment of, the IB field. A few ideas from the conference paper were included in our Aharoni and Brock (2010) editorial essay. In the remaining paragraphs of this tribute to Yair, I have thus excerpted from Aharoni and Brock (2008), trusting that these ideas will be no less relevant today.

"Ricardo Had No Internet" (Some Excerpts)

In this paper, we argue that theories in social science in general and in IB in particular are not true under all circumstances. Instead, these theories depend on the environment in which the organization operates. Changes in the political situation, economic variables, institutions, political regimes, and technology — even accumulated knowledge within firms — entail shifts in the ways international business is carried out. Firms are learning organizations and can adapt to the changing environment. Theories are therefore true for some time but rarely hold forever.

It is clear that breakthroughs in technology — along with many of the abovementioned developments like trade agreements, reduced transport costs, and cross-cultural awareness — have presented a range of managerial options scarcely considered less than a generation ago. For example, international sourcing has become the norm rather than curiosity, and detailed information about distant consumers is instantly available online. These changes were largely unpredicted by business researchers in general and IB scholars in particular. The impact of these changes proved several conventional wisdoms wrong. In 1900, it was true that people cannot fly — but soon thereafter, in North Carolina, it was proven very wrong. In the same way, many IB theories tended to assume at least implicitly that the world would forever remain largely the same. These theories thus turned out to be less universally valid and therefore less resilient than claimed.

We should point out some theoretical domains rarely encountered in our research literature, namely the effects of power and politics within MNEs as well as the use of political strategies by MNEs (Boddewyn, 1988, 1992). Most researchers tend to portray the MNE as "an efficient organizer of resources across national borders" with management theories based on "the fiction of mechanistic causal relationships" (Barner-Rasmussen *et al.*, 2007: p. 94, 101). However, it may well be that political stewardship is a crucial resource for the effective management of an MNE, which needs some protection from governments to survive. As Ashok Kapoor reminded us in the very first edition of *JIBS*, "The art of politics … can become as important, or even more important, to the success of an investment negotiation as hard-headed technical and financial calculations" (1970: pp. 27–28, citing Williams, 1965).

All the above does not mean that the traditional IB theories are wrong. They were right at a certain technology, culture, and political system. Thus, Ricardo was right and innovative 200 years ago, but given the Internet and other changes to the IB context, a multinational firm can invest in Portugal instead of exporting. Johanson and Vahlne were right in the 1970s (at least with regard to Scandinavian-based MNEs), but today's technology allows firms to skip internationalization stages, even to be born global. Most of today's powerful service multinationals could not exist without the trade concessions negotiated in the 1994 Uruguay Round. And MNEs from India and China are made possible by contemporary ICT, which enables firms to break down their value chains and thus leads to increasing uses of outsourcing by established MNEs and the increasing modularization of products and services. Today's MNEs are also facilitated by the concentration and globalization of retailing, by a more fluid international market for professional services, and by a more open market for international control, allowing the acquisition of foreign firms (for details, see Williamson & Zeng, 2009).

In short, for our field to progress, researchers need to take care not to overstep theoretical boundaries. We should all be careful to specify under what conditions (e.g., country, culture, economic, and political/legal environment) a theory is meant to apply. Also, because we researchers are naturally products of our environment, theories may be specific to national context, size, and culture.

Concluding thoughts

The main thesis advocated in this paper is perhaps trite if not obvious. Unfortunately, it is frequently ignored. International business theory is rarely, if at all, universally true. Rather it is a derivate of the extant environment. Technological advances, institutions, macroeconomic changes, and political regimes may all impinge on firms working in the international field that adapt to the changing conditions. Perhaps, the only variable that may be constant is the process of decision-making of managers, as discussed above. Unfortunately, this process is rarely studied. Again, researchers would do well if they clearly define the geographical, cultural, political, and other environmental conditions under which their theory holds.

Not long ago, Vernon (1994: p. 227) said that he tended to "remain cautious about the future of international business" because of the overwhelming complexity of comparative national and international markets. Since then, our technologically enabled information processing capabilities have given us more of a capability to access and comprehend these issues. While IB scholars are not expected to be prophets, we present some humble proposals as a basis for more realistic assessment of extant realities.

We all need to define carefully the terms used and their applicability (multinational; global or US). We must make explicit all implicit assumptions and carefully define the conditions under which the phenomenon is true (for example, China's much-vaunted growth is concentrated in coastal areas, not for the whole of China). We should show the consequences of changes rather than predicting them. And IB research has to be multidisciplinary, taking into account cultural factors, technological advances, political, economic, organizational, and managerial issues.

In all sciences, especially social sciences, scholars have ongoing struggles with keeping up with advances in thinking, knowledge, and context. Thus, in the most prestigious scientific journals — over double the age of *JIBS* — one will still find articles debating the definition of constructs like intelligence, health, planet, embryo, and vacuum. So too, in our relatively young field, we need to invest in clarifying our basic concepts. Exciting developments in the commercial world, fueled by the penchant of business journalism to focus on extraordinary stories, make it tempting to follow rhetoric rather than apply rigorous scientific methodology. Only with explicit assumptions and clear definitions would we be able to advance the theory and be able to predict.

Not only did Ricardo have no Internet, but all concepts of information and markets in his time were different from what they are today. Similarly, markets for IB scholarships are developing beyond what was considered a generation ago. According to John Dunning (2006: 3), "our field of study is at a watershed in its evolution" in that it is favorably poised among social sciences to capitalize on global social, technological, and economic changes. Thus, we return to our well-worn theme, that for a scientific field to progress, we need clear definitions and assumptions. IB researchers need to revisit the terms like international, multinational, global, and transnational, preferably following the footsteps of Miller and Freisen's (1984) taxonomic approaches that apply clustering techniques to populations of organizations and environments. The highly complex nature of contemporary MNEs will no doubt make this an arduous research direction. A suitably large research project is called for. Fortunately, there is a growing realization that large research teams are needed to tackle large projects — as illustrated by the recent GLOBE studies (House *et al.*, 2004).

In closing, IB has certainly made major strides toward scholarly legitimacy in its first generation as an academic field. To continue this trend, we need to follow Buckley & Lessard's (2005) advice to shore up

IB-specific theory development along with issue-driven research. MNEs have become learning organizations. They are able to survive competition and preserve high margins because of their ability to learn and adapt to the changing environment, achieving dynamic capabilities. Whereas, a generation ago, it was more common for MNEs to extract rent from existing resources and knowledge developed at home; today, they are learning and developing new capabilities in globally coordinated networks. If MNEs can adapt, IB theory too should adapt to changing environments. We can do no better than conclude with the words of Gary Hamel:

> "… unlike the laws of physics, the laws of management are neither foreordained nor eternal — and a good thing, too, for the equipment of management is now groaning under the strain of a load it was never meant to carry. Whiplash change, fleeting advantages, technological disruptions, seditious competitors, fractured markets, omnipotent customers, rebellious shareholders — these 21st century challenges are testing the design limits of organizations around the world, and are exposing the limitations of a management model that has failed to keep pace with the times." (Hamel & Breen, 2007: x)

References

Aharoni, Y. 1999. Internationalization of professional services: Implications for accounting firms. In Brock, D. M., Powell, M. J. & Hinings, C. R. (Eds.) *Restructuring the Professional Organization: Accounting, Healthcare and Law*. London: Routledge, pp. 20–40.

Aharoni, Y. & Brock, D. M. 2008. Ricardo had no internet: Exploring the elusive context of IB theories. Paper presented at the Academy of International Business conference, Milan, June/July.

Aharoni, Y. & Brock, D. M. 2010. International business research: Looking back and looking forward. *Journal of International Management*, 16(1): 5–15.

Barner-Rasmussen, W., Piekkari, R., Scott-Kennel, J. & Welch, C. 2007. New perspectives on the multinational corporation. *Academy of Management Perspectives*, 21(3): 93–101.

Boddewyn, J. 1988. Political aspects of MNE theory. *Journal of International Business Studies*, 19(3): 341–363.

Boddewyn, J. 1992. Political behavior research. In Buckley, P. J. (Ed.) *New Directions in International Business*. Brookfield, VT: Edward Elgar, pp. 81–87.

Boussebaa, M. & Faulconbridge, J. 2019. Professional service firms as agents of economic globalization: A political perspective. *Journal of Professions and Organization*, 6(1): 72–90.

Brock, D. M., Powell, M. J. & Hinings, C. R. 1999. *Restructuring the Professional Organization: Accounting, Health Care & Law*. London: Routledge.

Buckley, P. J. & Lessard, D. 2005. Regaining the edge for international business research. *Journal of International Business Studies*, 36(6): 595–599.

Dunning, J. H. 2006. New directions in international business research. *AIB Insights*, 6(2): 3–9.

Hamel, G. & Breen, B. 2007. *The Future of Management*. Boston: Harvard Business School Press.

House, R. J., Hanges, P. J., Javidan, M., Dorfman, P. W. & Gupta. V. 2004. *Leadership, Culture, and Organizations: The GLOBE Study of 62 Societies*. Thousand Oaks, CA: Sage.

Kapoor, A. 1970. Negotiation strategies in international business government relations: A study in India. *Journal of International Business Studies*, 1(1): 21–42.

Miller, D. & Friesen, P. H. 1984. *Organizations: A Quantum View*. Englewood Cliffs, NJ: Prentice Hall.

Skjølsvik, T., Pemer, F. & Løwendahl, B. 2017. Strategic management of professional service firms: Reviewing ABS-journals and identifying opportunities for future research. *Journal of Professions and Organization*, 4(2): 203–225.

Vernon, R. 1994. Contributing to an international business curriculum: An approach from the flank. *Journal of International Business Studies*, 25(2): 215–227.

Williams, S. 1965. Negotiating investments in emerging countries. *Harvard Business Review*, January-February: 89–99.

Williamson, P. & Zeng, M. 2009. China's emerging multinationals: Emerging through new global gateways. In R. Ramamurti and J. V. Singh (Eds.) *Emerging Multinationals from Emerging Markets*. Cambridge: Cambridge University Press, pp. 81–109.

https://doi.org/10.1142/9789811287510_0042

Chapter 42

A Tribute to Prof. Yair Aharoni

Avishai Gal

JIM — The Strategy Club, Tel Aviv, Israel

Personal Note

When I first met Yair, I was a graduate student at the Faculty of Management, Tel Aviv University. The program required all students to write a graduate thesis under the auspices of one of the faculty members and I decided to ask Prof. Yair Aharoni to become my thesis advisor. I approached him with some apprehension since he was the distinguished founder and prominent Dean of the Faculty, and I did not know him personally. Yair listened patiently to my request, and to my surprise and great relief, he agreed.

Since then, in the following 30 years, our paths crossed in various ways, professionally, and, mainly during the last 10 years, also personally, as I had the privilege of becoming his friend, despite our age difference.

Yair was the "Founding Father" of "Business Strategy" in Israel. He laid the foundations for this topic and mindset in both academia and senior management development programs and fostered its advancement and integration in Israel's leading businesses and companies since the 1970s. The enormous contribution of Yair to the state of Israel was recognized in 2010 when he received the Israel Prize for Management Sciences.

Together with his friend and colleague, Prof. Seev Hirsch, who also passed away recently, Yair was a pioneer and an acclaimed researcher and scholar in International Business Studies and was mostly interested in the management, strategy, and growth of international and global companies, especially those that originated in a relatively small country, such as Israel.

CEO of JIM (1981–1987)

After Yair had served as Dean for many years, and simultaneously holding the Issachar Haimovic Chair in Business Policy, he was appointed CEO of JIM — the Jerusalem Institute of Management. His appointment occurred after JIM was relocated from Jerusalem to Tel Aviv and became affiliated with the Leon Recanati Graduate School of Business Administration.

JIM was established in 1975 by Harvard Business School faculty and Israel's industry leaders, in cooperation with the Hebrew University of Jerusalem and later with the Faculty of Management of Tel Aviv University. It was an independent applied research and management development organization and the first, and for many years, the only organization in Israel that provided managerial development for senior managers and board members in Business Strategy and General Management.

In his capacity as the CEO of JIM, Yair initiated numerous public programs with Israel's business leaders and senior managers and developed in-house programs with major companies. Most of these programs were planned by Yair and JIM's staff and led by the Harvard Business School faculty, who wanted to contribute their vast methodological and practical knowledge to Israel's business sector, companies, and senior managers. Israel's management echelon was very determined then but somewhat lacked conceptual and methodological management know-how, especially concerning management and business in an international environment.

Some of these companies, especially the first generation of Israel's technology-based businesses, such as Scitex, Indigo (digital printing), Elscint (medical equipment), Iscar (high-end production tools for the metal industry), ECI, RAD (communication equipment), ORMAT (clean-tech, energy), Netafim (aggrotech, irrigation dripping systems), and even Teva (pharmaceuticals), to some extent, eventually became international technology or share leaders in their markets. They further became informal "incubators" for spin-offs and entrepreneurs, many of which were former employees, creating the critical mass that enabled, among other factors, the creation of "Israel Startup Nation". This process triggered the international emergence of Israel's high-tech sector, which now includes industries, such as electronics, ICT, digital printing, cleantech, aggrotech, pharmaceuticals, and biomed, as well as software and cyber, among others.

Yair was also involved, through JIM, in senior management development programs conducted in several Israeli consumer goods companies, such as Keter Plastics (plastic furniture and storage products) and the Strauss Group (food industry), that later became successful international firms, against all odds, even though they did not have inherited technological advantages. Others were acquired by global companies, such as Osem (food industry), which was acquired by Nestlé.

In 1987, JIM, under the leadership of Yair, conducted a comprehensive study, in cooperation with Telesis and Professor Seymour (Sy) Tilles, aimed at creating a vision and strategy for the economic growth of Israel. The study was commissioned by the Manufacturers Association of the "Histadrut" — the Israeli trade unions' association — which at that time was a dominant player in the Israeli economy, together with the sector of government-owned companies, the Operation Independence Task Force, and the Executive Board of JIM.

The study was based on interviews with 150 Israeli managers, including most of Israel's then major exporters. At that time, only a relatively small number of companies exported their products, and most had not yet moved the internationalization process beyond that stage. The researchers also interviewed 125 customers, competitors, and partners of Israeli companies in North America and Europe.

Based on the results of this research, JIM, headed by Yair, in cooperation with his co-researchers, published a comprehensive report for Israel's policymakers and the business sector, named "Export-led Growth Strategy for Israel" (see Appendix A).

The recommendations presented in the report emphasized the need for a roadmap, detailing an export-led strategy of both policymakers and the business sector. While the very detailed set of recommendations was not fully implemented, especially not by the government decision makers, the report was widely acclaimed and had a long-term impact on the mindset of Israel's public administration.

The main impact of the report, from my perspective, was on Israeli companies that were seeking to expand their sales to develop their markets outside Israel. These companies were encouraged by the report to perceive export and later internationalization, as viable growth strategies.

Even up to 15 years later, until the end of the 1990s, C-level managers from various parts of the Israeli economy, as well as researchers and students, came to JIM, asking for a copy of the report. Actually, we were left with only two copies, which we do not intend to give away.

JIM — The Strategy Club

About 35 years ago, in 1982, under Yair's leadership, JIM founded the Strategy Club. This club served initially as a meeting place for the first group of strategic planning managers, who worked for leading Israeli businesses. This group participated in an educational trip to Harvard Business School, organized by JIM, aimed at teaching them the fundamentals of strategic planning. Later, as the concept of business strategy evolved, and strategic thinking replaced strategic planning, senior managers joined the club.

At present, the club is a meeting place for CEOs and company owners, in the areas of Business Strategy and Management, with special focus on International Business. The mission of the Club is "to learn from the experience of others". Club members gather once a month for informal meetings, hosted by inspirational business leaders, as well as CEOs and owners of leading Israeli companies, at their own facilities.

The CEO presents the situation and development of the company and its strategy, referring mainly to sustainable strategic and managerial changes and their implementation processed and "lessons learned". This is followed by an open and informal discussion with the club members.

Yair and JIM in the Post-Yair Era

"Following" Yair, I joined JIM in 1988. However, it was about a year after Yair left JIM and returned to his full academic duties. Nevertheless, we met again and worked together on projects and developed programs together, as Yair remained an active participant in some of JIM's programs as a lecturer, providing in-house seminars. He also gave seminars that were part of strategic processes, aimed at enhancing the managerial and strategic capabilities of the company's C-level managers, CEO, and sometimes Directors, who participated in the various programs.

As an important legacy of Yair's era in JIM, I decided to maintain and develop JIM's Strategy Club, of which Yair became a dedicated honorary member, attending almost all of our meetings.

In 1998, JIM started to prepare practical case studies on leading Israeli companies, mainly international and global firms, based on the Strategy Club meetings. That also followed Yair's legacy, to some extent, since he formerly established the "Israel Institute for Business Research", which became part of the Faculty of Management and aimed at documenting Israeli companies to create a database for management researchers and students. However, the Institute was later closed, thus creating a vacuum in the systematic documentation of Israeli international and local companies, especially from the perspective of strategic and managerial decision-making and "lessons learned".

Yair and I, with our dear friend, the late Prof. Seev Hirsch, who was a former Academic Manager of JIM, frequently discussed the advancement of JIM'S ICS — Israel Case Studies — project. The project's goal is to develop JIM's case studies database, digitalizing it, for International Business researchers, especially within the context of emerging economies, students, and C-level managers. However, both Yair and Seev passed away this year, and JIM will have to pursue the fulfillment of ICS without their valuable support.

As Yair became older, it was difficult for him to arrive by himself to the club's meetings. Over time, I would pick him up before the meeting and bring him home afterward. This precious time allowed us, during the last decade or so, to discuss various issues that were important to both of us.

One of the frequent topics that were raised, which usually resulted in a very vivid conversation, often shared with Seev, who sometimes joined our car rides, was the dilemma that we all found fascinating: "exit vs. independent growth". This dilemma concerned the growth strategies of international companies, mainly those originating in small countries. A question we would frequently debate was if internationally growing, scaling up companies from small countries, such as Israel, should use an exit strategy and merge with a large international company, or if they should aim for independent growth.

Memories of Conversations with Yair

This is a free translation of Yair's verbal comments on the dilemma of exit vs. growth as an independent company, which is faced by successful international and global companies from small countries.

Yair referred to this frequent and popular debate, which occurred and is still sometimes raised in Israel's economic environment, almost each time a growing and scaling up international company has been acquired by a large foreign multinational or a private equity fund.

Both Yair and Seev, his friend and colleague, shared a passion for this unsolved debate that involves strategic, financial, industrial policy, values, and cultural aspects.

Yair's comments were recorded by Ms. Nili Avneri, the Strategy Club Manager, following the Club meeting, held in 2017, with Mr. Amotz Yarden, founder and then CEO of Sintec Media, a multinational Israeli fast-growing software company, that develops BMS — Broadcast Management Systems — and provides services to broadcasters, media companies, publishers, and multichannel video providers, with worldwide R&D and marketing subsidiaries.

Sintec Media was acquired twice by US private equity funds. The CEO, Mr. Yarden, shed light on the absence of local financing sources for fast-growing international Israeli companies, after the startup's venture capital stage, which constitutes a major obstacle for choosing the path of maintaining independent international growth.

Yair's Comments

"I was very excited by Amotz's statement that the majority of Israel's high tech managers are hoping for a fast exit.

The only person I have met that stated that he strives to be "the 2nd Teva" [the Israeli Pharmaceutical multinational, before the crisis] was Dov Moran [a notable and predominant Israeli entrepreneur, the inventor of the flash drive and Disk On Key and founder of M-Systems], but he also sold the company to a U.S. competitor later [SanDisk, in 2006].

The hopes of Amotz that the financing gap will be closed by local sources, such as institutional investors, backed by the government, raises several questions.

First, it is not clear if an Israeli-owned company acts differently than a foreign-owned company. In theory, the manager should strive to achieve the maximum return on investment. If such ROI could be achieved by moving the manufacturing from Israel to countries where labor costs are significantly lower, he should do it — whether it is an Israeli or a Chinese company.

Therefore, it is not clear what the difference is between an Israeli and a non-Israeli company. Even if the manager himself wants to act on the basis of his personal views, or sometimes his "patriotic" values — Zionist values in this case — there is a large chance that the Board will force him to act differently, or even fire him.

It is clear, however, that the state has an interest to secure employment and to preserve know-how and maybe it is right, in some cases, to have a law that prevents foreign investment — for example, to prevent the acquisition of company like RAFAEL [one of Israel's three largest defense companies] by an investor from hostile country.

Even such a law is not so simple. A law that permits restricting or preventing foreign investment, based on national defense considerations, exists only in the U.S., Canada, Germany, and Australia.

Apparently, only small countries, seeking foreign investments, fear that such a law will discourage multinational companies, that the state has an interest in their direct investments.

In Israel, a former MK (Member of the Knesset — the Israeli parliament), Professor Avishai Braverman, tried to promote such a law, but the government objected, arguing that prohibiting the sale of shares contradicts the freedom of private property rights.

Amotz thinks that the problem will be solved if Israeli institutional investors finance international growth following the startup-VC stage. However, if they acquire shares, who will prevent them from fulfilling their goal and make a profit, by later selling these shares to foreign investors?

Another problem is that most of the entrepreneurs are interested in fast exit, since, among other reasons, they excel in entrepreneurship, but they do not know how to manage large companies. Unfortunately, "the Israeli character" encourages entrepreneurship, but is less suitable for managing large firms, with rigid procedures and standards.

As long as businessmen are measured by their capabilities to achieve maximum profit, it will be difficult to integrate value-based principles, even if the institutional investors acquire shares in growing, scaling-up companies, since they would materialize their profits.

What is left, then, is only the option of receiving loans from the institutional investors, without voting rights. However, the extent of such loans is limited, and usually does not meet the full needs of a growing international company.

I hope that in the future, men wiser than I will find a solution for balancing national interest, political power, and managing businesses."

Appendix A

"Export-led Growth Strategy for Israel

The Message of this Report

Over the past 40 years, the public leadership of Israel has led the people of Israel on a series of successful quests which have required vision, determination, energy and intelligence to accomplish.

- The establishment in a hostile environment of the state of Israel from the ashes of the Holocaust;
- The creation of an impressive defense establishment to protect the state;
- The transformation of seemingly useless land into a garden of bountiful food and a source of useful minerals;
- The development of industry to bring self-sufficiency in food, clothing, and shelter and the conveniences of modern day life to the people of Israel;
- The forging of an educational and research establishment unparalleled for a small nation.

All of these missions have been accomplished by people who felt that they must be independent and self sufficient, for the non-Jewish world had often not been hospitable to Jewish people.

After three decades of startling accomplishment, Israel's economy stagnated in the late 1970s and 1980s. The leaders of Israel had to borrow from abroad increasingly to maintain the living standards of the Israeli people, creating an uncomfortable dependence.

This report discusses a new quest which must be undertaken to assure Israel's economic prosperity. Israel has one of two choices for its economic future: dependence on or interdependence with the rest of the world. Israel is too small a country to be an independent economic island and still be prosperous. The scale required to develop, manufacture and market goods in today's world is too large. Israel must trade extensively and successfully.

Israel exports now, but unlike many small countries in Europe, its exports are not large and do not command a high value in the international economy. Achieving prosperity through increased high value exports is the quest addressed in this report.

This report is long and technical but it really has only four simple but powerful messages:

- The goal of increased exports must become a national priority;
- The strategy and culture of most Israeli firms need to change from import substitute, defense supplier or raw material developer to focused builder of international competitive advantage;
- Israelis must learn to market their products better;
- The uneasy relationship which exists between the Israeli government and Israeli businesses must be modernized: the businesses must be allowed to function more independently.

This report is offered as a call to action. Its specific recommendations are presented with our firm belief that they can be of help to Israel in its quest. However, more important than adopting any one of the recommendations is the understanding by all concerned that Israel's future depends on achieving economic prosperity through increased high value added exports.

Israel's choice is between economic dependence and stagnation or economic interdependence and prosperity. The choice will be made soon."

Printed in the USA
CPSIA information can be obtained
at www.ICGtesting.com
CBHW072013160324
5441CB00001B/4

9 789811 287503